SOUTHERN BIOGRAPHY SERIES

Bertram Wyatt-Brown, Editor

Senator Allen Ellender
of Louisiana

Senator Allen Ellender of Louisiana

A BIOGRAPHY

THOMAS A. BECNEL

Louisiana State University Press
Baton Rouge and London

Designer: Melanie O'Quinn Samaha
Typeface: Galliard
Typesetter: Impressions, a division of Edwards Bros., Inc.
Printer and binder: Thomson-Shore, Inc.

The author is grateful to Thomas Wright for permission to quote from the papers of the late Elward Wright.

Some of the material in this book first appeared, in different form, in the following publications and is reprinted with permission: "Allender J. Ellender, Consensus Politician," *Louisiana History,* XXXII (Summer, 1991), 229–38; "The Ellenders: Pioneer Terrebonne Parish Family, 1840–1926," *Louisiana History,* XXVI (Spring, 1985), 117–27; "Louisiana Senator Allen J. Ellender and IWW Leader Covington Hall: An Agrarian Dichotomy," *Louisiana History,* XXIII (Summer, 1982), 259–75; "Fulbright of Arkansas Vs. Ellender of Louisiana: The Politics of Sugar and Rice, 1937–1972," *Arkansas Historical Quarterly,* LXIII (Winter, 1984), 289–303.

Library of Congress Cataloging-in-Publication Data
Becnel, Thomas, 1934–
    Senator Allen Ellender of Louisiana : a biography / Thomas A.
Becnel.
        p.   cm. — (Southern biography series)
    Includes index.
    ISBN 0-8071-1978-4 (alk. paper)
    1. Ellender, Allen Joseph, 1890–1972. 2. Legislators—United
States—Biography. 3. United States. Congress. Senate—Biography.
I. Title. II. Series.
E748.E38B43   1996
328.73'092—dc20   95-35101
[B]   CIP

for

Abigail Brown Becnel

(born November 11, 1993)

Contents

Illustrations

Preface

When I first saw the Allen J. Ellender Papers, they were in cardboard boxes stacked six- and seven-high in the cramped archives of the old Polk Library at Nicholls State University in Thibodaux, Louisiana. The papers had arrived from Washington, D.C., shortly after Ellender's death in July, 1972. With them came—fortuitously—Florence LeCompte, the senator's longtime personal secretary and family friend, to assist archivist Philip Uzee. Uzee introduced me to LeCompte and to the expansive Ellender collection. Originally I examined the papers for information on agriculture, politics, and other phases of national and international affairs from 1937 to 1972. In time I decided to write a biography of the senator.

The collection, now housed in the spacious Allen J. Ellender Memorial Library at Nicholls State, is available to researchers. Archivists who came after Uzee—Michael Forêt and Carol Mathias—continued to provide the friendly assistance I needed. Reference librarian Marie Sheley and interlibrary-loan librarian Francine K. Middleton also facilitated my research tasks.

I am indebted also to archivists of other collections. At the Lyndon Baines Johnson Library, archivist Claudia Anderson unraveled for me the mysteries of the Johnson Papers and photocopied materials I needed. Longtime friend Wilbur Meneray, head of the Manuscripts Collection at Tulane University, helped me with the Barrow Family Papers and shared his expertise on the papers of Hale Boggs, deLesseps Morrison, Sam Jones, and F. Edward Hebert. Judy Bolton at the Louisiana and Lower Mississippi Valley Collections at LSU sent printouts of computerized archival searches for materials on Ellender. Myrna Whitley, who processed the Russell Long Papers at LSU, took time to locate materials in the collection relating to Ellender. Sandra Biedler, head of Special Collections at the Chester Fritz Library at the University of North Dakota, helped familiarize me with the Milton Young Papers.

I am grateful to Nicholls State University for reducing my teaching load so I could research my topic and for granting me a sabbatical to write the biography.

Nicholls Distinguished Service Professor Emeritus Alfred Delahaye has been my friend and patient copy editor since he helped me with my study of the sugar industry more than fifteen years ago. A trained journalist and an avid reader of political biographies, Delahaye studied history under Francis Butler Simkins, T. Harry Williams, and Richard Kirkendall. His careful reading and timely advice saved me from embarrassing errors and provided new perspectives for viewing the Cajun senator. He also helped select photographs and plan their layout. Kerry Boudreaux, print and press supervisor of Student Publications and Printing at Nicholls State University, and campus photographer Adrian Gauthier duplicated photographs for use in the book.

A number of critics have provided helpful advice. William Cooper, former editor of the Southern Biography Series, has for years encouraged my efforts. He and several anonymous readers have alerted me to errors or oversights. Margaret Dalrymple, editor-in-chief and assistant director of LSU Press, has provided competent, professional assistance from her review of early versions of the study to final stages of preparation. John Easterly, managing editor at the Press, and freelance coordinator Catherine Landry directed the work through production. Anne R. Gibbons, my copy editor, was invaluable. Talented and easy-going, she weeded out typos and spelling errors, revised the footnotes to conform to Press style, and alerted me to a number of inconsistencies.

Of the many people who knew Ellender and shared their impressions and information with me, none was more knowledgeable or helpful than Flo LeCompte. She, better than anyone else, will know if this study is reliable. Dr. Allen Ellender, Jr., facilitated use of photographs at Southdown Museum in Houma and located additional materials on his father and mother to add to the voluminous Ellender collection in the Nicholls State University Archives. These favors he performed without ever once suggesting what I should write about his father. Others in Ellender's inner circle whose insights expanded my knowledge of the senator include Betty and Frank Wurzlow, Jr., George Arceneaux, Jr., Wallace Ellender, Jr., Charles Caillouette, Randolph Bazet, Elward Wright, M. L. Funderburk, Viola Lynch Ellender, and Irving Legendre, Jr.

I alone am responsible for errors of fact, judgment, or interpretation.

The dedication is to my daughter Abigail Brown Becnel, who was born just as I was completing the final stages of this work. Her mother is Houma attorney Dixie C. Brown. Besides being a loving wife and a devoted mother, Dixie has provided legal insights and asked probing questions that have inspired and sustained me over the years.

PART ONE

Louisiana

I

HARDSCRABBLE
(1890–1905)

A low-pressure system settled over south Louisiana during the last week in September, 1890, bringing rain, high humidity, and unseasonably warm weather. The rain helped sugarcane farmers, the New Orleans *Daily Picayune* noted, but the oppressive heat killed a mule pulling a wagon on Tchoupitoulas Street in the city.

In Washington, D.C., a delegation of Louisiana businessmen flocked to the Capitol when Congress began discussing a tariff schedule and sugar imports. Accusing the Republicans of conspiring against Louisiana raw-sugar producers, the group wanted to prevent inexpensive, duty-free raw sugar from flooding American markets and damaging the Louisiana sugarcane industry. The chairmen of the Senate Finance Committee and the House Ways and Means Committee directed tariff legislation with help from the Speaker of the House.

Allen Ellender did not become involved in the controversy, because this Gilded Age political struggle of the nineteenth century was not of his era. He was not born until Wednesday, September 24, 1890, the day the Republican-controlled Congress was concluding work on the tariff. For nearly half of the twentieth century Ellender would be closely involved in government sugar policies. But in 1890 Senator Nelson Aldrich of Rhode Island, chairman of the Finance Committee, and William McKinley of Ohio, House Ways and Means Committee chairman, guided the tariff bill to passage.

The McKinley Tariff placed sugar on the duty-free list and compensated domestic sugar growers with a bounty of two cents per pound. A reciprocity clause allowed the president to impose duties on imported sugar when conditions warranted. However, the McKinley Tariff set high duties on manufactured goods, and it handicapped farmers selling agricultural products abroad. These provisions would have displeased Allen Ellender had he been in Congress then. Senator Randall Lee Gibson of Louisiana led the fight to have the bounty apply to the 1890 sugar crop, but the measure was scheduled to take effect on March 1, 1891, after the Louisiana crop would have been sold. Robert Ruffin Barrow, Jr., a Terrebonne Parish sugar grower, collected $2,389 in 1892 from the sugar bounty for 119,464 pounds produced at Myrtle Grove Plantation.

Benjamin Harrison was president of the United States in 1890 and Francis T. Nicholls was serving his second term as governor of Louisiana. Senator Gibson helped Nicholls annihilate the infamous Louisiana Lottery Company. The last major conflict between Indians and federal troops was fought at Wounded Knee, South Dakota; Ellis Island was about to open; Queen Victoria ruled in England; and Mrs. Jefferson Davis awaited the October release of the first volume of the life of her husband.[1]

The Ellenders lived in coastal south Louisiana fifty air miles southwest of New Orleans on land built by the Mississippi River when it overflowed and deposited sandy, alluvial soil in fan-shaped deltas on the fringes of the Gulf of Mexico. The many bayous flowing southward through their native Terrebonne Parish into the gulf were distributaries of the Mississippi River. Once cleared of cypress and hardwood forests, the land was ideally suited for sugarcane cultivation.

Wallace and Victoria Ellender, probably unaware of the tariff struggle in the nation's capital, were expecting their first child before the 1890 sugarcane grinding season. Victoria gave birth to a healthy son on September 24 in a little Acadian cottage on Hardscrabble Plantation (where the name came from remains a mystery). The tract of land was owned by the Ellender brothers on both banks of Bayou Terrebonne, two miles north of Montegut, a sleepy little fishing and sugarcane village deep in the French bayou country of south Louisiana. Wally and Victoria named the baby Allen after Allen Sanders (a neighbor to the south, who later became a partner of the Ellender

---

1. New Orleans *Daily Picayune*, September 9–25, 1890; Napoleonville (La.) *Pioneer,* September 13, 20, 1890; Thibodaux (La.) *Sentinel,* August 16, September 20, 1890; Mary G. McBride, "Senator Randall Lee Gibson and the Establishment of Tulane University," *Louisiana History,* XXVIII (Summer, 1987), 245–62; Thomas Becnel, *The Barrow Family and the Barataria and Lafourche Canal: The Transportation Revolution in Louisiana, 1829–1925* (Baton Rouge, 1989), 117.

brothers in a sugar factory called Lower Terrebonne Refining and Manufacturing Company). Joseph, Allen's middle name, was the most popular saint's name given to Catholic boys in south Louisiana.[2]

Both Wallace Ellender and Victoria Jarveaux were first-generation residents born in Terrebonne (which means "good earth" in French). Both spoke French and were Acadians. Wallace was thirty-three in 1890, Victoria twenty-one. They came from humble origins and knew how to work. Theirs was a simple life, close to the soil and the resources of the nearby bayous, bays, and marshlands.

Wallace had married Victoria in 1889, the year he and his brothers purchased Hope Farm, a fifteen-arpent-wide (an arpent is a French measurement slightly less than an acre) sandy ridge fronting on the left descending bank of Bayou Terrebonne about three miles upstream from Hardscrabble. A strong, muscular man nearly six feet tall and weighing just under two hundred pounds, Wallace managed Hardscrabble with the assistance of a nephew, Lee Ellender. Wallace was born with lesions on the ligaments of his fingers; for that reason he could never straighten them completely. Two of his sons inherited this crippling disorder, which they had corrected with surgery. Wally chewed tobacco scooped from a pouch with permanently crooked fingers.[3]

The likable Wally signed his three-hundred-dollar marriage bond to Victoria on December 13, 1889, in a neat hand, writing his name as "Elender." In May, 1890, several months before Allen was born, the Ellender brothers had given Ernest, Wallace's twin brother, power of attorney to conduct business for the entire family. (The oldest brother, Henry, had died during the Civil War.) The six Ellender brothers who became agricultural partners were Joseph, Thomas Jr., James, Ernest, Wallace, and David.[4]

Only in a general sense were the Ellenders Acadians. They qualified if one defines Acadians as French-speaking south Louisianians who were mostly uneducated Roman Catholic farmers and fishermen. But they were not direct descendants of the Acadians expelled from Nova Scotia in 1755 by the British during the French and Indian War. True Acadians had recogniz-

2. Thomas Becnel, "The Ellenders: Pioneer Terrebonne Parish Family, 1840–1924," *Louisiana History,* XXVI (Spring, 1985), 117–27; Randolph Bazet, interview, October 22, 1980.

3. Ernest Ellender, Jr., interview, November 14, 1980; Nelo Hebert, interview, November 18, 1980.

4. Terrebonne Parish Conveyance Book "MM," Folio 227, in Terrebonne Parish Courthouse, Houma, La., hereinafter cited as TPCB; M. L. Funderburk, interview, July 11, 1980.

able names: Arceneaux, LeBlanc, Broussard, Boudreaux, Blanchard, Hebert, and Landry are a few of the most common in south Louisiana. Other French speakers, from the West Indies, from France, from Canada, made their way to Louisiana and were amalgamated into what was later called Acadian life. Germans, Spaniards, and Americans also became a part of the cultural tradition.[5]

Victoria's father came from France; her mother was born in Louisiana, according to the Twelfth Census, conducted in 1900. Only five feet three inches tall but sturdy, Victoria was a hard worker. Cleanliness was an obsession. Strong and big-boned, she weighed about 140 pounds. When her son Willard brought his petite future wife to meet her, Victoria noticed the girl's delicate features. After the little redhead had left, Victoria posed a question to her son: "Mais [But], Willard, what can she do with those little hands?"

Wally liked to drink and dance and have fun, but he tended to be tight-fisted with his money. If he returned home with the smell of liquor on his breath and asked Victoria to dance, she would push him away, saying that she had work to do and no time for foolishness. Victoria learned to speak English somewhat imperfectly, and with a strong French accent; she was more comfortable speaking French.[6]

Wallace and his twin brother, Ernest, were born in 1857, the seventh and eighth sons of Tom Ellender and Catharine Roddy. By the time Wallace and Ernest came along, Tom was able to send them to school because he had Henry, Joseph, Thomas Jr., and George to help with farm chores. James, born a few years earlier in 1854, also attended school. When the Eighth Census was taken in 1860, Wallace and Ernest were only three years old. Henry, the oldest son, was the only family member who had attended school that year. In 1870, when the Ninth Census was taken, the twins, then thirteen, had been to school that year, along with James, who was fifteen.[7]

Tom Ellender came to the bayou country of Terrebonne Parish in the late 1830s during the transportation revolution, but he did not become a slave owner like the Barrows, Bonds, Shaffers, McBrides, Minors, and

5. See Carl A. Brasseaux, *The Founding of New Acadia: The Beginnings of Acadian Life in Louisiana, 1765–1803* (Baton Rouge, 1987); Brasseaux, *Acadian to Cajun: Transformation of a People, 1803–1877* (Jackson, Miss., 1992); Glenn R. Conrad, ed., *The Cajuns: Essays on Their History and Culture* (Lafayette, La., 1978).

6. Her Anglo-Saxon daughters-in-law agreed unanimously on this point.

7. Eighth and Ninth Censuses, Microfilm.

McCullams. On the eve of the Civil War Tom Ellender obviously was a yeoman farmer, not a member of the planter aristocracy, although his land was worth six thousand dollars and his other assets another one thousand dollars.[8]

Lower Terrebonne was then largely a wilderness area. Cypress trees covered the swampland, hardwoods the fertile sandy ridges along the major bayous that flowed from the Mississippi River. The entire region was delta land—built over the past five thousand years by silt deposited when the rivers and bayous overflowed. Clearing the land and planting a crop was hard work in the isolated bayou country. In the 1880s, before Louisiana's coastal wetlands subsided, Tom drove cattle to winter pasturage on Caillou Island, now an endangered barrier island separated by miles of open water from land's end at lower Bayou Terrebonne.[9]

Tom Ellender, the son of Thomas Elinger (the name had a variety of spellings) and Sarah Compting, was probably born in Lebanon, Ohio, in 1818. He was of German ancestry and spoke German. In time, he spoke both French and English, but, in the view of local Acadians, with a strange accent. Tom's wife, Catharine Roddy, was born in Terrebonne in 1820. In 1830 her father owned eighteen slaves and a tract of land on Bayou Petit Caillou. When Catharine and Tom appeared before Justice of the Peace Ernest Porche on February 24, 1840, to sign their marriage bond, Catharine, who could write, was twenty years old and the owner of property. Tom made his mark next to his name, written as Thomas Elinger.[10] The first public reference using the modern spelling of the name—Ellender—appeared in the conveyance records of Terrebonne Parish in 1848 when Tom and Catharine sold a tract of land on Bayou Petit Caillou for five hundred dollars. Thus Tom and Catharine, neither of whom was a true Acadian, were outsiders who learned the language and ways of their Acadian neighbors. In time they, too, were called Acadians.

In 1874 Tom Ellender paid $828 for a tract of land of two and a half acres fronting the left descending bank of little Bayou Terrebonne about fifteen miles below the town of Houma. The depth of the land was of little consequence then because the high land hugged the edges of the bayous that

---

8. Eighth Census, Microfilm.

9. Houma (La.) *Courier,* September 24, 1965, in "1965" Scrapbook, Allen J. Ellender Papers, Nicholls State University Library, Thibodaux, La., hereinafter cited as AEP.

10. Terrebonne Parish Marriage Book 1, Folio 286, in Terrebonne Parish Courthouse, Houma, La.

provided the avenues of transportation. There Tom would live out the remaining years of his life. In 1880 Tom bought Hardscrabble, where Allen would be born in a plain raised Acadian cottage. It had a porch across the front and an attic under the high gable roof. The ground floor probably had only two rooms—and it undoubtedly had no indoor bathroom. By this time the Ellender brothers were old enough to perform most plantation tasks. They operated a small sugar mill on Hardscrabble with little outside help. Each brother had a special duty to perform. Wallace served as overseer; Ernest kept the plantation accounts. Others worked in the fields, the plantation store, or in the sugarhouse.[11]

Tom Ellender had bought Hardscrabble from Jean Pierre Viguerie for twenty-five hundred dollars. Originally called Caillou Field, the plantation had been part of Point Farm, once owned by Robert Ruffin Barrow, a wealthy Terrebonne planter and canal tycoon. Contiguous to the Pointe au Chien road on the north, it measured five arpents fronting on both banks of Bayou Terrebonne.[12]

Old Tom Ellender was illiterate, but he had a sound grasp of economic concepts. His many sons provided the labor for his farm operations. None of his sons, not even the married ones, received a set salary from their father. Tom parceled out funds as needed from his single bank account. The simple life-style of the Ellenders allowed them to avoid debt except when necessary to purchase more agricultural lands. After the Civil War, Tom acquired additional lands when many wealthy planters lost their plantations.

Tom was keenly aware that his sons provided a labor advantage and he enjoyed joking about it. Periodically a factor (commission merchant), who bought sugar from planters and provided letters of credit for purchasing supplies from New Orleans, called on Tom to review accounts for the year. A visiting factor, upon reviewing Tom's accounts, asked why no funds had been budgeted to pay his workers. Tom gestured toward his genitals and with obvious delight replied: "I produce my own labor."[13]

In his mid-sixties Tom became partially paralyzed. He died at home on May 17, 1884, at age sixty-seven. Although the guiding strength of the family was gone, the Ellenders remained a close-knit unit. Under the leadership of Ernest, the brothers enlarged their land holdings. In 1886 they purchased a

11. M. L. Funderburk, interview, July 11, 1980; O. J. Robichaux, interview, July 7, 1980.
12. TPCB "EE," Folio 593; P. A. Champomier, *Statement of the Sugar Crop Made in Louisiana in 1859–60* (New Orleans, 1860), 28.
13. M. L. Funderburk, interview, July 11, 1980.

two-and-a-half-arpent tract next to Hardscrabble and fronting on both sides of Bayou Terrebonne.[14]

Tom Ellender's estate became known simply as the Ellender brothers' land, even though their only sister, Elizabeth, who suffered from bouts of insanity, was still alive. (She died in 1894.) The Ellender brothers continued to buy land and to expand their operations. Brotherly cohesiveness explains, in part, their success in holding on to sugarcane lands during hard times. They had learned from Tom the value of hard work and the importance of frugality. Once the Ellenders had paid off their mortgages, they avoided debt; they were consistently conservative and solvent. They continued to commingle their funds, for there was still only one Ellender account at the bank.[15]

Hope Farm, bought the year before Allen was born, proved to be a good investment for the Ellenders. It contained a high ridge, fertile and crescent shaped, and many acres of valuable timber on its swampy fringes. Under the leadership of Ernest, the brothers purchased sugarhouse equipment from Ralph Bisland in 1891 and land and equipment from Albert Viguerie in 1894. The deal with Viguerie involved selling Hardscrabble to Viguerie, then buying it back on the same day, with Viguerie's equipment and some additional acreage. The brothers owed Viguerie thirteen thousand dollars, which they repaid in time.[16]

Life for Wallace, Victoria, and young Allen improved as the family business prospered. Around 1907 they left the small Acadian cottage on Hardscrabble where Allen was born to settle into a new Victorian-style house on Hope Farm three miles up Bayou Terrebonne. The twins, Ernest and Wallace, built identical houses only shouting distance apart. By then Allen had four siblings: Claude, born in 1895; a sister, Walterine, born in 1897; Wallace Jr., born in 1902; and Willard, born in 1905. Allen and Claude, like their mother, were short and stocky.

The Ellender clan continued to be a close-knit group. The brothers maintained one bank account and authorized Ernest to buy and sell property for them; they even shared food items. Once a week the family butchered an animal to divide among family members. The families of Ernest and Wallace were especially close. They shared a telephone and became almost a single family. If one brother bought a watermelon for his family, he bought

---

14. TPCB "JJ," Folio 287.
15. M. L. Funderburk, interview, July 11, 1980.
16. TPCB "MM," Folio 564; TPCB "OO," Folio 41–B.

a second for his twin's family. If one twin was not back at home at the expected hour, the other worried about him.[17]

As Roman Catholics, the Ellenders attended Sacred Heart Church in Montegut when they lived on Hardscrabble. After they moved to Hope Farm, they became parishioners of Saint Ann's Church in Bourg. There is no indication that they attended services regularly or that religion strongly influenced Allen during his formative years. Travel by horse and buggy was difficult; trips to Houma, slightly more than ten miles away, were infrequent.[18]

In 1896 the Ellender brothers added to their land holdings by purchasing Aragon Plantation just upstream from Hardscrabble. The seller, Edward A. LeBlanc, received $20,000 for the tract on February 21, 1896, $8,000 in cash. LeBlanc, reluctant to sell, was unable to meet a mortgage payment due a New Orleans bank. Better to sell to the Ellenders, Ernest argued successfully, than to have the bank seize the property and sell it to someone else. In 1900 Ernest purchased from the State of Louisiana 881 acres of swamp lands contiguous to Ellender holdings for only $110.13, or twelve and one-half cents per acre.[19]

The Ellenders and their planter neighbors of lower Terrebonne lived modestly, enjoying few frills of the wealthy plantation families in upper Terrebonne. Allen Sanders, a neighbor, was his own overseer. The Champagne, Robichaux, and Viguerie families also had simple life-styles.[20]

By the turn of the century, the Ellenders enjoyed a status between that of the planter aristocracy and the masses of poor farmers. They were respected in Terrebonne as hard-working big landowners. Rogers' *Parish Directory* for 1897 indicates that they owned 2,500 acres, including 300 acres in sugarcane and 175 in corn. They produced 5,000 tons of cane in 1896. The Ellender brothers had ninety mules—forty-five teams—to perform the necessary chores on Hardscrabble and Hope Farm. At Hardscrabble the family transported sugarcane from one side of Bayou Terrebonne to the other on a narrow-gauge railroad bridge spanning the bayou.[21]

17. M. L. Funderburk, interview, July 11, 1980; Charles Caillouette, interview, November 23, 1979.

18. Wallace Ellender, Jr., interview, November 20, 1979.

19. TPCB "QQ," Folio 43; Ernest Ellender, Jr., interview, November 14, 1980; Nelo Hebert, interview, September 30, 1980; TPCB "TT," Folio 46–B.

20. Randolph Bazet, interview, October 22, 1980.

21. *Ibid.;* O. J. Robichaux, interview, July 7, 1980; M. L. Funderburk, interview, July 11, 1980; Rogers, *Directory of the Parish of Terrebonne, 1897, Containing a Historical Sketch of the Parish* (New Orleans, 1897), 28; Wallace Ellender, Jr., interview, November 20, 1979.

As a youngster Allen Ellender displayed some precocious instincts, but there were no public schools in the area where he could begin his formal education. He learned to speak English and French. Like his father and old Tom Ellender, he developed a clipped, rapid accent a bit different from the typical Acadian accent. Perhaps the German speech patterns of Tom, passed down to Wally in watered-down fashion, influenced Allen's speech. He became noted for a good memory and an ability to learn quickly. Victoria, never totally comfortable speaking English, addressed her children in French. At an early age family members began to call Allen "Sous-Sous" ("Little Pennies"). One family explanation for the nickname is that young Allen hustled family members and passersby for pennies. Another attributes the name to a dream Allen had of finding pennies under his bed—only to cry mournfully upon awakening to find none.

Allen remembered wearing a dresslike gown as a child. It was the kind Ellender boys and girls wore until they were old enough for more traditional garments that distinguished boys from girls. At an early age he wore eyeglasses below his thick, dark, curly hair. Undoubtedly, his doting parents spoiled him. There was no shortage of cousins to play with or of uncles to serve as role models. A lesson learned by all Ellender children, male and female, was the importance of work and frugality. Parental influences and attention never precluded the requirement that Ellender children must work. Early in life Allen developed a healthy work ethic and a desire to prove himself to his elders. He seemed eager to fulfill family expectations, and he enjoyed the praise he received for his efforts.[22]

The Ellender brothers used plantation funds to educate their children, but some Ellenders saw little value in education and chose not to send their children to school. Ernest and Wallace took the lead in establishing a school in the Hardscrabble area. They engaged Henry Ellender, son of Thomas Jr., to teach the local children and the many Ellenders. Henry, one of the oldest of old Tom's grandchildren, instructed Allen and Allen's cousins. The extent and quality of Henry's education is not known. Rogers' *Parish Directory* for 1897 lists him as principal of Laperouse Public School, twenty-one miles south of Houma. The assessment roll for Terrebonne Parish in 1898 indicates that he was twenty-four years old and a teacher. Apparently Allen attended the one-room school regularly. When Sidney Larrieu called at the Wallace Ellender home on June 11, 1900, to take the Twelfth Census, Allen was at school. He had attended for eight months the previous year.[23]

22. Florence LeCompte, interview, August 2, 1979.
23. Rogers, *Parish Directory*, 30.

Nelo Hebert was Allen's classmate at Henry's tuition-free school. Born the same year as Allen, possibly also on Hardscrabble Plantation, Nelo had vivid memories of his youth. His father, Amadee Hebert, about the same age as Ernest and Wallace, had worked for old Tom Ellender. Nelo attended Henry Ellender's school at Hardscrabble with Allen and about thirty other students. The books and the instruction were in English, but on the playground most students spoke French. Hebert remembered young Allen as somewhat of a busybody and a *rapporteur,* a tattletale. Young Allen's desire to please may have led him to reveal the shortcomings of his classmates. It is hard to imagine that he did not work hard at his studies and try to impress his teacher. Unlike Huey Long, who resisted authority figures even early in life, Allen, perhaps trying to compensate for being short, became a syco-phant, frequently demonstrating his willingness to work hard and follow instructions.[24]

In July, 1904, when Allen was nearly fourteen, his uncle George was killed by lightning at Hardscrabble. Having taken his horse to breed with a neighbor's mare, he found himself in a violent local storm. The lightning bolt killed George and his horse. A bachelor, George had written his will in 1902, bequeathing his property to the six Ellender partners: Joseph, Thomas Jr., James, Ernest, Wallace, and David.[25]

When not in school, Allen worked on small tasks around the plantation. Convinced that everyone should perform chores, Wallace Sr. required Allen to carry water, feed livestock, open gates, and perform similar tasks. When he was about twelve, Allen kept tally of sugarcane delivered to the mill; he had mastered a simple single-entry bookkeeping method. Allen despised hav-ing to get up early in the morning, especially on cold, wintry mornings, to make coffee for the family. The smell of coffee became repulsive to him, and he avoided one standard Acadian passion, the frequent consumption of strong black coffee. He did not consider the work itself repugnant, but rather a part of growing up in the Ellender tradition.[26]

24. Nelo Hebert, interviews, September 30, October 21, November 18, 1980; William I. Hair, *The Kingfish and His Realm: The Life and Times of Huey P. Long* (Baton Rouge, 1991), 40.

25. Burial of George Ellender, August 1, 1904, in Sacred Heart Catholic Church funeral records, Montegut, La.; Nelo Hebert, interview, September 30, 1980; M. L. Funderburk, in-terview, July 11, 1980; Terrebonne Parish Will Book "1A," Folio 125, in Terrebonne Parish Courthouse, Houma, La.

26. Florence LeCompte, interview, August 2, 1979; Frank Wurzlow, Jr., interview, April 9, 1980; George Arceneaux, Jr., interview, December 31, 1979.

When Allen outgrew Henry's one-room school at Hardscrabble, he received private tutoring from Andrew Bouvier, an outsider who had married a local woman and who ran a small private school for some years in Montegut, just south of the Ellender lands. Bouvier, a native of France, had been in a Catholic order of brothers, which he had left before settling in the bayou country. After teaching Allen as much as he could, Bouvier advised Wally to send him to a preparatory school in New Orleans before allowing him to enter college. Like many Acadian students, Allen had trouble with English grammar and syntax.

In 1905 Bouvier helped Allen enter St. Aloysius in New Orleans, a private Catholic high school with facilities for boarders. Willard, the last of Wally and Victoria's children, was born that year. Allen was fifteen. Ellender brothers' funds paid the tuition for Allen's four years at St. Aloysius. Extant records do not reveal how the short Acadian boy from lower Terrebonne Parish adjusted to life in a New Orleans boarding school. Undoubtedly, he worked hard and tried to please his teachers. During the holiday seasons he rode the train home and participated in the sugarcane grinding chores at the end of the year.[27]

As a young man growing up on the Ellender sugarcane lands stretching from just below Bourg to the Pointe au Chien road just above Montegut, Allen came in contact with many adult men who worked on Hope Farm, Aragon, Hardscrabble, and Point Farm. Impressionable and eager to please, he proved himself worthy of responsibility. What he heard from those associates about race must have influenced him more than his personal contacts with blacks, for the Ellenders hired few laborers and earlier had owned few slaves.[28] Young Allen came in contact with blacks from time to time, but few blacks resided in the domain of the Ellenders, then or now. Undoubtedly the prevailing white view of blacks had been influenced by spirited racial clashes at the end of the Populist Era in Louisiana. These, presumably, made a strong impression on young Allen.

Allen liked the blacks who worked for his father on the sugarcane plantation. Uncle Henry was the only name he knew for the stable hand "who

27. *Aloysian,* n.p., n.d., and New Orleans *Times-Picayune,* May 21, 1965, both in "1965" Scrapbook, AEP; Allen J. Ellender, interview by David Schoenbrun, July 3, 1962, pp. 4, 6, in "Ellender Personal" Folder, and Florence LeCompte, mimeographed biographical office sketch of Allen Ellender, 1972, both in Box 1123, AEP; Charles Caillouette, interview, November 23, 1979; Wallace Ellender, Jr., interview, November 20, 1979.

28. M. L. Funderburk, interview, July 11, 1980.

was born a slave and put me on mules when I was a tot." Allen also remembered Henry's wife, Clara. "I called her Aunt Clara and she was as kind to
me as my mother was," he said.[29]

Although blacks in lower Terrebonne called Allen by his nickname,
"Sous-Sous," their world and his were different and separate—just as the
color of their skin was different. Allen came to realize this as a teenager. He
communicated with blacks comfortably and dealt with them as individuals.
Blacks deferred to whites in many ways, Allen knew, and they suffered from
economic, social, and political discrimination. No doubt he shared the pa-
ternalistic impression of blacks as lazy, inferior to whites, unambitious, and
probably happy with their lot. He may not have realized how racial events
in the South in general, in Louisiana, and indeed in Terrebonne and neighboring Lafourche parishes shaped the prevailing wisdom of his day. These
events had occurred in the years shortly before his birth. Before Allen was
ten, blacks in Louisiana had been disenfranchised and the Republican Party
had virtually ceased to exist. In many ways white supremacists reasserted the
control they had enjoyed during the days of slavery.

The Louisiana Constitution of 1868 had given black men the vote, and
a number of blacks had held political office during Reconstruction. The Fif-
teenth Amendment, ratified in 1870, prohibited states from denying the franchise because of race, creed, or previous conditions of servitude. However,
racial violence—called bulldozing (which included the intimidation of black
voters and the stealing of their votes)—had become a reality in Louisiana
during the 1870s and a way of life after home rule in 1877 when the Bourbon
Democrats regained political control. The Bourbons relied on bulldozing and
economic pressure to deny the franchise to blacks.

The Thibodaux Massacre of 1887, a bloody strike and race riot in neighboring Lafourche, left at least thirty-five blacks dead. It must have troubled
the Ellender brothers, for it dealt mainly with a dispute over wages paid
primarily to black sugarcane laborers. Just the year before, Jim Brown, a
mulatto leader in Houma, had called a strike to protest attempts by big
planters to oust small black landholders. Covington Hall, a neighbor of the
Ellenders at Rural Retreat Plantation, contiguous to Hope Farm, was forced
in 1891 to leave his plantation because of a financial setback. Allen was only
one year old. Hall had heard from an uncle, Rodney Woods, about the strike.
Fearful of losing his entire sugarcane crop, Woods gave in to black worker

---

29. David Schoenbrun, "Casebook of a Southern Senator: Allen J. Ellender of Louisiana," *Esquire,* September, 1963, p. 108.

demands and was called disloyal to his class by neighboring planters.[30] No record exists of how the Ellenders felt about the violent incident, but they undoubtedly knew of the prevailing white sentiment toward black laborers who joined labor unions and called strikes during the grinding season.

Bulldozing, a standard practice in upland cotton areas, was never common in sugar country because sugar planters, needing tariff protection, supported the Republican Party. When Louisiana Populists formed a fusion ticket with Republicans in the 1896 gubernatorial election, the Democrats knew stealing black votes would not be as easy as usual. After winning the election, the Democrats decided the safest thing to do was to disenfranchise blacks and weaken the Republican Party. They used precedents allowed in the U.S. Supreme Court's 1890 *Williams* v. *Mississippi* decision to disenfranchise blacks. Writing property and literacy requirements for voting into the Louisiana Constitution of 1898, they accomplished their objective—the Republican Party in Louisiana disintegrated and Louisiana became part of the one-party Solid South. Blacks were only slightly less disadvantaged as free citizens than they had been as slaves, but white politicians, many of them demagogues, harped on the race issue, creating the impression that it was the most serious problem facing the state. The emotional issue of race diverted attention from serious deficiencies in education and other public services—and from half-hearted attempts to get Louisiana in step with twentieth-century America.

When Allen was ten, in 1900, New Orleans experienced a bloody race riot associated with a manhunt for Robert Charles, a black man who refused to be intimidated by a bullying cop. Charles was gunned down after several days of violence in New Orleans. This was the racial milieu in which young Allen Ellender matured.[31]

Extant records do not reveal whether Allen knew about these racial clashes, but he must have heard about them. When classmate Nelo Hebert was a young boy, blacks had to tip their hats to whites and could not loiter in public places. Hebert remembered an incident involving Demé McGraw, the son of Robert McGraw, a popular black who broke horses at Pecan Grove Plantation. Demé apparently refused to defer to whites and was re-

---

30. Covington Hall, "Labor Struggles in the Deep South" (Typescript in Manuscripts Section, Howard-Tilton Memorial Library, Tulane University, New Orleans, La.), 32–34, 40, 42.

31. William I. Hair, *Carnival of Fury: Robert Charles and the New Orleans Race Riot of 1900* (Baton Rouge, 1976).

garded as a "sassy nigger." Like most southerners of their time (and Missourian Harry Truman), the Ellenders referred to blacks as "niggers." On one occasion local whites shot and injured Demé, who survived the shooting, moved to Chicago, and never returned to Terrebonne. Hebert recalled other incidents in which blacks, having been threatened with violence, gave in to their white oppressors.[32]

Allen's brother Wallace Jr., recalling how deferential blacks were when he was a youngster, thought the races got along better then. He minimized discriminatory practices and convinced himself that blacks in that era were satisfied with their lot. By the time Allen was a teenager, blacks had lost the right to vote, were legally segregated, and were potential victims of lynching. Between 1896 and 1903 at least ninety-two lynchings occurred in Louisiana. Yet, at least in the rhetoric of southern demagogues, the black threat was the most serious problem confronting white southerners. Young Allen learned of race relations during his formative years, when segregation and discrimination were ever present and violence was not unusual. Like other values passed on to him by his family, this too he accepted as the order of things, a part of life that was harsh and perhaps unfair, but nonetheless the lot of the people inhabiting the good earth. His character was developing in a society based on blatant racism.[33]

32. Nelo Hebert, interview, October 21, 1980; David McCullough, *Truman* (New York, 1992), 247, 588.
33. Hair, *The Kingfish,* 67.

2

YOUNG LAWYER, YOUNG WIFE
(1905–21)

*A*llen Ellender was proud to call himself an Acadian, but in many ways he aspired to rise above the humble ambitions of most of his French-speaking neighbors. They were content to live close to nature, farming, fishing, and trapping. He was eager to learn and would learn things alien to his family and friends, but he wanted them to know that in most ways his values had not changed. He remained very loyal to the family unit. Many Acadians considered education unimportant to success and happiness. But Ellender realized the importance of education, thanks to the prodding of Wallace and Uncle Ernest.

Burdened by short stature and a decided French accent, Ellender nonetheless never became withdrawn, never developed an "Acadian complex." His shortcomings did not limit or diminish his ability to learn when he entered St. Aloysius High School in 1905. He had ventured a bit from home in his early schooling, and he had come in contact with many different people. He had demonstrated qualities of leadership and responsibility, performing tasks assigned by his father and uncles. He had also been one of the brightest local students, one of the most eager to succeed. At first he could not decide whether to study medicine or law. After a shaky first semester struggling with troublesome English courses, he made respectable grades. He had a good memory for details and learned that he could not translate directly from French to English.

After he graduated from St. Aloysius in 1909, he passed the entrance examination to gain admission to Tulane University the same year. He lived in an inexpensive boarding house near the campus. In 1913 he joined Pi Kappa Alpha, an academic fraternity, where he met Leander Perez, a bright

young fellow from Plaquemines Parish. Like Ellender, he came from a sec-
ond- or third-generation non-Anglo-Saxon family that had adjusted to life
in Louisiana's productive wetlands.[1]

Ellender brothers' funds financed Allen's college education. His brother
Claude, his sister, Walterine, cousins Ernest Jr. and Henry Jr., and others
also received educational funds from the account. To earn money during the
summer vacation, which was the slow season on a sugar plantation, Allen
and his cousin Thomas Ellender III (called Tommy) followed the wheat
harvest across Kansas, Nebraska, and the Dakotas, pitching wheat into wagons during long days in the Midwest heat. In 1910 Allen worked on the farm
of Ross Throop near Arlington, South Dakota.[2] Occasionally Allen ran into
a farmer who thought the Louisianian was too small to handle the heavy
work, but he would quickly demonstrate his strength and endurance. He
became somewhat of an overachiever as a laborer to compensate for his short
stature and as a student to offset his nonacademic Acadian upbringing.

Ellender earned additional money in college by posing as a model for
art classes. His muscular, compact body was ideally suited for the task. He
posed before mixed classes of men and women, sometimes only in a loin
cloth. Usually the pose was that of a runner poised to begin a race or of a
boxer ready for combat. He used his earnings to attend movies, musicals,
and stage shows. For fifty cents he could get a top balcony seat at the old
French Opera House in the French Quarter to hear some of the great singers
of the day. He also enjoyed legitimate theater productions. The Acadian boy
from the bayou country absorbed urban culture as part of his education, but
it never drastically altered his life-style or basic philosophy. Besides, attending
shows and theatrical productions allowed him to meet new friends, including
attractive young women.[3]

On Tulane Night in 1913 Ellender had a part in a theatrical production
called *Old Heidelberg,* as did Helen Calhoun Donnelly, a pretty redheaded

1. Florence LeCompte, interview, August 2, 1979; *Aloysian,* n.d., n.p., in "1965" Scrapbook, Allen J. Ellender Papers, Nicholls State University Library, Thibodaux, La., hereinafter
cited as AEP; Glen Jeansonne, *Leander Perez: Boss of the Delta* (Baton Rouge, 1977), 11.

2. Ernest Ellender, Jr., and Ellen Ellender Walker, interview, November 14, 1980; Henry
Ellender, Jr., interview, November 4, 1980; Ralph O. Hillgren, *Daily Argus Leader* (Sioux Falls,
S.D.), October 24, 1947, clipping in "1945–1947" Scrapbook, AEP.

3. Florence LeCompte, mimeographed biographical office sketch of Allen Ellender, 1972,
Box 1123, AEP.

student enrolled at Sophie Newcomb College, the Tulane University branch for women. When he first saw Helen, riding on a streetcar with her mother, Ellender told a companion at his side, "That is the girl I'm going to marry."[4]

After he graduated from Tulane Law School in 1913 with an LL.B. in civil law, Ellender returned to Terrebonne Parish, but not to the family house on Hope Farm. Instead, he moved to Houma, the parish seat, where he opened his law office. He was twenty-three years old, a bachelor, and the first of Tom's grandchildren to earn an academic degree or to complete professional training. His years in New Orleans had matured him and instilled in him a sense of self-confidence.

Allen enjoyed his status as the most educated of the Ellenders. Uncle Ernest and Wallace had established themselves in Terrebonne as successful, respected farmers and businessmen. Allen's brother Claude, then only seventeen, had planned to follow in his footsteps and become a lawyer also. Willard and cousin Ernest Jr. both wanted to be doctors and were pursuing schooling preparatory for medical school.[5]

On his return from New Orleans Ellender took lodging at the Campbell Jones boarding house at Lafayette and School streets in Houma, near the home of Thomas Wright and his nine children. He left the friendly confines of Hope Farm for small-town life in the seat of government for Terrebonne Parish. Before long Ellender became the law partner of Harris Gagné, a respected attorney in the town of thirty-five hundred residents.[6]

The Ellender brothers helped further Allen's career in a number of ways. Through their intervention he became attorney for the Bank of Terrebonne. On September 2, 1913, the mayor and board of aldermen elected Ellender attorney for the city as well.[7] Neither job paid well or seriously interested established attorneys, but Ellender was just getting started. He needed experience and clients, and clients gradually found their way to his office. Meanwhile, he became a landowner of sorts. In 1914 he bought a lot, just

---

4. Carl Schneider to Allen Ellender, August 14, 1961, "Agriculture, General—1961" Folder, Box 304, and Florence LeCompte, mimeographed Ellender biographical office sketch, 1972, Box 1123, both in AEP.

5. M. L. Funderburk, interview, July 11, 1980.

6. Elward Wright, interview, November 8, 1979.

7. Certificate of Appointment, "Ellender, Allen J. (Personal)" Folder, Box 4, AEP; M. L. Funderburk, interview, July 8, 1980.

below Houma, measuring ninety-five by fifty-five feet at a sheriff's sale for ninety-five dollars. In 1915 and 1916 he bought other small lots in town.

As a practicing attorney, Allen could readily check the parish conveyance records and review the financial arrangements of the Ellender brothers. Uncle Ernest had spearheaded their expansion plans, buying land for the six brothers with funds from the single Ellender bank account. Allen noted that Ernest alone held title to 881 acres of swampland purchased by the brothers in 1900 and paid for with joint funds. In June, 1914, Allen acted as notary for the transfer of the undivided five-sixths of the swampland from Ernest to his five brothers for five hundred dollars.[8]

Sometimes Ellender acted in a surprising and unconventional manner. In 1915 he was appointed district attorney for Lafourche and Terrebonne parishes to fill a vacancy. He enjoyed being the chief prosecutor for the large rural parishes but knew his chances for winning election in 1916 were slim. A local tradition required the district attorney to be from Lafourche, the district judge from Terrebonne. Nonetheless, Ellender decided to buck tradition and file for the D.A.'s position. Friends and supporters believed he was wasting his time by running. His opponent in 1916 was Thibodaux attorney J. A. O. Coignet of Lafourche. Accompanied by Wallace Jr., Allen campaigned aggressively but Coignet won easily. Ellender took his defeat graciously.[9]

Ellender had challenged the local political structure to achieve a personal goal—and had failed. He may have seen the race as an opportunity to receive political recognition for future campaigns. In 1916 Ellender met Randolph Bazet, an assistant in the clerk of court's office, and saw Bazet almost daily. In time they became fast friends. Like Ellender, Bazet loved to fish and hunt. Sometimes Allen's brother Claude joined them for a duck or snipe hunt. Allen proved to be a good shot with a double-barreled shotgun. An old outdoorsman remembered the time Allen shot an albino mallard, the only one either of them had ever seen.

Ellender, regarded by Bazet as strong and athletic, could walk long distances and work hard. Bazet and Ellender, resting during a long hike, once stopped to snitch a few stalks of sugarcane from a neighbor's patch. As Ellender skillfully stripped the hard outer peel from the chewable sweet pulp

8. Terrebonne Parish Conveyance Book 63, Folio 335, in Terrebonne Parish Courthouse, Houma, La., hereinafter cited as TPCB.

9. Randolph Bazet, interview, October 22, 1980; Elward Wright, interview, November 8, 1979; Wallace Ellender, Jr., interview, November 20, 1979.

with a pocket knife, he reminded Bazet that they had committed an illegal act by "severing a resource from the soil." [10]

In other ways, Ellender was stubborn and a creature of habit. He enjoyed fishing as much as hunting, partly because in south Louisiana he could fish almost year-round. But he had no knack for fishing; only his enthusiasm kept local experts from giving up on him. He mostly caught redfish and speckled trout by using shrimp, cut mullet, or minnows for bait. His main problem was covering the barb of the hook with the meaty part of the live bait instead of running the hook through a thin layer of skin. Fish took Ellender's bait—and spat it out easily because the barb of the hook, buried in the body of the bait, did not penetrate the mouth of the fish. He stubbornly refused to alter his fishing style, despite pleas from local experts. Ellender, as an outdoorsman, would usually consume what he shot or caught. [11]

At twenty-six Ellender was becoming established as a young Cajun attorney from a prominent family. He had held public office and had been defeated for elective office. He was impressive in appearance, despite his five-foot-four-inch stature. He weighed about 160 pounds. He wore a size sixteen shirt with thirty-three-inch sleeves. He smoked cigarettes and, like many men in the Acadian country, he drank, especially on fishing trips. He also chewed tobacco and used a spittoon in his law office on the second floor of the Bank of Terrebonne building. He loved the agricultural lands and outdoor activities. Ever energetic, he seemed confident but low-keyed in dealings with townspeople, many of whom called him "Sous-Sous." When blacks came to his office, they tended to ask for "Mr. Sous-Sous Ellender." [12]

Ellender's obvious lack was a wife. After all, in the Acadian country early marriages and large families were common. Surely Victoria and the other Ellenders must have wondered when Allen would marry and start a family. They may have been encouraged on January 16, 1917, when he bought a house on a lot, 96 by 266 feet, on East Park Avenue near Gouaux Avenue— for $2,738.89. Several days later he bought an adjacent vacant lot of the same

10. Randolph Bazet, interview, October 22, 1980; Cyprian Voisin, interview, October 2, 1980.

11. Jack Carlos, interview, July 8, 1980; Irving Legendre, Jr., interview, July 10, 1980.

12. Elward Wright, interview, November 8, 1979; Evans Pitre, interview, July 11, 1980; M. L. Funderburk, interview, July 11, 1980; Allen Ellender, Jr., interview, June 6, 1980; Frank Wurzlow, Jr., to Allen Ellender (memo), April 5, 1956, in "Agriculture, Cotton, 1956" Folder, Box 248, AEP.

size for $161.11. Soon the reason became obvious; the pretty redhead he had met at Tulane had accepted his proposal of marriage. On March 19, 1917, Ellender married Helen Calhoun Donnelly at St. Louis Cathedral in New Orleans. The Rev. O. Racine performed the ceremony; Uncle Ernest, a witness, signed the marriage certificate.[13]

Helen was born in New Orleans in 1895, five years after Ellender. She was of Irish-American ancestry and had two brothers and four sisters. Her parents had not always been wealthy, but they had become prosperous middle-class Americans, eager to provide their children with opportunities that had eluded them. After Helen graduated from high school, she enrolled at prestigious Sophie Newcomb College, studied the arts, and often played minor roles in musical and dramatic productions.

Ellender was only modestly successful when he took his city-girl bride to live in the sleepy rural fishing and farming town of Houma. Only a month after their marriage the United States entered World War I. As a married man, Ellender received a deferred draft board status. The young couple rarely attended parties or entertained at home. Yet they complemented each other. Helen enjoyed Allen's status and popularity—and strenuously discouraged his tobacco chewing; Allen admired Helen's social refinement, her poise, her bearing. Ambitious for Allen, Helen wanted him to achieve lofty political and professional goals. Meanwhile, Ellender remained a country fellow, somewhat lacking in social graces, more fond of hunting and fishing and farming than parties. He liked being close to nature.

Helen—rather high-strung, moody, and subject to extreme personality shifts—was intense and somewhat unpredictable. "She could cuss you one day; love you the next," her sister-in-law recalled. Another family member remembered that she was often "up" for a few days and then "down" for a few. When she was feeling good, she giggled and had fun. Her introverted manner led some to consider her snobbish and aloof; no one visited her without an invitation. Ellender, although impatient at times, was approachable and down to earth.[14]

Helen busied herself with household chores at 235 East Park Avenue in a pleasant section of Houma. Although the town was the parish seat of Terrebonne Parish, it was largely a rural community with few sophisticated urban niceties. There was no hospital, few people had telephones, and the

---

13. TPCB 66, Folios 119, 140; Terrebonne Parish Marriage Book 50, Folios 128–29, in Terrebonne Parish Courthouse, Houma, La.

14. Daisy Donnelly, interview, July 14, 1980; Viola Lynch Ellender, interview, July 14, 1980; M. L. Funderburk, interview, July 8, 1980.

town did not yet have natural gas for heating and cooking, even though it was in the center of some of the biggest oil and gas deposits in the world. Just across Bayou Terrebonne from her home was the courthouse and Ellender's law office above the Bank of Terrebonne. Helen liked cats and fed at least fifteen daily. At one time she fed a squirrel until someone killed it. She also liked flowers, occasionally driving out into the country to obtain compost for her flower beds.[15]

In 1917 Ellender formed a close friendship with Elward Wright, the oldest son of Thomas Wright, the postmaster of Houma. When Ellender first moved to Houma, Wright was a teenager. He had attended Louisiana State University in 1917, but had left the following year for military service. He returned to Houma after the war. Then the death of his father cast him in the role of main provider for eight brothers and sisters. Knowing that Wright wanted to become a lawyer, Ellender invited him to clerk in his office so he could learn procedure and read case law in preparation for taking the bar examination.

When Wright explained his need to increase his earnings because so many siblings depended on him, Ellender suggested that he open an insurance agency. With some financial assistance from Ellender, Wright formed the Elward Wright Insurance Agency and became a notary public. The two men became close friends, even sharing their personal belongings. Ellender had complete trust in Wright, who bought property in partnership with Ellender without signing any legal documents. "There was not a scratch on paper between us—not even a handshake," Wright recalled.

Ellender relied on his instincts to judge character. He was honest and he assumed that his close friends were as well. Like the Ellender brothers in their business dealings, he considered a man's word to be his bond, even though he had studied the civil code and knew written documents were more reliable.

Their usual arrangement was for Elward to become one-third owner and Ellender two-thirds owner of city lots that Elward bought for as little as one hundred dollars each. Sometimes the only way Elward could raise his one-third share of the cost was by borrowing from the Bank of Terrebonne, using as collateral a note endorsed by Ellender. Much property in Wright's name was actually Ellender's because eventually the two men negotiated a counter letter, a legal document establishing Ellender's claim to property in

15. Evans Pitre, interview, July 11, 1980; Nolan P. LeCompte, Jr., interview, June 17, 1980.

Wright's name. It was a mere legal formality, one Ellender soon forgot. "He never could have found that damn letter if he had to," Wright said.[16]

Even though Ellender had a deferred draft status, he tried to join the military service in July, 1917. He was rejected for medical reasons. During a physical examination on July 6, doctors at Touro Infirmary in New Orleans discovered a stone the size of a quarter in his left kidney. In April, 1918, Dr. Joseph Hume, upon examining Ellender, found a urinary tract infection caused by the stone. He recommended surgery, which he successfully performed on April 17, to remove the stone. After several weeks of recovery, Ellender resumed his legal practice. Why Ellender wanted to volunteer for military service is not clear. Perhaps his sense of noblesse oblige learned as a youth prompted him to join. He may have anticipated that an exemplary military record would enhance future political campaigns.

His recovery complete, Ellender wrote in July, 1918, to Louisiana congressman Whitmel P. Martin about securing a military commission in the Judge Advocate's Division, the legal branch of the military. Martin replied that the only possible commission Ellender could get was as a translator in the Marine Corps. Ellender was disappointed, uncertain that his formal French was strong enough to allow him to pass a competitive examination. Next he wrote to Tulane president A. B. Dinwiddie about joining the Student Army Training Corps at Tulane. He informed Dinwiddie about his efforts to enter military service, his surgery and recovery, and his determination to serve. "I am 27 years old, married and have no children." He added, "I have a very good little practice, which am willing to sacrifice at any time, to get into the service."

In September, Ellender wrote again to Congressman Martin to say that he was studying French, in case he decided to try to become an interpreter. Meanwhile, Dinwiddie apparently secured an appointment for him to the Tulane SATC program, and Ellender was ordered to report to Camp Martin in New Orleans on October 1, 1918. He remained in camp in an indefinite status until the war ended on November 11, after which he was dismissed, "without having been duly inducted or honorably discharged."

Ellender, unlisted as a discharged veteran on the Terrebonne Parish roster of veterans, thought himself entitled to that honor. He explained his dilemma to Congressman Martin, who wrote to the commanding officer at Camp Martin, complaining of grave injustice to Ellender. The camp commander replied that "Private Allen J. Ellender" was released in compliance

16. Elward Wright, interview, November 8, 1979.

with a telegram from the Provost Marshall, prohibiting the induction of men into the SATC after November 11, 1918, on orders from the president of the United States.

Fanfare associated with the war's end and the imminent return of dough-boys heightened Ellender's concern about his military classification. Believing an honorable discharge from the military important, he pursued the matter with typical determination, providing documents to prove his assertions. In the fall of 1919 he again wrote to Martin: "I am not asking for a commission, but only to be recognized as a private." Nonetheless, Ellender was never listed among parish veterans.[17]

In 1918 Ellender became involved in his greatest love after politics—farming. He and his cousin Tommy Ellender—with whom he had pitched wheat in the Midwest—bought a small farm from Henry Ellender, Thomas' brother and Allen's elementary teacher at Hardscrabble. The little tract just north of Houma on Coteau Road was a sandy ridge built by an ancient stream, once a distributary of Bayou Terrebonne. The ridge itself was narrow and most of the land was rich, poorly drained soil called "gumbo." Allen and Thomas paid Henry a total of twenty-four hundred dollars for the land, but they did not have the asking price in full. Henry held a mortgage for the balance due.[18]

In time Allen bought out Tommy's interest and added to the farm, embracing 450 acres in all. Much was not arable, being covered with second-growth timber of little value. Ellender solved the problem of clearing the land by selling firewood, cut by workers on a piece-rate basis, to owners of shrimp-drying platforms and to residential users in nearby Houma. He paid workers on his farm a dollar to cut a cord of firewood and an additional ten cents to haul it from the woods to the road running alongside his farm. Before Ellender paid workers for a cord, he always checked it; no one could cheat him by leaving holes in the cord. Two hearty workers could cut five cords a day with a double handsaw, called a *passe par tout* by the Acadians. Ellender received three dollars for a cord delivered to a shrimp-drying plat-form.[19] He was proud to be a landowner and a farmer. Like the Ellender

---

17. Allen J. Ellender to A. B. Dinwiddie, September 18, 1918, Ellender to Whitmel P. Martin, September 19, 1918, Martin to Ellender, July 18, 1918, Martin to Commanding Officer, Camp Martin, December 8, 1918, Eugene H. Morter to Martin, December 9, 1918, Ellender to Martin, September 24, 1919, all in "Ellender, Allen J. (Personal)" Folder, Box 4, AEP; Terre-bonne Parish *Record of Veterans of World War I,* in Terrebonne Parish Courthouse, Houma, La.

18. TPCB 68, Folio 385.

19. Evans Pitre, interview, July 11, 1980.

brothers, he used timber cut on his land to pay off the mortgage—and he still had the land.

In 1921 Ellender plunged into politics again. This time he successfully sought to become a delegate to write a new state constitution. Voters elected him to represent his district. Ellender and J. C. Dupont, also a delegate to the convention, appeared before a meeting of the Houma-Terrebonne Association of Commerce on April 16 so they could properly influence constitutional provisions concerning highways.

Although he played less than a major role in drafting the Constitution of 1921, Ellender, reliable and dependable, attended all seventy-nine sessions between March 1 and June 18. He served on a committee that drafted guidelines for the impeachment and removal from public office of officials convicted of certain offenses and crimes. He also served on the agriculture and immigration committees. Several minor provisions proposed by Ellender were incorporated into the document.[20]

New Orleans attorney Richard Dowling and Ellender hoped to write a short document in 1921. They wanted it to include general concepts and principles like those in the United States Constitution. But they wanted to keep Louisiana's civil system based on the Napoleonic Code. The two drafted a document of about thirty pages, but veteran legislators representing the special interests, mistrusting the goodwill of the legislature, blocked its adoption. Nonetheless, the maverick delegates mounted a spirited effort. "That was one of the strongest fights he made," Dowling said of Ellender.[21]

Before the convention, on February 7, 1921, Helen gave birth to a healthy son, whom she and Allen named Allen Jr. There was no hospital in Houma then; virtually all babies were born at home, often only with the assistance of a midwife. Helen had a difficult delivery—and without the benefit of anesthesia. The resulting pain and trauma made a lasting impression on Helen, who made clear her intention to bear no more children. Not only did she favor a small family of her own, but she also encouraged members of the Ellender clan to follow suit. After one family member delivered her fourth or fifth child, Helen remarked, "You have enough [children]."

Allen and Helen became doting parents. "Little Allen" enjoyed much love and attention, from his parents and from his cousins. Allen wanted other

20. *Official Journal of the Proceedings of Constitutional Convention of the State of Louisiana,* March, 1921, pp. 89, 91, 101, 104, 496; Houma (La.) *Times,* April 16, 1921.

21. Paul Atkinson, New Orleans *Times-Picayune,* July 30, 1972, in Box 1, and Lake Charles (La.) *American Press,* March 30, 1963, in "1963" Scrapbook, both in AEP.

children, but Helen did not. She feared another difficult delivery and was apparently content to lavish her affections on Allen Jr. But Helen was a Roman Catholic, and her religion prohibited use of birth control devices. She became pregnant again, but according to close family members she either miscarried or had a stillbirth.[22] Ellender never revealed exactly what transpired during the second pregnancy, but he once admitted to having accused Helen, in a moment of anger, of "killing my child." The Ellenders, Allen knew, were expected to have large families.[23]

Helen was hospitalized in Touro Infirmary in New Orleans during late January and the early part of February, 1922. She was in the hospital again from March 11 to 18, 1922. Among the detailed receipts, canceled checks, itemized bills, and other information Ellender kept on file is a record of her having required ambulance service on January 22. Three days later she underwent a surgical procedure that required the use of an operating room and anesthesia. During much of Helen's stay in the hospital, she required around-the-clock nursing care.[24] She may have had corrective surgery or undergone a dilation and curettage procedure after a stillbirth or premature delivery.

Helen made Little Allen the center of her life, an integral part of her every activity. She became visibly disturbed if she could not be with the boy on his birthday. Meanwhile Ellender was moderately successful with his law practice and his financial ventures. In 1919 his taxable income was $6,832 from his law practice; his sale of real estate yielded a profit of $1,923. He earned only $2,567 in 1922, but in 1924 his income increased to $6,760, swelled in part by a profit of $1,428 from the sale of vegetables produced on his farm.[25] The sugar industry, an important part of the Terrebonne Parish economy, began to experience difficult times in the early twenties. Even though the Ellender brothers had not been able to switch to an alternative crop, Ellender was experimenting successfully in small-scale truck gardening on his Coteau farm. He also took the lead in helping others make the agricultural adjustments needed for survival.

22. Allen Ellender, Jr., interview, June 6, 1980; Viola Lynch Ellender, interview, July 14, 1980; Daisy Donnelly, interview, July 14, 1980; M. L. Funderburk, interview, July 8, 1980; Frank Wurzlow, Jr., interview, April 9, 1980.

23. Confidential communication to the author.

24. See "Ellender, Allen J. (Personal)" Folder, Box 4, AEP, for extensive financial records, personal correspondence, business dealings, and family matters. Ellender kept scraps of paper on which he jotted notes to himself and calculated his income tax returns.

25. See Box 3, AEP, for Ellender's income tax returns, as well as copies of canceled checks, receipts, and penciled-in worksheets with his calculations.

3

LAWYER, FARMER, LEGISLATOR
(1921–28)

*I*n 1921 Ellender seemed destined to make his mark in Terrebonne Parish. He had a growing law practice and had served on the committee that wrote a new constitution. He owned a small farm, and he had an attractive wife and a young son. What more could he want? In addition, the Ellender brothers were prominent in farming and in banking. Wallace was a vice-president of the Bourg State Bank, and Uncle Ernest, who kept more than $200,000 on deposit in the bank for the Ellender brothers, became president of the Bank of Terrebonne in 1920.[1]

However, the sugarcane industry suffered a severe decline during the 1920s that affected the Ellenders and many other planters. The war years had been especially good for sugar farmers. Robert Ruffin Barrow, Jr., writing to his daughter Zoe in 1914 said, "We in the sugar belt will be in clover if the war keeps up. Sugar should go to 6 or 7[¢] per lb."[2]

The Ellender brothers and a number of neighbors in the southern part of the parish had pooled their resources to form the Lower Terrebonne Refining and Manufacturing Company during sugar's boom years. The company had a mill in Montegut and owned surrounding sugarcane lands as well. The Ellenders owned one-sixth interest in the company, along with

1. Robert Ruffin Barrow Papers, Box "1923," Nicholls State University Library, Thibodaux, La.; Houma (La.) *Courier,* Centennial Edition, May 10, 11, 12, 1934; M. L. Funderburk, recorded interviews by B. Bourg, R. Detro, and M. Forêt, typescript, n.d. [1988], 101 pp., Nicholls State University Archives, 3–5.

2. Thomas Becnel, *The Barrow Family and the Barataria and Lafourche Canal: The Transportation Revolution in Louisiana, 1829–1925* (Baton Rouge, 1989), 161.

investors Allen Sanders, Albert Viguerie, Charles Champagne, F. P. Guidry, and Hugh Suthon. Whitney Bank in New Orleans held a mortgage on the mill, the Federal Land Bank a mortgage on the land. Viguerie ran the mill, located near the bridge across Bayou Terrebonne in Montegut.

Sugarcane prices held through 1919, but in 1920 they began to fall sharply. By 1925 the price had dropped from about seventeen dollars per ton during the boom times to less than five dollars per ton. Blight and other hardships had reduced production. Mosaic disease struck in 1925, the year the parish suffered a hard freeze. Tropical storms swept over the parish in 1909, 1915, and 1926, flooding the cane fields. In the 1909 storm, Ellender remembered, the eye passed directly over them. The 1926 storm dumped three feet of water over Allen Sanders' plantation just below Montegut. Terrebonne Parish had twelve sugar mills; one ground the entire crop that season. In 1927 the great Mississippi River flood brought more high water to the already troubled farmers. By the end of the decade a number of mills had failed, including the one owned in part by the Ellender brothers. Barrow, so optimistic in 1914, became pessimistic about conditions at Myrtle Grove Plantation as early as 1923. "Burdened as I am with obligations, I can not see the light ahead," he wrote. Later that same year he wrote: "I am getting desperate. I am at the end of my resources and can go no further." That year Barrow, needing to remain solvent, conferred with Ellender about selling property for him. He told Ellender he wanted fifteen hundred dollars for a little tract in Lafourche Parish, but he would take twelve hundred if that was all Ellender could get for it.[3]

Sugar establishments even more prominent than those of Barrow or Lower Terrebonne also experienced hard times and failure in the early twenties. Canal Bank of New Orleans foreclosed on the estate of H. C. Minor, which included Southdown, Waterproof, and Crescent Farm plantations. In 1922 People's Bank foreclosed on Argyle Plantation on Bayou Black. Virtually every sugar plantation experienced economic difficulty.[4]

When the Ellenders and their partners in Lower Terrebonne Refining and Manufacturing Company failed to pay eighty-five thousand dollars in

3. J. Carlyle Sitterson, *Sugar Country: The Cane Sugar Industry of the South* (Lexington, Ky., 1953), especially the chapter "The Great Decline of 1906–1926"; M. L. Funderburk, interviews, July 8, 11, 1980; "Weekly Report from Congress," September 6, 1969, Box 1507, Allen J. Ellender Papers, Nicholls State University Library, Thibodaux, La., hereinafter cited as AEP; Becnel, *The Barrows and the B&L*, 171.

4. M. L. Funderburk, interviews, July 8, 11, 1980.

property taxes in 1922, they lost their mill and its accompanying acreage to South Coast, a large sugar corporation. Although the Ellender brothers experienced a financial loss, they did not lose the properties along Bayou Terrebonne they had acquired before the turn of the century. A number of banks that held mortgages on plantations in sugar country also suffered financial setbacks and even failure. In 1925 and 1926 two banks failed in Lockport, two in Thibodaux, two in Houma, and a number in New Orleans.[5]

When sugarcane farming went into the doldrums, Ellender's law practice suffered accordingly. So did the economy of the parish, then still based largely on the sugar industry. In 1922 Ellender earned only $2,567 and paid no federal income taxes; in 1923 he paid only $104.78 in taxes on an income of $5,321. Then he made significant adjustments on his Coteau farm. He abandoned sugarcane and switched to truck gardening, employing innovative techniques based on scientific farming. He relied on county agents and the Extension Service for advice. He succeeded at truck gardening, using tenant laborers. His main crop was potatoes, but he also planted beans and corn, and he experimented with other crops. George Arceneaux, the county agent for Terrebonne Parish, convinced Ellender to buy only certified seed potatoes, even though they were more expensive than local varieties. One early brand Ellender planted was "Nebraska," a hearty potato type that produced as many as 360 bushels per acre in a good year. Ellender usually had between 150 and 200 acres of his farm under cultivation.

Ellender made a profit from his farming ventures, using day laborers, pieceworkers, and tenant farmers. Some workers who cut firewood on the farm also worked in the fields. Felicien Marcel, an Acadian from the Coteau Road area, was one of the first to work for Ellender. Later his son-in-law, Evans Pitre, became one of Ellender's steadiest workers, along with another Marcel and a man named Crochet. Eventually O. J. Thibodaux farmed Ellender's land. Like the Ellender brothers, Allen was a hard taskmaster, demanding a day's work for a day's pay, but those who worked for him considered him fair and honest. No gentleman farmer, Ellender loved the land and willingly got his hands dirty. Pitre and others noted that he was strong, had great stamina, and knew quite a bit about fertilizer, plant diseases, and the technical side of farming. He also expected his workers to have the farm kempt and neat looking.

Potato farming differed from the routine Ellender experienced on a sug-

5. Henry Ellender, Jr., interview, November 4, 1980; Charles Caillouette, interview, November 20, 1979; M. L. Funderburk, interview, July 11, 1980.

arcane plantation, where about one-third of the cane crop was planted each year in August or September and harvested the next year in November. Potatoes were planted in January or February in south Louisiana and harvested in May or June. After the harvest, an energetic farmer could plant a bean crop and harvest it before potato planting in January. During harvesting season Ellender hired as many as one hundred additional laborers. At the height of his potato operation, Ellender planted between eight hundred and nine hundred sacks of seed potatoes. In a good year, one sack of seed potatoes could produce as many as twenty sacks of potatoes. Once harvested and graded, potatoes were placed in 100-pound sacks (they weighed out 101 pounds to be sure of meeting the standard) and shipped by rail, mainly to the Chicago area. The price Ellender received per sack varied widely from year to year, fluctuating between a low of sixty cents and a high of two dollars.

Evans Pitre, who was called Vin, remembered Ellender as honest but tight. "If he owed you a nickel, he paid it; if you owed him a nickel, he wanted his money," Vin said. When the books did not balance exactly, Ellender would say, "Vin, something isn't right." Then the two men checked things out to the penny. Pitre recalled that Ellender once promised him a thousand-dollar bonus if he could produce two thousand sacks of potatoes on a certain part of the farm. Pitre met his goal and handed Ellender his account books saying, "You owe me a thousand dollars." Ellender checked the account carefully and the next day handed Vin a one-thousand-dollar bill, the only one Pitre had ever seen.

Pitre knew that Ellender abhorred waste. When inspecting potatoes for shipment, Ellender hated to discard a potato simply because it had a scab, or slight deformity, on the skin. Rather than throw away such a potato, Ellender sometimes bit off the "scab" and tossed the potato into the approved bin. Pitre reminded Ellender that if an inspector for the Department of Agriculture discovered the bitten potato, he would reject the entire sack.[6] Sometimes the frugal farmer seemed penny-wise and pound-foolish.

Ellender had demonstrated the profitability of truck farming in Terrebonne Parish. In fact, he became a leader in proving it. Soon Terrebonne had three-day "potato tours," sponsored in part by the railroads, to bring in people eager to learn new ways of using the good earth. Ellender must have

6. Ellender income tax returns, Box 3, AEP; Evans Pitre, interview, July 11, 1980; O. J. Thibodaux, interview, July 8, 1980; Allen Ellender, Jr., interview, June 6, 1980; George Arceneaux, Jr., interview, December 31, 1979.

had mixed feelings, seeing the vast Ellender sugarcane lands remain essentially sugarcane fields; the owners merely hoped for better times, unwilling to make major adjustments other types of farming would require. Sugarcane production was such that when a plantation failed, it was sold intact to another investor rather than broken up into small tracts.

In other ways, too, Ellender was becoming a respected family leader on whose legal knowledge and political influence the family relied. Younger Ellenders were coming along, and they would need better schools for success in professional careers. Ellender's brother Willard, born in 1905, and his cousin Ernest Jr. both wanted to go to college, so Wally and Ernest persuaded the Terrebonne Parish School Board to hire M. L. Funderburk to upgrade the school in Bourg. Ellender's sister, Walterine, had met Funderburk at the State Normal School in Natchitoches and had recommended him to the family. The Ellenders boarded Funderburk at Ernest's house at Hope Farm. Funderburk paid twenty dollars per month and could use the family car when he needed it. He became attached to the likable Wally, whom he shaved every Saturday.[7]

In 1923 Ellender decided to run for a seat in the lower chamber of the state legislature. The parish was ready for a political change, he sensed. The prominent Dupont family seemed vulnerable. He had served with J. C. during the constitutional convention in 1921; now he was challenging Albert for the house seat. E. A. Dupont was a candidate for sheriff against F. X. Bourg and E. D. Theriot. In this, his third political campaign, Ellender developed a technique for reaching voters through personal contact. For political advice and assistance, he relied heavily on his brother Claude and on Elward Wright.

While Ellender campaigned in anticipation of the January 15, 1924, primary election, Helen busied herself with a bridge club and with the Louisiana Federation of Women's Clubs, which chose her to chair a committee at a state meeting in Lake Charles. On January 6, Ellender read a speech by Gabriel Montegut at a public gathering for Hewitt Bouanchaud, a candidate for governor against Henry Fuqua and Huey Long, the upstart public service commissioner from Winn Parish.

When Long campaigned in Terrebonne Parish in 1924, he had to search for local politicians to introduce him before making a speech. C. C. Duplantis, a deputy clerk of court in Terrebonne, toured the parish with Long,

7. M. L. Funderburk, interview, July 11, 1980.

who received only 461 votes in the primary. The candidate Ellender supported, Henry Fuqua, received only 298 votes in Terrebonne, but won the statewide race for governor. Ellender's victory over Albert Dupont was impressive: 1,107 votes to 284.[8] His popular appeal and aggressive campaigning had won the day against the old entrenched Dupont faction. Ellender would enter the state legislature, and the man he had supported would enter the governor's office.

When the Louisiana legislature was in session, Ellender had to be in Baton Rouge for several weeks at a time. Sometimes Helen went with him, but Allen Jr. was only three when Ellender took office, and taking him along was difficult. When she could not be with Allen, Helen was frequently unhappy and depressed. She felt lonely and insecure, sometimes becoming jealous and fearful, sometimes suspecting Allen was with other women in Baton Rouge. But she was proud of her husband, ambitious that he succeed. She filled scrapbooks with newspaper clippings describing bills he introduced or election victories.[9]

Only a month after his election triumph, Allen assisted in the dismantling of the Ellender brothers' property. The agricultural arrangement of the Ellender brothers, directed by Ernest after old Tom Ellender had died, was finally coming apart. What prompted the division was the unhappiness of the widow and children of one partner, Joseph, who died on June 6, 1923. His wife, Selma, and her ten children wished to end the partnership that Ernest overshadowed. After a family meeting, Selma and the children requested a partition of the Ellender property.

Education may have been the main point of contention. Ernest used partnership funds to educate Ellender children—Allen, Claude, Ernest Jr. But not all of the older Ellenders were educated, nor had they believed strongly in its value. Yet family funds were being spent on those who wanted an education. Allen handled the legal partition of jointly owned but undivided lands.

Essentially, each received a portion of the family lands, generally where he lived, except for Joseph's heirs, who requested money and no land. Each family received title to land and buildings, eleven or twelve mules, hay, corn, and a variety of farm equipment. James, Ernest, and Wallace received parts of Hope Farm, Thomas Jr.'s family got the southern part of Aragon that

8. *Compilation of Primary Election Returns of Democratic Party, 1924,* in Box 1297, AEP; Houma (La.) *Times,* November 17, 24, 1923, January 12, 19, 1924.

9. Daisy Donnelly, interview, July 14, 1980; Frank Wurzlow, Jr., interview, July 17, 1990.

had not gone to Wallace, and David received all of Hardscrabble. All six partners or their heirs signed the document, recorded in both Terrebonne and Lafourche parishes (some Ellender lands were in Lafourche). But before long some members complained of not having received a fair share of the partition.[10]

The legal division caused friction in the family.[11] Some felt that Ernest and Wally, who each received a five-by-thirty arpent tract of sandy, well-drained land, had fared better than David, who received fourteen arpents on Hardscrabble fronting both sides of Bayou Terrebonne. Hardscrabble was not so deep or so well drained as Hope Farm. All six families had received a portion of the back land bought by Ernest at the turn of the century. The families of Ernest and Wallace held on to all their lands.

Ernest Jr. and his sister believed some Ellenders had virtually given away their lands to receive cash instead. At the time of the partition the sugar industry had declined and with it land values as well. Later, some Ellenders unsuccessfully filed suits to recover lands signed away.[12]

After a family gathering on February 27, 1924, to sign legal documents relating to the partitioning of the family property, Allen was involved in an automobile accident that took the life of his cousin Evelia Ellender, the sister of Tommy and Henry; nieces and nephews called her Aunt Dod. A teacher at St. Frances de Sales Academy in Houma, Evelia was born in 1898. After the family meeting in Houma, Evelia was in Allen's car riding back to the Bourg area with him and attorney Adrian Caillouet. At Presquille, where Bayou Petit Caillou forks from Bayou Terrebonne, two small pontoon bridges cross both streams, only two hundred yards apart. Allen's car struck a guardrail on the Petit Caillou bridge and fell into about six feet of water. Allen and Caillouet extricated themselves from the car, but Evelia drowned. David Ellender's stocky son Carl (called Tabin), a passerby, pulled her from the car by her hair. Allen's old classmate Nelo Hebert was one of the first on the scene. He transported the body in his small truck to a doctor's office where she was pronounced dead. Caillouet was not hurt in the accident; Allen suffered bruises and was sent to bed to recover from concussion and shock.[13]

10. Lafourche Parish Conveyance Book 55, Folio 204, in Lafourche Parish Courthouse, Thibodaux, La.

11. Henry Ellender, Jr., interview, November 4, 1980.

12. Ernest Ellender, Jr., and Ellen Ellender Walker, interview, November 14, 1980.

13. Nelo Hebert, interview, October 21, 1980; Houma (La.)*Times,* March 8, 1924; Fay Chauvin, interview, August 13, 1991.

In time Allen overcame the shock of the accident that killed his twenty-six-year-old cousin. He enjoyed being in the bosom of his family again. Claude, a 1921 LSU Law School graduate, practiced law in Thibodaux for about a year before returning to Houma to work in Allen's office. A bachelor then, Claude lived at Davidson's boarding house on Main Street. In January, 1925, Allen advertised in the local newspaper that Claude had become his partner in the general practice of law. The office remained on the second floor of the Bank of Terrebonne building.[14]

When the legislature was not in session, Ellender had time for his family, his farm, and his law practice, which grew steadily if unspectacularly. He performed a number of legal services for Robert Barrow, Jr., the owner of the Barataria and Lafourche Canal Company No. 2. Barrow, experiencing financial problems from his sugarcane operations, was negotiating with the Corps of Engineers for sale of his canal to the federal government. Ellender's former law partner, Harris Gagné, served as Barrow's agent in dealing with the Corps of Engineers.

The law firm of Ellender and Ellender represented Robert Jr. in a separation suit filed against his wife, Jennie Tennent Barrow. The long, rambling document prepared by the Ellender attorneys, undoubtedly with considerable help from Barrow, was more notable for detailing personality clashes and wild charges than for setting forth fine points of law. The Ellenders also filed a suit for Barrow against R. R. Barrow, Inc., the land company Mrs. Barrow and her daughters now controlled. The Barrow women used the corporation to keep Robert from squandering the family wealth during his separation from Jennie.[15]

In July, 1925, Allen and two silent partners—Houma businessmen Charles A. Ledet and Lee P. Lottinger—formed a real estate partnership. For convenience's sake, Ellender alone negotiated with other parties. The partners purchased from Barrow a canal right-of-way across Houma from Bayou Terrebonne to Bayou Black. Barrow's old canal had become expendable when the Corps of Engineers completed a new cut about one-half mile south of the old canal. The partners paid Barrow $5,500 for the old canal right-of-way, which they planned to fill in and sell for town lots, according to the Houma *Times.*[16] The new owners hoped the narrow tract, situated on the

14. Thelma Ellender, interview, May 24, 1989; Houma (La.) *Times,* January 31, 1925.

15. Becnel, *The Barrows and the B&L,* 174–78.

16. Terrebonne Parish Conveyance Book 83, Folio 137, in Terrebonne Parish Courthouse, Houma, La., hereinafter cited as TPCB; Houma (La.) *Times,* July 18, 1925.

edge of the commercial section of the city, would become valuable real estate once it was filled in.

During the first week of July, Wallace contracted pneumonia; he died on July 16, 1925, at age sixty-seven. In August, Allen and Claude handled his succession. His sole heirs were Victoria and the children—Allen, Claude, Walterine, Wallace Jr., and Willard. Wallace's immovable property included the land on Aragon and Hope Farm partitioned in 1924. At the time of his death Wally owned twelve mules, a Studebaker Light Six automobile, twenty-five shares of Lower Terrebonne Refining and Manufacturing Company stock, and five shares of Bank of Terrebonne stock. He also owned five shares of Houma Brick and Box Company stock and ten shares of Terrebonne Ice Company stock. He owned $1,350 in liberty bonds and had $621.94 on deposit in the Bank of Terrebonne. He held notes from creditors that totaled $5,200.[17]

More blacks than whites attended Wally's funeral, Allen recalled. He attributed this to Wally's reputation for dealing squarely with all people. He remembered his father being called out in the middle of the night to check on ill blacks who worked for him; they knew they could rely on him in an emergency.[18]

While he was seriously ill Wally exacted from Willard a promise to enter college. Allen and Claude mapped out their younger brother's career choices. Early on, they had ruled out engineering and recommended medicine. They paid Willard's tuition at Tulane and bought his clothes as he began his long medical training. Allen considered Willard, fifteen years his junior, more like a son than a brother. Like his father, Willard had lesions on the tendons of several fingers that prevented him from straightening all fingers completely. A simple surgical procedure solved Willard's problem when he was quite young.[19]

Willard and Allen Jr. became companions, sharing in the social activities of Allen and Helen. Ellender continued to produce bountiful yields in his potato fields. He welcomed a group of USDA dignitaries to Houma for the annual Irish potato tour in 1927. On a number of occasions the Extension

17.   TPCB 83, Folio 210; Viola Lynch Ellender, interview, July 14, 1980; Ellen Ellender Walker, interview, November 14, 1980.

18.   Allen J. Ellender, interview by Larry Hackman, August 29, 1967 (Washington, D.C.: John F. Kennedy Library), 44.

19.   Allen Ellender to Julian C. Miller, June 26, 1967, "Sweet Potatoes, Dept. Agriculture—1967" Folder, Box 419, AEP; Ernest Ellender, Jr., interview, November 14, 1980.

Service selected Ellender the "potato king" for producing the greatest yield per acre. Helen continued an active role with the women's club. In May, 1926, she went to New Orleans to buy favors so her group could present gifts along the route to Atlantic City for its annual convention. Sometimes when the Ellenders vacationed in Abita Springs, north of Lake Pontchartrain where Helen's sister lived, Willard accompanied them.[20]

Willard shocked the Ellender clan when he eloped with Viola Lynch, the petite redhead with the little hands whom he had taken to meet Victoria earlier. Allen and Claude made Willard promise to continue his medical training, even though he now had marital responsibilities. After a family meeting at which almost everyone shed tears, Viola was fully accepted into the family. Allen and Claude continued to support Willard financially; they probably paid for the diamond-and-emerald ring he bought Viola, who was always called Vi. Willard often promised to repay Allen and Claude. "I'm keeping track," Allen always said when Willard expressed concern about his growing indebtedness. Whenever Willard offered to pay back a portion of what he owed, Allen's stock answer was, "You can do that later."[21]

As late as 1927, Ellender still hoped to obtain an honorable discharge from military service. Once again he appealed in writing to Third District congressman Whitmel Martin for help: "I enlisted in good faith and served to the best of my ability, and to now refuse recognition of that service[,] on account of the inefficiency of those in charge of me, does not seem fair and just." Martin assured Ellender of having presented his case: "Your record is clear that you made every effort to serve your country."[22]

Ellender announced his candidacy for reelection in 1927. Floodwater covered portions of the parish and sugar planters faced mortgage foreclosures on their plantations. Ellender became involved in several local and statewide races, although no one filed to run against him. He actively supported O. H. Simpson for governor, not Huey Long, the Winn Parish public service commissioner. Elward Wright, encouraged by Ellender, campaigned for mayor of Houma.

Houma, the hub of Terrebonne Parish, was an inevitable stopping point

20. Houma (La.) *Times,* May 22, 1926, July 23, 1927; Houma (La.) *Courier,* April 28, 1927.

21. Viola Lynch Ellender, interview, November 14, 1980.

22. Whitmel Martin to Allen J. Ellender, December 20, 1927, and Ellender to Martin, December 26, 1927, both in "Ellender, Allen J. (Personal)" Folder, Box 3, AEP.

for politicians seeking public office. In October, Riley Wilson, a candidate for governor, with active support from Roland Howell of Thibodaux, campaigned in Houma against free textbooks, which Huey Long advocated. On November 15 Governor O. H. Simpson and his running mate, F. O. Pavy of Opelousas, arrived for a big rally in Houma. Ellender opened it by commenting favorably about the governor with whom he had worked in close harmony.

Huey Long and his running mate, Paul Cyr, campaigned in Houma in early November, 1927, and again in January, 1928, appearing before enthusiastic audiences. A. J. Caillouet presided at one meeting, which could not accommodate all supporters eager to hear the dynamic campaigner. Huey entertained the crowd in English; Cyr addressed it in French.[23]

Long won the January 17 primary, carrying both Lafourche and Terrebonne parishes. Huey's flamboyant speeches, which emphasized a bright future for Louisiana, undoubtedly made a strong impression on voters. In south Louisiana the sugar industry was in a slump and banks had been failing for some time. Truck gardening flourished, but the oil and fishing industries were sluggish and still small scale.[24]

Huey's bold, imaginative style and his optimism about Louisiana's future had captured the hopes of the poor, who were eager for a brighter day. Huey challenged the old system of the Bourbon Democrats, who had produced so little and had downplayed Progressive Era reformers' efforts to improve roads, establish public schools, and attract industry to the South. Long astutely noted that north Louisiana and New Orleans each contained about 25 percent of the state's votes. The Acadian country had about 20 percent of the voters; the Florida parishes and central Louisiana contained about 15 percent each. Complicating matters further, north Louisiana was mainly white Anglo-Saxon Protestant; south Louisiana had large black, Acadian, and Catholic populations. In all but ten of Louisiana's sixty-four parishes the population was two-thirds or more Catholic, or two-thirds or more Protestant.[25]

23. Houma (La.) *Courier,* October 20, 27, November 3, 17, 1927, January 19, 1928; Houma (La.) *Times,* November 5, 19, 1927, January 14, 1928.

24. M. L. Funderburk, interview, July 11, 1980; Elward Wright, interview, November 8, 1979.

25. Michael L. Kurtz and Morgan D. Peoples, *Earl K. Long: The Saga of Uncle Earl and Louisiana Politics* (Baton Rouge, 1990), 3, 12; William I. Hair, *The Kingfish and His Realm: The Life and Times of Huey P. Long* (Baton Rouge, 1991), 129.

Ellender's business partner, Elward Wright, campaigned on the need to modernize Houma's finances and to establish fiscal integrity. In April, 1928, Wright received 532 votes to win the mayor's race; Reuben Chauvin with 157 and C. C. Duplantis with 149 were far behind.[26]

In the mid-twenties Ellender seemed to be making greater strides as a farmer and attorney than as a legislator. The Louisiana Legislature had produced no startlingly new or innovative programs in highway, education, welfare, or agricultural reform. Yet rural agricultural Louisiana had begun to experience bank failures and depression long before the stock market crash of 1929. The oil, shrimp, and oyster industries were still in their infancy. In contrast, Ellender prospered because of his hard work and intelligence. In 1925 his truck gardening and cordwood ventures brought in nearly $3,000. A real estate venture yielded a $3,000 profit. His law practice accounted for the rest of a total income of $8,065 that year. In 1926 and 1927 he earned $4,504 and $6,210, respectively, from his farm and legal ventures. His total federal income taxes for the two years combined came to less than fifteen dollars.[27]

Meanwhile, the Ellenders continued an active social life. In February, 1928, Helen visited relatives in Savannah, Georgia. In July, Allen, Helen, and Allen Jr. drove to the Atlantic Coast and to New York, where Allen hoped to call on Governor Alfred E. Smith, before continuing to New England and to Quebec. On October 19, the family attended the wedding of Claude to Thelma Bickham in St. Francisville.[28]

Ellender's confidence grew as his potato ventures succeeded. He willingly shared his expertise with neighboring and visiting farmers. In 1928 USDA experts chose his potato farm as the most productive in the area.[29] He was refining his views on other subjects as well. As he entered his second term in the Louisiana Legislature, he was confident that he could help to improve the plight of his impoverished state. However, he would have to work with an aggressive new governor—Huey Long—whose candidacy he had opposed.

26. Houma (La.) *Courier,* April 12, 1928.

27. Ellender income tax returns, Box 3, AEP.

28. Houma (La.) *Times,* February 11, 1928; Houma (La.) *Courier,* July 22, October 25, 1928.

29. Houma (La.) *Courier,* May 10, 1928.

4

WITH HUEY LONG
(1928–31)

*A*llen Ellender did not vote for John B. Fournet, Governor Long's choice for Speaker of the House when the Louisiana legislature convened in May, 1928, but Fournet won without his support. The Speaker allowed him to remain on the Agriculture Committee and appointed him to Judiciary, Printing, and Railroad committees. Later Huey told Ellender, "Young man, I know you voted against me. We are going to make you chairman of the Printing Committee for it." Long's half-joking comment about the unimportant Printing Committee was his way of sending a serious message to Ellender: join the team or be satisfied with menial legislative assignments.[1]

Could Ellender convert to Longism? Was there some common ground between him and Huey? Obvious differences existed between them, yet they shared areas of interest. Long's views on big business coincided partly with Ellender's concerns about monopolistic corporations victimizing the little people. Ellender remembered South Coast, the large sugar corporation, having gobbled up Lower Terrebonne Refining and Manufacturing Company, the failed family-owned sugar mill near his home town. Some of Huey's strongest opponents, the Bourbon Democrats in the big plantation delta parishes, were the same leaders whose control of Louisiana Ellender hoped to break. Additionally, Long granted oil leases favorable to Texaco, the company beginning to develop the tremendous oil and gas resources of Terrebonne Parish. Theoretically, at least, they were compatible. Why not join

---

1. Houma (La.) *Courier,* May 24, 1928; Charles T. Walsten, "Allen J. Ellender: Long Legislative Lieutenant, 1928–1936" (M.A. thesis, Louisiana State University, 1985), 5, 6.

Long, Ellender thought, and reap the benefits of an ambitious legislative program?

But Ellender's conversion to Longism came after a bitter confrontation with Huey over legislative and family matters. Long, on the telephone to Ellender, cussed him out because he had voted against a $150,000 appropriations bill to renovate the governor's mansion. Ellender, equally irascible, shouted back that he would slap Huey's face if he made these statements to him in person. The call ended abruptly, both politicians fuming.

During the telephone conversation, Long threatened to sabotage the medical career of Willard, then an intern at Charity Hospital in New Orleans, the state institution under Long's control. Not surprisingly, this struck a responsive chord with Ellender, who was financing the medical career of the young brother whom he considered more a son than a sibling. Ellender told other anti-Longites about his shouting match with Huey and his threat to slap Huey.

Ellender's Terrebonne friends were concerned that their representative and the governor had reached a political impasse. Long would do little for the parish unless it provided strong legislative support for his program. Sam Polmer, a Schriever businessman and a Long supporter, urged Ellender to mend fences with Huey. J. B. Dupont and other Houma business leaders suggested that a delegation from the parish drive to Baton Rouge to patch things up with the governor. Terrebonne Parish would suffer further economic distress if Highway 90 bypassed Houma. Additionally, the area needed a spokesman to persuade the Corps of Engineers to route the Intracoastal Canal through Houma, a concept strongly supported at the time.

Ellender discussed the problem with Elward Wright, mayor of Houma and an anti-Longite. Then Ellender, accepting Wright's suggestion, decided to confer with the governor alone rather than rely on a delegation from Terrebonne. When Ellender called for an appointment, Long responded politely; he said he would be happy to see him the next day. Before leaving for Baton Rouge, Ellender asked Wright to accompany him. Wright went along for the ride.

When Ellender and Wright arrived at Long's office, his secretary, Alice Lee Grosjean, invited them in cordially. Then Huey personally ushered them into his inner office. He apologized for losing his temper earlier in the week and, in conciliatory tones, told Ellender many things had led to his frustration. He had just had a political squabble with Shreveport *Times* editor John Ewing, and he had been nursing a vicious hangover besides. Wright watched as Huey applied his charm on Ellender, who seemed mesmerized by him.

Later Long, Ellender, and Wright walked a block or so to the Heidelberg Hotel for lunch. As usual, Long dominated the conversation. He blamed his need for a new mansion, in part, on his wife, who did not want to leave Shreveport to live in Baton Rouge. On the drive home, Wright observed, Ellender vacillated and rationalized his position toward Long. He told Wright Huey was not such a bad fellow after all. He was being converted to the Long cause, though he may not have been aware the metamorphosis was taking place.[2]

Soon Ellender joined the team and became a first-string player. He became a regular visitor at the mansion, ever ready with advice or help. He became Huey's close friend as well. Many of Ellender's relatives and closest friends disliked Long and refused to support him, including Claude, his wife Thelma, and Elward Wright. Ellender's conversion seemed incongruous for a legislator who had campaigned in 1924 and in 1928 against Huey. He and Harvey Peltier of Thibodaux, a wealthy lawyer-businessman, quickly noted the drive and appeal of Long, who at their age was already governor. However, Long advocated rapid change to get Louisiana in step with the times; he epitomized a revolutionary approach to government alien to Allen's Horatio Alger past and the conservative ways of Tom Ellender and his brothers.[3]

An impressionable and loyal disciple, Ellender acknowledged Long's leadership, captivated by his brilliance and by the ambitious plans Huey articulated so convincingly. He joined Long to reap future rewards and share in the power. The old political system seemed to have failed. Just as he had pitched in to reach goals set by the Ellender brothers, he joined Huey without questioning (or agreeing with) every detail and scheme.

M. L. Funderburk, the Terrebonne educator-banker, thinks Ellender and Peltier acquiesced as the Lafourche and Terrebonne business establishment drifted toward support for Long. To them, Huey seemed to offer hope for restoring the devastated economy. Besides, there was a power vacuum in Terrebonne that Ellender hoped to fill: The old sheriff had died, and no new political leader had emerged to replace him. Others simply credited the shift to Long's ability to attract talented men. Recent scholars credit Huey's brother Earl with winning over Ellender, Peltier, and other significant sup-

2. Elward Wright, interview, November 8, 1980; Florence LeCompte, interview, August 2, 1979; Walsten, "Allen J. Ellender," 10.

3. Florence LeCompte, interview, August 2, 1979; Elward Wright, interview, November 8, 1979; Thelma Ellender, interview, June 30, 1980; Claude Duval, interview, December 18, 1979.

porters. (Ellender ranked only Lyndon Johnson and Sam Rayburn in the same league with Earl Long in political dealing.) Older, entrenched politicians were solidly aligned against Huey; he needed new people to replace them and to counter their influence. Long did not control the legislature. In the House only eighteen of one hundred members were elected on the Long ticket. In the Senate only nine of thirty-nine.[4]

For the press, Ellender denied Huey had threatened to thwart Willard's career and offered a slightly different explanation of his conversion to Longism. But Caddo Parish assessor J. W. A. Jeter and Webster Parish assessor Max A. Sandlin testified in Huey's impeachment hearing that they were in Huey's office and heard him threaten Ellender over the telephone. Ellender had told the *Times-Picayune* he had met with Long, but there had been no threat. "In 1928 my constituents said, 'We expect you to help carry out Huey's program,'" Ellender remembered later. "I had already decided I would by the start of the 1928 session, I really had no choice anyway." Ellender also said: "When I found out that he [Huey] was serious about helping the people, I took my coat off and helped him." At any rate, Ellender eventually voted for the mansion renovation appropriation and Willard completed his internship at Charity Hospital.[5]

Ellender and other converts to Longism found themselves catapulted to positions of leadership even though they were neophytes. Legislative veterans generally opposed Huey; legislative newcomers generally supported him, their main shortcoming being their inexperience.[6] Leander Perez of Plaquemines Parish, also an ambitious young lawyer, joined Ellender and Peltier on the Long team.

Ellender became an effective legislator. In 1928 he introduced nineteen measures, seven of which were enacted into law. Most of his bills dealt with the judiciary system and uniform pay for clerks and judicial employees. One of his bills funded research at LSU to assist the economically troubled sugarcane industry. Another Ellender bill established seasons in inland waters for shrimp, oysters, and other seafood. A conservative coalition, led by Lieutenant Governor Paul Cyr, who had become a bitter foe of Huey Long, and

4. M. L. Funderburk, interview, July 11, 1980; Glen Jeansonne, *Leander Perez: Boss of the Delta* (Baton Rouge, 1977), 64; Michael L. Kurtz and Morgan D. Peoples, *Earl K. Long: The Saga of Uncle Earl and Louisiana Politics* (Baton Rouge, 1990), 35, 39; T. Harry Williams, *Huey Long: A Biography* (New York, 1969), 279.

5. Walsten, "Allen Ellender," 10–11, 4, 6.

6. Williams, *Huey Long,* 297.

former congressman J. Y. Sanders of Baton Rouge, blocked most social leg-islation intended to help the poor.

Ellender's first Longite bill came in the special session of December, 1928. It set the salaries of state supreme court judges. Huey signed the bill into law before the year ended. The legislature also passed tax measures to finance better roads and to provide free school books. In a special session in March, 1929, Huey tried to pass inheritance and paving taxes and a five-cents-per-barrel tax on oil, but he could not muster the two-thirds vote nec-essary to amend the Louisiana Constitution.[7]

When the legislature was not in session, Ellender returned to Houma to family, farming, and his legal practice. His son, who turned seven in 1928, now attended the Lawton Academy, a private school in Houma with a good reputation. The Winder sisters conducted it. Graduates of Peabody College in Nashville, they stressed Latin and classical studies. Allen Jr., who visited many places with his mother, was an indifferent student. He had been spoiled and indulged by his parents, and he lacked discipline. Even though Ellender's legislative responsibilities took him away from home with increas-ing frequency, he occasionally took Little Allen to the Coteau farm to watch the potato harvest, to fish in the nearby bayou, or to hunt for Indian artifacts with Randolph Bazet along the natural levees.[8]

Allen and Helen often consulted with Little Allen's teachers at Lawton, wanting progress reports and suggestions on how to help the youngster improve. When Allen Jr. became interested in scouting, Helen became in-volved as well. She went on a practice hike with him and once slept with him in his tent pitched in their back yard.[9]

Ellender's growing importance as a Longite did not cause him to take on airs or to alter his way of dealing with people. He did little favors for those he had befriended earlier. Claude Duval, a youngster who lived around the corner from Ellender during his bachelor days in Houma, recalled that Ellender took him to see his first LSU-Tulane football game. Duval, whose father had died when he was a child, lived just a few blocks from Elward Wright, whom he also admired.[10]

Meanwhile, Ellender had become a minor celebrity because of his suc-cessful potato crops. Local newspapers took note of the production awards

7.   Walsten, "Allen Ellender," 6–8.
8.   Randolph Bazet, interview, October 22, 1980.
9.   Florence LeCompte, interview, June 11, 1980.
10.   Claude Duval, interview, December 18, 1979.

he frequently won because of his potato know-how. He showed Huey Long a picture of his Coteau farm, explaining that his success resulted from planting top-quality seed potatoes, Nebraska certified. Long inquired about planting potatoes at Angola, the sprawling state penitentiary on the banks of the Mississippi River forty miles north of Baton Rouge. Ellender told Huey he had ordered a carload of seed potatoes which he would let Clay Dugas at Angola have at his cost, three dollars per sack. Ellender told Dugas in a letter when and how to plant for maximum production. Ellender bragged of having produced 340 bushels per acre in the previous season. A farmer needed slightly more than four sacks of seed potatoes to plant one acre of land, Ellender wrote. He even offered to go to Angola to help Dugas, but he wanted Dugas to be ready for planting when he got there.[11]

When the Louisiana Legislature convened in 1929, Huey and his legislative lieutenants realized their ambitious program—schools, roads, bridges, textbooks, charity hospitals—cost more than the tax structure could bear. Huey attempted to broaden the base by taxing sales, beer, wine, cigarettes, oil, corporations, franchises, fishing and hunting licenses—and he searched for even more revenue sources. Brash and unorthodox, Huey challenged the old order in Louisiana by championing the cause of the little man. His fight against the oil giant, Standard Oil, which operated a huge refinery in Baton Rouge, symbolized the struggle between the wealthy corporations and the people. To achieve his goals, Huey made political changes and offended people. He abolished the poll tax, thereby breaking the back of many courthouse political cliques. He supported candidates who opposed recalcitrant sheriffs, assessors, or clerks of court. The Bourbon Democrats and their allies, the Old Regulars, or Choctaws, in New Orleans opposed Huey at every turn. With the support of big business and big oil, they attempted to impeach him in 1929.

Although Huey championed the cause of the little man, many of his friends and supporters were wealthy businessmen: Mayor Robert Maestri of New Orleans, oil men Seymour Weiss, Louis Roussell, and William Helis of New Orleans, James A. Noe of Monroe. Huey did not break the back of the old power structure; he browbeat it into submission and then welcomed its

---

11. Allen J. Ellender to Clay Dugas, January 5, 1929, and countless receipts, canceled checks, and the like to prove where Ellender had obtained the potatoes and how much he had paid for them, all in "Ellender, Allen J. (Personal)" Folder, Box 4, Allen J. Ellender Papers, Nicholls State University Library, Thibodaux, La., hereinafter cited as AEP.

members into his organization. His famed Share Our Wealth program seemed like a socialistic dream, but he never tried to implement it. He developed a highly personal organization that used patronage extensively. Relying heavily on severance taxes on gas and oil, royalties, and state leases, Huey created the impression among voters that state services were free. When oil and gas revenues declined, taxpayers balked at supporting taxes commonly used in other states—property, state income, gasoline—to fund government operations. Eventually, Long passed a number of regressive measures: sales, beer, and cigarette taxes. Using graft extensively, Huey's organization proposed legislation to tax and regulate the oil industry. Then legislators collected huge gifts that the industry spent fighting such legislation.[12]

The impetus for impeachment came in the special session of the legislature Huey called in March, 1929, to pass a tax on oil and other revenue measures that required a two-thirds vote of both houses. Getting a two-thirds vote was almost impossible. On realizing the tax package was not going to pass, the Long forces decided the best course of action was to adjourn the legislature sine die. Anti-Longites, hoping to frustrate Long by soundly defeating his tax measures, decided to prevent hasty adjournment of the legislature. Lieutenant Governor Paul Cyr, Charles Manship, the owner of two important Baton Rouge newspapers, and former governor J. Y. Sanders spearheaded the anti-Long effort. Huey had committed fraud by granting lucrative leases to Texas Oil Company, Cyr suggested in the Senate.

Speaker John Fournet planned the adjournment vote in the House on Monday, March 25. If the House adjourned, the Senate would have little choice but to follow suit. The result was a vicious confrontation that became known as Bloody Monday. It frustrated the Longites and set the stage for impeachment charges against Long.

A faulty voting machine in the House and human error contributed to the imbroglio. The clerk's failure to clear the voting machine had produced an inaccurate count that was not discovered until later. Pandemonium broke loose when Fournet announced a favorable vote, declared the house adjourned, and stepped down from the dais. The vote was incorrect, the anti-Longites screamed. Longites and anti-Longites exchanged blows. One anti-Longite, Clinton Sayes of Avoyelles Parish, walked on desk tops to reach the podium, receiving a bloody forehead along the way. Sayes said a Longite

<hr />

12. Kurtz and Peoples, *Earl Long,* 6–7, 9, 11, 13, 132, 186, 269.

hit him with brass knuckles, but Ellender said a fan blade struck Sayes, whose blood splattered Ellender, seated at his desk.

Finally quiet was restored for a roll call vote, and the House remained in session; the Senate too voted against adjournment. Conservative legislators in the House drew up impeachment charges against Huey. The Longites called them the Dynamite Squad. Among the charges was one alleging that Huey had ordered his bodyguard, "Battling" Bozeman, to assassinate J. Y. Sanders.[13]

Ellender was one of Huey's many attorneys in the impeachment struggle. Others included John Fournet of St. Martinville, House leader J. Cleveland Fruge, Harvey Peltier of Thibodaux, Leander Perez of Plaquemines Parish, John Overton of Alexandria, and Lewis Morgan of Mandeville. Many charges against Long contained little substance and were dropped. Article Ten dealt directly with Ellender. It detailed Huey's abusive telephone threat to wreck Willard's medical career. Ellender having denied the accusation, the House dropped this charge, even though two assessors testified to having heard the threat personally. In time the House reduced the number of charges from nineteen to eight.

In April, 1929, the House formed itself into a committee of the whole to conduct the impeachment hearing against Huey. After Peltier discovered an old law permitting defense attorneys to cross-examine witnesses who appeared before the House, Ellender and Peltier questioned many witnesses. On the fifth day of the hearing, April 10, Ellender himself took the stand to explain his dispute with Huey over appropriating funds to renovate the old mansion. Judge Robert Butler of the Seventeenth Judicial District Court in Houma testified that Ellender had told him of Huey's threat to Ellender. Now a Long supporter, Ellender downplayed his dispute with Huey.

Committed to defending Long, Ellender was forced into overlooking a number of shady practices and possibly exposing himself to charges of perjury. In his testimony Ellender concentrated on the political dispute over renovation of the mansion without mentioning Willard. His statement, given staccato-like in long run-on sentences, seemed strained and unconvincing.

After the first conversation, as Judge Butler just stated, I was a little mad at the Governor and the attitude of the Governor, so I decided to call him

13. Williams, *Huey Long,* 356–62; Allen J. Ellender, interview by T. Harry Williams, Louisiana and Lower Mississippi Valley Collections, Louisiana State University, Baton Rouge.

> up again, which I did, and I asked the Governor what did he mean by
> talking to me as he did, Gentlemen, after he had talked to me, that if he
> would talk to me as he had over the phone in my presence I would possibly
> slap his face.

Softening his statement considerably, Ellender conceded only the possibility
of slapping Huey. Huey's hangover explanation came out as Huey's inade-
quate sleep the previous night. Ellender quoted Huey as having said, "Allen,
don't get mad about it; I meant no harm, but I want you to come to Baton
Rouge and I would like to see you and show you and other members of the
legislature the exact condition of the mansion."

Ellender continued, "[Then Huey said,] by the way, they are now about
to begin demolishing the old home, and that I would have an opportunity
to find out the exact condition about it." Later he and Huey looked at the
partly demolished mansion. "I agreed with him then and there that I thought
it was advisable for him to take a vote on the mansion, and[,] provided he
could get the funds—I then told him if he could show me where he could
get the funds, I would gladly change my vote." According to his testimony,
Ellender went to Huey's secretary, got a mail ballot, changed his vote on
the appropriation to renovate the mansion, and tore up his original ballot.

The anti-Longites pressed Ellender on Huey's threat to impede Willard's
medical career. Ellender referred to two telephone conversations with Huey.
When asked who first mentioned Willard, Ellender said that he had mentioned Willard to Huey in the first conversation. In the second conversation
Huey had asked, "What about your brother?" Assuming Huey wanted to
know what he wanted for his brother, Ellender said for Willard to advance
solely on his own qualifications. Huey's tactics were not abusive to a legislator, Ellender testified before leaving the witness stand.

During the proceedings Ellender told how a legislator could defend himself against critical charges made by the chief executive of the state:

> I would go to the court about it. I am not trying at this time, Gentlemen
> of the Committee, to defend any of the acts of the Governor that he may
> have done or may have committed individually. Let Mr. Chas. Manship
> make a charge in the criminal courts of this state against the Governor. That
> is the remedy that he has and not an impeachment trial here.[14]

14. *Proceedings on Impeachment Hearings Before the Committee of the Whole of the House of
Representatives, State of Louisiana,* Baton Rouge, 1929 (transcript in State Archives, Baton Rouge,
La.), Vol. IV, p. 19, Vol. V, pp. 22–43.

The House voted fifty-nine to thirty-nine to impeach Huey; thus 59 percent opposed Huey. The upper house of the state legislature, the Senate, would hear the case against the governor. If two-thirds, or twenty-six of the thirty-nine members, found him guilty, he would be removed from office. Overton, Ellender, Peltier, and Perez focused on how many votes Huey needed to foil the impeachment attempt—the number was fourteen.

Huey's team worked feverishly in his defense. Ellender questioned many witnesses in the House. Huey had made political threats as a private citizen, Ellender told the press, not as governor of the state; therefore, he had committed no impeachable offense. Perez, under the general direction of John Overton, wrote legal memoranda for Ellender and Peltier. Perez favored a delaying tactic that would have forced the Senate to vote on the charges after the legal adjournment date of April 5. Then Huey could claim that an illegally convened body had voted on his fate.

Soon all of these legal maneuvers became irrelevant, for the Longites discovered a device to render the whole impeachment process ludicrous. Huey and Perez, with assistance from others, came up with the idea of a round-robin. It would be a petition signed by fourteen or more senators pledged to support Huey. It could thus undermine the whole process, especially if it surfaced before the Senate formally decided Huey's fate.

Long had asked Ellender to draft the round-robin document. The impeachment was a politically motivated, illegal attempt to remove Huey from office, Ellender's statement asserted simply. He got Helen to check his handiwork; Huey made minor revisions. Meanwhile, Longites sought fourteen senators to sign the document—fifteen senators signed. Huey's opponents then had the impossible task of getting the twenty-six votes needed for conviction. The round-robin, conceived by Huey and Perez and drafted by Ellender, thwarted the impeachment attempt. Before Huey's enemies had fully prepared their case against him, the governor had rendered their efforts moot.[15]

Ellender had played an important role in defending Huey in the impeachment crisis. In only a few months he had become part of Long's inner circle, one of Huey's trusted lieutenants. He must have taken pleasure in introducing a measure to formally end the impeachment. In a special session in September, 1930, Ellender introduced a resolution to repeal the impeachment

15. Williams, *Huey Long,* 381, 397, 401; Jeansonne, *Leander Perez,* 66–67; Walsten, "Allen Ellender," 11–13.

charges against Huey and to discharge the board conducting the hearing. The vote on Ellender's resolution was seventy for, twenty against.[16]

The Houma *Courier,* aware of Ellender's growing status in the Long organization, reported his achievements. He was in Baton Rouge for a conference with the governor in February, 1929, the society page reported. In April the press reported the House's vote of confidence in Ellender after he had explained the sale of seed potatoes to Angola. Huey had decided in May to pave roads in both Houma and Thibodaux because Ellender and Peltier could not decide which community should receive the hard-surfaced road.[17]

In the spring of 1930, anti-Long forces tried to remove John Fournet as Speaker of the House. Removal leaders included Lieutenant Governor Paul Cyr, former governor John M. Parker, and Esmond Phelps, publisher of the *Times-Picayune.* Fournet weathered the storm by a 55-to-44 vote. In the Senate, too, the Longites prevailed, electing Alvin O. King of Lake Charles president pro tempore. Ellender became chairman of the Joint Judiciary Committee, which included members from both houses of the legislature. In addition, he became a floor leader.[18]

In 1930 Ellender made little headway with Huey's road-bond amendment, which needed a two-thirds vote for passage. Huey favored a constitutional convention to bring the matter before the people. Meanwhile, Ellender moved to change the House rules to permit the road-bill passage by a majority vote rather than a two-thirds vote. When Speaker John Fournet ruled the motion admissible, the House exploded with anger and confusion. During the commotion, Ellender mounted the dais and offered to withdraw his motion if the House agreed to hear his bill the following week. The anti-Longs agreed. Ellender's bill was passed the next week by a 56-to-42 vote.[19] However, the measure soon failed in the Senate. Ellender had taken a chance with a bold step; it was a calculated risk, but he took it.

Huey Long decided to run for the U.S. Senate against Joseph Ransdell in 1930, even though he had two years remaining in his four-year term as governor. He selected Ellender and Harvey Peltier as his statewide campaign managers, believing the campaign issues would be the failed recent session of the legislature. In the New Orleans area Robert Maestri and Joseph O'Hara served as regional managers. Ellender and Peltier campaigned vig-

16. Walsten, "Allen Ellender," 13.

17. Houma (La.) *Courier,* February 28, April 11, May 9, 1929.

18. Walsten, "Allen Ellender," 16–17.

19. Williams, *Huey Long,* 451–52.

orously in their districts, reminding voters how Huey had brought them free textbooks, paved roads, and better education. Huey conducted much of the campaign himself, employing various state agencies and public bodies to generate support for his candidacy.[20]

In the days before voting machines, election commissioners played an important role in guarding against vote stealing. Each candidate for high office appointed election commissioners. The Old Regulars, or Choctaws, the New Orleans organization supporting Ransdell, entered eleven dummy candidates in the race, each planning to withdraw once he had appointed friendly commissioners. Aware of the tactic, Ellender found twenty-three dummies to enter the Senate race so they could name commissioners. When Mayor T. Semmes Walmsley of the Old Regulars realized what was happening, he called Ellender in for a friendly conference. The opponents agreed to an equal number of election commissioners and withdrew the many dummy candidates.

Huey won a smashing victory over Ransdell in the September 9 primary, 149,640 to 111,451.[21] But he could not take his seat in the U.S. Senate. Huey knew his opponents in Louisiana would claim he had vacated the governor's office upon taking the oath of office in Washington and would immediately swear in Lieutenant Governor Cyr as governor.

Meanwhile, Ellender enjoyed some success directing legislation. His most important Long measure in the regular session of the legislature in 1930 was House Bill 365, a four-cents-per-gallon tax on gasoline bought in Louisiana. The House passed the bill in June, the Senate cleared it in July, and it became law when Huey signed it shortly thereafter. Some bills helped Terrebonne Parish directly. One Ellender measure called for a license fee for trapping fur-bearing animals. Another called for improving roads in the parish; another appropriated forty thousand dollars for sugarcane research at LSU and ten thousand dollars for potato research in Terrebonne Parish. Huey once said half-jokingly that "You could buy Allen Ellender with a sack of potatoes," a reference to charges that Ellender benefited from research to increase potato production. Ellender had a contract to sell potatoes to Angola at "market prices," but actually received a higher price promised by Huey, Drew Pearson claimed in his nationally syndicated column. However, Ellender's financial records indicate no profit from his potato sales to the prison.

20. Walsten, "Allen Ellender," 18, 21–23.
21. Williams, *Huey Long,* 464, 479–80.

In a special fall 1930 session, Ellender directed House Bill 4 through to passage. It provided for gravel and shell roads and new bridges throughout the state. In September the House passed the measure by a vote of seventy-seven to twelve. The Senate soon passed the measure as well. By the end of the year Ellender was firmly entrenched as one of Huey's most effective supporters. He and Harvey Peltier and Public Service Commission Chairman Wade O. Martin often consulted with Huey on important matters. Ellender began to harbor hope of succeeding Huey as governor, once the Kingfish went to Washington to claim his U.S. Senate seat.[22]

The impeachment crisis behind him, Ellender made a final but futile attempt to secure an honorable discharge from military service. Shortly after the death of Whitmel Martin on April 6, 1929, he asked Helen's sister Mrs. Rose Pardee, who worked in Washington in government service, if she could get his file "pertaining to my discharge from the Army" from Martin's papers. Then, in a more conversational tone, he spoke of driving to Nebraska to visit the potato fields before going on to Winnipeg for a vacation.[23]

Ellender's financial status had improved in the 1920s even though the overall economy continued downward. His farm turned a profit, his legal practice was growing, and his investments were profitable. The Houma tract Ellender had bought from Robert Barrow, Jr., proved a good purchase. In 1927 the Houma Brick and Box Company paid Ellender and his partners one thousand dollars for a section between High and Academy streets. In 1929 Joseph Ane paid five thousand dollars for a section between Main and School streets. In 1930 the partners sold three other parcels for about one thousand dollars each.[24]

While the struggles over Long's program were in progress, Allen Jr. fractured his skull while playing at a neighbor's house on October 30, 1931. Ten-year-old Allen Jr. and a playmate had bumped heads. A terribly upset Helen summoned Dr. R. W. Collins, who found young Allen semicomatose

22. Randolph Bazet, interview, October 22, 1980; Walsten, "Allen Ellender," 17, 19, 20; Drew Pearson, Washington *Post,* March 22, 1943, in "Allred" Folder, Box 198, "Ellender, Allen J. (Personal)" Folder, Box 4, both in AEP. Ellender kept copious records to prove that he had not profited from the sale of potatoes to Angola. Even when the price of seed potatoes rose from $3.00 to $3.50 per sack, he honored his promise to Clay Dugas and sold at the original price agreed upon.

23. Allen J. Ellender to Mrs. Rose Pardee, July 26, 1929, in "Ellender, Allen J. (Personal)" Folder, Box 4, AEP.

24. Terrebonne Parish Conveyance Books 87, Folio 275; 92, Folio 33; 93, Folios 219, 458; 94, Folio 35, all in Terrebonne County Courthouse, Houma, La.

at 7:30 P.M. Collins telephoned Willard at Charity Hospital in New Orleans, then rushed his young patient to the New Orleans institution. Examinations and X-rays indicated an extensive stellate skull fracture. The boy would recover fully, doctors believed, but only after a long convalescence. They recommended that he remain at Charity, where Willard could monitor his progress. Allen Jr. spent a month at Charity under Willard's careful supervision, prompting the anti-Long forces to accuse Ellender of using Charity Hospital for his personal needs.[25]

Allen Jr. recovered fully and resumed his boyhood activities. When Helen was not sharing in his scouting or schooling, she had time for her plants, her cats, and her family's social goings-on. She and Willard's wife, Vi, became good friends, occasionally shopping together in New Orleans. Once at an auction at a St. Charles Avenue mansion, Helen bought an old grand piano for one hundred dollars. Vi, whose husband had not yet established himself in a private medical practice, settled for a small Dresden piano with a bid of ten dollars.[26]

In the summer of 1931 Huey's lieutenants waited eagerly for his blueprint for the 1932 gubernatorial election. Long would be a U.S. senator; someone would be Huey's candidate for governor of Louisiana, Huey's successor. Huey's shoes were big indeed—whom would he choose to fill them?

---

25. Allen Ellender, Jr., interview, June 6, 1980; unidentified newspaper clippings, August 20, 1932, in "1928–1936" Scrapbook, AEP.

26. Viola Lynch Ellender, interview, July 14, 1980.

5

SPEAKER OF THE HOUSE AND HEIR APPARENT (1931–35)

$\mathcal{L}$ong planned to govern Louisiana while he served in the U.S. Senate; consequently, he wanted a loyal supporter in the governor's mansion. His most likely choices in the 1931 gubernatorial election were Speaker John Fournet of St. Martinville, Alexandria attorney John Overton, and senate floor leader O. K. Allen of Winn Parish, who was chairman of the state highway commission. Huey selected Allen, knowing he would take orders without question. Allen Ellender claimed Huey had promised to support him for lieutenant governor. Unfortunately, Huey had also promised second spot on the ticket to Fournet and to his brother Earl Long.

Before Long announced his decision, he telephoned Ellender in Houma at about ten o'clock one night to ask him to come to New Orleans immediately, saying that he was in a political quandary. When Ellender arrived at Huey's Roosevelt Hotel suite, Huey said Fournet would not accept anything less than lieutenant governor. "Let Fournet have it if it will bring peace to the party," Ellender responded. When Long asked Ellender if he wanted to be attorney general, Ellender declined, saying, "Let [Mansura attorney Gaston] Porterie [have the position]." Ellender refused other offers, saying he supported Huey because he believed in his legislative program. Huey advised him to return to the legislature then and "we'll elect you Speaker."[1]

1. Allen J. Ellender, interview by T. Harry Williams, Louisiana and Lower Mississippi Valley Collections, Louisiana State University, Baton Rouge, La., hereinafter cited as "name of interviewee, interview by Williams"; Michael L. Kurtz and Morgan D. Peoples, *Earl K. Long: The Saga of Uncle Earl and Louisiana Politics* (Baton Rouge, 1990), 52.

Content to bide his time, Ellender decided to wait until 1936 to seek a statewide office. In July he told a Longite in the legislature, "I was supposed to be on the State Ticket, but it seems as though I will be displaced." He went on to explain, "I was offered the Attorney General's post, but have declined it." But he added confidently: "I fully expect to run for some 'High' office in 1936." Porterie, having accepted Huey's offer to be his candidate for attorney general, asked Ellender for his support. At the bottom of his letter, he wrote in longhand, "I do not feel I need to write you the above letter. I am running for the job you refused." [2]

In October, 1931, Cyr had himself sworn in as governor of Louisiana, claiming Huey had surrendered the governorship when he was elected U.S. senator. Long, angered by Cyr's audacity, consulted Ellender and Thibodaux attorney Harvey Peltier. The south Louisiana politicians, applying the same logic Cyr had used, came up with an answer. Cyr was no longer lieutenant governor because he had taken the oath as governor; therefore, Alvin O. King, the president pro tempore of the state senate and a Longite, could take the oath as lieutenant governor. King, claiming Cyr had vacated the office, did just that. Before King and Cyr settled their dispute in court, Huey was sworn in on January 25, 1932, as a U.S. senator. Cyr's full term of office expired before the court ever rendered a decision on the Cyr-King controversy.

Huey, remembering the painful defection of Lieutenant Governor Paul Cyr, did not want either Earl Long or Allen Ellender on the ticket, Fournet said. "I can't afford to have either one of those so and so's on my ticket," Fournet claimed Huey said. "Imagine what Earl, who is not as smart as Cyr, and Ellender, who is ten times smarter than Cyr and no better, will do to Oscar Allen," Huey said. Other Longites, too, believed Huey's bitter dispute with Cyr made the Kingfish reluctant to place Ellender in a high-level position. Ellender had a mind of his own and firm convictions about earning the good things in life solely through honest labor.[3]

Momentarily denied the opportunity to seek a statewide position, Ellender sought reelection to the state legislature in the January, 1932, Democratic primary. His only alternative to magnanimous political patience was to chal-

2. Allen Ellender to Alvin O. King, July 7, 1931, and Gaston Porterie to Ellender, July 16, 1931, both in "Ellender, Allen J. (Personal)" Folder, Box 4, Allen J. Ellender Papers, Nicholls State University Library, Thibodaux, La., hereinafter cited as AEP.

3. Charles T. Walsten, "Allen J. Ellender: Long Legislative Lieutenant, 1928–1936" (M.A. thesis, Louisiana State University, 1985), 26–29; John Fournet, interview by Williams.

lenge Long, a struggle he did not relish or think he could win. Instead, he defeated Morris Lottinger, receiving 1,638 votes to his opponent's 1,221. O. K. Allen became governor, John Fournet lieutenant governor. When the legislature convened on May 8, Ellender was elected Speaker of the House by acclamation. He was the last Speaker to preside over the House in the old capitol and the first in the new skyscraper capitol Huey had constructed.

As speaker Ellender presided over two regular and eight special sessions of the legislature. The majority of administration bills were designed either to finance new state programs or to break the back of the Old Regular organization in New Orleans. New taxes included levies on alcoholic beverages, automobile licenses, gasoline, public utilities, and corporations. Reprisal measures aimed primarily at Mayor T. Semmes Walmsley and the Choctaws brought New Orleans to its knees. Huey, through the legislature, forced New Orleans to accept a commission form of government, assessed the city an extra tax on water and sewage, increased the business license tax in the city, granted the governor police power over the city, and reorganized the Orleans Levee Board. These measures weakened the anti-Long forces, whose hopes were buoyed momentarily by the defection of Earl Long from the Long organization.[4]

As Speaker of the House Ellender tried to impose some of his money-saving plans on the legislature. Charles Frampton, writing for Long's *Louisiana Progress* weekly newspaper, claimed Ellender had saved the House $14,613.49 in operating expenses. Meanwhile, Ellender criticized the Senate for hiring a porter and for paying him $2.50 a day to sweep a space that "you could jump across." The frugal speaker added, "We do not want such a condition in the House of Representatives." George Vandervoort of the *Times-Picayune* quoted a Lafourche Parish legislator who said Ellender cut operating expenses but wasted funds on the construction of a new capitol.[5]

In 1932 O. K. Allen moved into the governor's mansion and Huey Long moved to Washington. Even though Huey's political activities had ostensibly shifted to the national scene, few observers believed he had loosened his tight rein on Governor Allen.

In the summer, Huey chose John Overton to run for the U.S. Senate against Louisiana's senior senator, New Iberia attorney Edwin Broussard. Without consulting Overton, Huey appointed Ellender and Peltier to be his campaign managers. Roosevelt Hotel manager Seymour Weiss handled the

4. Walsten, "Allen Ellender," 32–33.
5. Various newspaper clippings, in "1928–1936" Scrapbook, AEP.

finances for the campaign. Overton won the seat. When questionable election discrepancies surfaced, Broussard asked the Senate to investigate; in the ensuing hearings, Ellender admitted having made inadvertent errors on the election forms he submitted. He also acknowledged—to New Orleans newspapers—having used dummy candidates in the election against Broussard. Seymour Weiss quietly provided campaign funds as needed, Ellender said. Earl Long testified during the hearing to shady practices by the Longites. Only Weiss could account for how campaign funds were expended, Ellender and Peltier testified.[6]

During the hearings Ellender spoke of his religious practices. Asked if he were a member of the Kingfish's lodge, Ellender replied he knew nothing of Long having a lodge. When asked if he went to church, Ellender answered no—not in fifteen or twenty years.[7]

With help from Earl Long, anti-Long forces in 1934 hoped to remove Huey's legislative lieutenants and ultimately to impeach Governor O. K. Allen. For a while it appeared the anti-Longites would succeed—at least in removing Ellender as Speaker of the House. In April the anti-Long faction had forty-seven names on a round-robin to dump him in favor of George K. Perrault of St. Landry Parish, who had the support of the anti-Longites when the legislature convened in May, 1934. Huey's conservative opponents had formed an organization called the Square Deal; its goal was to elicit labor and popular opposition to Long. State A.F. of L. leader E. H. Williams refused to cooperate with the anti-Longites but thought the Square Dealers had the votes to oust Ellender.

The Longites sought ways to retain Ellender as Speaker. In a caucus on the sixth floor of the Heidelberg Hotel in Baton Rouge, Long, Governor Allen, Ellender, and others considered plans to foil their opponents. One plan was to have Attorney General Gaston Porterie rule that a two-thirds majority was needed in the House to remove the Speaker. Long and Governor Allen considered sealing off the capitol with the state militia to prevent the anti-Longites from appearing. "Huey, if you proceed with that plan, I'll be thrown out for sure," Ellender protested excitedly. "They are looking for

6. T. Harry Williams, *Huey Long: A Biography* (New York, 1969), 594, 604–605; New Orleans *Item,* February 7, 1933, in "1928–1936" Scrapbook, AEP; Walsten, "Allen Ellender," 31; James Paul Leslie, "Earl K. Long: The Formative Years, 1895–1940" (Ph.D. diss., University of Missouri, 1974), 109.

7. Unidentified newspaper clipping, n.d., in "1928–1936" Scrapbook, AEP.

an issue and that will furnish them with one." Indeed, the Longites agreed to a more sensible approach. They called in Earl for a conference with his brother and other leaders. The Long brothers reconciled their animosities, and the plan of Huey's opponents lost momentum. On May 13, Ellender won election as Speaker, getting fifty-eight votes to Perrault's fifty-four. Shortly thereafter, Earl, a skilled lobbyist, helped Ellender push through taxes on oil, liquor, and utilities.[8]

National matters also required attention. Ellender joined Huey Long in supporting Franklin Roosevelt for president. The New Deal seemed to offer more hope for ending the Great Depression than anything the Hoover administration advocated. Roosevelt, like Huey, was innovative, open to new ideas and approaches. Between election day in November, 1932, and inauguration day in March, 1933, bank failures increased at an alarming rate. The mere threat of failure sometimes triggered a run on a bank, sometimes causing even a sound bank to fail when most depositors lined up to demand all their money. The governor of Michigan declared a bank holiday in order to avert the collapse of the entire banking system. Business and bank failures, poverty, unemployment, and fear gripped the nation as Roosevelt prepared his inaugural address.

As attorney for the Bank of Terrebonne, Ellender understood the threat of bank failures. Terrebonne's three banks experienced financial woes because they held mortgages on sugar plantations in a depressed sugar economy. The Bank of Houma, the oldest, chartered in 1910, had lasted until 1924 when the Bank of Terrebonne took over its assets with no loss to depositors; stockholders suffered the brunt of the loss. The third bank in Houma, Peoples Bank, was in deep trouble because it held mortgages on big sugar plantations: Argyle, Crescent, Mulberry, Ridgeland, and Honduras. It failed. In New Orleans three of five banks failed. Only Whitney National Bank and American Bank and Trust survived the crisis. Hibernia, Marine Bank and Trust and Interstate Trust and Banking Company, and Canal Bank and Trust failed or were acquired by other banking institutions.

The financial problems of large New Orleans banks directly affected smaller local banks in the bayou country, which kept about 20 percent of their cash reserve requirement on deposit in a "correspondent bank." M. L. Funderburk of the Bank of Terrebonne became nervous when large New

8. Williams, *Huey Long,* 713–15; Walsten, "Allen Ellender," 34–35; Allen J. Ellender, E. H. Williams, interviews by Williams; Kurtz and Peoples, *Earl Long,* 62; Leslie, "Earl K. Long," 117–20.

Orleans banks faced runs. In New Orleans in February, 1933, he saw Hibernia Bank's depositors lined along the sidewalks of Carondelet and Gravier streets, clamoring to withdraw their endangered deposits. He hustled over to the office of Oliver Lucas, president of Canal Bank and Trust, which held some Bank of Terrebonne funds. Hibernia was sound and the Reconstruction Finance Corporation would provide emergency funds if a run occurred, Lucas assured him. Funderburk deposited some of his bank's funds in Marine Bank and Trust and Interstate Trust and Banking Company after noting no panic or threat of a run against that institution. Less than a month later, on March 9, President Roosevelt declared a bank holiday, closing all banks temporarily.

The Bank of Terrebonne, though solvent, needed a permit before it could reopen. State banks received permits from the state committee on banking, national banks from the federal Comptroller of the Currency. During the holiday, banks had to provide a statement for review by the state committee. In the meantime they could pay out no more than 5 percent of total deposits in emergency funds for families to buy groceries and necessities. About half of the Bank of Terrebonne's funds were in the Canal Bank and Trust; it would be unable to reopen after the holiday.

Ellender, busy with the legislature's Beer Session to vote in legal beer at the end of Prohibition, helped Funderburk arrange meetings with Long and state banking officials. He and Funderburk rode together to confer with Long, the state treasurer, and state banking officials. Long, having intervened to prevent a run on a Lafayette bank, was most eager to help sound banks reopen.[9]

Funderburk and state officials arranged to transfer Bank of Terrebonne funds to a sound bank that was acquiring the assets of the Houma institution's correspondent bank, Canal Bank. In the meantime the Bank of Terrebonne was allowed to use fifty thousand dollars in state severance taxes, collected by the sheriff in Terrebonne and deposited in the Bank of Terrebonne. Because the Bank of Terrebonne ultimately lost about fifteen thousand dollars, it had to reorganize and create a new bank. Stockholders could retain half of their stock, but would have to come up with thirty thousand dollars in cash. In April, 1933, the charter of Terrebonne Bank and Trust went into effect. Three years later, when oil revenue was flowing into state coffers, the state returned the fifteen thousand dollars the bank had lost in the initial reshuffling.

9. Williams, *Huey Long,* 543–45.

On the trip back to Houma after resolving Terrebonne's banking crisis, Ellender asked Funderburk to drive to his Coteau farm so he could check on his potato crop. Funderburk remembered sitting in his car on a cold night in February, 1933, as Ellender walked between the rows, checking the seed potatoes, running his fingers through the rich sandy soil. Ellender's propensity for direct contact with the good earth was well known to members of his family. Not only did he like to walk in the fields and stick his hands in the soil, he occasionally tasted the soil.[10]

As Speaker of the House, Ellender took an interest in national affairs. In February, 1934, he conferred with the legal department of the Public Works Administration office in Washington about a $4.5 million irrigation project for rice farmers in Allen Parish in southwest Louisiana. It involved irrigation, flood control, conservation, and the halting of saltwater incursion of coastal regions.[11]

In August, 1934, Ellender attempted questionable parliamentary maneuvers to move Louisiana legislation bogged down in debate and unlikely to pass. He proposed that a simple majority rather than two-thirds of the House could suspend the rules. Anti-Long forces protested loudly and stymied his efforts. Ellender threatened to have the House meet on Friday, and through the weekend if necessary, to get his package of bills considered. Ordinarily the legislature adjourned on Thursday evening and reconvened the following Monday. New Orleans legislators usually had their bags packed by noon on Thursday, ready to board the train for New Orleans shortly after adjournment. They quietly and secretly agreed to go along with Ellender if he allowed them to depart for New Orleans on the usual schedule. Ellender kept his plans secret from everyone, even Huey. A determined Huey got Ellender up early one morning to watch the sun light the sky up as they drove around Baton Rouge. When Huey asked about the legislative agenda, Ellender playfully told him to go to hell.[12]

In 1935 many Longites wondered whom Huey would choose to be his candidate for governor. Ellender expected Huey to choose him to replace O. K. Allen, prohibited by the Louisiana constitution from succeeding himself as governor. Long and John Overton were U.S. senators; Paul Cyr ob-

10. M. L. Funderburk, recorded interviews by B. Bourg, R. Detro, and M. Forêt, typescript, n.d. [1988], 101 pp., Nicholls State University Archives, 30–31, 48–49, 69–76; Florence LeCompte, interview, August 7, 1979.

11. Alexandria (La.) *Town Talk*, February 26, 1934.

12. Walsten, "Allen J. Ellender," 36; Allen J. Ellender, interview by Williams.

viously was no longer a member of the organization. Ellender, who had stepped aside in favor of Fournet in 1932, believed himself to be the logical choice. He had worked diligently and loyally for the organization; surely Huey would anoint him to run for the top spot. Ellender seemed to have the edge over his rivals, including Huey's brother Earl, ambitious but distrusted by the Kingfish. Earl had once defected and had even testified against the organization in the Overton hearings. Other rivals seemed less capable, had unscrupulous reputations, or were little known.

Ellender apparently overlooked some portentous signs. As late as early fall of 1935, Huey, unorthodox and often unpredictable, had made no formal announcement of his choice for governor. Ellender must have been aware of Huey's habit of promising high positions in the organization to several rivals—each sworn to secrecy about his imminent rise. The purpose was to assure a reserve of loyal, hard-working lieutenants. Even more important, Ellender may have failed to realize that Huey liked strong, innovative legislative leaders but docile figurehead executives. He wanted bland executives to fill posts that he technically or legally could not.

In May or June of 1935, Huey told Ellender he would be the preferred candidate for governor. However, the Kingfish may have made similar promises to New Orleans attorney Richard Leche, oilman James A. Noe of Monroe, Public Service Commissioner Wade O. Martin of Arnaudville, John Fournet, and Harvey Peltier. Not surprisingly, he asked Ellender to say nothing about his selection for the time being.

Later in the summer, Governor Allen called Ellender in for a political chat. He asked Ellender, who he assumed would be governor, if he would still be able to arrange oil deals on state lands when Ellender succeeded him. "I've been lucky in getting leases on state lands," Governor Allen said. "I have been able to get overrides on oil land. Can I keep on with that?" No, Ellender said. He told him it was not right to form dummy corporations to get low bids on state oil reserves. "If you got overrides, it [*sic*] should go to the state," Ellender said. "We'll see about it," the governor replied, suggesting Huey had approved his deals and would disapprove Ellender's puritanical objections.[13]

Long had permitted similar oil leasing arrangements for himself and a number of his followers; they profited unduly from oil resources that belonged to Louisiana citizens. Rapacious acts depriving the state of millions of dollars in mineral revenue did not violate Louisiana law. From 1914 until

13. Walsten, "Allen Ellender," 41–44; Allen J. Ellender, interview by Williams.

1936, the governor was the sole leasing agent for state-owned land and water bottoms. Huey, James A. Noe, and Seymour Weiss earned huge profits by acquiring leases from the state on the rich oil and gas deposits in Caddo Parish in north Louisiana. Later O. K. Allen, Simon Guidry of the Lafayette area, Harvey Peltier, and others in south Louisiana obtained inexpensive leases, which they, in turn, sold to major oil companies ready to develop the rich fields of coastal Louisiana. Ellender wanted no part of the unethical, but legal, leases. On May 21, 1924, long before he told O. K. Allen he would disallow such practices as governor, Ellender introduced a House concurrent resolution calling for a study of all sources of revenue and all expenditures by the Department of Conservation. However, his measure had been modified and stripped of restrictive provisions.[14]

Despite the sweetheart leasing arrangements by the Longites, oil rescued Terrebonne and other coastal parishes from the brunt of the Great Depression; no soup lines formed in Houma during the worst years of the 1930s. A number of pioneer oil men, wildcatters, had explored for oil in Terrebonne Parish in the late 1920s. They struck it in shallow sand domes in the coastal region. The forerunner of Louisiana Land and Exploration Company (LL&E) realized the viability of salt domes as oil resources and so leased much of the area. LL&E later sold its Terrebonne leases to Texaco for cash and a one-eighth override. The State of Louisiana received one-eighth, as did Win or Lose Corporation, the north Louisiana company owned by James A. Noe, and others.

In 1934 Noe purchased many acres of state land and formed Win or Lose, which held the mineral rights to the land. The state owned acres of coastal lands comprised of bays, lakes, marshes, rivers, bayous, swamps, and water bottoms. The subsurface resources were the property of the citizens of Louisiana. State law allowed the governor to lease these lands and water bottoms to the major oil producers. How much the taxpayers benefited from these leases depended on the honesty and integrity of the public officials who signed the leases. Noe donated thirty-one shares of Win or Lose stock to Huey Long. Even though Long built his reputation fighting against Standard Oil, his associate, Seymour Weiss, was a close friend of Louis LeSage, principal lobbyist for Standard Oil.[15]

14.   Brady M. Banta, "The Regulation and Conservation of Petroleum Resources in Louisiana, 1901–1940," 2 vols. (Ph.D. diss., Louisiana State University, 1981), II, 295, 489, 491–92, 494, 496, 506.

15.   Funderburk, recorded interviews (typescript, Nicholls State University Archives), 76; M. L. Funderburk, interview, July 11, 1980; Kurtz and Peoples, *Earl Long,* 46.

As early as June, 1934, F. Edward Hebert, city editor of the New Orleans *States-Times,* considered Ellender the top prospect to succeed as governor. Rather surprisingly, James A. Noe, Monroe businessman and partner of Huey Long in a number of oil deals, told the *Times-Picayune* in August, 1935, Huey had chosen him to be the next governor. Long had ruled out Richard Leche because he was a Roman Catholic and unlikely to impress voters in Protestant north Louisiana, Weiss surmised. Actually Long had reservations about any politician waiting to replace him: Fournet was too much of an Acadian, Martin a Catholic, Ellender too short, and Noe too closely associated with the oil industry.

But why would Ellender want to be a puppet governor, Long's next whipping boy? He must have observed the way Long treated Governor Allen, cussing him publicly and humiliating him openly and blatantly. Did he think Huey would treat him differently? Was he so enamored of Long's program that he would have suffered embarrassment to further it, or did his ego demand the title governor? After deferring to others in 1932 for the good of the Long cause, did Ellender now believe he was entitled to advancement?

These questions have no definitive answers, even in the voluminous papers Ellender left. Long's most accepting biographer, T. Harry Williams, admits that Huey spent lavishly, allowed his people to skim from the state, and grasped power needlessly, unable eventually to distinguish goals from methods. Yet roads, bridges, free textbooks, and adult education are but a few of Long's lasting accomplishments. Like the biographer Williams, Ellender must have considered Huey a mass leader—one with exceptional intelligence and insight and leadership. Dazzled by Long's brilliance and eager to be viewed a loyal follower, Ellender never questioned Long's hegemony, even in 1934 and 1935 when he helped push through the legislative bills that increased Long's grip on the state. He rationalized and supported the rapacious acts. He did not seem to question Long's motives any more than he would have questioned his father's management of a sugar plantation during his youth.[16]

The succession problem had not been resolved when the legislature convened in a special session Long told Governor Allen to call in September, 1935. Long wanted to provide financial aid to New Orleans, whose leaders had been browbeaten into submission. In the meantime, Long had fallen out

16. Williams, *Long,* x, 414–16, 820–25; William I. Hair, *The Kingfish and His Realm: The Life and Times of Huey P. Long* (Baton Rouge, 1991), 227–28, 240–41.

with Roosevelt and wanted to enact laws to control New Deal programs in Louisiana. He also wanted to gerrymander judicial districts of several anti-Long judges. He planned to eliminate the district of Benjamin Pavy, a bitter anti-Longite from St. Landry Parish in south-central Louisiana.

On Sunday night, September 8, while the legislature busied itself with its agenda, Huey conferred briefly with Ellender in the House at about 9:00 P.M. He asked Ellender to visit his twenty-fourth-floor suite once the House had adjourned. Huey wanted to discuss the upcoming gubernatorial election, Ellender assumed. Moments later Ellender heard the shooting that fatally injured Huey.[17]

Carl Austin Weiss, a prominent Baton Rouge physician and the son-in-law of Judge Pavy, shot Huey with a small-caliber pistol as he made his way down a marble corridor of the state capitol between the House and Senate chambers. Huey's bodyguards riddled Weiss's body with bullets as Huey stumbled down the back steps of the capitol and was driven to Our Lady of the Lake Hospital, about two hundred yards away. Huey's lieutenants hurried to the hospital to be near their wounded leader.

Ellender joined other Long supporters who hovered near Huey. They tried to explain who had shot him, and they interfered with his medical treatment. Dr. Arthur Vidrine, superintendent of the Charity Hospital in Louisiana, summoned surgeons from the Ochsner Clinic in New Orleans who specialized in gunshot wounds. Like other Longites jockeying to be near Huey, Ellender may have exaggerated how exclusive or extensive his hospital contacts with Long had been. "Allen, why was I shot?" he said Huey asked. Ellender called his brother Willard to come and evaluate the situation. "Huey, don't worry, my brother who is an expert in gunshots will be here and we will take care of everything," Ellender said. Vidrine assumed Willard would fly to Baton Rouge, but there were no lights at the airport in Houma, and Willard drove. Like the doctors from New Orleans, he was late in arriving. After waiting several hours for surgeons more capable than himself, Vidrine, who had lined up blood donors and ordered hospital personnel to match and type blood, performed surgery on Long.

Vidrine allowed Ellender and others to remain in the operating room. "I saw the entire operation," Ellender recalled later, in his usual rambling, quick-fire type of delivery. "I saw everything, only one bullet. Huey kinda fat. Vidrine would make a cut and clamp the blood vessel." Vidrine com-

17. Walsten, "Allen Ellender," 38, 39.

pleted the surgery shortly after midnight, just as Willard arrived from Houma. "Examine Huey and tell me," Ellender told his brother.

Willard assisted with a direct blood transfusion from James A. Noe, given with some difficulty because Huey's veins were collapsing because of shock. Huey failed to rally even after receiving about one and one-half pints of blood, Willard noted. Huey was bleeding internally, he surmised, and so asked Vidrine, in the presence of Dr. Jimmy Rives, if he had catheterized Huey. Vidrine answered no. When Vidrine ordered the catheterization at 6:30 A.M. Monday, the urine was "grossly bloody." Willard told Ellender, "Within a few hours Huey will be dead because he [Vidrine] failed to empty the bladder." Further examination indicated kidney damage, but by then the Kingfish was delirious and too weak to undergo additional surgery. He died at about 4:00 A.M. on Tuesday, September 10, 1935.[18]

As Louisianians underwent the emotional catharsis Huey's death and funeral engendered, Longites struggled to hold together the highly person-alized organization Huey had run in his unique manner. Who among them had the maturity, the bearing, the strength of character to lead the organi-zation? None matched Huey's intelligence, charisma, and perseverance, al-though they were unusually intelligent and highly successful. Ellender and Peltier were lawyers and legislative floor leaders. Governor O. K. Allen, Rich-ard Leche, Orleans Levee Board president Abraham Shushan, James A. Noe, Seymour Weiss, Share Our Wealth spokesman Gerald L. K. Smith, Earl Long had all wielded power in the organization.

As it turned out, no single Longite emerged as the obvious leader of the organization. Instead a number of them shared power and ruled as a makeshift team, nominally headed by Governor Allen. Ellender would have to overcome ambitious, strong-willed figures if he hoped to lead the orga-nization. He would have to proceed with caution and convincingly dem-onstrate his leadership to defeat his rivals. Any heavy-handed power grab was doomed to fail, as Smith soon discovered. When he attempted to wrest control of the faction, Long's lieutenants united against him and drove him from the state. But for a short time Smith played the dominant hand.

Smith's opportunity came when Seymour Weiss, who handled Huey's funeral arrangements, allowed him to deliver the eulogy at Huey's funeral on September 12, 1935. Ellender had been one of Huey's pallbearers, along with Governor Allen, John Fournet, James Noe, Wade Martin, Seymour

---

18. Allen J. Ellender, interview by Williams; Willard Ellender to Allen Ellender, March 19, 1963, in the possession of Timothy Ellender; Walsten, "Allen Ellender," 40.

Weiss, and Robert S. Maestri of New Orleans. Weiss later regretted his choice, for Smith delivered a stirring twenty-five-minute oration that made him well known. He praised Huey and urged continuation of his programs under the leadership of men Long had trusted. After the funeral, Smith kept himself in the public eye with mass meetings, radio broadcasts, a well-publicized telegram to President Roosevelt, a dramatic statement at the inquest into Huey's death, and wild charges of plots and intrigue masterminded by high-level public officials in Louisiana, in Washington, and on Wall Street.

Two rival cliques emerged. One faction, bent on continuing Share Our Wealth and on opposing the New Deal, included Smith, Noe, and Earle Christenberry, Huey's private secretary. Challenging them was a more conservative group consisting of Ellender, Maestri, Weiss, Shushan, Martin, and Fournet. They wanted to make peace with the Roosevelt administration and to dismantle the wealth-sharing movement. Initially, the rival groups could agree only to recognize Governor Allen as symbolic leader—for the time being.

Ellender seemed to have firm support from most Longites. On September 11 he told the *Times-Picayune* Huey had selected him to be the Long faction's 1936 candidate for governor. Political analysts for the newspaper seemed to accept his statement as a widely held belief among Longites, still in disarray after the death of their leader.[19]

For about ten days Ellender seemed to have Long-organization backing for governor. On the twenty-first the *Picayune* said Maestri, Weiss, Belle Chase attorney Leander Perez, and two important leaders from Jefferson Parish, Sheriff Frank Clancy and state senator Jules Fisher, supported Ellender. Earl Long, also an Ellender supporter, asked Longites to reject Richard Leche.[20]

On September 20, 1935, without consulting the major Longites, Gerald L. K. Smith endorsed James Noe for governor and Wade Martin for the U.S. Senate. The excluded Longites were surprised and angry. Smith expected to become Martin's secretary in Washington, they surmised, where he could control Share Our Wealth clubs and use franking privileges to maintain close communication with its members. Smith had stolen a march on Long's closest associates by announcing his strategy before they had devised their own.

Ellender was in bed with laryngitis in Houma when Noe announced for

19.   Walsten, "Allen Ellender," 43, 44.
20.   Leslie, "Earl K. Long," 131.

governor. Ellender fired back by quoting Huey Long: "The boy from down the bayou will be the next governor." That same day the New York *World Telegram* described Ellender as having the "verve and charm of a hitching post." The writer incorrectly claimed that Ellender made a fortune from his farm property and from oil wells.[21]

The overlooked Longites recovered quickly and responded after conferring in an all-night session in New Orleans. Ellender and Earl Long criticized Smith; Weiss and Maestri pressured Governor Allen into withholding support from Noe and Martin. Had Governor Allen joined the steamroller move to Noe and Martin, the remaining Longites might have been powerless to stop them.[22]

Ellender, always politically savvy, knew his ambitious political rivals would not agree to his hegemony. At Huey's funeral Helen had told her brother Charles Donnelly, "They're trying to push Allen aside." Rivals could quote Huey's dying promises to them, real or imaginary, without fear of contradiction. John Fournet remembered Huey's death-day words: "Now listen, quit quibbling with Wade Martin and Allen Ellender. Don't get crossed up with them. You're going to need them."[23]

The confusion over factions and choices diminished Ellender's chances of becoming governor. Leaders of the Long faction persuaded Governor Allen to reject the Noe-Martin ticket. In an all-night meeting at the Roosevelt Hotel in New Orleans, Governor Allen backed down and agreed to a revised ticket: Richard Leche for governor, Earl Long for lieutenant governor, and Ellender for the full Senate term. The governor, remembering his conversation with Ellender about oil deals, may have wanted to bypass Ellender because of his opposition to the oil leasing scams.

Noe knew he needed the support of other Longites. Angry over being bypassed by the Long faction, Noe nonetheless decided to stay in the race, thereby complicating matters a bit for the realigned ticket. Noe's strength was in the Monroe area; the Leche-Ellender group was strong in south Louisiana. Only John Fournet supported Noe.[24]

21.   Paul Harrison, New York *World Telegram,* September 21, 1935, and unidentified newspaper clipping, [September 21, 1935], both in "1928–1936" Scrapbook, AEP; Leslie, "Earl K. Long," 129.

22.   Glen Jeansonne, *Gerald L. K. Smith: Minister of Hate* (New Haven, 1988), 42–43; Allan P. Sindler, *Huey Long's Louisiana: State Politics, 1920–1952* (Baltimore, 1956), 118.

23.   Daisy Donnelly, interview, July 14, 1980; John Fournet, interview by Williams.

24.   F. Raymond Daniell, New York *Times,* September 19, 20, 1935.

Longites with ties to the lucrative oil leasing arrangements—Noe, O. K. Allen, Weiss, Peltier—saw in the chaos an opportunity to bypass the potentially dangerous Ellender, who had refused to condone the questionable leasing arrangements. Noe had sought the influence of Governor Allen and Harvey Peltier. Ultimately, compromise and accommodation prevailed and the Longites selected a unified ticket headed by Richard Leche. He may have been selected simply because he was acceptable to those who did not want Ellender. In Washington Ellender would be isolated from the politics of Louisiana oil.

Outmaneuvered by the oil moguls, Ellender accepted the nod for senator rather than for governor. His supporters and Noe's friends had agreed to support Leche to keep peace in the faction. Noe and Martin had ruined Ellender's chance for the top spot by threatening a party split; Maestri, Weiss, and O. K. Allen had been repelled by his straitlaced position on state oil leases.[25]

Why had Ellender, who had been considered the favorite until Smith confused the arrangement, agreed to accept anything but governor? Had he again demonstrated political patience for the good of the organization, or did he have no choice? Only by challenging them directly—asserting that he was Huey's choice and announcing his plans to campaign on that basis— could Ellender have seized the initiative. Without the assertiveness of a Huey Long (not to mention his financial chest), he agreed to a lesser spot on the ticket. He had not campaigned in Protestant north Louisiana and established a political base for himself, the way Huey had brazenly carved a spot in the Cajun country. Ellender decided against challenging his rivals for political leadership. Once again he would bide his time, hoping his chance for the position would come later.

Even after compromise and agreement, Ellender's position was not altogether secure. He was shocked to learn on October 23 that Governor Allen had changed his mind about supporting the revised lineup for the 1936 elections. The governor shattered the political truce by announcing his intention to run for the full Senate term. Ellender would withdraw because Governor Allen had decided to run, a New Orleans newspaper reported a week later. Governor Allen "had put over a 'fast one' that eventually would force Ellender to withdraw from the race."[26]

---

25. Walsten, "Allen Ellender," 44, 49, 51, 53–55.
26. New Orleans *States,* October 31, 1935, in "1928–1936" Scrapbook, AEP.

Ellender, returning from north Louisiana early in November, announced "under no circumstance" would he withdraw from the Senate race. He affirmed his intention to run even if he got "only one vote." Again the Longites, including Ellender, gathered in Baton Rouge. At a meeting in the governor's office, Maestri and Weiss attempted to dissuade the governor from running. They told him they would not support him over Ellender. Earl Long, too, spoke in support of Ellender saying, "You can't double-cross this man Ellender." Ellender had made clear his firm intention to back down no further for the sake of party unity. "I have stepped aside for party unity and harmony, but this time I'm not going to do it." [27]

Governor Allen relented under the barrage and decided not to run for the Senate. Again there was peace among the Longites. Ellender promised to support the ticket and campaign for a better old-age pension and improved sugar legislation. He had been frustrated in his efforts to gain high executive office, but for the time being at least, he was content to play the cards dealt him.

Before his Senate race, Ellender had made a trip to Washington in 1935 to confer with Secretary of Agriculture Henry A. Wallace about increasing sugarcane allotments for Louisiana growers. "All is well for the president in Louisiana," he said, indicating the Longites intended to end the political feud Huey had waged against the New Deal. [28]

In light of the political machinations before the January 21, 1936, election, Ellender not surprisingly turned to a trusted friend to manage his Senate campaign and to help develop an organization of his own: Elward Wright. There was no doubt about Wright's loyalty and honesty, so his business partner became his campaign manager. Ellender could hardly expect loyalty from his Long associates. As one of Huey's trusted leaders, Ellender had seen what the organization could accomplish during a campaign. Likewise he had seen organizational support sprout gossamer wings and vanish when ambitious rivals vied for power. He was unlikely to forget his feelings of hopelessness and betrayal as the Longites jostled for power. If he could develop a strong organization of his own, he could avoid future imbroglios like the one he had just survived. [29]

The Longites, promising to carry on in the tradition of the martyred

27. Walsten, "Allen Ellender," 56, 57–59; New Orleans *Item,* November 2, 1935, in "1928–1936" Scrapbook, AEP; Leslie, "Earl K. Long," 132.

28. Atlanta *Constitution,* December 5, 1935, in "1928–1936" Scrapbook, AEP.

29. Elward Wright, interview, November 8, 1979.

Huey Long, won convincingly. Ellender won a smashing victory over two opponents in the January 21 Democratic primary. He received 364,931 votes to 167,471 for Congressman John Sandlin of Minden, and 4,177 for Irving Ward-Steinman, a political unknown. In Terrebonne Parish he received 77 percent of the vote and in Lafourche, 66 percent. Other Longites won easily. Richard Leche became governor, Earl Long lieutenant governor. Ellender believed the Longite victory vindicated Huey.[30]

Governor Allen was expected to appoint Ellender to fill Huey's unexpired term, thereby assuring him a slight advantage in seniority over senators who would take their seats in January, 1937. However, just one week after the election James A. Noe became governor, Governor Allen having died suddenly on January 28, 1936. Huey had appointed Noe lieutenant governor when John Fournet had vacated the position to become a Louisiana Supreme Court justice. Now Noe could get even with Ellender and the New Orleans leaders who had derailed his chance to succeed Huey. Even though Noe's tenure in office would end in May, 1936, he was governor nonetheless. To Ellender's chagrin, he appointed Huey's widow, Rose, to fill the Kingfish's unexpired Senate term, denying Ellender an opportunity to gain a slight advantage in seniority over his colleagues. This vindictive maneuver confirmed the fears of Weiss and Maestri that Noe was too uncontrollable and unpredictable to run the Long organization. Their selection of Leche now seemed sensible. They probably felt the same way about sending Ellender to Washington, away from the inner workings of Louisiana government.[31]

As 1936 came to an end, Ellender mused over the political storms he had weathered. Political infighting among the Longites had nearly done him in, but he had survived the internecine struggle in a relatively secure position, that of U.S. senator from Louisiana. Like Harry Truman, he had been denied the state house and been elected senator instead, but he still had a prestigious position securely in hand.[32] As a U.S. senator he would, after all, be filling the shoes of Senator Huey Long.

30. *Compilation of Primary Election Returns,* January 21, 1936, in Box 1297, AEP; Allen Ellender to John Fournet, January 27, 1936, in "Allen J. Ellender" Folder, Box 10, John Fournet Papers, Louisiana and Lower Mississippi Valley Collections, Louisiana State University, Baton Rouge, La.

31. Walsten, "Allen Ellender," 60; F. Edward Hebert, *Last of the Titans: The Life and Times of Congressman F. Edward Hebert of Louisiana* (Lafayette, La., 1976), 108–109; Kurtz and Peoples, *Earl Long,* 79.

32. David McCullough, *Truman* (New York, 1992), 32.

PART TWO

Washington

6

SENATOR ELLENDER

(1936–38)

*I*n December, 1935, a month before Allen Ellender won his U.S. Senate seat, the Leche-Long-Ellender ticket was openly courting Roosevelt and New Deal leaders, Turner Catledge of the New York *Times* reported. A major concern of the group, he suggested, was an Internal Revenue Service probe of the Long organization. Clearly, the survivors of Huey Long's organization favored cooperation with the New Deal rather than opposition to it.[1]

Shortly after the Long faction won its victory at the polls in January, 1936, Ellender met with Longite financial manager Seymour Weiss, New Orleans mayor Bob Maestri, Governor Richard Leche, and Lieutenant Governor Earl Long at the Roosevelt Hotel. They decided to end the feud with the New Deal. Several Longites met with James Farley in February; soon thereafter the Long organization abandoned Share Our Wealth and endorsed Franklin Roosevelt. The transition was not difficult; Huey himself had been a New Deal supporter until he fell out with Roosevelt over control of jobs in Louisiana.[2]

In June, 1936, Senator-elect Ellender attended the Democratic National Convention in Philadelphia as a delegate. His win in the Democratic primary in January was tantamount to victory; the Louisiana Republican Party had few members and no candidate of its own in the November general election. Ellender said he was supporting Roosevelt.[3] The Long organization would

---

1. Turner Catledge, New York *Times,* December 19, 1935.

2. Michael L. Kurtz and Morgan D. Peoples, *Earl K. Long: The Saga of Uncle Earl and Louisiana Politics* (Baton Rouge, 1990), 11, 47, 81, 82.

3. New York *Times,* June 24, 1936.

not continue to feud with Roosevelt, Ellender and Seymour Weiss told the press in Philadelphia. Ellender did not consider himself committed to fighting Long's posthumous political battles. "Huey Long was personally ambitious and saw in his feud with a president a means of advancing his own presidential ambitions," Ellender said. "I always thought that Huey was subordinating the best interest of the state to his own ambitions." Weiss added a final observation, "There is no one in Louisiana with national ambitions. We want to do the best we can for our state."

These observations angered Longites in the state legislature, who threatened political reprisals against Ellender and Weiss. The two delegates dashed off a telegram to Speaker Lorris Wimberly, refuting statements attributed to them. "We have not said anything derogatory of our late leader." The wire added: "We desire for the people of our state to know that if Huey were alive we would be following him." Both delegates signed the statement. In a second statement Ellender denied having criticized Huey. Hostile New Orleans papers may have exaggerated their statements in an attempt to embarrass the Long organization, Harvey Peltier reminded legislators, shielding his old friends.[4]

Ellender was sworn in on Tuesday, January 5, 1937. Senators Harry Byrd of Virginia and John Overton of Louisiana escorted him, Carter Glass of Virginia, and Dennis Chavez of New Mexico, and a few others to the podium to be sworn in. Henry Cabot Lodge of Massachusetts and John H. Bankhead of Alabama were also new members sworn in that day, after reelected veterans had taken the oath. Lyndon B. Johnson was one of the newcomers taking the oath in the House.[5]

The day Ellender took office the United Auto Workers, of the CIO, was conducting a sit-down strike against General Motors in Flint, Michigan. Ellender, calling the strike, which created a national sensation, "un-American, and nothing short of a hold-up," aroused the ire of such labor leaders as John L. Lewis, head of the United Mine Workers and president of the CIO. When the Seventy-fifth Congress convened on January 5, Ellender's desk was behind that of William Borah of Idaho, a Senate veteran who remembered Huey Long vividly. Huey was bright and quick and one of the most capable men in the Senate, Borah told Ellender.[6]

    4. New Orleans *Item,* June 25, 1936, in "1928–1936" Scrapbook, Allen J. Ellender Papers, Nicholls State University Library, Thibodaux, La., hereinafter cited as AEP.

    5. *Congressional Record,* 75th Cong., 1st Sess., Vol. 81, Pt. 1, January 5, 1937, p. 6.

    6. Allen J. Ellender speech, Box 1827, AEP; Allen J. Ellender, interview by T. Harry

As a Longite, Ellender had helped Huey fight the New Deal, but as a farmer Ellender saw the positive changes the New Deal brought to the agricultural South. The Agricultural Adjustment Act provided mechanisms for raising farm prices, subsidizing farmers, and eliminating tenant farming. The Public Works Administration (PWA) and its successor, the Works Progress Administration (WPA), created millions of jobs and constructed parks, schools, courthouses, and countless other needed public facilities. The Tennessee Valley Authority prevented flooding and, with the help of the Rural Electrification Administration (REA), provided cheap electricity for the rural southern countryside. Other New Deal programs solved the banking crises, helped industry recover, created a labor-relations policy to settle labor disputes, aided indigent college students, and regulated public utilities.

If Ellender had been blinded to these realities by Huey's hatred of Roosevelt, he recovered quickly after Long's death. Roosevelt's easy victory in 1936 convinced him of the enviable position FDR enjoyed. He could have won the presidency without the South, which nonetheless was a solid part of his political coalition, along with organized labor, city bosses, blacks and other minorities, and liberal intellectuals. Besides, the schism between the urban northern wing and the southern wing of the Democratic Party had been healed. Even southerners voted to change the two-thirds rule in the Democratic nominating convention, which had for years given the South a veto of sorts in the nominating process.[7]

Breaking with Huey's policies was surely less than difficult for Ellender. After all, he had reluctantly become a Longite in 1928 after succumbing to threats, flattery, and Huey's ambitious blueprint for Louisiana. Even when he was a loyal Longite, his family and friends remained unconverted. His brother Claude and his sister-in-law Thelma never liked Huey; Elward Wright voted for Huey only once, for senator in 1930, and then only to get him out of the state. Now, without Huey, Ellender could assume a more natural political stance. He was on his own. If he ever hoped to be governor of Louisiana, he had to master the ways of the Senate and serve the people of Louisiana effectively.[8]

Williams, Louisiana and Lower Mississippi Valley Collections, Louisiana State University, Baton Rouge, La.

7. Robert A. Garson, *The Democratic Party and the Politics of Sectionalism, 1941–1948* (Baton Rouge, 1974), 7.

8. Thelma Ellender, interview, June 30, 1980; Elward Wright, interview, November 8, 1979.

Ellender hoped to become a part of the New Deal, which included in its ranks congressional leaders from the South whom he admired. He favored imaginative and innovative programs, especially those likely to solve the farm problem. FDR was more malleable and less liberal than many assumed. His gestures toward black leaders, southerners realized, were more symbolic than real. And the president had caved in to the cotton section of the U.S. Department of Agriculture, which had resisted reforms meant to bring greater benefits to black sharecroppers and to reduce the influence of big planters.

The freshman senator supported FDR's second Agricultural Adjustment Act, the 1937 Wagner Housing Act, and the Fair Labor Standards Act (the minimum wage law), after agricultural workers were exempted from its provisions. During his first session in the Senate, he filibustered to kill an antilynching bill, opposed efforts to remove the poll tax, and criticized a bill to form a permanent Fair Employment Practices Commission. Sometimes Ellender received his political cues from the Long organization in Louisiana. He and Overton sided with Roosevelt and voted against the Wheeler Amendment to the Reorganization Bill of 1938. Former PWA director Harold Ickes believed a call by WPA director Harry Hopkins to Leche influenced the vote, but he did not know what promises the Roosevelt administration made to Leche and the Louisiana legislative delegation.[9]

From the outset, Ellender was a solid New Dealer. James Hilty, who conducted a systematic study of New Deal voting patterns on a wide range of topics, indicates Ellender was a team player. In all three sessions of the Seventy-fifth Congress, Ellender voted on the winning side on many issues. He voted for virtually all relief and welfare measures in 1937 and 1938: providing financial aid for housing, extending the Civilian Conservation Corps (CCC), lowering matching funds by states for work-relief, creating the U.S. Housing Authority. He backed measures to regulate business, such as the Guffey-Snyder Act. He supported revenue and taxation bills and those expanding public power facilities. He favored the appointment of Hugo Black of Alabama to the Supreme Court and the Neutrality Act of 1937. He voted for acts to expand financial assistance for housing and allow the president to continue relief work in areas unable to afford the requisite 25 percent in matching funds. As signs of impending war surfaced in Europe and Asia,

9. Garson, *The Democratic Party,* 6; Richard Davies, *Housing Reform During the Truman Administration* (Columbia, Mo., 1966), 35; Harold L. Ickes, *The Secret Diary of Harold L. Ickes* (2 vols.; New York, 1954), II, 345.

Ellender voted for increasing naval appropriations and other preparedness measures.[10]

In 1937 Ellender joined twelve other freshman senators pledging support for Nebraska senator George Norris' progressive reforms. Ellender became a cosponsor—with many others—of the National School Lunch Act FDR signed into law that same year. The act governed surplus agricultural commodities, winning wide support from farm interests.[11]

Like Majority Leader Joseph T. Robinson, Ellender supported Roosevelt's court-packing plan. Robinson considered it moderate, but opponents, rousing intense opposition to the scheme, felt it would remove checks and balances built into the American system of government. Richard B. Russell, Jr., who had come to the Senate in 1933, opposed the scheme. Ellender's support for the plan was prompted more by efforts to win favor with administration leaders than by philosophical considerations. He generally supported presidential appointments and legislation unless doing so posed major problems for constituents. As a senator, Ellender, like Russell, decided to eschew grandstanding in the style of Huey Long to become a workhorse rather than a showhorse, maneuvering quietly behind the scenes to produce legislation. Neither Ellender nor Russell took a stand on an issue until his constituents voiced solid support.[12]

Ellender was lukewarm, at best, on a federal minimum wage law, but he voted for the Fair Labor Standards Act of 1938 nonetheless. In a rambling, convoluted radio broadcast titled "The Wages and Hours Problem" and delivered over the Mutual Broadcasting System on June 5, 1938, Ellender explained the development of tariff, income tax, labor, and federal reserve policies. Discussing their evolution in simplistic terms, he used conspiracy theory to explain how the Federal Reserve System had been created to prevent Wall Street bankers from victimizing farmers with exorbitant interest

10. James W. Hilty, *Voting Alignments in the United States Senate, 1933–1944* (1 vol. with appendix; University Microfilms International, 1979), A-135–41, A-104–107, A-242–44, A-211–13, A-187–89, A-299–305, A-265–69, A-441–43.

11. Richard Lowitt, *George W. Norris: The Triumph of a Progressive, 1933–1944* (Urbana, Ill., 1978), 330n; James Finley to David McKinzey, November 15, 1968, "Food Stamp Program, Department of Agriculture, 1968" Folder, Box 441, AEP.

12. Simeon Henkle to Joseph T. Robinson, February 15, 1937, Box 226.1, and Robinson to R. W. Robins, February 27, 1937, Box 255.2, both in Joseph T. Robinson Papers, Special Collections, University of Arkansas Library, Fayetteville, Ark., hereinafter cited as JTR; Gilbert C. Fite, *Richard B. Russell, Jr., Senator from Georgia* (Chapel Hill, 1991), 116, 125; "Supreme Court" Folder, Box 569, AEP.

rates. He had similar theories for antitrust laws. Acknowledging a need for some kind of wage-and-hour legislation, Ellender was not sure Congress had authority to set uniform rates nationwide. He preferred the old way of setting rates, by the law of supply and demand.[13]

Somewhat of a political maverick, Ellender had no blueprint for his Senate career. Instead, he responded to constituents and followed the lead of influential southern senators who devised agricultural, labor, and racial policies. Like them, he learned to embrace the programs the New Deal had to offer his state and to criticize those he disliked. He could blame extremists— liberals, communists, integrationists, greedy Wall Street adventurers—for suggesting programs he opposed. Often inconsistent and iconoclastic, Ellender sometimes called himself a Longite, sometimes a loyal New Dealer. Always he sought popular support.

Ellender did not fall into a neat category in his first year in the U.S. Senate. Clearly a New Dealer, he voiced heated opposition to some programs, using arguments first advanced by Huey Long. In other matters, such as race, organized labor, poll taxes, and antilynching legislation, Ellender took stands diametrically opposed to views he and Long had both supported. He drew closer to the agricultural establishment, the power structure of modern farming, which had a direct influence on the lives of sugarcane and cotton farmers. He heard often from the American Sugar Cane League and other farm lobby groups.

Like Huey Long, Ellender favored federal aid to education. However, race and religion, he discovered, intruded into education bills. Roman Catholics, claiming their tax dollars entitled them to educational benefits, opposed education bills prohibiting aid to religious schools. In Louisiana, Huey, devising the now widely accepted child-benefit theory, had solved a delicate religious issue when Catholics opposed his free textbook program. Under it, the state provided books to all Louisiana children, regardless of the school they attended. Ellender, a forceful advocate of separation of church and state, would have limited aid to books and bus transportation. When critics asked him to vote against the Harrison-Black-Fletcher Bill in 1937 because it discriminated against Catholics, he asked for specific proof of unfairness.[14]

13. "Farm Act, Administrative Rulings" Folder, Box 301, AEP.
14. Henrietta Koop to Allen Ellender, July 17, 1937, and Ellender to Koop, May 14, 1937, both in "Harrison-Fletcher Bill" Folder, Box 156, AEP; Ellender to Charles F. Buck, Jr., June 7, 1938, in "Federal-Aid-to-Education-Bill" Folder, Box 461, AEP.

Aware of widespread poverty in many sections of the country, Ellender favored educational aid to states to equalize opportunities for all Americans. Black Protestant ministers would support such a bill, they wrote to say, only if it included guarantees that the states would expend monies for black schools in the same proportion as for white schools. Willing to accept the stipulation, Ellender reminded the Georgia Association of Negro Colleges and Secondary Schools that schools had to remain open for eight months of the year to qualify for funds.[15]

Ellender, who never capitalized the word *Negro,* supported racial segregation and other discriminatory measures that prevented blacks from enjoying freedoms and opportunities generally available to most Americans. In dramatic fashion his views on race became widely known during the Seventy-fifth Congress.

By 1937 most southerners favored making lynching a federal crime, according to a Gallup poll. Even Senator Harry Byrd of Virginia favored such legislation. But opposition to the measure encompassed much more than just an attempt to stop an antilynching bill. It involved broader questions: federal meddling in southern racial questions, fear of future black political activity in the South, and concern about elevating the racial question into a national debate. On racial matters Ellender had preconceived notions; he ignored the consensus, no matter what the polls revealed.

Yet Ellender's racism was essentially traditional, neither vindictive nor mean. A product of his times, he, like most white southerners, opposed granting more rights and privileges to blacks, whom he considered inferior. Like many segregationists, he professed to like blacks personally. He softened his stance somewhat by saying his real opposition was to intrusion by the federal government into the affairs of the states.

In 1938 Ellender joined a filibuster of a federal antilynching bill that would have made lynching a federal crime. During the January, 1938, filibuster Ellender was assigned by Richard Russell of Georgia to a team of southern senators who planned to hold the floor day after day until supporters of the antilynching measure gave up hope of passage. During the debate, Ellender introduced a bill to ban marriage between members of different races. It failed. Younger and more energetic than most senior senators, Ellender held the floor longer than anyone else. Filibustering for a total of

15.   E. H. Lambert to Allen J. Ellender, April 29, 1937, and Ellender to Georgia Association of Negro Colleges and Secondary Schools, March 9, 1937, both in "Harrison-Fletcher Bill" Folder, Box 570, AEP.

twenty-seven hours and forty-five minutes over a period of six days, Ellender amazed his Senate colleagues and sent his staff frantically scurrying for materials on race for him to read from the floor.

Even after a hard day of filibustering, Ellender would rise early the next morning for eighteen holes of golf, return home for a quick shower, and be on the Senate floor at 10:00 A.M., ready to continue with his seemingly endless speeches. He exhausted his staff, who found his drive and his stamina incredible. One staffer described him as "tough as a mule." (When he was on vacation, years later, Ellender could not understand why staffers Frank Wurzlow, Jr., and George Arceneaux, Jr., refused to join him at 6:00 A.M. on a Saturday for one of his favorite recreations—planting trees on the Houma golf course.)[16]

From the outset Ellender appreciated the difference between politics in Washington and Baton Rouge. He contrasted legislative techniques in the nation's capital with those in the Louisiana legislature for a Long supporter. "When Huey was living, he took matters in his hands and appeared in person before his committees," Ellender explained. "Up here the wishes of the President are put through by various departmental heads who act as his agents."[17]

Ellender had learned about the Senate from Huey Long. He approached his Senate duties with tenacity and unbridled energy—just as he had done when faced with earlier challenges. Former senator Ransdell, who had lost his seat to Huey but still lived in Washington, offered advice when Ellender sought it. Ransdell was a gentleman, Ellender discovered, eager to share his knowledge of how to function in the nation's capital. Ellender, feeling guilty, remembered the severe criticisms he and Huey had uttered about Ransdell. John Overton, veteran Longite whom Ellender had helped to win a Senate seat in 1932, was beginning his fifth year. Willing to help, Overton always reminded Ellender who was senior senator.[18]

Seniority, determining as it did the pecking order in the Senate, was all important. Ellender had a rudimentary knowledge of parliamentary proce-

16. Ickes, *Secret Diary,* II, 303; Frank Wurzlow, Jr., interview, April 9, 1980; Thelma Ellender, interview, June 30, 1980; Boxes 1022 and 1827, *passim,* AEP; George C. Rable, "The South and the Politics of Antilynching Legislation, 1920–1940," *Journal of Southern History,* LI (May, 1985), 213, 216, 217.

17. Allen J. Ellender to Harry D. Wilson, January 15, 1937, in "FSA Farm Tenancy" Folder, Box 321, AEP.

18. Florence LeCompte, interview, August 2, 1979.

dure, which could bewilder a newcomer, and in time would master it. He demonstrated patience and showed proper deference to powerful committee chairmen, knowing this was expected of Senate freshmen. Ellender enjoyed one advantage: he was a Democrat and Democrats controlled both houses of Congress. Each committee had roughly the same percentage of party members as the Senate itself, which meant that all committee chairmen were Democrats.

A committee chairman controls legislation in various ways. Sometimes he does not call his committee to meet at all, thereby stalling or killing a bill he dislikes. He also sets the agenda, the order in which bills get considered. This allows him to push his favorite bills, bury his least favorite. He appoints chairmen of subcommittees and knows the legislative histories of important bills on such vital topics as agriculture, foreign policy, banking, and the like. Because senators from the one-party South generally won reelection time after time, they enjoyed a great advantage in seniority over senators from states with a strong two-party system. Therefore, southerners controlled the committees and wielded power disproportionate to their numbers. Often they were conservatives who favored racial segregation. Most senators were Protestant, well educated, upper middle class, and from small towns. Like Ellender, many senators were lawyers. Then as now, committees could have a symbiotic relationship with the executive branch. The State Department traditionally influences the Foreign Relations Committee, the USDA the Agriculture Committee.[19]

Allen and Helen quickly discovered the complications of moving to Washington, D.C. They would have to find housing for the family, a school for Allen Jr., and a staff to man Ellender's office—all requiring time and planning. And Ellender would have to give up his Houma law practice; Baton Rouge was close to Houma, but Washington was not.

Helen never liked the frenzy of political activity swirling around Baton Rouge when Huey was in town and the legislature was in session. She grudgingly accepted the idea of moving into an even bigger fishbowl in the nation's capital. Visits to Louisiana would permit links with friends and family, who could, in turn, also visit Washington, Allen assured her. Because Allen Jr. had completed his prep school training and would enter Virginia Military Institute, Helen found moving at least palatable. She would be near

19. Donald R. Matthews, *U.S. Senators and Their World* (Chapel Hill, 1960), 16–21, 23, 33–35, 159–66, 168.

her son, whose education and extracurricular activities she had closely supervised. In addition she could visit her sisters Rose Pardee and Lola Crabbe, both widows, who lived and worked in Washington. Even though she dreaded being uprooted to Washington, Helen realized Allen's political career had made a giant leap. Ambitious for him, she wanted him to take himself seriously at all times. She discouraged his drinking, tobacco chewing, and his modest persona as Sous-Sous, the simple Acadian outdoorsman. She wanted him always to be Senator Ellender, the serious political leader charged with weighty governmental responsibilities.[20]

As Ellender's business partner and closest political associate, Elward Wright had been an integral part of the law firm of Ellender and Ellender even though he was not an attorney himself. Wright, though mayor of the city of Houma and the owner of an insurance agency, nonetheless performed many legal duties for Claude and Allen, especially when the latter was with Huey Long. "I was actually practicing law—without a license," Wright admitted later. When Ellender won the Senate seat, Wright passed the Louisiana bar examination and became a legitimate member of the Ellender and Ellender law firm. He inherited many of Allen's cases when the Ellenders moved to Washington.[21]

Ellender asked Herbert Wurzlow, the chief deputy to the clerk of court in Terrebonne Parish, to go to Washington as his secretary and office manager. Herbert said no but recommended his brother Frank Jr. for consideration. After a single interview, Ellender offered the job to Frank, who accepted. Like Ellender, Frank was only five feet four inches tall, less muscular but quiet and soft-spoken. After finishing high school in 1926, Wurzlow attended Soulé Business College in New Orleans, where he learned stenographic skills, bookkeeping, and office management. The Wurzlows, like the Ellenders, were descendants of yeoman German immigrants who had migrated to Terrebonne during the transportation revolution, the expansionary boom before the Civil War. He did not speak French. Ellender, not one for pretension, called Frank simply his secretary. (Today the title would be administrative assistant.) Joining Frank in the office but only briefly was Billy Sullivan, Helen's nephew from New Orleans.[22]

For only $50 per month Ellender rented a spacious second-floor apartment at 2633 16th Avenue (at the intersection of Connecticut Avenue). The

20. Florence LeCompte, interview, August 2, 1979.
21. Elward Wright, interview, November 8, 1979.
22. Frank Wurzlow, Jr., interview, April 9, 1980.

Dominican embassy occupied the floors below the structure overlooking Meridian Hill, a beautiful little park between the apartment and the Capitol down a slope to the south. The landlord had lowered the rent from $150 per month to $50 because the building needed renovation; his plan was to remodel and design smaller apartment units. The Ellenders rented furniture for $15 per month. Wurzlow, a bachelor, rented an apartment in Georgetown until the Ellenders invited him to move into their large facility. Wurzlow remained under Allen and Helen's roof until 1940, when he married Betty Chauvin of Houma.[23]

Allen and Helen did not become active participants in the party circuit in the nation's capital. Free food and liquor were readily available to members of Congress, Ellender quickly realized. He also understood how lobbyists used entertainment to influence legislation. For a time, he and Helen drank and mixed occasionally with the elite, but Helen, quiet and shy, disliked seeing Allen drink at parties, sipping cocktails. Besides, Ellender did not always handle liquor well and sometimes drank to excess. Basically, the Ellenders enjoyed staying home. They enjoyed listening to music and going to movies; there was little time for much more, because Ellender spent long hours in committee hearings and meetings or in the office tending to correspondence from constituents.

On weekends the Ellenders drove to the VMI campus at Lexington, Virginia, to see Allen Jr. Young Allen eventually asked them to visit less frequently. He was being teased by classmates, and he needed time to study and tend to personal matters. Occasionally the parents played hosts at parties for their son and his campus friends. While Allen Jr. was at VMI Ellender made a pact with his son: he would not smoke or drink so long as his son did not smoke or drink. Allen Jr. agreed. His father released him once from his pledge so he could enjoy fully a prom he planned to attend.[24]

Eager to learn about agricultural policy before beginning his Senate career, Ellender had attended a regional farm conference of the Agricultural Adjustment Administration in 1936 and made known his intention to improve the plight of tenants and sharecroppers. "When I go to the Senate,

23. Frank Wurzlow, Jr., interviews, January 3, April 9, 1980, April 6, 1992; Allen Ellender, Jr., interview, June 6, 1980; John Gilliot to Allen J. Ellender, July 31, 1939, Ellender to Gilliot, August 1, 1939, Ellender to Mrs. R. Golden Donaldson, August 1, 1939, all in "Apartments" Folder, Box 986, AEP.

24. Frank Wurzlow, Jr., interview, April 9, 1980; Allen Ellender, Jr., interview, June 6, 1980; Florence LeCompte, interview, June 11, 1980.

I'm going to do all I can to help them," he said. Then he wrote to Senate Majority Leader Joseph T. Robinson of Arkansas to request appointment to the Agriculture Committee. "Practically all of my spare time has been devoted towards trying to solve the problems of the farmers of my State," Ellender wrote." Overton told Robinson: "He [Ellender] has a very thorough knowledge of agriculture, both theoretical and as a practical and successful farmer."[25] Robinson assigned Ellender to the Committee on Agriculture and to the Committee on Education and Labor.

The modern agricultural establishment, a vested interest group representing various elements of the farm economy, includes the USDA, agricultural colleges, the Extension Service, and a vast array of farm lobbies representing sugarcane, cotton, rice, dairy, wheat, feed grains, tobacco, peanuts, and many others. The American Sugar Cane League lobbies as the voice of the domestic sugar industry.

Ellender supported the Sugar Act of 1937, the basic law governing the domestic sugar industry. The United States produces about half of the country's sugar needs; imports provide the remainder. The act allocates import quotas to friendly nations. The Sugar Division of the USDA regulates sugar prices and exercises control over producers by establishing child-labor and other restrictions that must be met before a producer can qualify for benefit payments. The USDA conducts annual hearings to gather information for setting "fair and reasonable" wage rates for sugarcane workers. Because agricultural work is seasonal, it is exempt from child-labor and other labor laws. Although the Sugar Act prohibits child labor, it nonetheless affords less protection for uneducated rural sharecroppers than the Wagner Act provides for factory workers on the assembly line.[26]

Gordon McIntire of the Louisiana Farmers' Union tried to improve working conditions for sugar workers. He offered several recommendations, among them that growers should support mandatory school attendance laws and not shorten the school term to coincide with the harvest season. McIntire accused the Works Progress Administration and other agencies of altering their labor policies for the convenience of sugar growers. To a certain extent, he was right. James Crutcher, a WPA administrator, had agreed to

25. Memphis *Commercial Appeal*, March 9, 1936, in "1928–1936" Scrapbook, AEP; Allen Ellender to Joseph T. Robinson, November 9, 30, 1936, and John Overton to Robinson, November 12, 1936, in Box 206.7, JTR.

26. Thomas Becnel, *Labor, Church, and the Sugar Establishment: Louisiana, 1887–1976* (Baton Rouge, 1980), 35–36.

a plan worked out by the American Sugar Cane League and officials from the Louisiana State Employment Service. Crutcher explained to Ellender how the plan worked. "If necessary, we will close down sufficient projects and influence the workers, as far as possible, to accept temporary employment in the canefields," he wrote. "The workers will be told that their jobs on W.P.A. will be waiting for them as soon as they return from harvesting the cane crop." When a New Orleans newspaper in January, 1938, charged Ellender with having a hand in coercing WPA workers into cutting sugarcane, Crutcher, in "personal and confidential" letters to Ellender, claimed the criticisms of Ellender were unwarranted.[27]

Ellender had worked with Crutcher, trying to get WPA projects, such as a swimming pool for Houma, and jobs for some of his constituents. Crutcher usually indicated his willingness to bend federal rules a bit for political expediency. There were no black supervisors over white WPA laborers, he once assured Ellender; whites would have resented such arrangements, he agreed with Ellender.[28]

Aware that cotton farmers had evicted tenants rather than share benefit payments with them, Ellender wanted to make sure the Sugar Act did not discriminate against landless tenants on sugar plantations. He was suspicious of South Coast, the corporation that had bought out Lower Terrebonne Refining and Manufacturing Company, the mill partly owned by the Ellender brothers. Mervin Polmer, an old Longite who ran a plantation store in north Terrebonne, wrote awkward but informative letters to Ellender about the tactics of large growers. "The [American] Sugar [Cane] League does not properly represent the small tenant cane grower in matters of this kind," he wrote, "so It's up to you to take care of the Underdog small Cane farmer and see if you Can't help them."

However, Ellender received little correspondence from tenants and their spokesmen—and a great volume from the sugar establishment. Usually the demand was for larger benefit payments for growers and lower wages for their laborers. Trying to maintain balance between the dissimilar groups, Ellender spelled out to Clarence Bourg, the Cane League's principal lobbyist, his basic philosophy regarding agricultural programs. "I have asked for better

27. Becnel, *Labor, Church, and the Sugar Establishment,* 36–37; Rodney Dutcher, New Orleans *States,* January 18, 1938, J. H. Crutcher to Allen Ellender, January 20, 1938, both in Box 29, AEP.

28. J. H. Crutcher to Allen Ellender, June 28, 1937, Box 29, and Ellender to Crutcher, October 19, 1938, in "WPA, General" Folder, Box 34, both in AEP.

prices so that those who employ can be in a position to pay better wages," he wrote.

When Ellender backed down on strict enforcement of child-labor provisions of the Sugar Act, his popularity with tenants and their spokesmen declined. His 1937 amendment to the act reduced penalties for violations considerably. Allowing growers to receive full benefit payments despite child-labor violations encouraged growers to "give up social responsibility," McIntire complained. In 1938 Ellender directed a Thibodaux sugar factory manager to Section 14 of the Sugar Act, which allowed for compensating disabled workers at a lower rate of pay.[29]

Ellender's support for the Schriever Project, an experimental Farm Security Administration communal sugar program in Terrebonne, won back some support from tenants and small growers. All participants in the project were white. The project did nothing for blacks in the area, the Rev. Edward A. Ford, a missionary of the Presbyterian Church, complained to Ellender.[30]

Sheltering Civilian Conservation Corps and Rural Electrification Administration projects in Louisiana meant retaining a few jobs in the depressed state. The CCC would keep its drainage camps in Ville Platte, Iowa, Abbeville, Lafayette, and Thibodaux to help 175,000 people with 535 miles of ditches, Senator John Overton and Ellender announced in May. Earlier in the year the CCC director admitted "these drainage ditches and laterals would never be built except for the personal benefit and profit that the individual land owners expected to receive from them." In 1938 the REA and the South Louisiana Electric Cooperative Association would spend $110,600 to build 113 miles of electric lines for 400 customers in Terrebonne, Lafourche, and Assumption parishes, Ellender announced. Several rural lines ran from Houma out to rural communities like spokes on a wheel.[31]

Ellender and Harvey Peltier complained about Civilian Conservation Corps engineer B. O. Childs, who rejected some CCC drainage projects

29. Irving Legendre to Allen J. Ellender, August 2, 1938, and Ellender to Legendre, August 8, 1938, both in "Wage and Hour Division, Rulings—Correspondence, #1, 1938" Folder, Box 94, AEP; Becnel, *Labor, Church, and the Sugar Establishment,* 38–42.

30. Edward A. Ford to Allen Ellender, n.d. [1938], in "Farm Security Administration" Folder, Box 321, AEP; James D. Holley, "Old and New Worlds in the New Deal Resettlement Program: Two Louisiana Projects," *Louisiana History,* XI (Spring, 1970), 162.

31. Robert Fecher to Allen J. Ellender, February 4, 1938, and May 31, 1938, news release, both in "Civilian Conservation Corps" Folder, Box 561, AEP; "Rural Electrification Adm. L.A. #8" Folder, Box 61, AEP; one of the author's students, Matt Leonard, wrote a class paper on REA, April 17, 1990.

because they benefited only private land owners. Ellender, griping to Childs because a certain canal "could drown out many farms in the Coteau section" (where Ellender's potato farm was located), told Peltier, "So long as such men are retained we will be unable to place our friends in safe positions." Most of Ellender's mail regarding the CCC was requests to keep camps in certain areas open or pleas to give abandoned buildings at CCC camps to local governing bodies.[32]

Ellender's love of the land continued in Washington, but there he could not enjoy the planting or the harvest or run his fingers through the soil and taste its richness and goodness. Like Populist leader Tom Watson of Georgia, he seemed most relaxed when he was close to the soil. Elward Wright noted his reluctance to sell land except at an exceptional price, for he believed land was greater security than any other investment.[33]

Ellender enjoyed vicariously the excitement of the grinding season by telephoning Wallace Jr. (known in the family as Brother), who farmed the family sugarcane lands on Bayou Terrebonne. Sometimes he called Brother twice a day. Occasionally he would say, "Hold the line; I have to run for a vote." On his return about five minutes later, he would resume the conversation. At first Brother mistook Ellender's calls for attempts to manage the family sugar operation by long-distance telephone; he resented the intrusions. Soon Brother came to understand Allen was lonely for the excitement of the harvest; he gladly allowed his brother to share the seasonal euphoria, even if only by long distance.[34]

Sometimes Ellender called Irving Legendre, Jr., in Thibodaux to ask questions in rapid order. Are you making money? Can you survive? Is there enough fertilizer available at a reasonable price? Do you have enough fuel? Legendre, too, knew Ellender was doing more than merely checking with a constituent back home. He wanted to be part of the routine he had observed every fall of his life.[35]

Early in the 1937 session Julius Dupont, president of the Houma-Terre-

32. Allen Ellender to B. O. Childs, August 18, 1938, Childs to Ellender, November 18, 1938, and Harvey Peltier to Ellender, November 22, 1938, all in "CCC Camps" Folder, Box 34, AEP.

33. C. Vann Woodward, *Tom Watson: Agrarian Rebel* (New York, 1938), 346; Elward Wright, interview, November 8, 1979.

34. Florence LeCompte, interviews, August 2, December 18, 1979.

35. Irving Legendre, Jr., interview, June 18, 1980.

bonne Chamber of Commerce, wrote to Ellender about his dream of a deep-water canal from Houma to the Gulf of Mexico. He said the potato crop promised to be a bumper one, and the market price seemed to be good. Humble Oil had drilled a well on the Ellender tract at Montegut, which he heard "would be the largest field in the world" because of preliminary geologic evidence. "I know with your royalty in this field this will be good news."[36]

When Ellender returned to Louisiana from Washington, he invariably stopped at his Coteau farm on the way to Houma, regardless of the weather, regardless of the time of day or night. Claude and Thelma, who sometimes drove him from the New Orleans airport, remembered waiting in the car late at night as Ellender walked among the rows, often sifting the earth through his fingers. Others pressed into chauffeuring the senator knew he never varied his ritual, no matter how tired he was. Preoccupied with his agricultural inspection, Ellender never inquired how his driver fared.[37]

By the end of his first two years in the Senate, Ellender had generally established his views on race, labor, agriculture, and other programs. He had abandoned the quixotic ways of Huey Long to become a conservative southern senator. In his opinion, this was the most sensible way of serving his constituents.

36. Julius Dupont to Allen Ellender, March 12, 1937, in "Houma Ship Canal" Folder, Box 17, AEP.

37. Thelma Ellender, interview, June 30, 1980; Florence LeCompte, interview, August 2, 1979.

7

PERSEVERING DESPITE THE
LOUISIANA SCANDALS
(1939–40)

*A*llen Ellender returned to Washington, D.C., in January, 1939, eager to begin the Seventy-sixth Congress. He had relaxed at home, visiting friends and family, fishing, planting trees, and looking over his Coteau farm. In addition, he had consulted with local and state leaders about their concerns and needs; he had also checked the political climate in Louisiana. At holiday dinner tables, he had begun to enjoy discussing matters from a national and international perspective with immediate family and nieces and nephews. Despite his global outlook, however, he still wanted to live in the governor's mansion and personally direct the activities of the Pelican State.

Ellender would resign his Senate seat to run for governor of Louisiana, newspapers in Washington and New Orleans reported early in 1939. Not true, Ellender insisted. A loyal supporter hoped he would run in 1940, but in April Ellender told another follower he would not run for governor but would remain in the Senate, because he was "in a better position up here to help my people."[1]

After weighing his options, Ellender, in deference to Lieutenant Governor Earl Long, decided against running for governor in 1940. Long planned to seek the top post. Ellender, remembering how Earl had sup-

---

1. William Porteous, Jr., to Allen Ellender, March 6, 1939, Box 1813, and Ellender to Brother Peter, April 5, 1939, in "Sugar—S. J. Res. 190, Comments" Folder, Box 251, both in Allen J. Ellender Papers, Nicholls State University Library, Thibodaux, La., hereinafter cited as AEP.

ported him against Noe and Wade O. Martin in the Longite dogfight after Huey's assassination, deferred to Earl because he had two years remaining on his Senate term. He could seek the state house in 1944 with the support of Earl, ineligible as governor to succeed himself. This seemed the most sensible plan to follow.

Meanwhile, agriculture continued to be Ellender's major focus. He spent endless hours explaining the inner workings of the comprehensive Sugar Act. With the help of the Congressional Reference Service, the Sugar Division of the USDA, the American Sugar Cane League, countless growers, and labor representatives, Ellender became an expert on the act. He thought parts of it worked poorly, so he developed ideas to improve it. He tried to balance the interests of consumers, workers, raw sugar producers, and East and West Coast refiners who wanted to import low-cost raw sugar from abroad.

Perhaps without realizing it, Ellender gravitated toward leaders of the Cane League rather than to spokesmen for plantation workers who mostly represented blacks. The Cane League relied on a paid staff and a lobbyist in Washington; agricultural unions, not covered by most labor legislation, struggled to exist. Ellender, whose family owned sugarcane lands, had more in common with the sugar establishment than with agricultural unions. In the South unions were not widespread, less than traditional, and rarely a strong political force. Besides, many of the laborers they represented were black.

Cane League officials applauded Ellender for helping to get the Sugar Act of 1937 passed. An improvement over the Jones-Costigan Act of 1934, in the view of the League, it allocated domestic production quotas based on acreage, not sugarcane tonnage. The act, in effect, raised the quotas for Louisiana farmers, who fertilized generously to produce more cane on fewer acres—460,000 tons in 1937, a substantial increase over the 260,000 tons in 1934.

Ellender had developed a legislative style of his own, for he had matured and had mastered the inner workings of the Senate. A team player, he worked closely with the Democratic leadership in Congress and supported Roosevelt on a number of issues. He believed the president should have a free hand in making appointments; consequently, he voted to confirm most presidential nominees without much inquiry.[2]

But if Ellender pushed too hard in his attempt to gain benefits for cane

2. Frank Wurzlow, Jr., interview, April 9, 1980.

growers, especially those who did not abide by restrictions, he risked pressure and bad publicity unleashed by Roosevelt and Secretary of Agriculture Henry A. Wallace. In at least two instances, they prevailed. In January, 1939, Ellender introduced a measure to exempt cane growers from acreage restrictions so they could qualify for benefit payments. Wallace said such exemptions would make adjusting supplies of mainland cane impossible. Payments were conditional, Wallace then explained. If a grower agreed to certain labor and production controls, he qualified for benefit payments. "It should be understood, of course, that there is no restriction on the production of sugar cane by any who does not desire to apply for such government payments," Wallace said. He cited big Louisiana producers who received as much as $195,000 annually in payments.[3]

When sugar growers planted more than their domestic acreage quotas, the Sugar Division ordered the excess crop acreage plowed under. Growers, bitter in their complaints, resorted to political solutions. Secretary Wallace stood firm: Growers would not receive conditional benefit payments unless they met acreage restrictions. Selling over-quota cane could result in the loss of the entire benefit payment, Ellender warned growers. Taking their case to the press, growers, for a time, had New Orleans journalists believing the Sugar Act was a repressive measure. Wallace responded by releasing the names of plantations who received large benefit payments under the act. Realty Operators and South Coast both received more than $150,000 per year.

Ellender, resenting charges and insinuations of being apathetic to cuts in production, responded to sugar growers by reminding them of his efforts on their behalf. Aware of rapidly shifting political fortunes, he reminded one critic: "When I returned to Louisiana in 1937, I was hailed as a hero for having had the Sugar Bill signed."[4]

Ellender, having observed and learned from respected committee chairmen, stressed conciliation and compromise, not confrontation and rhetoric. Impatient with rambunctious, heavy-handed lobby techniques, he resented intrusion by political leaders in Louisiana into what he considered his domain. During the controversy over sugarcane acreage reduction in 1939, he

3. Henry A. Wallace to E. D. Smith, March 10, 1939, "Cotton—1939" Folder, Box 301, AEP; New Orleans *Times-Picayune*, April 9, 13, 1939.

4. Thomas Becnel, *Labor, Church, and the Sugar Establishment: Louisiana, 1887–1976* (Baton Rouge, 1980), 74–76.

criticized Governor Richard Leche and New Orleans mayor Robert Maestri for sending a harsh telegram to President Roosevelt and to Secretary Wallace when growers received orders to plow under over-quota cane. "We need both the President and the Secretary of Agriculture in this crisis," he wrote, "and we can't afford to use such tactics as were suggested in the telegram." He told Maestri to tell Leche "not to permit some of those overenthusiastic sugar planters to barge in and make our fight harder in Washington." When a sugar industry spokesman asked him to make a speech in the Senate against the soft drink industry's pleas for low sugar prices, Ellender replied, "puffing off" on the Senate floor did little good. "I have been keeping in touch with Clarence Bourg [chief lobbyist for the Cane League] regarding developments in the sugar industry, and have taken steps suggested by Clarence."[5]

Ellender's office staffers, headed by Frank Wurzlow, Jr., considered Ellender something of a taskmaster but easy to talk to and get along with, provided they worked hard and remained loyal to him. He put in long hours to do his congressional homework; consequently, he did not have to rely on staff or interest groups to tell him how to vote on a measure. Once he made a decision about an issue, he was tenacious. When angry, he would never curse or scream at staff members; instead, he would keep his own counsel and say little. He hated to have to dismiss an employee, even one obviously inept or incompetent. He had confidence in Wurzlow and allowed him to complete a task unimpeded, once he had given him instructions. He learned to distinguish issues and personalities. He could disagree strenuously with a colleague on one matter and be a staunch ally with him on another. He dealt effectively with members of both parties.[6]

The outbreak of war in Europe in September, 1939, made Ellender's work on behalf of the sugar industry easier. Roosevelt, using his emergency powers, suspended domestic sugar quotas but reminded growers not to expect unlimited production in the future. He persuaded the Senate to pass Joint Resolution 225, so a farmer could harvest 100 percent of his domestic quota plus twenty-five acres without suffering a cut in benefit payments. Realizing the opportunities provided by the Sugar Act, Ellender turned to sugarcane production on part of his Coteau farm. Wurzlow asked the Terrebonne Parish county agent to check Ellender's farm to determine what the

5. Allen Ellender to Robert Maestri, March 24, 1939, in "Sugar, S. 69 and S. Res. 10" Folder, Box 251, AEP; Becnel, *Labor, Church, and the Sugar Establishment*, 78.

6. Frank Wurzlow, Jr., interview, April 9, 1980; George Arceneaux, Jr., interview, December 31, 1979.

senator needed to do to receive the maximum possible soil conservation payment.[7]

Ellender's jousts with Wallace and the USDA over domestic allotments drew him closer to the Cane League, which provided him technical assistance in his continuing clashes with the Sugar Division. Often the League sent Ellender a "suggested letter," which he forwarded to the USDA, sometimes without alteration. Ellender wondered if his own benefit payments for 1939 would be questioned because he used over-quota cane from one tract to seed another tract. The USDA, considering each of the two tracts as "a farm," threatened to withhold payment. Ellender wrote to Dr. Joshua Bernhardt of the Sugar Division: "Now Doctor, I am asking that you be practical."

Ellender resisted efforts to limit the size of benefit payments to farmers. Senators Harry Byrd and Carter Glass of Virginia, along with Josiah Bailey of North Carolina, opposed price supports and minimum wages. Byrd, believing sugar growers received excessive payments, wanted to limit maximum payments to a grower to $5,000 per year. He failed to impose limits, even after the maximum was raised to $10,000 and finally to $50,000. Limiting the size of payments was based on the concept of subsidizing the small family farm and the notion that large agribusiness ventures needed no subsidies. Ellender, realizing that many sugar, cotton, and wheat farmers received much more than $50,000 per year, helped defeat the limit.[8]

When not fighting acreage restrictions or conducting committee business, Ellender toned his muscles in the Senate gymnasium. Sometimes he and Secretary Wallace hit a punching bag together. They once tied on boxing gloves and sparred for photographers. In a mock bout, Ellender dispatched Wallace to the floor, thereby earning the nickname "Little Bull."

Ellender also attracted headlines when his Labor Committee subcommittee conducted hearings on discriminatory promotions of attractive secretaries, to the consternation of their less attractive counterparts who received no promotions. In April Ellender criticized Secretary of the Interior Harold Ickes for allowing Marian Anderson, the black opera singer, to sing on the grounds of the Lincoln Memorial; she had been denied access to Constitution Hall by the Daughters of the American Revolution.[9]

7. Frank Wurzlow, Jr., to C. C. Couvillion, April 27, 1939, in "AAA, General, 1939" Folder, Box 464, AEP.

8. Becnel, *Labor, Church, and the Sugar Establishment*, 74–77; Robert A. Garson, *The Democratic Party and the Politics of Sectionalism, 1941–1948* (Baton Rouge, 1974), 3.

9. Random newspaper clippings, Washington *Post*, April 8, 1939, all in "1939–1940" Scrapbook, AEP; David Schoenbrun, "Casebook of a Southern Senator: Allen J. Ellender of Louisiana," *Esquire*, September, 1963, p. 106.

When Allen Jr. marked his eighteenth birthday in February, 1939, Allen and Helen drove to Lexington to visit him at VMI. Allen presented his son a unique gift: an album filled with the autographs of President Roosevelt, members of the cabinet, justices of the Supreme Court, and ninety-six senators who had served with the Houman during the Seventy-fifth Congress. (While Allen Jr. was away at school, the album "disappeared.") [10]

Meanwhile, Ellender tended to personal and business matters close to home. He advised a friend, concerned about a mortgage held by Realty Operators, on how to obtain a clear title to her property. The company, he said, had written off her debt: "They no longer expect to collect." She should talk to Claude or Elward about selling her land to a third party, who could then resell it free of encumbrances. He also forwarded to the secretary of war a secret code formulated by Helen's brother C. A. Donnelly; military experts rejected it as impractical. [11]

When the Louisiana Scandals broke on June 29, 1939, Ellender was in Washington, partly insulated and somewhat isolated from the shenanigans of the Longites in Louisiana. He had accepted requests from Louisiana political leaders from time to time, but he had also rebuked them for incursions into his bailiwick. In April, 1938, Ellender wrote to President Roosevelt requesting the appointment of Governor Richard Leche to the federal bench for the Eastern District of Louisiana. Roosevelt said he would consider Leche for the post. Then on June 29, Leche resigned as governor of Louisiana "for health reasons." That same day Ellender wrote to U.S. Attorney General Frank Murphy, asking him to withdraw Leche's name from consideration. He wrote a similar letter to Roosevelt the next day. [12]

Leche, it soon became clear, had resigned amid charges of fraud and political corruption. Apparently he was at the center of a major scandal. Ellender, finding himself on the defensive, quickly disassociated himself from Leche. "Just as soon as I discovered that Governor Leche was involved in

10.   Washington (D.C.) *Times-Herald,* March 22, 1939, New Orleans *Times-Picayune,* February 8, March 23, 1939, all in "1939–1940" Scrapbook, AEP; Allen Ellender, Jr., interview, April 6, 1992.

11.   Allen Ellender to Mrs. L. J. Barrios, January 27, 1939, in "Miscellaneous B" Folder, Box 986, AEP; Ellender to Harry Woodring, April 19, 1939, and Woodring to Ellender, April 27, 1939, both in "Miscellaneous D" Folder, *ibid.*

12.   Allen Ellender to Franklin Roosevelt, April 12, 1938, Roosevelt to Ellender, April 20, 1938, Ellender to Frank Murphy, June 29, 1939, and Ellender to Roosevelt, June 30, 1939, all in Box 1297, AEP.

scandals, I immediately went to the President, in person, and asked that his name be withdrawn," Ellender wrote. Then he and Senator Overton submitted three names for consideration to fill the judgeship: Adrian J. Caillouet, William J. O'Hara, and Lewis L. Morgan, all Longites.[13] (Caillouet, who had been in Ellender's car in a 1924 accident, received the appointment.)

The scandals toppled many prominent Longites. In addition to Governor Leche, off to prison went George Caldwell, superintendent of construction at LSU; Abraham Shushan, president of the Orleans Levee Board; Seymour Weiss, Huey's financial manipulator; and James Monroe Smith, president of LSU. The anti-Long faction was ecstatic; finally, the corruption of the Long crowd had been exposed. Anti-Longites sought evidence to implicate Ellender, Earl Long (who became governor when Leche resigned), and other Long followers.

Try as they might, anti-Longites could not implicate Ellender in the Louisiana Scandals. Ellender was simply an honest man, honest beyond doubt. He truly was uninvolved in corruption, especially that associated with both Huey and Earl Long. According to FBI records, Huey and Earl received funds from organized crime for many years. The Louisiana Scandals of 1939, which decimated the Long organization and sent many of its leaders to prison, did not touch Ellender. FBI files on Ellender, which are somewhat revealing on foreign affairs, never associate him even remotely with political scandal. Neither Huey nor Earl—for good reason—kept written records documenting their financial manipulations. Ellender, on the other hand, kept copious records, every record, never discarding a scrap. His papers—more than two thousand boxes in all—contain detailed financial records of virtually every transaction he ever made. His personal income tax returns, complete with penciled-in doodling and calculations, are there. Deductions for a lost mule, a fire, or profits from a sale are all in the collection. His files contain rent accounts collectible, itemized cost lists, and old hospital receipts and canceled checks. If Allen Ellender was a crook, the evidence would be clear, for he had the most complete paper trail ever left by any Louisiana politician. Actually, voluminous records indicate simply that he was as honest as he was frugal. Even the criticized potato deal at Angola proved to be beyond criticism or challenge. In 1936 the potato crop at the prison farm brought in $91,000, second only to sugarcane, which brought in $137,000, an audit at the penitentiary shows.[14]

13. Allen Ellender to R. T. Douglas, June 8, 1940, in "Miscellaneous D" Folder, Box 322, AEP.

14. See Michael L. Kurtz and Morgan D. Peoples, *Earl K. Long: The Saga of Uncle Earl*

Ellender's detailed income tax records, replete with penciled work sheets and tallies, reveal his gradual accumulation of property—and his frugal ways. Over the years his income increased steadily. In 1934 his total income was $8,033, of which $941 came from his farm. He paid $90.73 in federal income taxes. In 1935 he earned $10,568, largely because of a $3,293 profit from farm operations. The figures fluctuated somewhat over the years: $15,000 in 1936, $21,000 in 1937, $16,000 in 1938, $12,000 in 1939 (the year the Louisiana Scandals broke). That year Ellender's income came from his $10,000 Senate salary, $1,844 from rents and royalties, and from farm operations, which suffered a loss of $3,063. Ellender lost two mules in 1939 for which he claimed a deduction of $190.[15]

Part of Ellender's income came from oil leases, but they were not leases on state lands or water bottoms (land below a lake or stream owned by the state). As Julius Dupont had suggested in 1937, the Montegut area became a productive field. In 1938 Barnsdall Oil Company paid $6,400 in royalties to the estate of Wallace Ellender. Claude told Allen on February 17, 1938, "Lake Long's second well came in yesterday," indicating big-find potential for the field contiguous to Ellender lands. Claude turned down a $4,000 lease offer for one-half interest in the mineral resources on a five-arpent tract of Aragon Plantation. Noting how the oil boom had increased land values, Claude observed: "It is strange, that several years ago, we would have sold the whole property for $3,500, and now we turn down $4,000 for half the minerals."

The oil money brought badly needed cash to the Ellenders. "I see in your letter, that you would prefer Mamma keeping all the money," Claude wrote. "I have, therefore followed your wishes in the matter." Later he wrote with some concern, "Mamma has purchased a Plymouth car, and is very anxious to learn how to drive it." Victoria, then 69, would have difficulty driving because of her failing eyesight, Claude knew. He tossed in news about being stranded overnight on a fishing trip: "Willard rescued us next morning." He also noted, "The weather is now very warm and potatoes should be coming out."[16]

and Louisiana Politics (Baton Rouge, 1990), xiv–xv, 80–89, 125–26, 137–38, 183, 190–91, 193, 271–72, for information on the Longs and organized crime; Angola audit, February 15, 1937, "Prisons—Louisiana State Penitentiary, Angola—Audit (1936)" Folder, Box 2060, in Richard Leche Papers, Louisiana and Lower Mississippi Valley Collections, Louisiana State University, Baton Rouge, La.

15. Box 3, AEP.

16. Claude Ellender to Allen Ellender, n.d. [February, 1938], February 17, 25, 1938, all in "Scurto Case" Folder, Box 1843, AEP.

Obviously Ellender, busy in Washington taking care of his constituents, had no part in the shady operations of the Leche administration. Would he now finally emerge as the true heir of Huey Long to lead the state? Or had Ellender been so indelibly branded a Longite that he, too, could be toppled by the anti-Long forces eager to regain control of Louisiana? Ellender contemplated his options as the first session of the Seventy-sixth Congress moved toward adjournment in the fall of 1939. He would have to tread lightly with political friends and enemies upon his return to Louisiana for the holidays. He was wiser now, a respected senator; reelection would not confront him until 1942; both the presidential election and the governor's race were in progress.

In explaining his place in the Long organization, Ellender soon developed a simple, consistent refrain: I believe the guilty should be punished; I should not be judged by the corruption of others; I am proud of the part I played in the Huey Long program for the people of Louisiana.

FBI records indicate close ties between the Long organization and organized crime. Seymour Weiss, the organization's link to Mafia figures Carlos Marcello and Frank Costello, was a friend of FBI director J. Edgar Hoover and was never investigated by the FBI. He may have been an informer who provided insider information on the scandals. Weiss and Robert Maestri had ties to gambling and prostitution in New Orleans even before they met Huey Long. Sheriffs Frank Clancy in Jefferson and L. A. Mereaux in St. Bernard parishes were in on the take. James Brocato, Huey Long's bodyguard known as "Diamond Jimmy Moran," had close ties to the ring.[17]

Leche and Weiss became entangled in oil pipeline deals in violation of the Connally Hot Oil Act, a proration bill designed to limit the amount of oil entering the market. Weiss received ten cents per barrel from oil man Freeman W. Burford, who owned a pipeline running from Longview, Texas, to Caddo Parish, for oil shipped on Burford's pipeline. Weiss shared in the cash kickback with Leche. Federal authorities indicted Weiss, Leche, and Burford.[18]

The scandals led to close scrutiny of WPA projects in Louisiana. James A. Crutcher, the WPA administrator for Louisiana who curtailed WPA projects during the sugarcane grinding season to help growers reduce their labor costs, played golf with Governor Leche and was accused of using WPA funds

17. Kurtz and Peoples, *Earl Long,* 88–89, 137–38.
18. W. C. Feazel to Allen Ellender, September 23, 1942, in "Justice—Paroles, Leche, Richard W." Folder, Box 126, AEP.

and personnel to perform private work for the governor and his friends. Congressman Everett Dirksen of Illinois, who served on an investigating House subcommittee of the Appropriations Committee, noted, "I have followed up on the thing pretty well, particularly this fellow Crutcher who was running around loose down there." Wondering if Louisiana would bring charges against Crutcher, Dirksen observed, "he diverted those funds to unlawful purpose." The U.S. attorney general investigated charges of misusing more than $7 million in WPA funds, including $3.8 million on the Board of Levee Commission of the State and $807,000 for the Southern Yacht Club.[19]

Louisiana officials had been under investigative scrutiny for some time by both the Justice Department and the Internal Revenue Service. Agents intensified their efforts when Leche resigned and Earl Long became governor. Heading the investigation was O. John Rogge, the head of the Special Criminal Investigation Unit of the Justice Department. He was assisted by Elmer Irey, an IRS investigator, and Rufus Fontenot, the IRS collector for Louisiana.[20]

Former governor James A. Noe, who had been frustrated by the Longites after Huey's assassination and who had sabotaged Ellender's ambition to be governor in 1936, gained a measure of revenge on the Long faction by exposing their wrongdoings. He informed F. Edward Hebert, then city editor of the New Orleans *States,* about the diversion of building materials from the Louisiana State University campus to the homes of Leche and Caldwell. He took affidavits of WPA fraud in Louisiana to Drew Pearson, the syndicated columnist. When he visited the U.S. attorney in Washington, Noe also visited Ellender. His courtesy call on the junior senator must have been cool, for the two had become political rivals. However, Noe's visit implied de facto affirmation of Ellender's innocence in the growing scandal.[21]

Battered and caught off guard by the scandals, the Long organization nonetheless regrouped and chose a ticket for the 1940 election: Earl Long for governor and Harvey Peltier of Thibodaux for lieutenant governor. Earl and Peltier would carry on in the tradition of Huey despite some indiscretions by a few scoundrels, the Longites asserted.

The anti-Long faction chose Sam Houston Jones, a lawyer and reformer from the southwestern part of the state who was known and respected for

19. *Hearings Before the Subcommittee of the Committee on Appropriations,* 78th Cong., 1st Sess., 267–68, copy in Box 1289, AEP.

20. Kurtz and Peoples, *Earl Long,* 86–88, 93, 98, 102, 138.

21. F. Edward Hebert, *Last of the Titans: The Life and Times of Congressman F. Edward Hebert of Louisiana* (Lafayette, La., 1976), 121–27.

his honesty and integrity. Jones, crediting Long with bringing progress to Louisiana, said his father had voted for Huey. The anti-Longites declared the entire Long organization to be rotten; only total annihilation would allow honest government to emerge. With it would come audits of state finances and proof of just how much damage Huey's minions had done. James A. Noe also jumped into the race, and so did Hammond attorney Jimmy Morrison, who represented strawberry farmers in his district.

Ellender leaped into the gubernatorial fray with full force. Campaigning from Washington and in Louisiana, he predicted a first primary victory for Long and Peltier. He criticized Sam Jones and Noe, emphasizing an ongoing investigation of the Long organization by Attorney General Frank Murphy and Assistant Attorney General O. John Rogge. Ellender, wanting the investigation to stop during the election campaign to deprive the anti-Longs of fresh political ammunition, knew constant reminders of wrongdoing in the Long organization could affect election results. Ellender's critics accused him of sheltering crooks.

Ellender also waged a battle of sorts against the press, especially the anti-Long newspapers. In his view, they covered the scandals more dramatically than the situation warranted. New Orleans papers warned voters to guard against vote stealing and fraud in the Democratic primary scheduled for January 16, 1940. The hostile *Times-Picayune* published headlines detrimental to Ellender: "Ellender Protests Rogge Vote Probe" and "Ellender Rails at Press and Rogge." When Ellender implied Congress would pass legislation to curb the activities of vicious newspapers, the press fired back angrily. Ellender's desire to fight back caused him to revert to a Huey Long tactic of blaming the press for his political woes. For a man who fancied himself a fair-minded defender of the Constitution and separation of church and state, he showed little respect for other First Amendment rights. The Shreveport *Journal,* criticizing his assault on freedom of the press, said Ellender was wrong in predicting a victory for Earl Long and was lucky not to have to stand for reelection in January.[22]

Ellender, claiming Rogge would actually be supervising the election, added racial fuel to the debate over Rogge's investigation of voter irregularities. "If you people don't watch out, in 10 or 15 years the federal government will be in charge of all elections and the darkies will be voting," he said.

22. The "1939–1940." Scrapbook, AEP, contains numerous clippings. Shreveport *Journal,* August 14, 1939, Box 1813, and Box 1297 *passim,* AEP, contain many newspaper clippings, photographs, and editorials on the campaign.

Alluding to the Reconstruction period in Louisiana when carpetbaggers ran the state and blacks voted, Ellender had his speech criticizing the Rogge investigation printed in the *Congressional Record*. Wurzlow, forwarding one thousand copies and one thousand franked envelopes to Alice Lee Grosjean at Long headquarters, said she could use the envelopes to mail Ellender's speech to constituents, "provided you do not insert any other material."[23]

Sam Jones and Earl Long found themselves in the runoff of February 20, 1940; Noe and Morrison had been eliminated in the January 16 primary election. Long received 226,385 votes to 154,936 for Jones and 116,564 for Noe. Noe threw his support to Jones in exchange for promises to pay off his campaign debts and to share patronage with Noe's political friends. He lost little time in criticizing Ellender as a member of the corrupt Long organization. Ellender had recommended the fallen Leche for a federal judgeship, Noe reminded Louisianians. Using his Shreveport radio station to great advantage, Noe said Ellender opposed Rogge and the Justice Department only because "they are putting your people in jail."[24]

Ellender and other Longites knew Noe was under investigation himself for oil deals and possible income tax evasion. The Jones organization had tried to shield Noe from indictment because he was hurting the Longites and helping Jones, a correspondent told Ellender. Without mentioning Huey Long's links to oil, the Longites brought out Noe's control of Win or Lose Corporation, the oil company that fared so well at obtaining lucrative leases on state lands and water bottoms and, in turn, selling them to W. T. Burton of Texaco. Texaco had developed many of the fields of coastal south Louisiana. Ellender's files contained confidential information documenting Noe's earnings of $92,396 per year as president of Win or Lose; for Seymour Weiss, the vice-president, the earnings were identical. By comparison, the president of Standard Oil earned only $32,272 per year, and chief executive officers of major oil companies generally earned even less.[25]

Ellender searched futilely for corruption by Jones and the anti-Long faction. Using his Washington connections, he asked the War Department

23. New Orleans *Times-Picayune*, January 15, 1940, Box 1297, and Frank Wurzlow, Jr., to Alice Lee Grosjean, February 8, 1940, Box 1813, both in AEP.

24. Random newspaper clippings across Louisiana, January, 1940, Box 1298, AEP; Mark T. Carleton, "Four Anti-Longites: A Tentative Assessment," *Louisiana History*, XXX (Summer, 1989), 252.

25. W. C. Feazel to Allen Ellender, January 22, 1940, in Folder 6, Box 1813, AEP. Countless newspaper clippings can be found in Boxes 1297 and 1298 (the salary information is in box 1812), AEP.

for Sam Jones's World War I military records. The War Department, providing a sketchy outline of Jones's career, said such records could not be released, even to a senator. Ellender must have viewed with envy Jones's exemplary record.[26]

While in Louisiana campaigning for Long, Ellender maintained a hectic schedule of talks, meetings, and appearances in the remote corners of Terrebonne Parish. One day's itinerary included stops at Bayou duLarge at 10:00 A.M., at Petit Caillou at 1:30 P.M., at the Bourg School at 4:00 P.M., and at the Courthouse Square in Houma at 7:00 P.M. His supporters in the sugar industry noted his vigorous efforts in Long's behalf.[27]

Jones, in making the farm program a campaign issue, opened Ellender's eyes to harsh realities he may have overlooked. Mississippi received more benefit payments on cotton than Louisiana, Jones contended, because its congressional delegation was more astute than the Louisiana delegation, consisting of Longites. Noe accused Ellender of having abandoned the Louisiana sugar farmers during the acreage plow-under in 1939.

Mississippi senator Theodore Bilbo defended Ellender in a telegram to Jones: "Your statement reflects gross ignorance of provisions of the farm act and farming conditions in your state and mine." Bilbo's blast came in late January, after the first primary but before the runoff. In praising Ellender, Bilbo wrote: "There is no man in the Senate who has worked harder than Senator Ellender for the farmers of his state."[28]

Ellender asked the Cane League to say a few kind words in his behalf; but the lobby group, eager to avoid antagonizing anti-Longites, planned to stay neutral in the Long-Jones fight. An endorsement of Ellender would have been interpreted as endorsement of Earl Long. The League could not risk alienating Jones, whose campaign seemed to be picking up momentum. The lukewarm endorsements Ellender received from the League alerted him to an obvious truth, but one he had overlooked: Getting involved in political campaigns in Louisiana is fraught with peril; proceed cautiously.[29]

A week before the runoff columnist Drew Pearson wrote of a second

26. E. S. Adams to Allen Ellender, February 3, 1940, Box 1812, and office staff to Ellender, February 12, 1940, Box 1813, both in AEP.

27. Frank Wurzlow, Jr., to Wade Martin, January 2, 1940, Box 1813, and H. J. Marmande to Allen Ellender, March 14, 1940, in "Agriculture, Sugar Prices" Folder, Box 280, both in AEP.

28. Theodore Bilbo to Sam Jones (telegram), January 31, 1940, Box 1812, AEP.

29. Box 1297, AEP, contains many telegrams the Cane League sent Ellender in January, 1940; Florence LeCompte, interview, August 2, 1979.

Louisiana Purchase—one made during the campaign. Roosevelt had called off Rogge's investigation of the election at Ellender's request in exchange for support from the Long organization. Pearson's implication was clear: The organization was thoroughly corrupt and further investigation would topple more of its second-echelon leaders. Ellender was no better than most Long-ites, Pearson suggested, but he offered no evidence of wrongdoing. In fact, Ellender, who had succeeded in calling off Rogge during the heat of the campaign, had some political influence with Roosevelt, his column revealed.[30]

Jones narrowly defeated Long on February 20, 1940. Long and Peltier, Ellender noted, had not even carried Lafourche and Terrebonne parishes against Jones. Headlines underscored the margin of victory; editorials glorified the rejection of Longism and predicted significant reform. Happily Ellender had to return to Washington early in 1940.

In October a federal grand jury indicted former governor James A. Noe, national Democratic committeeman from Louisiana, for income tax evasion. It also indicted Seymour Weiss, the man who had financed many of Huey's political campaigns, on income tax evasion and other charges. Internal Revenue Director Rufus Fontenot had deferred charges against Noe until Jones had won the election, or so Ellender believed.[31]

When he had time to reflect on the political situation back home, Ellender realized some of his old friends had abandoned him, some had fallen short of his expectations, some were in prison. With the Jones administration in control in Louisiana, Ellender was still the junior U.S. senator—with two years remaining on his first term. He had to make political adjustments and move on. To a supporter Ellender wrote, "We lost the election, and as good Democrats we must bow to the will of the majority. It is to be hoped that Governor-elect Jones will carry out his campaign promises."[32]

As critics bemoaned the scandals, Ellender detached himself from the wrongdoers. To an anti-Longite who mused, "You and the rest of the 'Long' boys . . . will be lucky to hold your 'seat' till 1942," he replied sharply: "I am not personally responsible for what a few leaders might do in any par-

30. See "Miscellaneous La. Politics" Folder, Box 1813, AEP, for clippings on the alleged deal.

31. Monroe (La.) *News Star,* October 3, 1940, New Orleans *States,* October 16, 1940, both in "1939–1940" Scrapbook, AEP.

32. Allen Ellender to J. W. Wilson, March 9, 1940, Box 1813, AEP.

ticular parish in order to help a candidate." He repeated his standard line: "I hope that all of those who did wrong are punished." Messages of support from loyal followers buoyed Ellender; the situation was not hopeless. One partisan thought Ellender had made a monkey of Senator "Cotton Ed" Smith of South Carolina in debate over farm spending. "They tell me he hasn't been the same since," he wrote, obviously delighted with Ellender's efforts on behalf of the sugar industry.[33]

A friendly correspondent wondered if Ellender had noted the number of Jews involved in the scandals. Even as he rejected a Jewish conspiracy, Ellender replied condescendingly: "The Federal Government convicted ten persons, seven of whom were Jews." He added, "I have nothing against the Jews, but in our case they were very unscrupulous in using some of our officials to obtain money from the State." He continued: "Seymour Weiss, Abe Shushan, Monte Hart, and several other Jews took advantage of the situation and grafted from the State."[34]

As state Democratic committeeman, Ellender attended the state Democratic convention in Baton Rouge in June, 1939, hoping to deliver a speech endorsing President Roosevelt for an unprecedented third term. However, the convention chose Governor Jones to head the delegation to the national convention in Chicago and loudly denounced Ellender whenever he tried to speak. Booing delegates prevented him from speaking, even when he tried to discuss his conversation with Roosevelt about sugar legislation. Unable to continue, he said in desperation: "That's all right—you can boo, but he's going to be your next president." His prepared speech, titled "Why Elect Roosevelt" (he never completed it), defended FDR as a champion of human rights and blasted Republicans for sponsoring class legislation. As though to assert some measure of independence from Roosevelt, Ellender said he would vote against the confirmation of Frank Murphy, his old rival in the scandals investigation, for appointment to the Supreme Court.[35]

FDR overcame the two-term barrier by trouncing Wendell Willkie in

33. Daniel Brooks to Allen J. Ellender, February 1, 1940, and Ellender to Brooks, February 7, 1940, both in "Miscellaneous La. Politics" Folder, Box 1813, AEP; Bentley Mackay to Allen J. Ellender, n.d. [September, 1940], in "Agr-Sugar-General, '40 & '41" Folder, Box 39, AEP.

34. Pierre Besset to Allen Ellender, March 16, 1940, in "Miscellaneous A" Folder, Box 322, AEP.

35. James Domengeaux, interview, December 23, 1980; "Miscellaneous, Presidential Campaign—1940" Folder, Box 50, and newspaper clippings, n.d., in Box 1813, "1939–1940" Scrapbook, all in AEP.

November, 1940. By then the Phony War in Europe had erupted into a genuine confrontation. Hitler's forces seemed to threaten all of Europe; Japan seemed emboldened and encouraged by the aggression of its Axis counterpart.

The threat of war in Europe alerted Ellender to foreign affairs. Knowing his expertise in this area to be limited, he wisely deferred to his seniors on the Foreign Relations Committee. In 1938 he had asked his office staff to gather materials for a file on the foreign indebtedness of the United States. He appeared in a photograph with veteran Senators Hiram Johnson of California and Key Pittman of Nevada, who favored retaining a U.S. embargo on arms shipment to warring nations. Ellender criticized Hitler and called for a repeal of the embargo. Acquiescing to Johnson and Pittman, Ellender began his comments with "We have heard the big guns of the Senate, now it's time for the popguns." He was backing FDR on this issue, but he was showing Senate leaders he knew his place.[36]

Ellender's voting record indicates his continued support for Roosevelt. In the second session of the Seventy-sixth Congress he and Senator Robert Wagner of New York had perfect success scores, voting on the winning side in every roll call vote. Ellender voted to eliminate the cash-and-carry provisions of the arms embargo (in October, 1939), for preparedness measures (in August, 1940), for increasing agricultural appropriations, for extending executive authorization on measures to stabilize the dollar and enact reciprocal trade agreements, for investigating oppressive labor practices, and for increasing work relief and welfare payments to the states. Ellender surprised his colleagues and constituents by getting in step with Wagner, the "pilot of the New Deal," whose base of support was urban industrial America.[37]

As the Congress ground toward adjournment in the fall of 1940, Ellender found himself in a new political environment. He was the only top-level Longite untarnished and unscathed by the scandals and by the 1940 election. His influence in Washington had grown in the eyes of the president and Democratic leaders. Nonetheless Sam Jones, the anti-Longite, sat in the governor's office, lived in the governor's mansion, wielded the governor's power. With his Longite rivals rejected at the polls or disgraced by the scandals,

---

36. Unidentified newspaper clippings, 1939, Box 1297, and "Johnson Act" Folder, Box 561, all in AEP.

37. James W. Hilty, *Voting Alignments in the United States Senate, 1933–1944* (1 vol. with appendix; University Microfilms International, 1979), A-26–27, A-412–19, A-445–49, A-109–112, A-307–314, A-59, A-144–148, 142.

would Ellender emerge as leader of the Longites? Clearly he would have to distance himself from many people associated with scandal if he expected to win reelection in 1942. Perhaps if he became a senator for all the people, the anti-Long faction would not mount a major effort to oust him as the last vestige of Longism. A loss clearly would rule out his dream of running for governor in 1944. For now the main objective was to do a good job for all Louisianians as war clouds gathered ominously about the country.

Ellender, seated bottom step right, in the summer of 1911 in South Dakota, where he "pitched wheat."

Allen J. Ellender Collection, Allen J. Ellender Archives, Nicholls State University

Wallace and Victoria Ellender with children, 1909 or 1910, while Allen was away at school. Allen, third from the left, had himself added to the photograph. Wallace Jr. is on the far left, Claude fourth from the left, Willard in front between Victoria and Wallace, and Walterine at far right.
Allen J. Ellender Collection, Allen J. Ellender Archives, Nicholls State University

Allen with Helen's family, the Donnellys, about 1920. Helen is seated at far left in front of her husband; her mother, Mary Jane Hinds Donnelly, is seated next to her, with Lola Crabbe in front. Florence and husband Will Morgan are to the right of Mrs. Donnelly, and Rose Pardee is at the far right.

Allen J. Ellender Collection, Allen J. Ellender Archives, Nicholls State University

Allen in 1912 while attending Tulane University.

Allen J. Ellender Collection, Allen J. Ellender Archives, Nicholls State University

Helen Donnelly as a young woman.

Allen J. Ellender Collection, Allen J. Ellender Archives, Nicholls State University

Allen receives a hug from Helen on March 15, 1949, after filibustering 12 hours, 21 minutes, to kill a Senate bill.

Allen J. Ellender Collection, Allen J. Ellender Archives, Nicholls State University

Ten minutes after this photograph of Ellender and Long was taken on September 8, 1935, Long was fatally wounded by an assassin.
Courtesy Southdown Museum in Houma

Ellender and Long in 1933 at the hearings concerning John Overton's 1932 victory over Senator Broussard, achieved with Ellender's help.
Allen J. Ellender Collection, Allen J. Ellender Archives, Nicholls State University

Ellender with Governor
Richard Leche before
the Louisiana Scandals
broke in 1939.

Allen J. Ellender Collection,
Allen J. Ellender Archives,
Nicholls State University

Ellender in his potato
patch, about 1938.

Allen J. Ellender Collection,
Allen J. Ellender Archives,
Nicholls State University

Ellender after a successful duck hunt in 1938.
Allen J. Ellender Collection, Allen J. Ellender Archives, Nicholls State University

Ellender after a productive tarpon fishing trip in 1938.
Allen J. Ellender Collection, Allen J. Ellender Archives, Nicholls State University

Allen (fourth from right) and siblings: Claude, Willard, Walterine, and Wallace Jr., in 1960.

Allen J. Ellender Collection, Allen J. Ellender Archives, Nicholls State University

8

WAR AND REELECTION
(1941–42)

$\mathcal{A}$fter arriving in Washington in early January, 1941, Senator Ellender contracted a severe case of the flu. It kept him away from his office until mid-January.[1] By then the national preoccupation with war had insulated him from the political turmoil in Louisiana. Agricultural surpluses, once considered an economic problem, now seemed essential as the country prepared for war. Farmers, no longer required to limit production in order to qualify for benefit payments, grappled with a severe labor shortage. Unemployment disappeared.

Official U.S. policy was neutrality, but Roosevelt's 1940 election influenced senators and representatives at the start of the Seventy-seventh Congress to pass the Lend-Lease Act, an emergency measure designed to keep Britain and other European nations from falling to Germany. Britain seemed to be the only European power capable of slowing Hitler's juggernaut. From January until March, Congress debated Lend-Lease. Considered a Roosevelt supporter, Ellender surprised national observers by offering an amendment to Lend-Lease: "to prevent the president from using U.S. military force outside of the United States, its territorial waters and possessions." Ellender wanted to keep the country out of war, he insisted, not to restrict the president. "I am for aiding England to the limit of our ability, but our people must be made to realize that the aid, as now contemplated, is bound to lead us into actual warfare," he said, responding to thousands of concerned con-

---

1. Allen Ellender to Marcus DeBlanc, January 18, 1941, in "Hurricane Area" Folder, Box 570, Allen J. Ellender Papers, Nicholls State University Library, Thibodaux, La., hereinafter cited as AEP.

stituents who wanted to avoid war. On March 7, 1941, administration forces defeated his amendment easily. Nonetheless Ellender voted for Lend-Lease and for a $7 billion defense appropriations bill. Apparently he was content with token opposition to foreign policy.[2]

As German armies advanced on the Russian front in July, 1941, Ellender commented on Hitler and prospects for quickly ending the war. Europe would face a prolonged struggle if Hitler were not defeated by November, he said. "It is either knock out Hitler now or face such a [prolonged] situation," he said, without explaining how to get rid of the Nazi leader. "The only way we can keep war from our shores," he said, "is to furnish England and her allies with the best implements of War." Meanwhile, he recommended strengthening U.S. military bases.[3]

The Japanese attack on Pearl Harbor on December 7, 1941, astounded the United States, which declared war on December 8. Ellender, having voted for Roosevelt's declaration of war, joined a congressional delegation inspecting the damage wrought by the surprise attack a week after the strike. The Houma *Courier* published a photograph of him casting a wreath on the waters above the sunken USS *Arizona* at Pearl Harbor and quoted him as saying he would concentrate on winning the war. British tactics and policies vexed Ellender as the war progressed. He had voted for aid to Britain, but he became disenchanted—in Ellender's phrase "nauseated"—by what he thought was British apathy after the fall of Tobruk, Libya, to Gen. Erwin Rommel's Afrika Korps in June, 1942.[4]

Like other southerners in Congress, Ellender worried about the influence of organized labor on Roosevelt. CIO leader Sidney Hillman, who had urged labor to support FDR in 1940, headed the Office of Production Management and therefore conferred frequently with the president. Another agency, the War Labor Board, recognized unions and equalized wage differentials in the textile industry.

Civil rights spokesmen angered Ellender even more than labor leaders

2. Los Angeles *Evening Herald and Express,* January 16, 1941, Washington (D.C.) *Evening Star,* March 7, 1941, Washington *Post,* March 8, 1941, Paul Mallon, New York *Journal and American,* March 12, 1941, all in "1941" Scrapbook, AEP; James W. Hilty, *Voting Alignments in the United States Senate, 1933–1944* (1 vol. with appendix; University Microfilms International, 1979), A-316–20, A-421–29.

3. New Orleans *Times-Picayune,* July 20, 1941, and Monroe (La.) *Times,* July 25, 1941, both in "1941" Scrapbook, AEP.

4. Houma (La.) *Courier,* December 16, 1941, in "1941" Scrapbook, and Chicago *Daily Tribune,* June 26, 1942, in "1942" Scrapbook, both in AEP.

did. Three prominent black leaders—A. Philip Randolph of the Brotherhood of Sleeping Car Porters, Walter White of the NAACP, and Lester Granger of the Urban League—announced plans for a July 1, 1941, march on Washington by 100,000 blacks. The purpose would be to publicize war industry hiring and job practices discriminatory to blacks. Eleanor Roosevelt, former National Youth Administration head Aubrey Williams, New York congressman Fiorello LaGuardia, and other liberals tried to dissuade proponents from marching. After Roosevelt in June, 1941, signed Executive Order 8802, creating the Fair Employment Practices Commission, black leaders called off the march. A part of the Office of Production Management, the commission had authority to cancel government contracts to enforce racial hiring guidelines. However, its annual budget was only eighty thousand dollars.

Ellender, Richard Russell, Jr., of Georgia, and other segregationists blocked attempts to make the FEPC a permanent organization and kept its budget small. They opposed the Soldiers' Voting Act of 1942 until it had been so weakened that it could not be used to enfranchise blacks in the armed forces.[5]

Ellender's political opponents in Louisiana prevented him from capitalizing on local hiring practices. He had little influence over jobs in Louisiana war plants early in the war. Governor Sam Jones and former governor James A. Noe controlled hiring at Fort Polk, the military facility near Leesville in Vernon Parish, through the Louisiana Employment Office, which handled job placement. It served as a clearinghouse for jobs at Fort Polk; also instrumental was W. Horace Williams, the primary contractor at the military facility. Jones had convinced many labor leaders to sever political ties with the Long faction.

In July, 1941, Ellender met with Earl Long and New Orleans mayor Robert Maestri at the Roosevelt Hotel to discuss the labor situation at Fort Polk. Federal regulations did not require Williams, Ellender complained, to clear all jobs through the Louisiana Employment Office, which discriminated against Longites. Ellender asked Williams to hire some of his friends. To accommodate Ellender, Williams fired Speedy Rhodes, a personnel officer sympathetic to Jones. Observing Jones's tendency to brag about his gubernatorial accomplishments, Ellender wrote, "I would not at all be surprised

5. Gilbert C. Fite, *Richard B. Russell, Jr., Senator from Georgia* (Chapel Hill, 1991), 180; Michael I. Sovern, *Legal Restraints on Racial Discrimination in Employment* (New York, 1966), 9; Robert A. Garson, *The Democratic Party and the Politics of Sectionalism, 1941–1948* (Baton Rouge, 1974), 14–15, 17, 18, 20–22, 29–30, 44–52, 63–73.

if he claimed credit for having originated both the Lend-Lease Act and the Selective Service Act."

State Federation of Labor leader E. H. "Lige" Williams had defected to Jones, and Ellender claimed to wonder why. "As you know," Ellender wrote Williams, "I have a 100% labor record in Washington which shows that I have been doing all in my power to help organized labor." Ellender may have voted for the minimum wage law and tried to extend WPA projects, but he had labeled the sit-down strikes un-American, blamed John L. Lewis for many problems, and worked to weaken child-labor provisions of the Sugar Act and other labor laws. An Ellender supporter said, "The labor situation is awful. Jones and Noe and their representatives are in control."[6]

Union leaders knew Ellender was not a friend of organized labor, but they considered him more open-minded than Jones. When the governor sent the state police to scrutinize pickets at a Gulf States Utilities plant in Baton Rouge, the Carpenters' Union complained of harassment. Although union bricklayers disliked Marion T. Fannally, Jones appointed the contractor to the Board of Commerce and Industry. In the muddled hiring and labor situation, Ellender tried to find jobs for supporters in shipyards and on military bases. "I am in hopes that we will be able to obtain a few jobs for our friends," he wrote to an old Longite early in the war.[7]

As workers flocked to jobs in shipyards, war plants, and new industries, the sugar industry faced a disastrous manpower shortage. The Cane League, needing alternative labor sources, sought Ellender's help. War industries paid higher wages than the WPA, the Civilian Conservation Corps, the Farm Security Administration, and agriculture. Working with the United States Employment Service, Louisiana WPA administrator James Crutcher established a policy in 1942 for using WPA workers in agricultural jobs. Ellender told a sugar executive to notify his parish welfare director if he needed field workers. "I had several released to my farms in that manner," he wrote.

6. Thomas Becnel, *Labor, Church, and the Sugar Establishment: Louisiana, 1887–1976* (Baton Rouge, 1980), 24–25. See "General Somervell Investigation" Folder, Box 198, AEP, for many details of the Camp Polk situation. Ellender to Paul Fink, October 16, 1941, in "War, National Defense, General #2" Folder, Box 50, and New Orleans *States,* July 16, 1941, in "1941" Scrapbook, both in AEP.

7. See Box 333, AEP, for countless letters about jobs. Allen Ellender to Earle Christenberry, February 26, 1941, in "General Information" Folder, Box 77, John A. Collum to Ellender, July 27, 1941, in "National Labor Relations Board, General" Folder, Box 53, Joseph McCurrain to Ellender, February 26, 1942, in "Wages and Hours, General, 1942" Folder, Box 333, all in AEP.

The League inquired about using displaced Japanese Americans who had been removed from their West Coast homes and confined to camps in the Midwest as a security measure. When these efforts failed, the League considered importing workers from Mexico, Jamaica, and the British West Indies. This caused racial problems to surface because some governments did not allow their citizens to work in the segregated South. Next, the League inquired about using German prisoners of war in the cane fields, but Ellender called the plan impractical and counter to military rules. Some proposals to solve the wartime labor shortage were blatantly selfish or discriminatory. Several growers wanted black soldiers to be furloughed during cane-harvesting season. Others wanted to exempt workers from the military draft or to abolish child-labor restrictions. Soon angry letters poured into Ellender's office criticizing Lafayette congressman James Domengeaux's bill to remove all child-labor provisions from the Sugar Act. Ellender replied, "I have taken no interest in this legislation. It was originated by Congressman Domengeaux." Frustrated by the volume of job-conflict mail, Ellender told workers and employers to consult the National War Labor Board to solve problems.[8]

His letter notwithstanding, Ellender favored easing restrictions on child labor during the cane-harvesting season. Farm boys in their teens were more experienced agricultural laborers than outside contract laborers, he wrote USDA officials. Young boys, Cane League president F. Evans Farwell explained, could help farmers avoid waste and win the war. The League wanted to hire youngsters to stack sugar cane across rows in bundles for mechanical loaders to lift into wagons. After authorities eased the rules in 1942, an army of young men, cutting cane after school and on Saturdays, "saved the crop."[9]

Military installations and war plants in Louisiana, Ellender quickly realized, could help end vestiges of the Great Depression. War industries—chemical plants, shipyards, and defense bases—sprang up in Louisiana's suitable environment. Shipyards in New Orleans found themselves building twenty-five new ships, projects that would add approximately $50 million to the economy. Construction at Fort Polk would add another $8 million to

8. Becnel, *Labor, Church, and the Sugar Establishment*, 38, 82. For a multitude of letters on the labor shortage, see Allen Ellender to Harriet G. Johnson, October 27, 1942, in "Sugar Act of 1937, To amend—S. 3237 and S. 3236—Child Labor" Folder, Box 251, and "Farm Labor" Folder, "Labor—General 1942" Folder, both in Box 333, all in AEP.

9. Allen Ellender to Claude Wickard, April 2, 1942, in "Agr., Sugar, General, 1942" Folder, Box 280, and F. Evans Farwell to Marvin Jones, January 10, 1944, in "War Food Admin., #2" Folder, Box 445, both in AEP; Verne Pitre, "Saving the Crop," in *Grandma Was a Sailmaker: Tales of the Cajun Wetlands* (Thibodaux, La., 1991), 95–97.

the economy. The Arkansas-Louisiana Electric Cooperative would build a generating plant "in the natural gas fields in Louisiana," REA administrator Harry Slattery said. Ellender claimed credit for new plants—an ammonia plant in Monroe, a flying-boat assembly plant in New Orleans, chemical plants in several places, a synthetic rubber plant in Baton Rouge, the Higgins shipyard in New Orleans, and a base in Houma to house dirigibles, or blimps, which patrolled the Gulf of Mexico searching for German submarines. As the country shifted to a wartime economy, Ellender's constituents experienced shortages of gasoline, tires, automobiles, fuel, building materials, even manpower problems. They wrote letters to him outlining their difficulties.[10]

In May, 1941, Governor Jones sent Ellender a frantic telegram. The Higgins shipyard in New Orleans had closed and workers had been laid off, all because of an engine shortage and too few orders. A few days later, Ellender replied with good news: The Navy, considering Higgins' work better than that of ship-building plants in New Jersey, would sign a contract with Higgins Industries to build twelve PT boats. In September, Ellender's brothers Claude and Willard joined others to form the Houma Boat and Contracting Company, Inc., a boat-building firm. It received subcontracts from New Orleans shipbuilder Andrew Higgins. Ellender's influence gave the company an unfair advantage over competitors, columnist and radio commentator Drew Pearson charged.[11] The senator did not profit from the venture.

During the war Ellender received unusual, patriotic, and even bizarre requests, which he coordinated with John Overton of Alexandria, the senior senator. One impediment to joint action was Overton's refusal to switch to daylight saving time like other senators; consequently he began work one hour later than Ellender and ended his work day one hour later. The tire shortage proved a major problem for car dealers. Before surrendering a repossessed automobile, owners usually replaced the new tires with old ones. Patriotic inventors frequently offered their devices to the government free of

10.   Harry Slattery to Allen Ellender, July 7, 1941, in "Rural Electrification Administration, Ark-La Project" Folder, Box 61, AEP; New Orleans *Times-Picayune,* January 10, 1941, "1941" Scrapbook, *passim,* Box 1827, *passim,* and "1942" Scrapbook, *passim,* all in AEP.

11.   Sam Jones to Allen J. Ellender (telegram), May 16, 1941, and Ellender to Jones, May 20, 1941, both in "Allen J. Ellender—U.S. Senator" Folder, Sam Houston Jones Papers, Special Collections, Howard-Tilton Memorial Library, Tulane University, New Orleans, La.; Terrebonne Parish Record of Incorporation, III, 45, at Terrebonne Parish Courthouse, Houma, La.; Drew Pearson, text of radio broadcast, February 28, 1943, in "Allred" Folder, Box 198, AEP.

charge. Tractor dealer H. B. Naquin of Thibodaux developed a workable incendiary bomb, based, unfortunately, on principles similar to those already in use. Shrimp fishermen requested travel permits to enter restricted coastal fishing grounds, but the Coast Guard did not have the film needed to make identification photographs. "I hope you will do all you can to help us out," one fisherman wrote, "as you know we are having a bad season now on account of the sub-marines. We can't go in the Gulf to fish," he exaggerated. Ellender asked the War Production Board for help.[12]

Patriotic citizens offered genuine but humorous ideas for waging war against submarines in the Gulf of Mexico. Ellender received hundreds of impractical proposals for antisubmarine devices. A Grand Isle citizen wanted to convert the only road on the island into a landing strip for use by planes to patrol the Gulf of Mexico. One writer suggested draping nets suspended on steel rods welded to the sides of the vessels to ward off torpedoes. Why not make greater use of the "submarine-proof intracoastal waterway which now stands 90% idle?" asked one sensible writer. Ellender forwarded reasonable proposals to the appropriate military and administrative agencies. Fighting submarines required special equipment and highly trained personnel, Secretary of the Navy Frank Knox replied. "No one would agree, for instance, that we ought to send untrained men armed with shotguns out to meet a panzer tank brigade and yet," he wrote, "that is what some think we ought to do in combating submarines."[13]

During the war Ellender helped small landowners clarify mineral rights to land acquired from the U.S. government. Workers in the experimental Farm Security Administration sugarcane project (the Schriever Project) had acquired forty acres of land when the project ended in the early 1940s. The FSA retained 75 percent of the mineral rights and the owners 25 percent. Selling or leasing land with this arrangement would have been complicated, Ellender knew. He helped landowners acquire full mineral rights to their small tracts.[14]

12. Florence LeCompte, interview, September 6, 1977; R. L. Riviere to Allen J. Ellender, February 4, 1942, in "Office of Price Administration, #2" Folder, Box 50, "Commerce Dept., National Inventors Council, Gen." Folder, passim, Box 280, Ellender to War Production Board (telegram), August 7, 1942, in "War Production Board, Nat'l Defense, #4, 1942" Folder, Box 429, and Desire Theriot to Ellender, June 8, 1942, in "Labor Department, General, 1942" Folder, Box 333, all in AEP.

13. N. I. Ludwig to Thomas J. Flanagan, July 15, 1942, and Frank Knox to Ellender, July 11, 1942, both in "Civil Aeronautics Authority" Folder, Box 280, AEP; T. P. Chandler to Ellender, June 6, 1942, in "Submarine Menace, 1942–43" Folder, Box 198, AEP.

14. Box 1289, passim, Box 614, passim, both in AEP; James D. Holley, "Old and New

Servicemen and their families wrote to Ellender to express their fears and unhappiness about war-related inconveniences. He provided information or referred them to officials who could solve their problems. While Allen Jr. was an ROTC student at VMI, Ellender successfully amended a compulsory military training bill to exempt senior ROTC students and graduate students from the draft. It deferred him until he had completed his studies. Commissioned at graduation, Allen Jr. did not report for active duty until he completed his medical training at Tulane University in 1944. Unable to visit often with his parents during the war, Allen Jr. frequently wrote to them and telephoned.[15]

The Terrebonne Ice Company and the Houma Brick Company both became involved during the war in controversies over wage-and-hour legislation. This was especially significant because Ellender had inherited an interest in the companies. Houma attorney Claude B. Duval handled claims against Ellender by the Office of War Production (OWP). The Wages and Hours Division of OWP ruled the brick company, whose business was mainly retail, exempt from the regulations, Duval informed Ellender. The ice company, Duval said, was subject to the law because its seafood and vegetable products entered interstate commerce. "Your name was never mentioned in connection with the Terrebonne Ice Company," Duval reassured him. Ellender could resolve the problem, Duval said, by writing checks for back pay to ice company employees.[16]

Despite his busy schedule, Ellender participated in political activities. On April 25, 1941, he spoke at the unveiling of the statue of Huey Long in the Capitol in Washington in a spot reserved for former senators. A number of anti-Longites, objecting to its cost, fifteen thousand dollars, walked out when Ellender began his speech. Undaunted, he continued, praising Huey. In June, he joined congressional leaders at the funeral of Mississippi senator Pat Harrison. Ellender quietly tried to assist Longites convicted in the Louisiana Scandals. Unfavorable publicity about Louisiana slowed his efforts to obtain pardons for oil tycoon Seymour Weiss, former Orleans Levee Board

Worlds in the New Deal Resettlement Program: Two Louisiana Projects," *Louisiana History,* XI (Spring, 1970), 162.

15. Allen Ellender, Jr., interview, June 6, 1980; Virginia Military Institute *Cadet,* September 16, 1940, in "1939–1940" Scrapbook, AEP.

16. Robert T. Amis to Baird Snyder (memo), September 13, 1940, in "Wage and Hour Rulings—1942" Folder, Box 333, and Claude Duval to Allen Ellender, January 15, 1941, in "Wage and Hour Division, Houma Ice Company" Folder, Box 53, both in AEP; Claude Duval, interview, December 18, 1979.

president Abraham Shushan, and former LSU construction superintendent George Caldwell. To former governor James A. Noe, who was seeking help for Weiss, Ellender explained: "As I suggested to you the other day, the Justice Department would have to pass on the matter, and [Attorney General Francis] Biddle is so scared of publicity and of Louisiana politics that he would not, in my opinion, turn a peg to help us." In May, 1942, Ellender called Shushan a friend who "is not a criminal by nature." The Justice Department did not grant pardons until convicted felons had been off probation or parole for four years.[17]

Ellender had to reassure his friend Caliste Duplantis of Houma, who feared he would not receive the postmaster appointment Ellender had promised him. "Every Senator is accorded the privilege, I understand, of naming the postmaster of his own domicile," Ellender said. "Nothing need be said about that, but let them go on and attempt to give trouble and we will see where they land." Duplantis became postmaster. Columnist Drew Pearson sent investigator Bob Brothers to Houma, Duplantis reported later, to gather information about Ellender, who Pearson suspected was receiving graft from war plants.[18]

As his first term in the Senate neared its end, Ellender hoped that he had endeared himself to voters. He knew he could not rely on old political allies to help his reelection campaign, for the Long organization, beset by scandal, was in serious disarray. He would have to face his opponents on his own and with his own organization.

According to the *Christian Science Monitor,* in 1942 Ellender had supported New Deal programs, but his success score (the times he voted with the winning side) had declined considerably. Conservative Democrats— Carter Glass and Harry Byrd of Virginia, Millard Tydings of Maryland, Alben Barkley of Kentucky, and James Byrnes of South Carolina—were gaining in strength. Ellender had joined them frequently, especially on civil rights

17.   F. Edward Hebert, *Last of the Titans: The Life and Times of Congressman F. Edward Hebert of Louisiana* (Lafayette, La., 1976), 163–64; Frank Wurzlow, Jr., to Sam Jones, June 26, 1941, in "Allen J. Ellender—U.S. Senator" Folder, Sam Jones Papers; V. L. Caldwell to Allen Ellender, August 9, 1941, in "Justice, Department of, Paroles" Folder, Box 53, Ellender to James A. Noe, June 12, 1942, Walter Ulrich to Ellender, May 15, 1942, Dave Shushan to Ellender, May 18, 1942, and Ellender to United States Board of Parole, May 7, 1942, all in "Justice, Department of, Paroles" Folder, Box 333, all in AEP.

18.   Allen Ellender to Caliste Duplantis, February 4, 1941, in "Post Office Department, Houma" Folder, Box 333, and Caliste Duplantis to Ellender, July 15, 1942, Box 1814, both in AEP.

legislation. Ellender had voted for repeal of the embargo on military hardware, enactment and then extension of the military draft, the sending of troops abroad, Lend-Lease, providing ships for Britain, and repeal of neutrality laws. Domestically he had voted for the Tennessee Valley Authority, extension of WPA relief, FDR's governmental reorganization bill, farm parity, and outlawing use of labor spies by management. In August, Ellender voted against appropriating $100 million for federal highway construction.[19]

In the summer of 1942 Ellender turned his attention to his own reelection campaign. "You have been selected by acclamation as my campaign manager," Ellender wrote Elward Wright in July, thereby officially opening his campaign. To reduce the burden he was placing on his old friend, Ellender promised that his brother Claude and Frank Wurzlow, Jr., would help prepare for the September 8 Democratic primary. Ellender hoped to disseminate information from a number of government agencies—National Youth Administration, Rural Electrification Administration, Social Security, Farm Security Administration, Agricultural Adjustment Administration—to prove he had served his constituents with diligence and effectiveness. The people were more interested in winning the war, he observed, than in political campaigns. After Ellender filed for the office, he returned to Washington.[20]

Before he had assembled pertinent political information, Ellender made an embarrassing political move in May, 1942, against anti-Longites serving simultaneously on military duty and in the Louisiana legislature. He forwarded to Secretary of War Henry Stimson details about 1st Lt. W. D. Cotton of Rayville, an Army reservist, who had been called to active duty. Cotton, a state senator, and Maj. deLesseps S. Morrison of New Orleans, a state representative, both leaders in the Jones organization, had received furloughs to attend sessions of the legislature. Ellender complained because Cotton had appeared on the floor of the legislature in uniform, Ellender being unaware that military leave policy applied to all military personnel in the state legislature. Ellender had already sent his complaint to Washington when Shreveport *Times* editor John Ewing wrote to explain the leave policy. Stimson, in the meantime, had canceled the leaves "in view of the urgency of war conditions."

19. *Christian Science Monitor,* June 16, 1942, in Box 1820, AEP; Hilty, *Senate Voting Alignments,* 51, 57, A-29–31, A-78, A-83, A-170–71.

20. Allen Ellender to Elward Wright, July 11, 1942, and Ellender speech, August 26, 1942, both in Box 1814, AEP; "1942" Scrapbook, *passim,* AEP.

After Governor Jones complained to the War Department, President Roosevelt had the leaves restored. Stimson, upon reinstating them, explained that the leaves had been canceled "through an administrative error." Ewing, not one to consider the uniform issue important, thought Ellender had erred. "It was a dirty trick," an anti-Longite thought, for Ellender to be the foil of the Maestri crowd and to forward letters about Cotton to the War Department. Except for an unfavorable editorial in the *Item,* the imbroglio received slight newspaper coverage. Ellender had committed a political blunder and was probably content to let the matter lie after the leaves had been restored.[21]

To avoid being caught in confrontations like the Cotton incident, Ellender decided on a policy of neutrality in local elections. He would run as a bipartisan spokesman for all Louisianians. He did not want to antagonize Sam Jones and have to campaign against him. He hoped to avoid entangling alliances with candidates, even with those who had been his allies in the past. "I am absolutely insistent in that matter," Wright told a supporter, "and I will be absolutely consistent in it." To friends seeking endorsements, Wright explained, "There are several candidates [for local races], and the Senator has supporters among each group." When Clem Sehrt, Earl Long's law partner, asked if he could list Ellender on political posters, Wright said no. Ellender asked Hammond attorney Jimmy Morrison to remove the senator's name from his flyers. Ellender "has not aligned himself with any local candidates in this campaign," Wright wrote.[22]

For political expediency and other reasons Ellender did not sever all ties with the Longites, even though they were reeling from effects of the scandals. After all, only a handful of Huey's supporters had been convicted of crimes. And Ellender was not privy to Huey's financial deals—his questionable links to organized crime and shady oil-leasing schemes, which were not widely known by the public at the time. Huey had run a highly personalized and unusual organization; without Huey perhaps Ellender could in time become leader of a reorganized, cleaned up Long faction. At any rate, where could Ellender turn? He had been a floor leader and visible member of the Long organization; the anti-Long reformers had no place for him.

21.   Allen Ellender to Henry L. Stimson, May 26, 1942, John Ewing to Ellender, July 2, 1942, Robert Daspit to Ellender, June 24, 1942, and Stimson to Ellender, July 2, 1942, all in "Sen. W. D. Cotton" Folder, Box 988, AEP; New Orleans *Times-Picayune,* July 7, 1942, in "1942" Scrapbook, AEP.

22.   Elward Wright to Joseph Tritico, August 14, 1942, Wright to Sidney Harp, August 3, 1942, Wright to Clem Sehrt, August 14, 1942, all in Box 1814, AEP.

Then there was the idea of a program for the people of Louisiana. The anti-Long faction had no program but opposed every Huey Long measure, even the good ones, because of Long's personality and brusque manner of dealing with people. A number of anti-Longites, years later, admitted that this blind opposition to roads, bridges, and free textbooks prevented them from stopping Long and his legislative agenda.[23]

Ellender's Washington staff wrote letters to governmental agencies requesting data—number of employees, locations of plants, expenditures by parishes. Ellender, preparing speeches and news releases, sent summaries to John Overton, who promised to make a statewide radio broadcast for the junior senator. Ellender accepted endorsements from prominent leaders, but simply would not endorse anyone in return.[24]

Ellender avoided some prospective supporters and dealt cautiously with others. A Cane League official, pledging support, said "four Jones Congressmen" would campaign for him. Ellender, penciling instructions for his staff on the letter, wrote, "Thank him on return. Do not be specific." When a lawyer from Hammond requested a $100 retainer to get "some of the Jones votes no matter how we get them," Ellender was even more cautious. Replying evasively to the attorney, Ellender penciled to his staff, "I would not like to hook up with this party."[25]

In June, Ellender learned who would be his opponent: E. A. Stephens, a New Orleans Buick dealer. He was a Jones supporter and a vocal critic of Mayor Maestri. An Ellender fan concluded, "He'd be a push-over for you." A native of Virginia, Stephens had attended William and Mary and was a former president of the Board of Commissioners of the New Orleans Dock Board. Several people, including a DeRidder *Enterprise* journalist, provided information about him. St. Mary Parish sugar grower John Caffery, Jr., was his campaign manager in the Third Congressional District. Stephens' campaign chief in north Louisiana was Harvey G. Fields, a resident of Farmerville and a former United States attorney for the Western District, who had prosecuted some of the Longites in 1939 and 1940.[26]

23. William I. Hair, *The Kingfish and His Realm: The Life and Times of Huey P. Long* (Baton Rouge, 1991), 164.

24. John Overton to Frank Wurzlow, Jr., August 10, 1942, in "Radio Time" Folder, Box 1814, AEP.

25. Frank Barker to Allen Ellender, January 17, 1941, in "Agriculture, Sugar, 1942" Folder, Box 280, AEP; Leon Ford to Ellender, May 8, 1942, Ellender to Ford, May 22, 1942, both in Box 1816, AEP.

26. Shirley Wimberly to Allen Ellender, June 23, 1942, in "National Housing Agency, 1942" Folder, Box 333, AEP; John McKay and Mrs. H. M. Barrett to Allen Ellender, n.d., Box

Stephens attempted to associate Ellender with scandal by charging Ellender with profiting from the Houma Boat Company, recommending Leche for the federal bench, and trying to impede O. John Rogge's investigation of the scandals. Caffery called Ellender "an ugly part of the corrupt group against whom Louisianians arose a while ago in resentment." Dubbing Ellender "Little Bull," Stephens said a vote for Ellender in 1942 would be a vote for Maestri for governor in 1944. He called Ellender "Maestri's Ellender." He also called him Maestri's stooge.[27]

Wurzlow, after returning to Houma in July, 1942, to assist the campaign, asked the staff in Washington to find a letter in which Fields offered to support Ellender. He also wanted to know how much the Caffery family sugar factory, Columbia, in Franklin, Louisiana, had collected in sugar payments. Caffery charged Ellender with failing to pass adequate sugar legislation. But the Caffery family, Wurzlow discovered, received $23,000 in 1937, $19,000 in 1938, and $16,000 in 1939 in sugar payments. Ellender used the information in his stump speeches.[28]

Calling himself a Jeffersonian (he meant states' rights) Democrat, Ellender responded to Stephens' campaign charges in thirty-minute radio talks over stations WDSU and WNOE in New Orleans, KWKH in Shreveport, and WJBO in Baton Rouge. The Dock Board, Ellender said, lost money under Stephens' direction. A victory for Stephens, Ellender told voters, would give Virginia three senators. He proudly accepted endorsements from Mayor Maestri and the Regular Democratic Organization in New Orleans. Defending the Houma Boat Company, New Orleans shipbuilder Andrew J. Higgins said it provided jobs to local people. Ellender bragged about his successful involvements, including WPA and housing projects and benefits to agriculture.[29]

Racial issues surfaced during the campaign but gave no edge to either

---

1822, Frank Wurzlow, Jr., to Ellender staff, July 31, 1942, Box 1814, and Box 1827, *passim,* all in AEP.

27.   Box 1827, *passim,* Stephens radio speech, August 31, 1942, Box 1822, and speeches and newspaper clippings, in "1942" Scrapbook, all in AEP; Carolyn Glynn, interview, March 14, 1988.

28.   Frank Wurzlow, Jr., to Mrs. [?] Long, July 31, 1942, Box 1814, and Florence LeCompte to Wurzlow, August 3, 5, 1942, Box 1818, all in AEP.

29.   Allen Ellender speeches, Box 1827, and random newspaper clippings, Box 1815, AEP; Bentley Mackay to Ellender, August 26, 1942, and Andrew J. Higgins speech, August 7, 1942, both in Box 1819, AEP.

candidate; neither rose above traditional demagoguery. Stephens, currying support from white voters, accused Ellender of favoring social equality for blacks. Not to be outdone, Ellender bragged of filibustering against the "pernicious anti[-]lynching bill" and said, "I invite the unknown critic who is asking how I stand on the negro issue to read some of my speeches on the subject." Ellender was correct; he had not changed his racial stance once he became a senator on January 5, 1937. Ellender wrote to FBI director J. Edgar Hoover in February, 1942, for information about Noel Siwel, a black journalist who had criticized Ellender in *Sepia Socialite,* a black New Orleans newspaper. Ellender asked if the FBI had a file on Siwel. Hoover said no, adding that the FBI would take no action in a Louisiana political matter.[30]

Subtly and quietly the agricultural bureaucracy helped in the campaign. Truman Ward of the USDA promised to mail thirty thousand agricultural bulletins with a cover letter from Ellender no later than September 3, just five days before the election.[31]

Ellender accumulated a healthy campaign fund. Contractor W. Horace Williams of north Louisiana, once considered loyal to Sam Jones, collected $8,200 for Ellender, although T. L. James of Ruston refused to contribute. W. C. Kemper of the Cane League gathered funds from the sugar interests. According to an official list submitted to a Senate committee investigating campaign contributions, Claude Ellender had contributed $3,000, W. Horace Williams, $2,500, and sugar growers from $100 to $300—all for a total of $12,985. The actual sum received was undoubtedly higher; Wright did not officially record all cash contributions. Thanking E. F. Creekmore of the New Orleans Cotton Exchange for a $250 contribution in July, Wright wrote, "At the moment, it does not appear that the Senator has serious opposition." During the campaign Ellender made $10 and $15 donations to churches that asked for contributions.[32]

Ellender's optimism grew as his campaign chest filled and as reports told of poor attendance at Stephens' meetings. Only fifteen people attended a

30.   Stephens radio speech, August 31, 1942, Box 1822, and Allen Ellender speech, August 26, 1942, Box 1819, both in AEP; Allen Ellender to J. Edgar Hoover, February 24, 1942, and Hoover to Ellender, March 4, 16, 1942, all in "Justice—General, 1942" Folder, Box 33, AEP.

31.   Frank Wurzlow, Jr., to Martha Sims (telegram), August 24, 1942, Box 1818, AEP.

32.   "U.S. Senate Special Comm. to Investigate Senatorial Campaign Contrib., 1942" Folder, and W. Horace Williams to Allen Ellender, August 25, 1942, both in Box 1823, AEP; E. F. Creekmore to Ellender, July 14, 1942, and Elward Wright to Creekmore, July 24, 1942, both in Box 1827, AEP.

Stephens rally in Bossier City, an Ellender supporter said. Ellender asked an old friend in the USDA, "What do you hear about my election? Reports reaching me are very favorable. If my opponent has any support it must be in hiding. I expect to carry every parish in the State next September 8th." [33]

Staffers nonetheless worked as though Ellender were an underdog. In August, Martha Sims in Washington was receiving telegrams inquiring about unanswered letters written in July. Everyone was working at a fevered pace, she told Wurzlow, but "the trouble seems to be that there are only 24 hours in a day." Wurzlow sympathized but offered no solution. "You will have to take care of important government mail in Washington. Impossible to handle here in heat of campaign," he replied. Working on Sundays, from 8:30 A.M. to 5:00 P.M. and then from 7:00 to 10:00 P.M. as well, Wurzlow complained, "We are snowed under here and can handle only campaign work." Clearly Ellender campaigned as energetically as he did most other things. To relieve his overworked staff, Ellender hired Florence LeCompte, called Flo, of Bourg on Bayou Terrebonne near the Ellender lands. Short and petite, Flo spoke Acadian French. Bright and hard working, Flo at twenty-seven had ten years of office experience. Like many women during the war, she took a typing test at the local post office to qualify for secretarial work in the nation's capital. She and a woman friend arrived in Washington in March, 1942.[34]

Ellender trounced Stephens on September 8. He did not carry every parish in the state, but he did receive 72 percent of the votes cast, beating Stephens by 218,141 to 102,900. He received more than 90 percent of the votes in Terrebonne Parish. He lost St. Landry Parish by 239 votes and St. Bernard by 101. Obviously pleased, he wrote to thank many contributors and friends who had helped in the campaign and asked for names of overlooked workers.[35]

Ellender's successful strategy meant that his Senate seat was safe for six more years, that is, unless he decided in 1944 to seek the goal he had coveted since 1932—the governorship of Louisiana. Jones did not prove popular,

33. Numerous reports, August, 1942, Box 1814, AEP; Allen Ellender to Bentley Mackay, August 21, 1942, in "Immigration and Naturalization Serv. 1942" Folder, Box 333, AEP.

34. Martha Sims to Frank Wurzlow, Jr., August 18, 1942, and Wurzlow to Sims (telegram), August 29, 1942, both in Box 1818, Houma (La.) *Courier*, March 10, 1967, in "1967" Scrapbook, all in AEP; Florence LeCompte, interview, June 20, 1991.

35. Report of Secretary of State to Sam H. Jones, Governor of Louisiana, Results of Democratic Primary on September 8, 1942, p. 6, Box 1824, AEP; Allen Ellender to John Overton, September 9, 1942, Box 1818, and Box 1816, *passim*, AEP.

partly because Louisiana voters had only a fleeting interest in political reform. The war had created shortages Jones could not remedy. Ellender could delay his ultimate decision until Jones's tenure as governor was nearing its end.

9

WINNING THE WAR
(1943–46)

$\mathcal{E}$llender returned to Washington in January, 1943, feeling optimistic indeed. Of the Longites who had sought reelection since the scandals, only he had won. The country, now engrossed in full war production, began to sense victory. Moving up in seniority, Ellender became chairman of the Claims Committee, which handled damage claims of citizens against the government. He also enhanced his ranking on the Agriculture Committee.[1]

Untainted by scandal and reelected in 1942 by an impressive margin, Ellender once again assessed his chances of becoming governor of Louisiana in 1944. In January, 1943, New Orleans journalist Hermann Deutsch predicted that Ellender would resign from the Senate and run for governor without opposition from the Jones organization. An anti-Longite would run for the Senate without opposition from the Old Regulars, Deutsch suggested. Ellender had supported former governor Earl Long in 1940, sincerely hoping that he would win and then support Ellender in 1944. However, after losing to Jones, Earl wanted to run again. Until Earl made up his mind, Ellender remained noncommittal.

In July, 1943, Ellender, convinced Earl and Hammond attorney James Morrison would enter the governor's race, told a supporter he had decided to keep his Senate seat. But he did not publicly announce his decision until September.[2]

---

1. Sam Jones to Allen Ellender, January 18, 1943, and Ellender to Jones, January 27, 1943, both in "Claims—General" Folder, Box 581, Allen J. Ellender Papers, Nicholls State University Library, Thibodaux, La., hereinafter cited as AEP.

2. Orville Priestly to Allen Ellender, July 29, 1943, and Ellender to Priestly, July 30, 1943, both in "Agriculture, Rice—1946" Folder, Box 27, AEP; "Senator Ellender, Governorship"

Ellender suspected labor racketeers in Louisiana had turned against him for supporting the Smith-Connally Act, which authorized presidential seizure of war plants on strike. Union members supported Earl Long despite shipbuilder Andrew Higgins' efforts to win union support for Ellender, who had alienated union workers by openly criticizing Lewis. "As a member of the Labor Committee of the Senate," Ellender said, "I had the opportunity to stab labor if I desired, but I did not do so. I was one who did all in my power to prevent any hurtful amendment to the Wagner Act, which is really and truly a godsend to labor." Refusing to concede the labor vote, Ellender said, "I cannot make up my mind that the bulk of labor is against me and if I do become a candidate, my guess is that these labor leaders will be put in their place by an almost solid vote for me in the coming campaign."[3]

As it turned out, Earl Long did not run for governor either. Unable to win the endorsement of New Orleans Longite Robert Maestri, Long ran instead for lieutenant governor on a ticket headed by Lewis Morgan of Covington, a political unknown, against country singer Jimmie Davis, from north Louisiana, and Morrison. Because the Longites had not chosen him, Ellender decided to remain neutral. "I do not expect to take any active part at all, as I am much too busy here in Washington," he explained. Davis, the anti-Longite candidate, won the 1944 race. Ellender, the only Longite who could have been elected governor, must have felt like telling the Long faction, "I told you so." But he did not. He had passed up his best chance to seek the governor's office since 1936. Had he been too cautious, or had he correctly decided that the old Long organization was too badly splintered to be of help? Unsure of Longite support, Ellender chose to remain in the Senate.[4]

During the war, an anti–New Deal coalition, the Southern Bloc, opposed Roosevelt on race and labor policy. Siding with southerners on some

---

Folder, *passim,* Box 408, AEP; Hermann Deutsch, New Orleans *Item,* January 29, 1943, Houma (La.) *Terrebonne Press,* July 30, 1943, Monroe (La.) *Morning World,* September 22, 1943, all in "1942–1943" Scrapbook, AEP; Michael L. Kurtz and Morgan D. Peoples, *Earl K. Long: The Saga of Uncle Earl and Louisiana Politics* (Baton Rouge, 1990), 118.

3. Minute Book, United Brotherhood of Carpenters and Joiners, Local 2258, October 4, 1943, union headquarters, Houma, La.; Allen Ellender to Fred G. Benton, October 5, 1943, in "Gubernatorial Campaign—1944" Folder, Box 408, AEP.

4. Allen Ellender to William T. Bennett, December 17, 1943, in "War Department, General, 1943" Folder, Box 18, and "Gubernatorial Campaign, Lewis Morgan" Folder, Box 408, both in AEP; Kurtz and Peoples, *Earl Long,* 117; Houma (La.) *Courier,* March 30, 1944, in "1944" Scrapbook, AEP.

measures, Ellender supported Roosevelt on others. Realizing the importance of seniority, he never encouraged third-party movements. He rejected overtures from antilabor agitator John U. Barr, who had formed a Harry-Byrd-for-president committee. He dismissed as political rhetoric Governor Sam Jones's March, 1943, *Saturday Evening Post* article "Will Dixie Bolt the New Deal?" suggesting a Louisiana defection from the Democratic camp.[5]

By the end of the Seventy-eighth Congress, Ellender's success scores — the times he voted on the winning side on roll call votes — had declined. Nonetheless, his rating on a conservative-liberal scale was closer to the political center than that of many of his southern colleagues, according to historian James Hilty. Rating senators from the Seventy-fifth through the Seventy-eighth congresses, Hilty used a scale of + 1.0 for most liberal, − 1.0 for most conservative. Ellender's .43 was considerably lower than liberals Edward Costigan, Colo. (.93), Hugo Black, Ala. (.84), Robert Wagner, N.Y. (.65), and Alben Barkley, Ky. (.54). But he was less conservative than John McClellan, Ark. (− .84), Millard Tydings, Md. (− .78), Carter Glass, Va. (− .63), and Walter George, Ga. (− 30). Harry Truman, Mo., and Carl Hayden, Ariz., both scored .42, a fraction less liberal than Ellender. Joseph Robinson, Ark. (.25), John Overton, La. (.17), and Richard Russell, Ga. (.13) were lower.[6]

By January, 1945, victory over the Axis powers was imminent. In the Pacific, the Japanese navy had suffered major defeats; in Europe, German units had retreated before Gen. Dwight Eisenhower's forces. Ellender, involved increasingly in the legislative process, had become somewhat predictable. He voted to limit funds for FEPC and against making it a permanent organization. He voted for farm legislation but against labor measures.

Ellender voted for presidential appointees even when they espoused views different from his own. This distorted his image as a typical southern conservative. In January, 1945, Franklin Roosevelt submitted two names to the U.S. Senate for confirmation: Henry A. Wallace for secretary of commerce and Aubrey W. Williams to head the Rural Electrification Administration. In heated debate the Senate confirmed Wallace but rejected Williams.

5.   Robert A. Garson, *The Democratic Party and the Politics of Sectionalism, 1941–1948* (Baton Rouge, 1974), 95, 101–104.
6.   James W. Hilty, *Voting Alignments in the United States Senate, 1933–1944* (1 vol. with appendix; University Microfilms International, 1979), 296–97, A-33, 143, 144, 147.

Ellender voted to confirm both candidates. His support for Williams was surprising and courageous.

An outspoken and capable administrator, Williams received the backing of the CIO, the NAACP, and other liberal groups. Ellender defended Williams against charges of being a communist and an inept administrator. Some early Williams supporters—John Bankhead of Alabama, Richard Russell of Georgia, and J. William Fulbright of Arkansas—backed down because of racial pressure from home. Although he shared the concerns of his southern colleagues on race and labor, Ellender wanted the president to have a free hand in choosing his subordinates. Bucking the Farm Bureau Federation, Ellender supported Williams despite a preponderance of mail against confirmation. He wanted REA to have capable leaders.[7]

Vice-president Harry Truman of Missouri became president when Roosevelt died at Warm Springs, Georgia, on April 12, 1945, only weeks after the Williams nomination failed. In May, Allied military forces on the continent celebrated V-E Day; in August the war in the Pacific ended.

Converting to a peacetime economy after the war created problems for President Truman. Farmers thought the government showed undue favoritism to labor; businessmen complained of red tape and curbs on prices and profits. Labor wanted price controls and collective bargaining but no wage restrictions. When Truman played the role of strikebreaker, organized labor became angry. Farmers wanted high prices for commodities; businessmen hated price controls. Consumers, concerned about inflation and the black market, complained about shortages. At war's end, industrialists, wanting subsidies to continue, tried to disguise the size of their subsidies and prevent public scrutiny.[8]

Truman made John L. Lewis a scapegoat for the country's economic distress. Crippling railroad and steel strikes led the president to enjoin the United Mine Workers from striking and prompted him to bring legal action against Lewis. The strikes came as he was eliminating wage controls, meat

7. John A. Salmond, "Postscript to the New Deal: The Defeat of the Nomination of Aubrey W. Williams as Rural Electrification Administrator in 1945," *Journal of American History*, LXI (September, 1974), 417, 420, 422–23, 428, 431, 433; Gilbert C. Fite, *Richard B. Russell, Jr., Senator from Georgia* (Chapel Hill, 1991), 170; "Rural Electrification Administration, Aubrey Williams" Folder, Box 446, and Box 412, *passim*, AEP; George Arceneaux, Jr., interview, December 31, 1979.

8. Barton Bernstein, "Economic Policies," in *The Truman Period as a Research Field*, Richard S. Kirkendall, ed. (Columbia, Mo., 1967), 90–91, 94, 96.

price regulations, and emergency housing for veterans. Ellender enjoyed a friendly relationship with Truman, always outspoken and direct. The two men did not always agree on race and labor issues, but they understood their areas of disagreement. Ellender respected Truman, but Roosevelt was the president he most admired.[9]

Ellender's position with organized labor had deteriorated during the war years. Like other southerners, he disliked CIO leader John L. Lewis, calling him a "Mussolini of mines" during the sit-down strikes. He credited Lewis for his change of attitude toward labor. In May, 1943, Lewis' United Mine Workers demanded wage increases in excess of Little Steel Formula 15 percent guidelines. Shortly thereafter, Congress passed the Smith-Connally (War Labor Disputes) Act. Ellender, favoring legislation to "curb the power of would-be labor dictators like Lewis," voted for it. The act provided for a thirty-day cooling-off period before a union could go on strike and outlawed political contributions by unions. Roosevelt vetoed the bill, but Congress overrode the president 244 to 108 in the House, 50 to 25 in the Senate. Ellender wrote, "I am actively supporting [bills] to prevent labor unions from exacting tribute from management."[10]

Ellender later changed his mind about Smith-Connally because he did not like to see unions capitalize on a provision of the bill to call for strike votes, "all at the expense of the Federal Government." By December, 1945, he favored repeal of Smith-Connally because unions, without incurring expenses, could call for a strike vote to demonstrate the threat of a strike. Although Ellender proclaimed himself for the working man and against labor racketeers, he was against providing twenty-five dollars per week in unemployment compensation for twenty-six weeks. He also voted against increasing the minimum wage from forty cents per hour to sixty-five cents.[11]

In the summer of 1946 Senator Francis Case of South Dakota introduced a bill to create a federal mediation board and to make unions liable for any breach of contract. The Case Bill provided for a thirty-day cooling-off period before a strike could be called. While the Senate considered the bill, Truman requested authority to draft striking railroad workers. After talking to Tru-

9. *Ibid.*, 99–100, 102, 105–106; Elward Wright to Allen Ellender, April 15, 1946, in "Fur Industry, 1946" Folder, Box 153, AEP; Frank Wurzlow, Jr., interview, April 9, 1980.

10. Thomas Becnel, *Labor, Church, and the Sugar Establishment: Louisiana, 1887–1976* (Baton Rouge, 1980), 25; Garson, *The Democratic Party,* 38–40.

11. Becnel, *Labor, Church, and the Sugar Establishment,* 180, 181–82; Allen Ellender to J. Paul Treen, December 3, 1945, in "Labor Problems" Folder, Box 581, AEP.

man about the bill, Ellender voted for it and endorsed it in writing. "I wish to make it clear that I am supporting the President's proposal without qualification and without reservation," he wrote. "He must be sustained lest the power of a few labor leaders will become paramount to Government itself and nothing short of anarchy will follow."

While Truman was addressing the Senate, he received word that the rail strike had been settled. Later the Senate passed an even stronger version of the original Case Bill, which Truman promptly vetoed. It would have created a new labor department and given management the right of injunction. Robert Taft had supported the Case Bill but had objected to denying workers basic rights long enjoyed. Ellender and his southern colleagues disagreed with the president's action, but they did not have the votes to override. The Case Bill "would have ended the immunity from anti-racketeering and antitrust laws which labor unions have enjoyed for so long," Ellender told a supporter. The bill would have created a separate mediation board for labor and established a sixty-day cooling-off period before a strike could begin. Ellender's constituents worried about strikes during the summer of 1946.[12]

During the war big farmers feared that the labor shortage enhanced the bargaining position of blacks. They criticized the WPA and the Farm Security Administration, even though neither group hired many workers. They encouraged the USDA to organize a farm labor committee to investigate manpower shortages.[13]

Ellender's sugar industry constituents became more vocal as the manpower shortage worsened. Early in the war Ellender had been unreceptive to the idea of using POW labor, mainly because he realized the deficiencies of plantation housing. The military required hot and cold running water, bathroom facilities, electricity, and other amenities usually not found in houses of black sugarcane workers. Furthermore, military rules prohibited prison camps within 150 miles of the coast. Refusing to admit defeat simply

12. Garson, *The Democratic Party,* 156–64; Allen Ellender to Harry Truman, May 28, 1946, in "Ellender" Folder, General File 704, Truman Library, Independence, Mo., hereinafter cited as HST; Truman Veto Message on *Case* Bill, June 11, 1946, in "Education and Labor Committee—*Case* Bill" Folder, Ellender form letter, n.d., Shreveport *Times,* June 5, 1946, in "Strikes—1946" Folder, all in Box 211, AEP; James T. Patterson, *Mr. Republican: A Biography of Robert A. Taft* (Boston, 1972), 305–306, 307; Allen Ellender to C. C. Tassin, June 19, 1946, and Ellender to George Goodman, June 19, 1946, both in "Education and Labor Committee—*Case* Bill" Folder, Box 211, AEP.

13. Pete Daniel, "Going Among Strangers: Southern Reactions to World War II," *Journal of American History,* LXXVII (December, 1990), 889, 893.

because growers could not comply with military rules, the Cane League launched a campaign to circumvent the rules. Succumbing to a barrage of letters, petitions, telegrams, and editorials, the War Department changed its POW labor policy. Military authorities decided to build side camps, or branch camps, in lieu of regular prison camps. Ellender served as spokesman for the sugar industry before various government agencies, bureaus, and departments. Meanwhile, the War Department worked closely with the United States Employment Service.

Before long seven or eight side camps—some were abandoned Civilian Conservation Corps camps—sprang up in sugar country less than fifty miles from the Gulf of Mexico. Cane League officials, although they agreed among themselves that POW labor was efficient, officially requested wage reductions to POWs because "the German prisoner cannot perform anything like the amount of work that free labor does." The Army rejected requests for wage cuts and refused league requests to change the method of compensating POWs from an hourly basis to a piece-rate basis.

German POW labor made planters less dependent on Negro laborers, whose bargaining position improved as wartime shortages continued. Frank Barker of Lockport, chairman of the Cane League labor committee, asked Ellender to help get furloughs for black soldiers to harvest cane. In August, 1943, Ellender instructed Wurzlow, "Without giving the matter any publicity at all, which as you know has been our usual course, try to find out what can be done toward securing a lot of the colored soldiers who are encamped in various parts of the South." Wurzlow, who himself was drafted later in the year, failed to locate surplus black soldiers to harvest sugarcane. Noting the influence of POWs on black workers, a Cane League director observed, "I am also told that the presence of the prisoners has served to wake up the negroes to some concern about more prisoners being brought in to take over their jobs entirely. As a result the negroes are working better and are staying on the job throughout the week." The Cane League applauded Ellender for convincing the War Food Administration to raise the price of sugarcane by thirty-four cents per ton in 1943 and eighty-five cents per ton in 1944.[14]

Some sugar growers hoped to continue using POW labor after the war ended, but President Truman wanted all war prisoners repatriated by June,

14. C. J. Bourg to Allen J. Ellender, September 2, 1943, in "War Department, Prisoner-of-War Labor, 1943–44" Folder, Box 18, AEP; Becnel, *Labor, Church, and the Sugar Establishment,* 83–86.

1946. By then, the president reasoned, returning GIs would be job hunting. As the POW labor force declined, the league considered importing Jamaican and Mexican laborers and setting up a permanent labor-supplying organization. In September between 300 and 350 Jamaicans would be coming to Louisiana, Ellender informed a sugar grower. Optimistic about the future of the sugar industry, Ellender told Harvey Peltier of Thibodaux, "I don't believe you would make a mistake in remodeling your factory."[15]

By the latter stages of the war, Ellender had cultivated a conservative stance on a number of issues. However, he supported Hill-Burton to provide adequate medical assistance to every class of citizens. The American Medical Association (AMA) opposed Hill-Burton and other bills to subsidize hospitals and public health facilities and labeled supporters of the measure advocates of socialized medicine. "Because I was honest and sincere in my beliefs, I was accused of being in favor of socialized medicine," Ellender told the AMA. "It is my honest opinion that if you simply assume a negative attitude you are going to get the worst of it." The next year, Ellender opposed S. 1606, the Wagner-Murray-Dingell Bill, because it did not give either the patient or the doctor free choice. Critical of compulsory health insurance, Ellender favored a voluntary system. "I am definitely opposed to socialized medicine," he wrote.[16]

Race, too, figured in a growing antiadministration coalition led by southern conservatives. Truman decided to support a permanent FEPC, which had eliminated racial wage differentials and discriminatory hiring practices. But segregationists viewed any racial change as a challenge to segregation itself.

Roman Catholic archbishops Robert E. Lucey of San Antonio and Joseph Francis Rummel of New Orleans supported FEPC, which every president after Roosevelt kept alive by executive order. Georgia senator Richard Russell of the Appropriations Committee limited FEPC funds to half a million dollars or less. Robert Taft, favoring a temporary organization with

15. Becnel, *Labor, Church, and the Sugar Establishment,* 88, 89; Allen J. Ellender to D. Thibaut (telegram), September 5, 1946, in "Agriculture, General, 1946, #2" Folder, Box 27, AEP.

16. Allen Ellender to Edwin L. Zander, August 20, 1945, in "S. 191—Public Health Service Act" Folder, and Ellender to George F. Fasting, June 19, 1946, in "S. 1606" Folder, both in Box 581, AEP; New Orleans *Times-Picayune,* April 30, 1949, in "1949" Scrapbook, AEP; Virginia Van der Veer Hamilton, *Lister Hill: Statesman from the South* (Chapel Hill, 1987), 136–38.

powers of persuasion only, also opposed a permanent FEPC. Taft's biographer thought he did not appreciate the plight of blacks. When Senator John Overton began a three-week filibuster of an FEPC bill in January, 1946, Ellender joined in resisting "that nefarious bill." [17]

Ellender had not maintained a consistent position on the poll tax. In the Seventy-eighth Congress, the House passed an NAACP-backed anti–poll tax bill; Ellender joined the Southern Bloc to kill the bill in the Senate. As a supporter of Huey Long, he had helped to eliminate the poll tax in Louisiana; now he voted against a federal bill to outlaw the discriminatory measure. Officially he had not changed—he still opposed the poll tax, he said—but state law, not federal mandate, should end it. Federal encroachment, he said unofficially, would lead to the "degradation of our race." In other words, he had changed his position, but for the record, he had not changed; he was making a racial adjustment.[18]

As an agrarian Ellender had no problems supporting a free lunch program. The Ellender-Russell Bill, cosponsored by Ellender and Richard Russell in May, 1945, was signed by Truman on June 14, 1946, as the School Free Lunch Act. Using surplus farm commodities, the USDA assumed one-half of the cost of school lunches. Matching funds from the states provided the other half. Since New Deal days, Ellender had advocated using surplus farm commodities in a federally subsidized lunch program. An early federal effort, using tariff revenue, had provided surplus commodities for school lunches in an experimental program.[19]

Proud of the Free Lunch Act, Ellender frequently had to defend its limitations on aid to parochial schools. New Orleans archbishop Joseph Francis Rummel, wondering why the lunch bill disallowed federal funds for equipment and classes in private schools, communicated extensively with him on the subject. In a three-page letter, Ellender explained state and federal guidelines. "I hope that you understand my position," he wrote. He quoted

17.   Michael I. Sovern, *Legal Restraints on Racial Discrimination in Employment* (New York, 1966), 103; Louis C. Kesselman, *The Social Politics of FEPC: A Study in Reform Pressure Movements* (Chapel Hill, 1948), x, 23–24, 141, 168, 172; Patterson, *Mr. Republican,* 304–305; Garson, *The Democratic Party,* 28, 90–93, 137–44, 172–87; F. Ray Marshall, *Labor in the South* (Cambridge, Mass., 1967), 228; Allen Ellender speech, May 19, 1950, in "Speeches, 1950" Folder, Box 105, AEP.

18.   Garson, *The Democratic Party,* 31, 34–36, 42–44; Allen Ellender to Gessner T. McCorvey, n.d., Box 1407, AEP.

19.   Thibodaux (La.) *Comet,* n.d., in "1945–1947" Scrapbook, AEP; Fite, *Richard Russell,* 186–87.

the Louisiana Constitution and federal regulations on aid to a religious denomination. Despite a heavy volume of mail from Catholics, Ellender stuck to his view that the child-benefit theory did not extend beyond textbooks, bus transportation, and foodstuffs for school cafeterias. Doing more, he reasoned, would violate separation of church and state by benefiting the institution, not the child.[20]

During the war Ellender made a number of inspection tours of U.S. embassies abroad, his first being shortly after the Japanese had bombed Pearl Harbor. He returned from a 42-day congressional tour of thirty Asian and European countries on August 6, 1945, the day the United States dropped its first atomic bomb. The war against Japan was going well, he reported, but China was "hopeless." Warring factions seemed unable to settle their differences and graft was rampant in China, he reported. American goods shipped to China were frequently stolen. A number of German and Japanese personnel remained in China. Ellender left for another tour of the Pacific in June, 1946. He celebrated the inauguration of the Philippine Republic in Manila on July 4. He made his way to Japan and China, returning in August after visiting north Africa and parts of Europe. Flo LeCompte did not expect him in Washington until late September.[21]

In August, 1946, the Senate appointed Ellender to chair a special committee to investigate charges against Mississippi senator Theodore Bilbo of intimidating blacks attempting to register to vote. Favoring only a state investigation of the charges, Ellender claimed Bilbo's critics wanted to win influence with black leaders and civil rights organizations. Bilbo, using only speeches to win reelection, not violence or coercion, had broken no election laws, Ellender said. In the investigation Ellender clashed with Taft, whom he admired. Ellender threatened to filibuster unless resolution of Bilbo's status was delayed until after the Mississippian had undergone cancer surgery at Ochsner Foundation Hospital in New Orleans. Ellender prevailed; the committee eventually cleared Bilbo of all charges.[22]

20. Joseph Francis Rummel to Allen Ellender, February 15, March 11, 1946, and Ellender to Rummel, February 28, 1946, all in "School Lunch and Milk Program" Folder, Box 211, AEP.

21. New Orleans *Times-Picayune,* August 5, 1945, in "1945–1947" Scrapbook, AEP; Allen Ellender to H. W. Hillyard, June 24, 1946, in "*Case* Bill" Folder, and "Claims, General" Folder, both in Box 581, AEP.

22. Garson, *The Democratic Party,* 206–210; unidentified clippings, August, 1946, in "1945–1947" Scrapbook, AEP; Allen Ellender to L. M. Haynie, November 29, 1947, in "Legislation, Strikes, 1947" Folder, Box 594, AEP. FBI File 62-81810 contains newspaper clippings dealing with Ellender's investigation, but like so many FBI records obtained through the Freedom of Information Act, significant pages are either missing or completely blacked out.

During the war Ellender received a tremendous volume of mail. Ignoring no correspondent, he answered constituents on a wide variety of wartime requests. He helped a Catholic priest who wanted to buy a new car but who did not have a trade-in required by a New Orleans Ford dealer. After receiving a letter from Ellender, the dealer "found" a car for the priest. He assisted old friends, like Plaquemines Parish boss Leander Perez, with jobs, postal appointments, nominations to the military academies, military transfers, early releases from military service, flood protection, disaster relief, and funds for canals, locks, and erosion control. He helped communities obtain propane gas for home heating.[23]

The Navy had expropriated land south of Houma for a base to house dirigibles, or blimps, used to patrol the Gulf of Mexico for German submarines. Schriever businessman Mervin Polmer informed Ellender in 1943 that landowners whose property had been seized had not been paid by the federal government. Ellender dashed off letters to the Justice Department and to the navy. His constituents soon had their money.[24]

Americans frequently complained about Office of Price Administration (OPA) policies and regulations. Retailers disliked Maximum Price Regulation 339 (rayon hosiery) and MPR 208 (work clothes). The OPA set different prices for wholesalers, chain stores, and independent retailers. "We are sunk," a Houma retailer wrote Ellender, if chain stores undersell us. Correspondents, complaining of the hardships of gasoline rationing, believed corruption and black market operations were widespread, but they rarely provided proof of their allegations. Ellender had opposed gas rationing until a study conducted by Bernard Baruch convinced him of its necessity. While he was recovering from food poisoning at Bethesda Naval Hospital on June 22, 1943, Ellender corresponded with a constituent about the OPA price of beans.[25]

Ellender, believing senators could be friends despite political differences, shipped twelve hundred pounds of potatoes to acquaintances in Washington

23. Raymond A. Wegmann to Allen Ellender, September 15, 1943, in "Office of Price Administration, General, 1943" Folder, Box 375, AEP; "Petroleum Administration for War, 1944" Folder, *passim,* and Florence Bruner to Ellender, June 12, 1943, in "Miscellaneous, 1948, Ellender Family" Folder, Box 76, AEP; Glen Jeansonne, *Leander Perez: Boss of the Delta* (Baton Rouge, 1977), 113–14.

24. "Justice—General—1943" Folder, *passim,* Box 126, AEP.

25. Allen Ellender to Julian McPhillips, June 29, 1943, in "OPA, 1943" Folder, Ellender to Leon Wolf, April 1, 1943, in "Office of Price Administration, 1943" Folder, P. H. Ferguson to Ellender, May 4, 1943, in "OPA, 1943" Folder, all in Box 116, AEP.

when foodstuffs were in short supply during the war. Drew Pearson, calling him "Potatoes" Ellender, incorrectly accused Ellender of profiting by selling potatoes to the Louisiana penitentiary. However, government supports for perishables at 90 percent of parity, Pearson reported correctly, had produced huge surpluses and gigantic spoilage problems.[26]

Despite the wartime environment, Ellender did not earn huge profits from his farming operations. In 1943, for instance, he earned $4,213 on gross farm sales of $22,746. His expenses exceeded $10,000 spent for wages, seed, fertilizer, taxes, and equipment. In fact, since the 1930s, his income had grown only moderately: $16,226 in 1941; $18,197 in 1942; and $21,467 in 1943.[27]

The manpower shortage struck Ellender's office in 1943. He lost Wurzlow—who had received a temporary deferment in March—to the military draft late in 1943. His capable office manager went to Officer Candidate School and was commissioned a first lieutenant in the army at Camp Lee, Virginia. He served on active duty until the end of the war in the quartermaster corps.[28] Like everybody else, Ellender had to adjust. He hired Augusta Peters from Shreveport in north Louisiana to help in the office.

Cooking became Ellender's trademark during the war. Terrebonne Parish clerk of court Randolph Bazet thought Ellender picked up the practice from Numa Montet, a Thibodaux congressman noted for his Louisiana dishes. Ellender practiced in Betty Wurzlow's kitchen on Saturdays, experimenting with recipes borrowed randomly. He may have gone to the Wurzlows because typically he would leave behind a messy kitchen—and Helen disliked having to clean up after him. Some of Ellender's best recipes came from people who received no credit. He borrowed a number from Mr. and Mrs. Calvin Rhodes who ran the City Cafe on 505 East Main Street in Houma. When Allen and Helen came to the cafe for a meal, they sometimes sent Allen Jr. to the movie theater nearby with young Riley Rhodes, who later had a restaurant of his own on Barrow Street. Riley gave Ellender his shrimp okra gumbo recipe, only to see it appear later as a creation of Senator Ellender. Flo provided the recipe for pecan pralines, which Ellender made

26. Drew Pearson, Washington *Post,* March 22, 1943, in "Allred" Folder, Box 198, AEP; New Orleans *Times-Picayune,* May 23, 1943, in "1942–1943" Scrapbook, AEP; Allen J. Matusow, *Farm Policies and Politics in the Truman Years* (Cambridge, Mass., 1967), 125–31.

27. Box 3, AEP.

28. Frank Wurzlow, Jr., interview, April 9, 1980; unidentified newspaper clippings, March, 1943, in "1942–1943" Scrapbook, AEP.

famous in Washington and Louisiana. After years of practice, Ellender's repertoire included typical Acadian dishes: gumbos, omelettes, courtbouillons, jambalayas, stews, pralines, and a number of fish and wild-game dishes. Ellender liked being the center of attention when he cooked, but he disliked seeing guests raise the lids of his pots.[29]

While Allen and Helen were in St. Louis in March, 1944, fire damaged much of the interior and a brick rear outside wall of their home in Houma. Helen's mother, Mrs. Charles M. Donnelly, and her sister Mrs. L. J. Barthet lived in the house. Quick work by the Houma Fire Department controlled the blaze. "Quite a few pieces of fine furniture that Helen had been gathering here and there for the past twenty-five years were ruined, some of them completely burned," Ellender wrote. His in-laws moved in with Claude and Thelma temporarily; their white spitz joined Helen, who sent a one-hundred-dollar check to the volunteer fire company. Ellender, remaining in Louisiana to settle insurance claims and arrange repairs, apologized to constituents in April for not answering his mail: "I had the misfortune of losing a part of my home by fire." Eager to observe the repair work, Ellender had to search for scarce building materials in May.[30]

Hunting and fishing continued to provide recreation for Ellender. He hunted grouse in North Dakota with Republican senator Milton Young, a member of the Agriculture Committee. He sent a pair of mallards shot in Louisiana to President Roosevelt and gave the president's thank-you note to the hunt organizer as a memento. Urging a businessman to call before visiting in September, 1944, Ellender said, "I usually go out fishing twice a week and I want to be sure that I will be around when you come."[31]

Ellender quietly aided Longites convicted in the scandals of 1939. Aware

---

29.   Byrne Ellender Legendre, interview, July 10, 1980; Frank Wurzlow, Jr., interview, April 9, 1980; Henry Ellender, Jr., interview, November 4, 1980; George Arceneaux, Jr., interview, December 31, 1979; Thelma Ellender, interview, June 30, 1980; Viola Lynch Ellender, interview, July 14, 1980; Noble Rogers, interview, June 30, 1980; Jack Carlos, interview, July 8, 1980; Florence LeCompte, interview, August 2, 1979; Randolph Bazet, interview, October 22, 1980; Riley Rhodes, interview, January 7, 1992.

30.   Allen Ellender to John E. Coxe, April 22, 1944, in "School Lunch Program—Hearings" Folder, Box 580, AEP; Houma (La.) *Courier*, March 30, 1944, in "1944" Scrapbook, AEP; Ellender to Richard Leche, May 31, 1944, in "Justice—Parole, Leche, Richard W." Folder, Box 126, AEP.

31.   Unidentified clippings, [November, 1944], in "1944" Scrapbook, AEP; Allen Ellender to Henry Kraak, September 5, 1944, in "Ellender, Allen J." Folder, and Ellender to Milton Young, October 8, 1945, in "Thank You" Folder, both in Box 989, AEP.

of the danger posed by active intervention on behalf of a convicted felon, he nonetheless maintained ties to former governor Richard Leche. Attorney General Francis Biddle feared unfavorable publicity. "I understand that Drew Pearson gets much of his dirty stuff through some source in the Justice Department," Ellender told Leche. He secured for Leche a transfer from the federal prison at Atlanta to an institution in Texarkana, where his family could more easily visit. Leche penciled long letters to Ellender, and Ellender sent chatty replies.[32]

In 1945 Ellender intervened in a dispute between education leaders in Louisiana to prevent the state from losing almost $400,000 in matching federal funds if State Superintendent of Education John E. Coxe and Frank Godchaux, president of the State Board of Education, did not settle their dispute over vocational education monies. By late September, Coxe and Godchaux came to terms, and U.S. Commissioner of Education John W. Studebaker released $800,000 for Louisiana vocational schools. Meanwhile, Shreveport *Times* editor John D. Ewing criticized Ellender for supporting S. 1080, a bill allowing state control of federal education funds. Ewing felt all federal education bills increased the possibility of racially integrated schools.[33]

On August 29, 1946, Ellender's mother, Victoria, suffered an early morning heart attack at home. Willard informed Allen by telephone, declaring her survival chances to be poor. Claude and Thelma, vacationing in the Rocky Mountains, had not been contacted. As Allen made arrangements to visit his mother, Flo LeCompte asked the FBI to help locate Claude and Thelma. The FBI finally reached them in Manitee Springs, Colorado. After Willard talked to Claude, he and Thelma drove to Houma in their 1942 Buick. Victoria, seventy-seven, died the next day. She was buried next to Wallace in the cemetery of St. Ann's Church in Bourg. Her four sons, her son-in-law, and a nephew were pallbearers. President Truman sent Allen a note of sympathy.

Victoria had continued to live alone in the family home Wallace had built on Hope Farm. The old house had become run down and neglected in recent years. Walterine and her husband, Charles Caillouette, who lived

32. Allen Ellender to Mrs. Richard Leche, October 3, 1942, Ellender to Leche, May 31, 1944, May 8, 1945, all in "Justice—Parole, Leche, Richard W.," Folder, Box 126, AEP.

33. Allen Ellender to John D. Ewing, July 23, 1945, and Ellender to John E. Coxe, September 22, 1945, both in "S. 1080" Folder, Box 591, AEP.

in Houston, thought the Ellender men had paid too little attention to their mother in her advanced years. Charles replaced broken screens, painted, and performed odd jobs when he and Walterine visited Victoria. After Victoria died, Walterine had to drive 335 miles from Houston, Charles complained, to place flowers on her grave because her brothers had neglected to do so.[34]

During the war, when Walterine and Charles visited Houma, they always left with their car loaded down with seafood, vegetables, and other items from Hope Farm, which was managed by Wallace Jr. Once on bidding them adieu for their return to Houston, Helen stood next to a pasture where Brother's bull, named Logan, grazed. Noting how the Caillouette car was loaded like a gypsy wagon, Helen wondered if they would have taken Logan if they had room for him. She sent a telegram to their home in Houston, which they found on arrival: "You forgot Logan!" Momentarily angry about the biting telegram, Walterine eventually took good-natured kidding about it, all of which became in time part of an oft-repeated family tale.[35]

Victoria's death made Ellender aware of his own mortality. He clarified property held in partnership with Elward Wright. In September and October, 1946, Wright filed counter letters in the Terrebonne Parish Courthouse, explaining legal technicalities of property held in his name, but owned in part by Ellender. Lots purchased by Wright were actually only one-third his, the documents explained. Ellender's ownership share was two-thirds, the documents made clear.[36]

From time to time, Ellender had taken an interest in legislation affecting the military status of medical students. In 1945, when Allen Jr. was on active duty, the senator amended a selective service bill to provide deferments for medical and graduate students. After the war, Ellender asked the War Department about a promotion for Allen Jr., then an army lieutenant. When the Pentagon said Allen Jr. and others Ellender had inquired about were low on the promotion list, he let the matter rest.[37]

After ten years in the Senate, Ellender still longed to be governor of

34. D. M. Ladd to Director, August 29, 30, 1946, FBI File 62-81810; Charles Caillouette, interview, November 23, 1979; Harry Truman to Allen Ellender, September 3, 1946, Post-Pres. Gen. Files, Box 559, HST; Houma (La.) *Courier,* September 5, 1946.

35. Florence LeCompte, interview, December 2, 1991.

36. The first letter, dated September 2, 1946, can be found in Terrebonne Parish Conveyance Book 151, Folio 656, the second, dated October 2, 1946, in Book 154, Folio 369, both in Terrebonne Parish Courthouse, Houma, La.

37. Clarke Fales to Allen Ellender, October 29, 1946, in "Miscellaneous, Ellender Family, 1946" Folder, Box 76, AEP; *Congressional Quarterly,* January–February–March, 1945, p. 331.

Louisiana. "I am still being urged to run for Governor in the next election and I am giving the matter most serious consideration," he wrote in June, 1946. Despite Earl Long's defeats, the Long organization had not proclaimed Ellender its leader. Only if the Longites rallied behind him, Ellender decided, would he enter the race for governor.

Although Ellender maintained the image of the frugal, honest southern agrarian, he had allowed a certain amount of media hype to creep in and distort his public image. For instance, his cooking talents, while real, were not accurately depicted. The senator did not seem to consider the deception dishonest and did not correct the errors. He came to take himself a bit too seriously, succumbing to the glitz and imagery of campaigns and lobbying in the nation's capital. After all, a certain amount of myth-making was expected of a senator.

Back in Louisiana, Ellender planned to relax in his usual way—touring the state, planting trees, fishing, hunting, and visiting friends and relatives. Once again he would consider his political options, this time at his leisure in the bayou country. "I want to get into every nook and cranny of Louisiana," he told an old friend. He would have to think the matter over carefully before deciding on a course of action.[38]

38. Allen Ellender to Nathan Bolton, June 1, 1946, in *"Case* Bill" Folder, Box 581, Richard Leche to Ellender, June 12, 1946, and Ellender to Leche, June 18, 1946, both in "Miscellaneous, Ellender, Allen J., 1945" Folder, Box 408, and "Louisiana Governorship for '48" Folder, *passim,* Box 76, all in AEP.

10

THE TRUMAN YEARS
(1947–48)

$\mathcal{S}$hortly after convening in January, 1947, the celebrated Eightieth Congress erupted into struggles over foreign policy, race, labor, and states' rights. Meanwhile, Allen Ellender's perennial political dilemma—to run for governor or seek another Senate term—would be complicated by a presidential election. Eleven years earlier, in 1936, when he grappled with presidential, gubernatorial, and senatorial races, Ellender had been ousted from the gubernatorial race. Concentrating on his legislative agenda in 1947, he said little about the forthcoming election in Louisiana.

The president's political problems continued. Blunter and more outspoken than Roosevelt, Truman could not hold together the Democratic coalition FDR had built. Trouble lurked on many fronts: labor wanted concessions, southerners resented civil rights bills, and Republicans controlled both houses of Congress (245 to 188 in the House, 51 to 45 in the Senate). Supported unenthusiastically by a fragmented party, Truman faced reelection in 1948.

Truman's racial proposals, based in part on a National Urban League report, shocked Ellender and southern segregationists. The president's committee on civil rights, which prepared a report titled "To Secure These Rights," recommended abolishing segregation in the armed forces, passing antilynching legislation, and establishing a permanent FEPC. In January, 1947, Richard Russell led the Southern Bloc in a filibuster against a permanent FEPC. The president's racial program, Ellender thought, was designed to dissuade Henry A. Wallace from running and to keep blacks from leaving the party. Liberal intellectuals supported civil rights measures.[1]

1. Richard Davies, "Social Welfare Policies," in *The Truman Period as a Research Field,*

Truman's labor policy also antagonized the South because it discouraged legislation to weaken or destroy safeguards established by the Wagner Act. Conservative Republicans and southern Democrats joined forces to promote labor measures akin to the Case Bill, which Truman had vetoed in 1946.[2] They drafted a new measure in 1947 bearing the names of Senator Robert Taft of Ohio and New Jersey congressman Fred Hartley.

The Taft-Hartley Bill, popular with congressmen who objected to the disruptive strikes of the postwar era, outlawed featherbedding (pay for work not performed) but restricted organized labor in several ways. It removed antiunion citizens' committees from National Labor Relations Board jurisdiction by changing the definition of *employer*. It outlawed secondary boycotts and prevented strong unions from helping weak ones. It permitted unfair labor practices charges against unions to linger before being settled. It denied men on strike the right to vote in representation elections. It permitted states to pass right-to-work laws. The bill required unions to submit financial reports, thereby exposing their weaknesses to industry. And by guaranteeing the rights of nonunion workers, it suggested that workers did not need unions.[3]

Although he opposed some harsh aspects of the bill, Ellender supported Taft-Hartley. "Industry as a whole has made huge profits since the war," he said. Believing that the Wagner Act gave labor unfair advantages over management, Ellender favored correcting imbalances. He wanted to force the National Labor Relations Board to recognize independent unions as genuine unions. Taft moderated Ellender's views on anticommunist oaths, presidential seizure power, and allowing striking workers to vote in bargaining elections. The Senate passed Taft's bill on May 13 by a vote of sixty-eight to twenty-four. Twenty-one Democrats, including Ellender and sixteen other southerners, voted for it.[4]

Truman vetoed Taft-Hartley because it weakened trade unions and in-

ed. Richard S. Kirkendall (Columbia, Mo., 1967), 174; Robert A. Garson, *The Democratic Party and the Politics of Sectionalism, 1941–1948* (Baton Rouge, 1974), 220–25, 227, 235; Gilbert C. Fite, *Richard B. Russell, Jr., Senator from Georgia* (Chapel Hill, 1991), 213, 227–28, 230–31, 218; James T. Patterson, *Mr. Republican: A Biography of Robert A. Taft* (Boston, 1972), 313, 335, 336, 338.

2. Fite, *Richard Russell*, 227–28.

3. Garson, *The Democratic Party*, 215; Barton Bernstein, "Economic Policies," in *The Truman Period*, ed. Kirkendall, 107; Thomas Becnel, *Labor, Church, and the Sugar Establishment: Louisiana, 1887–1976* (Baton Rouge, 1980), 26.

4. Patterson, *Mr. Republican*, 356, 364, 366; Becnel, *Labor, Church, and the Sugar Establishment*, 26.

terfered with collective bargaining. Ellender said he would vote to override, which Congress quickly and easily did. Except for Congressmen Hale Boggs of New Orleans and Jimmy Morrison of Hammond, the entire Louisiana congressional delegation voted to override.[5]

Favoring Ellender's stand, some constituents called for a more restrictive bill. A more repressive measure, Ellender reminded them, would have received insufficient support to override a presidential veto. The National Catholic Welfare Conference, a group supporting the rights of workers, opposed Taft-Hartley. Ellender's files contain *Rerum Novarum,* Pope Leo XII's encyclical on labor. He had underlined in red the sections on socialism and communism.[6]

Meanwhile, Ellender again considered running for governor of Louisiana. He undoubtedly discussed the subject with Governor Jimmie Davis, who stopped by for a visit in April, 1947. Ellender, trying "to get right with labor," stalled in May about announcing his intentions. In July he went on a "pulse-feeling tour" of Louisiana. In August, while in New Orleans for an eye examination and a round of golf with baseball commissioner A. B. "Happy" Chandler of Kentucky, Ellender promised to announce "pretty soon" his intentions for the January 20, 1948, Democratic primary. Former governors Earl Long and Sam Jones, Hammond attorney Jimmy Morrison, and Secretary of State Wade O. Martin, Jr., had already announced. Finally, in mid-September, Ellender announced his decision: "Since most of the candidates are personal and political friends I have decided not to take part in the first primary." Although officially neutral in the race, Ellender quietly supported Earl Long. Senior senator John Overton endorsed Sam Jones. In October, 1947, Ellender thought Long's popularity in the Acadian country around Terrebonne Parish indicated he would win.[7]

Helen considered Earl Long a crude bumpkin, but when he was cam-

5.   Garson, *The Democratic Party,* 217–19; Becnel, *Labor, Church, and the Sugar Establishment,* 27; Edgar Poe, New Orleans *Times-Picayune,* June 20, 23, 1947, in "1945–1947" Scrapbook, Allen J. Ellender Papers, Nicholls State University Library, Thibodaux, La., hereinafter cited as AEP.

6.   John U. Barr to Allen Ellender, May 19, 1947, and Ellender to Barr, May 21, 1947, both in "Labor, 1947" Folder, Box 463, AEP; "Labor, 1948" Folder, *passim, ibid.*

7.   Edgar Poe, New Orleans *Times-Picayune,* April 12, 1947, E. M. Clinton, *ibid.,* May 11, 1947, Edgar Poe, *ibid.,* July 26, August 6, 1947, Houma *Courier,* September 26, 1947, all in "1945–1947" Scrapbook, AEP; Allen Ellender to Roy O. Martin, October 30, 1947, Ellender to R. T. Douglas, September 23, 1947, and Ellender to Earl Long, October 3, 1947, all in "Louisiana Governorship for '48" Folder, Box 76, AEP.

paigning in Houma, she invited friends to a formal political luncheon for Earl at her home. As guests milled about the house, Helen's cook, Eva, brought a tray of hors d'oeuvres into the formal dining room. Glancing at the fare, Earl announced in a loud voice, "I don't eat that." Later, on rejecting other items brought in, Earl proclaimed, "I don't eat most of this stuff." Furious but calm, Helen rang the little china bell used to summon the cook and said: "Eva, fry Mr. Long some eggs."[8] Earl won easily without visible support from Ellender—or Helen.

Governor-elect Long, coming to Washington early in May, 1948, talked privately with Ellender before accompanying him to visit President Truman. They discussed the 1948 election, in which both Truman and Ellender would face reelection. Southern Democrats, dissatisfied with civil rights and tidelands oil policies, contemplated third-party efforts. After the meeting with the president, Ellender took Long on a sight-seeing tour of Washington and to lunch at the Statler Hotel, where they talked for three hours.[9]

Long and Ellender undoubtedly discussed election year political nuances with Truman. Long remained a loyal Democrat because of his income tax problems and his desire to obtain additional Social Security funds for Louisiana. Eager to accept a compromise offer by the federal government on offshore oil lands, Long acquiesced to Leander Perez and his followers, who convinced him to hold out for bigger concessions. During Long's second term of office, from 1948 to 1952, more than 100,000 blacks registered as Louisiana voters.[10]

Less than two weeks after Long and Ellender's meeting with Truman, John Overton died at the age of seventy-two. He had undergone abdominal surgery at Bethesda Naval Hospital. Ellender served as a pallbearer for the old Longite whose first election campaign he had managed. Now the senior senator, Ellender asked for and received Overton's seat on the powerful Appropriations Committee. Long, planning to campaign for Huey's son, Russell, for the vacant Senate seat, appointed oilman William C. Feazel of West Monroe to fill the unexpired portion of Overton's term.[11]

8. Florence LeCompte, interview, December 2, 1991.

9. Paul Wooton, New Orleans *Times-Picayune,* May 4, 1948, in "1948" Scrapbook, AEP.

10. Michael L. Kurtz and Morgan D. Peoples, *Earl K. Long: The Saga of Uncle Earl and Louisiana Politics* (Baton Rouge, 1990), 148–49, 194; Glen Jeansonne, *Leander Perez: Boss of the Delta* (Baton Rouge, 1977), 319; Allen Ellender to Don Ewing, August 9, 1948, Box 1826, AEP.

11. Edgar Poe, New Orleans *Times-Picayune,* May 17, 1948, in "1948" Scrapbook, AEP; Kurtz and Peoples, *Earl Long,* 144.

Back in Washington, Ellender engaged in the political rhetoric of the new congressional session that began in January, 1948. He talked about race, labor, and foreign affairs. He was surprised—in his words "shocked"—by Truman's civil rights proposals, and he threatened a filibuster against these "obnoxious measures." The president "has completely surrendered to the labor bosses and labor racketeers," he said. He saw civil rights as a conspiracy: "I am convinced that the program was conceived by the Communist Party, which so cleverly propagandized it that a small group of so-called liberal and intellectual Negroes adopted and promoted it as the Negroes' own program for advancement." [12]

Ellender revealed his deep-seated racial prejudices when black labor leader A. Philip Randolph testified at a Labor Committee hearing. Refusing to call the president of the Brotherhood of Sleeping Car Porters Union "Mr. Randolph," Ellender called him simply "Randolph." When Randolph asked to be called "Mister," Ellender said he did not choose to use the courtesy title to address the witness. Both men adjusted and continued—Randolph answered Ellender's questions; Ellender used no name at all when he spoke to the labor leader. Like Richard Russell, Ellender assumed blacks to be inferior to whites. Neither senator advocated violence, race baiting, or crude slurs, but each feared "mongrelization" of the races would weaken the vigor of Anglo-Saxon traditions in the United States. Civil rights legislation, both believed, discriminated against the South, already unfairly accused of many wrongs. [13]

Ellender hedged on his labor stance, but on race he did not equivocate. Southerners working within the Democratic Party had for years blocked poll tax and antilynching legislation, he told a Dixiecrat. In a campaign radio speech, he explained the evil of civil rights bills. "They are the insidious means to an evil end," he said. "That end is complete and absolute social equality, an amalgamation of blood, a total erasure of the color line." For quick reference, Ellender kept near at hand black crime statistics and Article 94 of the Civil Code of Louisiana, which prohibited interracial marriages. Blacks could not govern themselves, he said; those who had gotten ahead in the world were part white. "Mongrelization" in Egypt, Brazil, and India had destroyed white civilizations, he believed. [14]

12.   Edgar Poe, New Orleans *Times-Picayune,* February 4, 5, March 4, 1948, in "1948" Scrapbook, AEP.

13.   New Orleans *Times-Picayune,* June 13, 1947, *Newsweek,* June 23, 1947, both in "1945–1947" Scrapbook, AEP; Fite, *Richard Russell,* 165, 167.

14.   Allen Ellender to William Caskey, August 9, 1948, Box 1825, AEP; Ellender speeches

On most other issues too Ellender had developed a political stance. During the war he had become critical of U.S. foreign policy and, in particular, of aid to Britain. He accused the British of getting "unnecessarily involved" in Greece after the Russians had driven the Axis forces out. If the British had not been preoccupied with the Aegean Peninsula, he thought, they could have driven the Germans out of North Africa. Like Richard Russell and Robert Taft, the conservative Republican from Ohio, Ellender supported the Marshall Plan and the Truman Doctrine to aid Greece and Turkey, but with reservations about high costs. "Fortunately, Senator Russell and I saw eye to eye in this foreign aid program," he wrote, "and we consistently voted against it after the European recovery [in the late 1940s]." [15]

Ellender fought the St. Lawrence Seaway project, the plan to connect the Great Lakes to the Atlantic, which he viewed as a competitive threat to Mississippi River traffic and the Port of New Orleans. It was not fair, he asserted, to tax Americans to pay for a waterway running mostly through Canada, since there was no guarantee of perpetual free U.S. access through it. [16]

From time to time Ellender joined Republicans in bipartisan legislation. He endorsed Taft's education bill introduced in February, 1947. "I am concerned that the federal government should and must come to the aid of the poorer states in providing adequate educational facilities for children," he said. "I take the position that education transcends state lines." Disingenuously adding his racial escape clause, Ellender said, "I am unalterably opposed to giving the federal government any direct supervision over state schools. I have always been insistent that any funds provided by the Federal Government should be administered by the individual states." Reiterating his support for the child-benefit theory, Ellender said, "I was in the Louisiana Legislature when that law was placed on the statute books and I approved of this position." Taft, promoting equality of educational opportunity, worried too about using public funds for religious schools. [17]

and statistical materials on race, in "Hospitals" Folder, "Civil Rights" Folder, both in Box 1442, AEP; Ellender radio speech, August 13, 1948, in Elward Wright Papers, in possession of Thomas Wright, Houma, La.

15. Chicago *Tribune,* December 7, 1947, in "1945–1947" Scrapbook, AEP; Fite, *Richard Russell,* 195, 222; Patterson, *Mr. Republican,* 370, 384–85; Hugh Cates, "Allen Ellender, Oral History No. 149," April 30, 1971, in Richard B. Russell Collection, Richard B. Russell Memorial Library, University of Georgia, Athens, 11, hereinafter cited as Ellender interview for UGA.

16. New Orleans *Times-Picayune,* February 18, 1948, in "1948" Scrapbook, AEP.

17. Allen Ellender to many Baptists, July 8, 1947, and Ellender to many constituents, March, 1948, both in "Federal Aid to Educ." Folder, Box 590, AEP; New Orleans *Times-*

Many Americans lived in substandard housing, Ellender realized. Since 1943, when the Louisiana senator served on a housing subcommittee with Taft and Robert Wagner, a liberal Democrat from New York, he took an atypical southern view of public housing legislation. Observers were surprised to see conservatives Ellender and Taft join the urban-liberal Wagner on housing. Real estate interests and Republicans in the House opposed housing legislation. In 1945, Wagner and Ellender introduced a measure to liberalize Federal Housing Authority mortgages and to build 1.2 million housing units per year for the next five years. In 1946 a similar bill, the Wagner-Ellender-Taft housing bill, would have provided 1.25 million units per year, slum clearance, easy FHA loans, and provisions for tenants to pay one-fifth of their income in rent. It passed the Senate but died in the House Banking and Currency Committee. In April, 1948, the Senate passed the Taft-Ellender-Wagner Housing Bill, a measure similar to the 1946 bill. Once again, the House rejected the bill.[18]

Before adjourning on June 21 for the national conventions, Congress renewed the military draft, passed a farm bill, and created the Department of Defense. It rejected universal military training, a civil rights bill, public housing, aid to education, and a higher minimum wage. Truman astutely blamed the Republicans and conservative southerners for labor, price-control, and race problems. Blocking repeal of New Deal reforms, Truman used executive action to strengthen some programs. On July 26, 1948, the president called the Congress into a special session—opening it one day after what Missourians call Turnip Day—to give the Republicans a chance to enact their platform. The Turnip Session produced no significant legislation, but it helped Truman shift blame to the Republicans. Minneapolis mayor Hubert H. Humphrey's civil rights speech at the Democratic convention symbolized Truman's racial stance.[19]

Dissident Democrats, meeting in Birmingham on July 17, 1948, formed the States' Rights Party—headline writers popularized the term Dixiecrats—and nominated Governor J. Strom Thurmond of South Carolina for president and Governor Fielding Wright of Mississippi for vice-president. Prom-

Picayune, February 2, 1947, in "1945–1947" Scrapbook, AEP; Patterson, *Mr. Republican,* 321–22.

    18.   Patterson, *Mr. Republican,* 315–20; Walter Johnson, ed., *The Papers of Adlai Stevenson* (8 vols.; Boston, 1973), III, 25n; Shreveport *Times,* April 21, 1948, in "1948" Scrapbook, AEP.

    19.   Davies, "Social Welfare Policies," in *The Truman Period,* ed. Kirkendall, 170–71, 179; Bernstein, "Economic Policies," *ibid.,* 106, 110–11; Garson, *The Democratic Party,* 278.

inent anti-Longites Sam Jones and Judge Robert Kennon of Minden joined Plaquemines Parish boss Leander Perez and third-party leader John U. Barr in the new party. Barr, a right-wing New Orleans businessman and an anti-Longite, also supported right-to-work legislation. Louisiana congressmen F. Edward Hebert of New Orleans, James Domengeaux of Lafayette, and Otto Passman of Monroe also joined. Ellender, Earl Long, and Russell Long did not associate with the splinter group.[20]

Southern conservatives joined the Dixiecrat movement for a number of reasons: race, labor policies, tidelands oil, foreign policy, communism, and states' rights. Seniority kept prominent southern Democrats from joining the movement. Based on orthodox membership in the major parties, seniority determined chairmanships and power in Congress. Party loyalty protected seniority; consequently, ranking party leaders generally ignored third-party movements. Even though Ellender agreed with the racial and tidelands policies of the Dixiecrats, he never considered bolting his party. Had Senator James Eastland of Mississippi withdrawn from the Democratic Party, he told Leander Perez, he would be removed as chairman of the Senate Judiciary Committee, which influenced civil rights legislation. Ellender, explaining seniority to supporters in north Louisiana, reminded them of a Louisiana law prohibiting a member of one party from participating in the primary of another party.

At a meeting of the Democratic State Central Committee on March 6, 1948, Perez and the Dixiecrats had tried to secede from the national party. But Ellender and Earl Long foiled the defection attempt. Ellender, Hale Boggs, Earl's brother George Long, and Orleans Parish Assessor Jimmy Comiskey received seats at the national convention.[21]

Several days after the Dixiecrats met in Birmingham, Ellender returned to Washington to oppose civil rights legislation. Claiming to be "not so happy" to be back in the capital, Ellender probably welcomed a chance to convince southern Democrats that his views on race had not changed, even though he spurned the Dixiecrats. Ready for a filibuster if necessary, he proclaimed, "I've got a 50-hour speech in my system." As a member of a five-man southern Democratic steering committee, he helped to block legislation. During time for "amending the journal" southerners took the

20. Kurtz and Peoples, *Earl Long,* 148–51; Fite, *Richard Russell,* 241; Garson, *The Democratic Party,* 258, 281, 298; Ellender interview for UGA, 9–10.

21. Kurtz and Peoples, *Earl Long,* 149–50, Edgar Poe, New Orleans *Times-Picayune,* November 24, 1948, in "1948" Scrapbook, AEP.

floor—and kept it all day. Because amending the journal was not considered an official "measure," opponents were powerless to invoke cloture.[22]

Despite the racial vituperation, Ellender's 1948 reelection campaign was typical of the previous one—and uneventful. Elward Wright, as usual, managed it with help from Claude and Wurzlow, who had left Ellender's staff after the war and was now first assistant to the Terrebonne Parish clerk of court. Ellender had a healthy campaign chest, and his opponent, Dixiecrat James Domengeaux, was little known statewide. Hoping to ignore the Dixiecrats and say as little as possible about Truman, Ellender decided to capitalize on his reputation as a friend of farmers and ordinary people. To a concerned supporter, Ellender wrote, "I don't see why we should get excited over Truman because he has no chance to be elected President."[23]

Although Ellender downplayed Truman's chances of winning, he in many ways was like the Missourian. Both were honest, outspoken, and direct, products of the land and content to call themselves farmers. Both as young men had referred to blacks as "niggers." Each had aspired to the governor's mansion, but had been selected to run for the Senate instead by forceful leaders whose organizations later floundered in scandal: Tom Pendergast's in Missouri; Huey Long's in Louisiana. Both came up under articulate mentors whose obfuscation frequently left listeners wondering what they meant: Franklin Roosevelt and Huey Long. Neither was considered brilliant, but both worked hard and achieved success with average ability.

Truman, however, had changed, most notably on civil rights legislation. Believing segregation policies discriminatory, Truman modified his racial position, calling for an end to discrimination and violence by implementing the findings of his Civil Rights Commission, "To Secure These Rights."[24]

A congressman since 1941, Domengeaux, knowing he did not have a chance against Ellender without support from deLesseps Morrison and other anti-Longites, admitted, "I was a cripple." He was a gambler reputed on Capitol Hill to be a first-rate poker player—he played for big stakes with Clinton Anderson of New Mexico and Everett Dirksen of Illinois. Domengeaux, thinking he would lose his House seat, took a chance on winning

22. Shreveport *Times,* July 26, 1949, in "1948" Scrapbook, AEP.

23. Allen Ellender to William Caskey, August 9, 1948, Box 1825, AEP.

24. David McCullough, *Truman* (New York, 1992), 194, 200, 247, 587–88; Ronald Steel, "Harry of Sunnybrook Farm," a review of David McCullough's *Truman* in *New Republic,* August 10, 1993, p. 39.

Ellender's Senate seat. A practical joker who once served muskrat at a Washington luncheon in an attempt to ridicule Ellender's culinary exploits, Domengeaux had a meager legislative record. When the League of Women Voters asked for a debate, Ellender refused with a curt reply: "I am not going to give him the opportunity of getting free advertisement at my expense." [25]

Domengeaux, saying Ellender was the candidate of the rich and the special interests, tried frantically to develop an issue. The *Times-Picayune* did not think he had much of a chance against Ellender, who said he supported Truman on most things. He would continue to oppose him on race and tidelands oil.[26] Though confident of victory, Ellender collected funds from his usual sources. Eager to separate campaign funds from other revenues, Ellender told Wright the "Public Relations" (or "Radio Account") was different from the Allen J. Ellender "Campaign Fund," which was not to have "money that was contributed to me for radio purposes" during the Taft-Hartley fight. Instead of returning unused campaign contributions, Ellender asked donors for permission to transfer surpluses to his radio fund. He spent approximately four thousand dollars annually to record radio broadcasts. Stations in Louisiana gave him free airtime.

W. Horace Williams, the north Louisiana contractor, gathered contributions from shipbuilder Andrew Higgins and from New Orleans businessmen Alfred Moran and Leon Heymann. A contractor who had given $1,000 to the radio fund balked at giving more. In midsummer Administrative Assistant Gilbert Fortier went to New Orleans to pick up $25,000. It would be used for radio ($8,000), parish expenses ($6,400), advertising ($3,000), travel ($2,500), stationery ($1,850), and mailing ($1,800). Limiting contributions to $5,000, Fortier refused gifts from banks, labor unions, and big corporations. He wanted to avoid gifts from "people who might feel that they have purchased the Senator body and soul because of small or large contributions." One campaign checkbook in Ellender's office showed a balance of $11,900.[27]

25. James Domengeaux, interview, December 23, 1980; Allen Ellender to William Caskey, August 9, 1948, Ellender to E. F. Creekmore, August 9, 1948, and Ellender to Martha Robinson, August 10, 1948, all in Box 1825, AEP; Kurtz and Peoples, *Earl Long,* 145.

26. Shreveport *Times,* July 27, 1948, New Orleans *Times-Picayune,* September 9, November 7, 1948, all in "1948" Scrapbook, AEP.

27. Allen Ellender to Elward Wright, July 29, 1948, Box 1825, Gilbert Fortier to Florence LeCompte, July 29, 1948, Box 1826, W. Horace Williams to Fortier, August 13, 1948, Box 1823, Ellender to Theodore Granik, October 29, 1948, in "Senator E., Personal" Folder, Box 993, all in AEP.

Because the Taft-Hartley fight had alienated organized labor, Ellender and Wright tried to differentiate between working men and unions. Professing to be for the working man but against corrupt labor leaders, Ellender wrote in 1948: "I have always done everything I could for the laboring man, and I am in favor of labor unions if they are administered properly, but many labor unions have been victimized by these racketeers." Industry, he said, could do something about inflationary wage increases. "In other words," he wrote, "if profits are much greater than they were before the war, it might be well for industry to think about reducing prices so as to offset the necessity for more wage increases." After examining congressional voting records, AFL president William Green and Louisiana Federation of Labor president E. H. "Lige" Williams designated Ellender an opponent of labor.[28] Realizing he would not get a union endorsement, Ellender voted for Taft-Hartley—and probably improved his reelection chances.

During the campaign Ellender labeled a bill sponsored by Senator Karl Mundt of South Dakota and Congressman Richard Nixon of California to more closely regulate the activities of communists in America "vicious." Claiming its "Gestapo methods" would deprive Americans of freedom of speech, Ellender explained that the bill would affect "not communists but good substantial American citizens who happen to be of liberal inclination and belief." Domengeaux called Ellender's statement a last-ditch effort to win labor support before the August 31 primary. As expected, Ellender won a lopsided 284,293 to 119,459 victory over Domengeaux, garnering nearly 62 percent of the votes cast.[29] But Earl Long—endowed with the Long name and winning the highest office in the state—had clearly established himself as the leading political figure in Louisiana.

Ellender had not neglected congressional legislation during the campaign. A major defender of the domestic sugar industry, he had used his influence in 1947 to delay removal of price ceilings and rationing controls on sugar until the end of October when Louisiana raw sugar went to market. Knowing prices would rise when wartime agencies removed controls, Ellender wanted his Louisiana constituents to share in the prosperity. Ellender

28. Becnel, *Labor, Church, and the Sugar Establishment*, 26; Elward Wright, interview, November 8, 1979; Allen Ellender to Gilbert Fortier, September 8, 1948, in "Miscellaneous Office Memos to and from Houma—1948" Folder, Box 76, AEP; various newspaper clippings, April 6, 1948, Box 1826, AEP.

29. Unidentified newspaper clippings, n.d., in "1948" Scrapbook, AEP; New Orleans *Times-Picayune*, September 9, 1948.

shielded the Sugar Act, scheduled to expire in 1948, with an amendment extending its life for three years.[30]

Senator Richard Russell of Georgia, wishing to give southerners an alternative to Truman, offered himself for the presidential nomination at the Democratic National Convention in 1948. Rejected strongly by delegates from the North, he lost, despite unusual support from Republican senator Milton Young of North Dakota, Ellender's close friend who claimed he was nearly banished from the Republican Party for campaigning for Russell among Senate Democrats. Russell would have been a good president, Ellender thought. As expected, the Democrats selected Truman.[31]

Truman's vitality in the 1948 presidential campaign surprised many political observers who had conceded the election to Republican governor Thomas Dewey of New York. The two third-party candidates—Progressive Henry A. Wallace and Dixiecrat J. Strom Thurmond—were expected to attract Democratic voters and hurt Truman's chances. At a press conference in May, Truman alluded to campaigning in Louisiana: "Senator Ellender invited me to pay a visit to the South, and I told him nothing would please me better if it could be arranged."[32]

Truman defeated Dewey in November in one of the closest political races in U.S. history. After the elections, Ellender struggled to keep the Dixiecrats—they carried Louisiana—from embarrassing the Louisiana Democrats and alienating the national party. Attempting to make peace with Truman and the Democrats, Ellender tried to convince Dixiecrats to cast their electoral votes for Truman. He failed. All the while, Ellender said he would continue to oppose Truman's racial policies.[33]

Despite the presence of a papal encyclical on labor in the senator's files, Ellender was not a religious person. Formal religion did not affect Ellender's thinking regarding social or political issues. Baptized in the Roman Catholic church, Ellender seldom attended church services and joined no congregation. Voters in south Louisiana assumed that he was a Catholic, those in north Louisiana that he was a Protestant. His ambition to become governor

30. Becnel, *Labor, Church, and the Sugar Establishment,* 35, 81.

31. Ellender interview for UGA, 9–10; Fite, *Richard Russell,* 241.

32. Patterson, *Mr. Republican,* 393, 394; Clark Clifford, *Counsel to the President: A Memoir* (New York, 1991), 120–22; *Public Papers of the Presidents of the United States: Harry S. Truman* (8 vols.; Washington, D.C., 1964), IV, 278–79.

33. Edgar Poe, New Orleans *Times-Picayune,* November 24, 1948.

of Louisiana prompted him to downplay his Catholic background and to list himself as a Presbyterian. Catholic candidates did not win Protestant votes in north Louisiana, so Catholics rarely became governor of Louisiana.[34] In addition to the religious deception, Ellender's congressional biographical sketch incorrectly stated his age (his date of birth was listed as 1891) and his military record (he was listed as a World War I veteran).

Ellender doubted basic Christian religious tenets. Professing to believe in God, he could not or would not accept some doctrines on faith. He once shocked Flo LeCompte by saying Christ was a good man but not God. "Why don't you become a Jew?" she shot back. Despising the commercialism of religion, he hated extravagant church ceremonies and displays, especially in areas where parishioners endured poverty.

A number of family stories explain Ellender's religious evolution and history. He soured on religion, one version suggests, while attending St. Aloysius. Perhaps rebelling at the school's compulsory church attendance policy, Ellender chose not to attend church after graduation. He had not attended in fifteen or twenty years, he said in 1932, which meant that his nonattendance began after he left St. Aloysius. Another story attributes his apathy to a priest's refusal to bury a divorced friend of Ellender's with full rites. Ellender may have decided to call himself a Presbyterian because he was impressed by the Rev. J. M. "Possum" Blackburn, a popular Presbyterian minister in Houma who hunted rabbits with Ellender and Charles Cail-louette, Ellender's brother-in-law. Blackburn refused to hunt on Sundays with Catholic boys who had not attended Mass. Fascinated by Presbyterian minister Peter Marshall, the Senate chaplain, Ellender read some of Marshall's writings and once proclaimed, "I belong to Peter Marshall's church." Despite these testimonials, he was not active in any church. "He was not a practicing anything," Allen Jr. recalled.[35]

Ellender helped his Catholic constituents in a number of ways. He assisted priests eager to acquire surplus chapels from deactivated military bases. The wooden structures usually wound up in rural country parishes. He sent Army-Navy football tickets—with a reminder that they were five dollars each—to two New Orleans priests attending Catholic University in Wash-

---

34. Frank Wurzlow, Jr., interview, April 9, 1980; Randolph Bazet, interview, October 22, 1980; Allen Ellender, Jr., interview, June 6, 1980.

35. Florence LeCompte, interview, September 4, 1979; Thelma Ellender, interview, June 30, 1980; Frank Wurzlow, Jr., interview, April 9, 1980; George Arceneaux, Jr., interview, December 31, 1970; Allen Ellender, Jr., interview, June 6, 1980.

ington. He conferred with railroad executives about obtaining free travel passes on their lines for Catholic nuns. Some lines accommodated the nuns, others refused. When the superintendent of schools for the Archdiocese of New Orleans asked him to prevent cuts in appropriations for school lunches, Ellender blamed Republicans for the cuts.[36]

The senator was health-conscious long before fitness became an American obsession. Because he was physically fit, he appeared younger than he was. He had quit smoking in the late 1930s and had reduced his alcohol consumption. He worked out regularly at the Senate gymnasium. He liked to strike a punching bag and once posed as a boxer for a free-lance photographer. He took up golf—a sport casually taken up by Huey Long—but avoided the courses where golfing congressmen gathered, especially the Army-Navy Country Club, Chevy Chase, and Burning Tree. Mostly he played at the Old Soldiers' Home, which had no greens fee or membership dues, with Republican senator Milton Young of North Dakota. More noted for determination than skill, the five-foot-four Ellender played year-round, regardless of the weather. Frank Wurzlow, Jr., remembers playing with ice on the ground. When he played with Wurzlow, whom he always beat, Ellender conceded three- and four-foot putts to himself.[37]

Helen had gradually become involved in the activities of Senate Wives, a social group interested in civic work. She chaired the Flowers and Decorations Committee in April, 1948, when Bess Truman was a guest. The group served ham, Louisiana strawberries, and cake. Like Allen, Helen displayed her culinary skills. A Washington newspaper once ran a three-column photograph of her cooking gumbo.[38]

For some time Allen and Helen had planned to move into more spacious accommodations in Washington. Anticipating a need for furniture, Helen sent pieces damaged in the 1944 fire to a New Orleans repair shop. The firm's outrageous delays in completing the task prompted Ellender to com-

36. Fite, *Richard Russell,* 214; Henry Bezou to Allen Ellender, May 27, 1947, and Ellender to Bezou, May 29, 1947, both in "School Lunch" Folder, Box 169, AEP; Charles J. Plauche to Allen Ellender, July 3, 1947, and Ellender to Plauche, July 7, 1947, both in "War Assets Administration, 1947" Folder, Box 42, AEP; Raymond A. Wegmann to Ellender, November 20, 1947, and Ellender to Wegmann, November 21, 1947, both in "Miscellaneous W 1947" Folder, Box 408, AEP.

37. Frank Wurzlow, Jr., interview, April 9, 1980; George Arceneaux, Jr., interview, December 31, 1979.

38. New Orleans *Times-Picayune,* April 29, 1948, and Lucia Brown, Washington *Post,* June 18, 1948, both in "1948" Scrapbook, AEP.

plain in 1947 and 1948; on one occasion he said a craftsman's word was not worth "a tinker's dam." Reporting on scarce and expensive housing in Washington, Administrative Assistant Gilbert Fortier said reasonably priced apartments rented quickly. Helen would have to see for herself the houses on the market. Russell Long paid twenty-six thousand dollars for a house near Rock Creek Parkway, north of the Capitol near the Walter Reed Army Medical Center, he said.[39]

In August, 1947, Ellender bought a Chevrolet sports coupe from a dealer in Maryland for Allen Jr., then a captain in the Army. Making all the arrangements, Fortier sent a check for $1,411.55 (and instructed the dealer to deliver the vehicle to Ellender's parking spot—No. 134—in the Senate garage). Ellender departed shortly afterward in his black 1946 Buick with congressional license plates for Seattle to join other senators for an inspection tour of the Pacific. While he was in Alaska, Helen's sister Mrs. Louis J. Barthet died at her home in Abita Springs north of Lake Pontchartrain, where the Ellenders had spent many peaceful vacation hours. Ellender's office tried unsuccessfully to notify him en route.[40]

When in Louisiana, Ellender was relatively free from congressional matters. He fished, hunted, and cared for business affairs. Upon leasing his Coteau land to tenant Harris Pitre in 1948, "a very good boy," Ellender gave up farming. He turned down offers to sell his royalty in a strip of land near the Lirette Gas Field in Terrebonne Parish. In November he inquired if the Post Office in Houma had office space he could use. Finding none available, the Public Building Administration advised him to rent private accommodations and send his invoices to the sergeant-at-arms of the Senate. Meanwhile, Ellender informed local realtors of various properties he had to rent or lease.[41]

When Harvey Peltier of Thibodaux inquired about prospects for the sugar industry in 1948, Ellender reiterated his faith in land. "The old saying that the best investment on earth is earth itself is something I would ponder

39. Allen Ellender to J. Herman, February 27, 1947–November 8, 1948, and Gilbert Fortier to Florence LeCompte, November 18, 1948, both in "Senator E., Personal" Folder, Box 993, AEP.

40. Gilbert Fortier to Allen Ellender, Jr., August 20, 1947, in "Senator E. (Personal)" Folder, Box 989, and unidentified newspaper clipping, n.d., in "1948" Scrapbook, both in AEP.

41. Allen Ellender to Arthur Gayle, December 9, 1948, Ellender to Mattingly Tractor and Implement Company, June 5, 1948, Ellender to John Todd, December 2, 1948, Edward F. McGinnis to Ellender, November 8, 1948, and Ellender to C. R. Patterson, November 8, 1948, all in "Senator E., Personal" Folder, Box 993, AEP.

for a long while before I would dispose of my cane lands, if I were in your place," he wrote. "If I had to choose between having a $100,000 farm and $100,000 in the bank, I would keep the farm any time." In the summer, Ellender paid $3,900 for thirteen town lots in Houma near the Intracoastal Canal.[42]

In 1935 Allen's brother Willard and their cousin Ernest had opened Ellender Memorial Hospital, a twenty-two-bed structure in a refurbished wooden building moved near Allen's home. In September, 1948, Allen asked Secretary of State Wade O. Martin for legal advice about establishing a hospital in Houma. The senator wanted to help his son, his brother, and several Ellender cousins who were doctors build a hospital. The doctors Ellender—known in Houma as Dr. Allen, Dr. Willard, and Dr. Ernest to avoid confusion—hoped to replace their private facility with a small public hospital. "It is my idea to erect a memorial to my father and late uncles," Allen wrote. The small Ellender hospital closed in 1954 when Terrebonne General Hospital, a public Hill-Burton–financed facility, opened.[43]

By the end of 1948, Earl Long was governor, but Ellender had won an impressive reelection victory. As senior senator, he would return to the Senate to complete work on housing and education bills he and Taft and Wagner had sponsored but failed to pass. He had coauthored the Free School Lunch Act of 1946 and would continue to be a significant voice on the Agriculture Committee. His standing in the Senate had grown; he was now more than just a senator. Perhaps he could now forsake the idea of becoming governor of Louisiana.

42. Allen Ellender to Harvey Peltier, June 10, 1948, in "Agriculture, Sugar, 1948" Folder, Box 177, AEP; Terrebonne Parish Conveyance Book 161, Folio 539, in Terrebonne Parish Courthouse, Houma, La.

43. Allen Ellender to Wade O. Martin, Jr., September 17, 1948, in "Senator E., Personal" Folder, Box 993, AEP; Allen Ellender, Jr., interview, November 18, 1991; Houma (La.) *Daily Courier,* July 1, 1979.

PART THREE

Worldview

II

The Death of Helen

(1949–50)

$\mathcal{T}$ ruman's surprising victory in the 1948 presidential election helped the Democrats regain control of both houses of Congress at the start of the Eighty-first Congress. On the Agriculture Committee Allen Ellender ranked second to Chairman Elmer Thomas of Oklahoma. The Legislative Reorganization Act of 1946 had abolished the Claims Committee, which Ellender had chaired. In order to remain on the Appropriations Committee, Ellender had to resign from the Education and Labor Committee (renamed the Labor and Public Welfare Committee).

Ellender's new responsibilities made demands on his time. The Appropriations Committee met every day, "practically all day long," Florence LeCompte told Elward Wright in April, 1949. The staff would not be going home for Easter, she said, because "the Senator won't take one day off." Noting the strain on Ellender, LeCompte was surprised to hear him admit to being tired. "The Senator, I think, is beginning to wear himself out," she noted. "He's always been so indestructible that it seems strange to hear him talk that way."[1]

At Ellender's request, Frank Wurzlow, Jr., returned to Washington when administrative assistant Gilbert Fortier retired in 1949. Both Betty Wurzlow and Ellender had encouraged Frank to become a lawyer. Frank,

---

1. Allen Ellender press release, January 8, 1947, Box 991, and Bascom Timmons, New Orleans *Times-Picayune,* January 6, 1949, in "1949" Scrapbook, both in Allen J. Ellender Papers, Nicholls State University Library, Thibodaux, La., hereinafter cited as AEP; Florence LeCompte to Elward Wright, April 8, 1949, in Elward Wright Papers, in the possession of Thomas Wright, Houma, La.

enrolling in night classes at American University, spent two years in prelaw training and three years in law school. In the meantime, George Arceneaux, Jr., had joined Ellender's staff as well. Arceneaux, a recent LSU journalism graduate, was the son of the former county agent who later headed the sugarcane experimental station in Houma. Young Arceneaux called Claude's wife "Aunt Thelma." She had been his Sunday school teacher at First United Methodist Church in Houma. When his military tour of duty ended, Arceneaux joined the staff and, like Wurzlow, registered for night classes at American University with the idea of becoming a lawyer.[2]

The agenda of the Eighty-first Congress included education, housing, agriculture, and labor legislation. Ellender hoped to pass education and housing bills he and Robert Taft of Ohio and Robert Wagner of New York had been unable to pass in the Eightieth Congress. Ellender respected both talented men of principle, but he had more in common with Taft, a conservative Republican, than with Wagner, a liberal Democrat. Like them, he displayed legislative flexibility.[3]

Ellender and Taft successfully cosponsored education bills in the Senate. But Senate Bill 472 died in the House in the Eightieth Congress and Senate Bill 246 died in the Eighty-first Congress. The identical bills, Ellender informed constituents, would have provided aid to primary and secondary education. Hoping to guarantee a minimum expenditure of $40 per educable student to all parts of the country, Ellender realized the cost would be about $300 million. Roman Catholics, who opposed bills banning aid to parochial schools, complained to Ellender. Bluntly asserting his views on separation of church and state, Ellender, as usual, told Catholic critics who pressed the point he could not support legislation contrary to the Constitution.[4]

Ellender also tried to help Americans who needed housing. He had supported public housing since the New Deal when he voted for the 1937 Housing Act. After meeting with members of the National Housing Agency during World War II, Ellender had studied housing needs near military installations and in urban centers. Houma mayor Elward Wright discussed

2. Frank Wurzlow, Jr., interview, April 9, 1980; George Arceneaux, Jr., interview, December 31, 1979.

3. James T. Patterson, *Mr. Republican: A Biography of Robert A. Taft* (Boston, 1972), 260, 329, 330, 332.

4. Allen Ellender to Joseph G. Boudreaux, April 21, 1947, in "S. 866" Folder, Box 568, and Ellender to S. C. Shaw, January 11, 1948, in "Federal Aid to Education, 1949" Folder, Box 604, both in AEP.

housing shortages for personnel assigned to the Navy dirigible base south of town.[5] Veterans' organizations and urban leaders generally supported public housing bills, but real estate groups and home builders, claiming public housing competed with private industry, usually opposed the bills. Housing bills, Ellender insisted, always gave private builders first priority for home construction.

In 1946 radio commentator Fulton Lewis criticized Ellender's bill, S. 1821, designed to provide "a decent home for every American." Ellender defended the act to create 100,000 units for distressed families of servicemen and for veterans and their families. Appearing on the "American Forum of the Air" in 1947 with Charles Stewart of the National Association of Real Estate Boards and Edward Carr of the National Association of Home Builders, Ellender said private industry had failed to meet the need for 1.5 million new homes each year. Housing bills generally included funds for research, slum clearance, farm dwellings, and low-rent public structures, as well as aid for private home financing through the Federal Housing Authority and the Federal Home Loan Bank Administration.[6]

Louisiana businessmen gave Ellender no support in 1946 when he appeared before the Real Estate Board in New Orleans for advice on housing legislation. "I was in a measure rebuffed, and received little if any help at all by way of making the bill acceptable to all interests," Ellender said. An attorney friend thought Ellender had won respect for courageously defending his bill. Because local governments controlled projects funded with federal monies, housing legislation backers usually avoided racial entanglements. Southerners in the House, whose constituents were mainly rural, opposed housing bills that provided little to benefit their districts.[7]

Ellender helped draft and pass the most important bill in Truman's Fair Deal, the 1949 Housing Act. He had served on a special housing and urban redevelopment subcommittee, whose August, 1945, report became the basis

5. "Temporary Housing for Veterans" Folder, Box 1318, and Box 145, *passim,* both in AEP.

6. Allen Ellender report to 79th Cong., 2d Sess., "Temporary Housing for Veterans," February 21, 1946, in Box 1318, AEP; Ellender radio speeches, May 20, June 2, 1947, in "S. 866" Folder, Box 568, AEP; Box 587, *passim,* AEP.

7. Allen Ellender to Lee F. Johnson, February 5, 1947, Ellender to Clem Bernard, April 18, 1946, and Bill Porteous, Jr., to Ellender, April 16, 1946, all in "S. 1592" Folder, Box 587, AEP; Richard Davies, "Social Welfare Policies," in *The Truman Period as a Research Field,* ed. Richard S. Kirkendall (Columbia, Mo., 1967), 172–73; Richard Davies, *Housing Reform during the Truman Administration* (Columbia, Mo., 1966), 11, 12, 24–26, 30, 33, 35–36, 113–14.

for the bill prepared by Wagner's aides and introduced by Ellender, Taft, and Wagner as an administration bill. Mayor Fiorella LaGuardia of New York supported the measure, which Ellender considered an important postwar domestic issue and the most effective and inexpensive way to deal with urban slums.

At a National Housing Conference, Truman blamed Republicans for killing early housing bills. When the Republicans included housing in their platform, he called the Turnip Session to give them a chance to pass a housing measure. "You remember what happened," Truman said. "Senator Taft himself turned against the bill, and asked the Senate to kill it, and the Senate did kill it." Later a "teeny-weeny" housing bill passed. Finally, Truman said, in 1949 Congress passed a good housing bill.[8]

Racial matters were as important to Ellender as housing was. From time to time he consulted FBI director J. Edgar Hoover for background information on people. Filibustering against Truman's civil rights package in 1949, Ellender took the floor at 11:26 A.M. on Monday, March 14, and held it for twelve and a half hours. At 7:00 P.M. he sent word to his staff: "I am still good for a few hours yet." Never even loosening his collar, Ellender kept a strong voice to the end. Occasionally he drank water. "Now I shall discuss the poll tax for a few hours," he said with a straight face. Ellender attributed his stamina to a breakfast of toast and broiled ham, consumed without coffee or juice. The wire services and weekly news magazines published a photograph of Helen kissing Allen as he ended his marathon speech.[9]

For a nonreligious person, Ellender was surprisingly cooperative and polite to Catholic priests and nuns, but when race and separation of church and state came up, he could be quite blunt. In 1949, upon explaining to Msgr. Maurice Schexnayder, pastor of St. Francis de Sales Church in Houma, details about obtaining a surplus military chapel, Ellender offered to donate a lot on the southeast corner of his Coteau farm for the chapel. But when the mother superior of Ursuline College in New Orleans criticized his racial views, Ellender responded aggressively. "I wonder how long you would maintain the Ursuline College in New Orleans if you were to admit colored girls to go to the same classes and occupy the same dormitories, if you have any, with white girls."

8. *Public Papers of the Presidents of the United States: Harry S. Truman* (8 vols.; Washington, D.C., 1966), VIII, 319–20.

9. FBI File 62-81810, March 10, 1949; Edgar Poe, New Orleans *Times-Picayune*, March 16, 1949, and *Time*, March 28, 1949, p. 19, both in "1949" Scrapbook, AEP.

The Rev. Thomas Shields, president of Loyola University in New Orleans, in asking Ellender to protect the tax-exempt status of private colleges, expressed concern about the status of Loyola-owned radio station WWL in New Orleans. "The revenue of WWL is Loyola's endowment," Shields wrote. Pending legislation, Ellender replied, would tax the station, but the university's losses could offset the profits of the station.[10]

As the number of black voters in Louisiana increased, Ellender became concerned about trends he considered dangerous to the political stability of the nation. "So-called civil right[s] advocates," he told FBI director Hoover, "are complaining and using the FBI to service their own purposes." Hoover, whose tone suggested he and Ellender had similar views on civil rights, replied, "Whenever a negro in any way has a run-in with the law he immediately contacts the National Association for the Advancement of Colored People or the Civil Rights Congress who immediately complains to the Civil Rights Section of the Criminal Division of the Department of Justice who in turn refer [*sic*] the matter to us for investigation."[11]

Ellender, fearing civil rights legislation would change a lifetime of racial practices he accepted, knew the number of black registered voters in Louisiana had increased after World War II, from 908 in 1940 to 28,177 in 1948.[12] If the trend continued, he would have to alter his racial position or concede the black vote to a campaign opponent. Neither alternative seemed acceptable to a practical politician who happened also to be a segregationist.

Ellender also had misgivings about immigrants. He opposed allowing displaced persons from Europe to swarm into the United States unchecked. Instead, Ellender favored a five-year ban on their coming. "I repeat, it is our sacred obligation to think of America first," he said, convinced that DPs

10.   Maurice Schexnayder to Allen Ellender, May 7, 1949, and Ellender to Schexnayder, May 14, 1949, both in "War Assets Administration—1949" Folder, Box 9, AEP; Ellender to Schexnayder, August 6, 1949, in "Miscellaneous, Sen. Ellender (Personal)" Folder, Box 227, AEP; M. Columba to Ellender, April 20, 1949, and Ellender to Columba, April 28, 1949, both in "Civil Rights—1949" Folder, Box 306, AEP; Gilbert Fortier to Cap Gresen, February 25, 1949, in "Miscellaneous, Fortier, G. J. (Personal)" Folder, Box 227, AEP; "Federal Aid to Education—1949" Folder, *passim,* Box 306, AEP; Thomas J. Shields to Ellender, September 11, 1950, and Ellender to Shields, October 2, 1950, both in "Taxes, 1950" Folder, Box 162, AEP.

11.   J. Edgar Hoover to Mr. Tolson, October 30, 1950, FBI File 62-81810; Kenneth O'Reilly, *"Racial Matters": The FBI's Secret File on Black America, 1960–1972* (New York, 1989), *passim.*

12.   Edward F. Renwick, "The Longs' Legislative Lieutenants" (Ph.D. diss., University of Arizona, 1967), 15.

faced neither death nor privation if they returned to their homelands. None-theless, he cooperated with Congressman Hale Boggs of New Orleans and the Cane League in their efforts to use the Port of New Orleans for DPs in order to reduce transportation costs to planters in south Louisiana. Ellender told a cane grower interested in having a former German POW worker return to his plantation as a DP that a former POW would not qualify as a displaced person.

It would be foolish, Ellender believed, to allow DPs to become Amer-ican citizens quickly and easily. Doctors, nurses, and professional people—all unlikely to be interested in agricultural work—were needed in Europe to rebuild their own countries. They should not be allowed to come to the United States simply because it was a rich nation. Fearing the French had selected the best of the DPs and left the less desirable for the United States, Ellender wanted to close DP camps in Europe in the summer of 1949. "They will stay in camps as long as we continue to feed them," he said. Senator Richard Russell, sharing many of Ellender's fears, thought immigrants from Asia and Africa would "dilute Anglo-Saxon culture." [13]

Ellender's thoughts, however, tended to be dominated by agricultural prob-lems. American Sugar Cane League lobbyist C. J. Bourg kept Ellender ap-prised of developments in the sugar industry. Rarely overlooking an issue affecting the domestic sugar industry, Bourg in 1949 advised the senator to exempt agricultural workers from National Labor Relations Board jurisdic-tion. "This year the NLRB is trying to eliminate this provision," Bourg wrote. "We are opposed to such elimination because we do not want any labor union interfering with our agricultural labor."

Postwar agriculture was changing dramatically, Ellender knew. Mecha-nization had eliminated many farm labor jobs and the small family farm was giving way to large commercial farms. Like other facets of the American economy, agriculture was subsidized. In Ellender's view, farmers should not

13. Allen Ellender radio broadcast, June 3, 1947, in "Speeches, 1948" Folder, Box 634, AEP; Hale Boggs to Ellender, October 26, 1948, E. J. Guidry to Ellender, July 21, 1949, Ellender to Guidry, July 25, 1949, all in "Displaced Persons Commission" Folder, Box 374, AEP; Hubert Lerschen to Ellender, February 5, 1949, Ellender to Lerschen, February 17, 1949, both in "Justice Dept., Immigration and Naturalization, 1949" Folder, Box 374, AEP; "Immigration, 1949" Folder, *passim,* Box 635, AEP; Ellender speech, March 11, 1950, in "Speeches, 1950" Folder, Box 105, AEP; New Orleans *Times-Picayune,* May 8, 1949, in "1949" Scrapbook, AEP; Gilbert Fite, *Richard B. Russell, Jr., Senator from Georgia* (Chapel Hill, 1991), 220.

have to apologize for that. Nor should there be limits on subsidies to big farmers.

Ellender liked Charles Brannan, the bald, personable secretary of agriculture who had directed the Farm Security Administration, but he disliked the Brannan Plan, a controversial agricultural program introduced in April, 1949, to reduce farm spending. The complicated program would have replaced price supports for commodities with income supports for farmers. Instead of allowing unlimited production of commodities at subsidized prices, the plan would have established a minimum income per farmer and a ceiling on the maximum amount any farmer could receive. The limit on payments, Brannan told Truman, would be a "hot potato." By July, Brannan had abandoned the limit in a compromise bill with George Aiken of Vermont, ranking Republican on the Senate Agriculture Committee. But the House defeated the Aiken-Brannan compromise.[14]

Limiting the size of benefit payments to farmers may have been a bigger factor in the defeat of Brannan's plan than most experts acknowledge. Cotton interests, wanting guarantees against a limit on payments, wrote the Agricultural Act of 1949 to replace Brannan's plan. It included the cotton snapback provision: If Congress placed a limit on payments to farmers, cotton farmers would automatically revert to the old system of price supports without acreage restrictions.[15]

Parity became a key word in farm policy. The agricultural establishment had invented parity to raise farm prices and income. Parity was set with a formula for determining prices by comparing current production costs and commodity prices to those of 1910–14, a good period for farmers. By raising farm prices, economists hoped to restore the ratio of industrial income to

14. Theodore Saloutos, in "Agricultural Organizations and Farm Policy in the South after World War II," *Agricultural History,* LIII (January, 1979), 391; Florence LeCompte, interview, June 23, 1981; "Brannan Farm Program" Folder, *passim,* Box 306, AEP; "General Farm Program," Hearings Before the Committee on Agriculture, 81st Cong., 1st Sess., Pt. 2, April 12, 1949, pp. 176, 192; "Agricultural Adjustment Act of 1949," Hearings Before Subcommittee of the Committee on Agriculture and Forestry, 81st Cong., 1st Sess., July 15, 1949, pp. 242, 244–45; Barton Bernstein, "Economic Policies," in *The Truman Period,* ed. Kirkendall, 113.

15. Julius Duscha, *Taxpayers' Hayride: The Farm Problem from the New Deal to the Billie Sol Estes Case* (Boston, 1964), 58–59; Reo Christenson, *The Brannan Plan: Farm Politics and Policy* (Ann Arbor, 1959), 178–79; Allen J. Matusow, *Farm Policies and Politics in the Truman Years* (Cambridge, Mass., 1967), 200–202; Murray Benedict, *Farm Policies in the United States, 1790–1950* (New York, 1966), 485–87; Varden Fuller, "Political Pressure and Income Distribution in Agriculture," in *Agricultural Policy in an Affluent Society,* ed. Vernon W. Ruttan *et al.* (New York, 1969), 256.

farm income at 1910–14 levels. Because parity increased farm prices substantially, the agricultural establishment agreed to accept less than 100 percent implementation initially.

In the wake of the Brannan Plan, Senator Clinton Anderson of New Mexico introduced a compromise measure with flexible price supports from 70 to 90 percent of parity. By October, fixed supports at 90 percent of parity prevailed and became the backbone of the Agricultural Act of 1949.

Ellender served on the conference committee to iron out differences between House and Senate versions of the 1949 farm bill. In mid-October he proposed supporting commodities at 90 percent of parity the first year, 85 percent the second, and 80 percent the third. Republican Milton Young of North Dakota and Democrat Richard Russell of Georgia went along with Ellender's compromise. Two agricultural innovations sprang up after the Brannan Plan failed: the Soil Bank and Public Law 480. The Soil Bank paid farmers to take acreage out of production. PL 480, called the Food for Peace Program, subsidized the purchase of surplus commodities by foreign nations. When Secretary Brannan suggested paying transportation costs to ship PL 480 commodities abroad, Ellender protested. "If we pass this too, then they would be up here next asking us to cook the food and then feed it to them," he said.[16]

Over the years Helen had tried to fit into Washington society, although she disliked much about it. Somewhat insecure and jealous, Helen hated the party circuit. She did not like Allen to drink and be around women who circulated among people in power. Happy but moody, Helen enjoyed the Senate Ladies' Club, sometimes called Senate Wives, a civic-minded social group promoting community projects, exchanging recipes, and meeting for teas and social events. Like the Senate itself, the club operated on a seniority system. In April, 1949, it selected Helen chairman, although some members had more seniority than she. One columnist, sensing a social snub, speculated that Mrs. Robert Taft had supported Helen for the top spot because she did not want Mrs. Millard Tydings to win. All ended well—Mrs. Tydings was ineligible under club rules to seek the post Helen won handily.[17]

16.   Jay Walz, New York Times, October 17, 1949; John Morris, New York Times, October 19, 1949; Fite, Richard Russell, 215; Duscha, Taxpayers' Hayride, 63–64; New York Times, December 3, 1950, in "1950–1951" Scrapbook, AEP.

17.   Washington Post, April 24, 1949, Paul Wooton, New Orleans Times-Picayune, August 8, 1949, Edgar Poe, New Orleans Times-Picayune, June 9, 1949, New Orleans Times-Picayune, July 6, 1949, all in "1949" Scrapbook, AEP.

Ever eager to promote Louisiana agricultural and seafood products, the Ellenders always specified creole items at their social functions. For a 1949 luncheon Helen wanted to serve Louisiana navel oranges. Allen ordered fifty of the large citrus fruit for her from a New Orleans produce dealer he knew. Several days later, fifty cases of navel oranges arrived in the nation's capital. As honest as he was frugal, the senator was in a quandary. He wanted to pay a just debt, but he had ordered fifty oranges, not fifty cases. Undaunted, Allen told Helen to select fifty nice fruit; then he offered the remainder to Magruder's, a fancy grocery with delicatessen items, at his cost plus shipping. Magruder's bought the oranges; Allen paid the New Orleans produce dealer.[18]

In June, Helen accompanied Allen on a trip to Europe, where they visited Pope Pius XII. Helen's ancestral home, Ireland, not as clean or as prosperous as she had always imagined, disappointed her.

Back at home, friends and family members realized that Helen was ill. Incapacitated with increasing regularity by violent headaches, she sometimes stopped at Allen's office, so tired and ill after shopping that she had to rest on a sofa until she had recovered a bit. Suffering memory loss, she once walked into a public building in New Orleans and became so disoriented that she did not know who she was or where she was. Before Allen fully realized the seriousness of her illness, Helen feared her ailment would take her life.[19]

Allen, sometimes impatient with her forgetfulness and frailty, was for a time oblivious to Helen's illness. Once, in the presence of Richard Russell and a party of men and women, Allen walked ahead of Helen, completely ignoring her. The gentleman bachelor Russell, calling Allen to task, stated in a voice loud enough for all to hear, "If you won't walk with your wife, I will." Randolph Bazet's wife, May, a close friend, said Helen preferred to remain in Louisiana when she was not feeling well.

Although Allen was somewhat aloof, the Ellenders were a closely knit and sentimental group. Helen was disappointed if she had to be away from Allen Jr. on his birthday, so she usually found ways to be with him. When he was on military duty in Puerto Rico in the late 1940s, she flew there to celebrate his birthday. Misplacing a battered old leather shaving kit at the Roosevelt Hotel in 1948, Ellender asked hotel manager Seymour Weiss to

18. Betty Wurzlow and Frank Wurzlow, Jr., interview, April 14, 1992.

19. Viola Lynch Ellender, interview, July 14, 1980; Frank Wurzlow, Jr., interview, April 9, 1980; Daisy Donnelly, interview, July 14, 1980.

find the kit, which Helen had given him as a birthday present twenty-five years earlier. Weiss found it and returned it to his old friend. Ellender had a picture of Helen on his desk signed, "I'm looking at you devotedly—Helen."

Helen's headaches persisted during the European trip and grew more severe after her return. She told Allen, "It's in my head, Allen, and I expect the end soon." Reluctant to face reality and eager to cheer her up, Allen cited anemia as her problem. Allen Jr., surmising eye problems, scheduled an appointment for her at the Ochsner Clinic in New Orleans. A doctor there suspected a brain tumor, but Helen made Allen promise never to ask her to submit to brain surgery. Insisting on returning to Washington, Helen entered the Yater Clinic for extensive tests. Unable eventually to take even a short walk without becoming faint, Helen did not want people to know the severity of her illness. Feeling dizzy after a stroll, she told Allen, "Let's not move because I don't want the people sitting on the porch of our apartment house to know my condition."

A tumor at the base of Helen's brain proved to be the cause of her headaches, disorientation, and memory lapses. After conferring with her doctors, both Willard and Allen Jr. believed surgery too dangerous, for it would kill or paralyze her.

On Wednesday, September 28, 1949, Helen, although suffering from a severe headache, visited Allen's office. The next day she entered Doctors' Hospital in Washington. Allen summoned his son to her bedside. At about 7 P.M. she lapsed into unconsciousness. Heeding the advice of experts at Ocshner and Yater, Ellender agreed to a simple but dangerous test, an X-ray "with some of the spinal fluid and brain fluid extracted and replaced with air." Helen did not recover from the test. She died at 2 A.M. on Friday, September 30, before Allen Jr. arrived. She was fifty-four. Allen, in near shock on seeing her, rubbed her hands as though she were alive. He seemed unable to realize she was gone.

At 6:25 that night the body left the city that Helen had never liked. It traveled aboard a special funeral coach attached to the Louisville and Nashville Crescent Limited. It was accompanied by Allen, Allen Jr., Frank Wurzlow, Jr., Gilbert Fortier, Representative Henry D. Larcade of Opelousas, and members of Ellender's staff. The body arrived in New Orleans on Saturday, October 1, at 8 P.M. On Sunday Helen's wake was conducted at P. J. McMahon and Son Funeral Home at 4800 Canal Street. Her casket was surrounded by banks of flowers.

Her funeral service, a requiem High Mass sung by Monsignor Schexnayder of Houma at St. Louis Cathedral, began at eleven o'clock Monday. New Orleans archbishop Joseph Francis Rummel attended, along with priests from the bayou country. Then, the cortege made its way to the Donnelly family tomb in St. Louis Cemetery, where Helen had asked to be buried. The family sent the flowers to New Orleans hospitals. "That's the way Helen would have wanted it," Vi Ellender said.

Harry and Bess Truman sent a message of condolence. Ellender thanked Bishop Charles Greco of Alexandria for his prayers and concern. "I never learned until after her death that she had done so much for so many people while she lived," he wrote. "However, after I learned what suffering she would have had to undergo had she lived, I realized she would have preferred to go as she did." On returning to Louisiana, Ellender spent time with Claude and Thelma, Willard and Vi, and Allen Jr. and the grandchildren. He liked to discuss world affairs with his nieces and nephews, whom he welcomed warmly whenever they came to visit.[20]

Ellender maintained close ties to family and friends. In May, 1950, he visited Helen's mother, Mary Jane Donnelly, then eighty-four years old, at Abita Springs. Mrs. Donnelly was seriously ill after suffering a heart attack. He wrote thank-you notes to Houma residents who had contributed books to the Terrebonne Parish Public Library in Helen's memory. During his stay in Louisiana, he provided inaccurate military information for a biographical questionnaire. "I served in World War I in the Infantry, and was released at the grade of Top Sergeant," he wrote. "I have never been in the reserves."[21] Technically Ellender had never served on active duty nor been honorably discharged from military service.

20. Allen Ellender to Charles Greco, February 6, 1950, in "Mrs. Ellender" Folder, Box 105, AEP; Ellender to Seymour Weiss, April 26, 1948, in "Senator E., Personal" Folder, Box 993, AEP; Ellender to Harry and Bess Truman, October 17, 1949, Ellender to Mrs. Arthur Vandenberg, October 13, 1949, Ellender to Ella Hooper, February 21, 1950, and mimeographed office obituary, all in "Mrs. Ellender" Folder, Box 1004, AEP; Harry Truman to Ellender (telegram), September 30, 1949, PPF 559, in Harry Truman Papers, Truman Library, Independence, Mo.; Thelma Ellender, interview, June 30, 1980; Viola Lynch Ellender, interview, July 14, 1980; Randolph Bazet, interview, October 22, 1980; Daisy Donnelly, interview, July 14, 1980; Florence LeCompte, interview, June 20, 1991; Edgar Poe, New Orleans *Times-Picayune,* October 1, 1949; Houma (La.) *Courier,* October 7, 1949.

21. New Orleans *Times-Picayune,* May 21, 1950, in "1950–1951" Scrapbook, AEP; Allen Ellender to Glen Douthit, August 8, 1950, in "Sen. Ellender—Misc." Folder, and many letters to friends, August 8, 1950, in "Mrs. Ellender" Folder, both in Box 1004, AEP.

As Ellender grew in power and influence in Washington, he did not forget the frugal ways of his early days on a sugarcane plantation in Terrebonne Parish. He lived modestly, and he hated waste. He would return from Louisiana fishing and hunting trips carrying ice chests filled with ducks, geese, fish, shrimp, and oysters for his parties. His apartment was not air-conditioned and he did not have a maid. Allen Jr., just beginning his private medical practice in Houma, dared to buy a Cadillac, but he hid it from his father as long as he could. Later, when Allen Jr. bought a new car, he chose the same color as the old model, hoping his father would not notice the new purchase. He did not want to hear a lecture on how the old car could have lasted a few more years.[22]

Ellender enjoyed receiving little gifts and mementos from friends and leaders of foreign countries he visited. He knew the difference, however, between small presents and expensive ones with unspoken commitments. When Lafayette patent medicine tycoon Dudley LeBlanc told him to buy the best suit he could find and send the bill to him, Ellender replied with a polite no-thanks letter. "I believe I have an ample supply of clothes at the present time," he wrote. At about the same time, Ellender quibbled with a department store over a four-dollar refund not credited to his account.[23]

Once, on returning from vacation, Ellender complained that his apartment needed cleaning. Florence LeCompte volunteered to clean it. Softhearted and totally loyal, Flo often got stuck with jobs no one else wanted to do. On another occasion when Flo was on vacation, Ellender complained about his dirty apartment to secretary Augusta Peters. She sent her maid to clean the senator's apartment, but she sent a bill for services rendered. Ellender, paying a just debt, never complained about his apartment in front of Peters again. When Willard and his wife visited Ellender in the heat of summer, they slept at Flo's apartment, which was air-conditioned.[24]

Not only was Flo generous and loyal, she could cook as well. She was single and did not seem to mind working long hours at the office. Ellender, never a very good driver, always seemed more eager to gaze about than to concentrate on the road ahead. Flo, scared to be in a car with Ellender behind the wheel, assumed the driving task herself. Sometimes after leaving

22. Florence LeCompte, interview, December 2, 1991.

23. Dudley LeBlanc to Allen Ellender, September 3, 1949, and Ellender to LeBlanc, September 16, 1949, both in "Thank-You Letters and Greetings" Folder, Box 998, AEP.

24. George Arceneaux, Jr., interview, December 31, 1979; Viola Lynch Ellender, interview, July 14, 1980.

the Senate Office Building, Ellender and Flo went out to eat Chinese food. Ellender liked most types of food, except Mexican dishes, which upset his stomach.[25]

Ellender, popular with the ladies, who considered him gallant, still cooked, and he entertained political acquaintances and dignitaries. Staffers wondered if he would remarry. George Arceneaux, Jr., thinks he had idealized Helen as a wife and created an image no other woman could ever emulate. Ellender's busy schedule left little time for socializing and courting.[26] From time to time, Ellender did appear in public with attractive women. He courted a woman journalist in Washington briefly. He escorted a woman friend from Louisiana to a political function of Earl Long. Willard's wife, Vi, and her daughters were never sure whether Ellender's women companions were social, business, or political acquaintances. Vi, knowing Flo to be totally loyal and dedicated to Ellender, hoped the two would marry. But Flo's relationship with Ellender was based on trust and friendship, not romance. Flo handled all his personal mail, including financial matters. She helped him prepare his formal dinners and occasionally went with him to social functions. Eager to see the movie *The Sound of Music,* Flo told Ellender that long hours of office toil entitled her to see it. "Pick a day, and we'll go," Ellender said. He enjoyed the movie so much that he went to see it five times. Whenever grandchildren showed up in Washington, Ellender took them to see *The Sound of Music.* Flo was undoubtedly Ellender's closest woman friend. Among men, Senator Milton Young of North Dakota was his best friend in the capital.

For a time after Helen's death, Ellender had several women in his life. Flo, trying not be judgmental or selective, assumed he would settle down in time. Although Flo had definite notions about the women he escorted, she did not try to impose standards on Ellender or voice maternal concerns. "It wouldn't have done any good," she said. When describing some of his women acquaintances, however, Flo used such terms as "aggressive," "pushy," and even "tramp."

Flo considered one of Ellender's relationships disastrous. Grace Johnson of Virginia, she thought, was an unfortunate companion. For a time Ellender and Johnson, who had worked for Senator Carter Glass of Virginia on the Appropriations Committee, socialized about Washington. Later Ellender hired her for committee work when Glass left office. Johnson, domineering,

---

25. Florence LeCompte, interview, September 25, 1980.
26. George Arceneaux, Jr., interview, December 31, 1979.

manipulative, curious, and troublesome, caused dissension among committee staffers. They disliked her intensely after Ellender sent her on European
junkets, which brought unfavorable publicity to Ellender and to the committee. Calling Johnson a hell-bent freeloader, *Time* criticized her two 20-
day trips to Paris for the Appropriations Committee. Grace, "fiftyish, tough-
talking, weight-throwing, $10,000-a-year staffer and longtime friend of
Louisiana's Democratic Senator Allen J. Ellender," investigated shops, bars,
and restaurants. She and her woman companion, "leaving a wake of empty
bottles, empty pockets and nail-chewing functionaries," gathered little useful
information, *Time* said.[27]

Ellender did not return to Washington early in January, 1950, for the
opening session of Congress. He remained in Houma to settle Helen's estate
and on January 20 became ill with the flu. He canceled a civil rights debate
with Minnesota senator Hubert Humphrey on "Town Meeting of the Air."
Flo had expected him in Washington at the end of the first week in February.[28] Truman's legislative success rate had not been impressive, but the president had hopes for his Fair Deal. Civil rights legislation was always under
consideration, and a new term—McCarthyism—came into vogue as the Cold
War heated up.

Despite Grace Johnson's extravagance, Ellender had become a persistent
critic of wasteful and costly government programs. He opposed spending
$20 million to construct a new Senate office building. He favored renovating
the old structure, possibly by air-conditioning the basement. Calling Truman's compulsory health insurance socialized medicine, Ellender outlined for
the American Medical Association alternatives to the Truman health program—a voluntary system, grants-in-aid to states, possibly expansion of the
Louisiana charity hospital concept. When labor demanded repeal of the Taft-
Hartley Act, Ellender said Congress would consider changes other than those
recommended by labor bosses. For the first time, Ellender wondered if REA,
designed originally to bring electricity to rural and remote areas, had expanded to the point of putting private utility companies out of business.

When Ellender's administrative assistant, Gilbert Fortier, retired in December, Ellender did not name Wurzlow to fill his slot. Instead he assigned

27. Viola Lynch Ellender and Susan Ellender Stahl, interview, July 14, 1980; Florence
LeCompte, interview, December 2, 1991; *Time,* January 7, 1957, p. 15.
28. New Orleans *Times-Picayune,* January 31, 1950, in "1950–1953" Scrapbook, AEP; Florence LeCompte to Robert Bulliard, January 28, 1950, in "B" Folder, Box 1004, AEP.

some of Fortier's duties to Wurzlow and some to Flo. Like Richard Russell, Ellender did not overpay his staff. As part of his economy move, he spent less on office staff than did most senators.[29]

During the Easter recess spent in Louisiana, Ellender criticized Wisconsin Republican senator Joseph McCarthy, whose anticommunist tactics attracted headlines. Ellender labeled "ridiculous" McCarthy's charges against suspected communists. "The fact that a man belonged to an organization that later turned semi-Red is no reason to charge him with being a Communist," Ellender said. But when the subject shifted to race, he added a less-than-sensible justification for opposing civil rights measures—blacks in the South were treated better than blacks in the North.[30]

Ellender maintained contacts with political friends back home. Freshman senator Russell Long was doing quite well, he told Governor Earl Long in February, 1949. Alluding to Louisiana tax problems, Ellender offered no solution. When a Longite from New Orleans asked Ellender to help James A. Noe of Monroe with appeals to the Federal Communications Commission for radio station WNOE, he complied. "I have done and will continue to do everything possible to assist our good friend, Jimmie Noe," he said magnanimously. Roosevelt Hotel manager Seymour Weiss asked Ellender to assist New Orleans labor consultant Charles Logan to arrange an appearance before a Senate labor hearing. Ellender told Weiss to send "our mutual friend" to see him.[31]

While in Louisiana in October, 1950, Ellender bought a modern, air-conditioned apartment in Washington. He paid $13,776.80 for Apartment 306-G, at 3900 Connecticut Avenue, in a cooperative complex called Tilden Gardens. Harry and Bess Truman had rented an apartment in the complex in 1935 for $150 per month. Wurzlow, handling the sale for him, negotiated also for a covered parking spot nearby. Ellender paid a $1,000 down pay-

29. Washington (D.C.) *Times Herald,* May 10, June 8, 15, 1949, New Orleans *Times-Picayune,* April 30, June 6, 1949, Washington (D.C.) *Daily News,* May 30, 1949, Edgar Poe, New Orleans *Times-Picayune,* December 22, 1949, all in "1949" Scrapbook, AEP; Fite, *Richard Russell,* 200.

30. New Orleans *Times-Picayune,* April 11, 1950, in "1950–1951" Scrapbook, AEP.

31. Allen Ellender to Earl Long, February 19, 1949, in "Miscellaneous, Sen. Ellender (Personal) 1949" Folder, and Ellender to Seymour Weiss (telegram), February 21, 1949, in "Miscellaneous, Appointments, 1949" Folder, both in Box 227, AEP; James E. Comisky to Ellender (telegram), January 10, 1949, and Ellender to Comisky (telegram), January 10, 1949, both in "Federal Communications Commission, 1949" Folder, Box 9, AEP.

ment, wrote a check for $4,776.80, and signed a promissory note for the $8,000 balance.[32]

Meanwhile, Flo reported from Houma that the senator "has been most kind and considerate with me, and everything here has been so very pleasant." However, when Allen Jr. returned to his burgeoning medical practice, Ellender became lonely and upset. "He is very much broken up now, though, about Allen's departure, and I certainly do feel sorry for him," she wrote. A few weeks later, Flo drove to New Orleans to meet Ellender, who flew in from Washington. They met Helen's sisters and placed flowers on Helen's grave, as is the custom in Louisiana on All Saints' Day.[33]

A few months earlier, in July, 1950, an Oklahoma election boosted Ellender's stature in the Senate. In a primary election, Mike Moroney defeated Oklahoma senator Elmer Thomas, the chairman of the Senate Agriculture Committee. Thomas had been a strong supporter of the Brannan Plan, which Ellender had helped defeat. Thomas' departure meant Ellender would be chairman of the Agriculture Committee when Congress convened in January, 1951, provided the Democrats maintained control of the Senate after the November 8 election. If the Republicans gained control, Aiken, the ranking Republican, would be chairman.[34]

The Democrats, by maintaining control of Congress in the November elections, assured Ellender the chairmanship of the Agriculture Committee in January, 1951. The new Congress faced important foreign and domestic tasks. Truman had failed to pass a civil rights program, medical care, educational reform, and the Brannan agricultural program. Surprisingly, he got a major housing bill, a new minimum wage act, social security extension, increased funding for reclamation and public power projects, and the National Science Foundation bill.[35] Truman, meanwhile, faced a barrage of charges from Senator McCarthy, who fostered fear of Communism for political advantage.

On June 24, 1950, the Cold War erupted into a hot military conflict when Korean forces north of the thirty-eighth parallel, attacking on a broad

32. Frank Wurzlow, Jr., to Allen Ellender, October 13, 1950, in "Sen. Ellender—Personal" Folder, Box 1004, AEP; David McCullough, *Truman* (New York, 1992), 214.

33. Florence LeCompte to Frank Wurzlow, Jr., October 17, November 2, 1950, both in "Houma Office" Folder, Box 1004, AEP.

34. New Orleans *States,* July 27, 1950, in "1950–1951" Scrapbook, AEP.

35. Davies, *Housing Reform,* x; Davies, "Social Welfare Policies," in *The Truman Period,* ed. Kirkendall, 154; Bernstein, "Economic Policies," in *The Truman Period,* ed. Kirkendall, 111.

front, overran much of the south, nearly capturing Pusan. Truman, condemning the invasion, ordered American soldiers into the area after the Security Council of the United Nations authorized a multinational force to maintain peace. The military situation in Korea deteriorated after Gen. Douglas MacArthur's brilliant Inchon landing in mid-September. In a surprise attack in late November, Chinese troops overran U.S. positions north of the thirty-eighth parallel as winter set in. MacArthur, reluctant to admit error, complained of enemy forces using "a privileged sanctuary" north of the Yalu River to deny him a complete victory. As 1950 came to an end, Ellender realized Americans were troubled about foreign affairs.

Meanwhile, in Louisiana Ellender visited friends and family, fished, and hunted ducks. Having celebrated his sixtieth birthday in September, he was in good health and had a great deal of energy and enthusiasm for life. Helen was no longer with him, but he had created a separate world for himself in the U.S. Senate, where he was senior senator from Louisiana, chairman of the Agriculture Committee, and a ranking member of the Appropriations Committee. He had lost his wife of thirty-two years, but he had many activities to occupy his mind.

12

CHAIRMAN OF THE
AGRICULTURE COMMITTEE
(1951–53)

*P*resident Truman, condemned by Republicans and conservative Democrats alike for many of the country's problems, suffered political setbacks in his last years in office. When he removed Douglas MacArthur from command in Korea, his antagonists said he was afraid to stand up to China. The Supreme Court ruled his seizure of the steel mills an unwarranted usurpation of power. Conservatives in his own party rejected many of his racial, labor, and social policies. On some measures, Ellender sided with the administration, on others he opposed the president.[1]

Early in the sessions, Ellender, a member of the Appropriations Committee as well as chairman of Agriculture, spoke out against waste and the rising cost of government spending. The FBI, one of the more expensive agencies, had forty-nine hundred agents, the Treasury three thousand, he said. The FBI's Ellender file (No. 62-81810) contained a newspaper clipping explaining that Ellender had publicized the previously secret information: "Sen. Allen J. Ellender, of Louisiana, has broken the silence."[2]

Congress produced more rhetoric than usual when it convened in the presidential election year of 1952. Ellender announced his presidential predictions: Dwight Eisenhower would not seek the presidency; Robert Taft would defeat Truman if the Missourian chose to run, which Ellender

---

1. Barton Bernstein, "Economic Policies," in *The Truman Period as a Research Field,* ed. Richard S. Kirkendall (Columbia, Mo., 1967), 130; *New Republic,* September 22, 1952, p. 17.

2. Buffalo (N.Y.) *Sun,* February 28, 1951, FBI File 62-81810.

doubted. As usual he proved to be a poor judge of presidential politics. Eisenhower ran, easily winning the Republican nomination over Robert Taft of Ohio and other aspirants. Truman, on the other hand, did not run; Governor Adlai Stevenson of Illinois won the nomination over Senator Estes Kefauver of Tennessee. Richard Russell of Georgia once again made an unsuccessful bid to win the Democratic nomination, supported incongruously again by Republican Milton Young of North Dakota.

Ellender respected Stevenson as a man, but disagreed with his views on tidelands oil and civil rights, and his willingness to change Senate Rule 22, which permitted unlimited debate. He told Senator J. William Fulbright of Arkansas he would vote for Stevenson but not campaign for him.[3] As it turned out, Eisenhower ran well in the South and won easily in November. The Democratic coalition forged by Franklin Roosevelt was falling apart. Ellender and his southern colleagues had helped to cause the demise of the Solid South.

Eisenhower's landslide victory in November, 1952, helped Republicans win control of Congress. In the Senate they held a 48–46 edge, which meant that when the Eighty-third Congress convened on January 3, 1953, George Aiken of Vermont would become chairman of the Agriculture Committee. Ellender would have to surrender the prize he had waited so long to get, and after holding it only two years. Aiken and the incoming secretary of agriculture, Ezra Taft Benson, favored flexible, low price supports for agricultural commodities. Ellender favored high, fixed price supports.[4]

Raised close to the land and for years a farmer himself, Ellender realized that agriculture had undergone enormous changes from the 1930s to the 1950s. By the mid-1950s mechanization had transformed agriculture from labor-intensive to capital-intensive. Farm tenancy, once a major problem for the South, shrank into insignificance, and mules became rare. In the eleven Confederate states plus Oklahoma and West Virginia the number of tenants

3. Washington (D.C.) *Times-Herald,* January 14, 1952, and various newspaper clippings, August, 1952, all in "1952" Scrapbook, Allen J. Ellender Papers, Nicholls State University Library, Thibodaux, La., hereinafter cited as AEP; Gilbert C. Fite, *Richard B. Russell, Jr., Senator from Georgia* (Chapel Hill, 1991), 278; Allen Ellender to J. William Fulbright, n.d., and Folders 13, 14, *passim,* in Box Control Number 78, J. William Fulbright Papers, Special Collections, University of Arkansas Library, Fayetteville, Ark.

4. Theodore Saloutos, "Agricultural Organizations and Farm Policy in the South After World War II," *Agricultural History,* LIII (January, 1979), 393; New Orleans *Item,* November 7, 1952, in "1952" Scrapbook, AEP.

declined from 1.8 million in 1936 to 750,000 in 1950 to 300,000 in 1959.[5] There were fewer farms than before, but they were bigger. The number of farms in the former Confederate states declined from 2.63 million in 1930 to 1.3 million in 1960 to 909,000 in 1970. In that same era the general farm population, too, had declined dramatically: 13.4 million in 1930 to 9.7 million in 1950 to 2.9 million in 1970.

The odyssey of those who left the land—"Farmers Left Behind," Gilbert Fite called them—has not been an American success story. Driven from the land (sometimes by New Deal programs ostensibly designed to help them), these human relics moved to town, to the periphery of the unskilled labor force. Economic studies beginning about 1949 indicated that many marginal farmers had eked out a meager existence on the land. In 1957 about 57 percent of southern farmers earned less than five thousand dollars per year.

Rural poverty was the subject of study by Alabama senator John Sparkman, who chaired a subcommittee investigating the phenomenon. But Congress did not seem to consider the problem important. Like many members of Congress from agricultural states, Ellender seemed to believe that small, inefficient farmers were better off leaving the land for other employment. A number of factors contributed to this prevailing viewpoint. The agricultural establishment was most comfortable working with efficient, educated farmers who were usually represented by influential lobby groups; consequently, most money went to big farmers in the form of price supports for commodities. Few funds were available for groups like the Farm Security Administration and the Farm Home Administration. Poor farmers were weak and unorganized. The haunting specter of race, too, entered the picture. Many poor farmers were black; white southern politicians for the most part ignored them.[6]

Ellender had come to realize the complicated reality of American broker politics and the part that the politics of agriculture played in the scenario. Many phases of the economy—agriculture, publishing, airlines, education, the military, shipping—were subsidized, competing for tax dollars. If farmers hoped to get their share of public largess, they would have to play the game

5. Jack Kirby, *Rural Worlds Lost: The American South, 1920–1960* (Baton Rouge, 1987), 51, 67, 68.

6. Gilbert Fite, *Cotton Fields No More: Southern Agriculture, 1865–1980* (Lexington, Ky., 1984), 211, 212, 214, 218, 223–25, 233, 234; Pete Daniel, *Breaking the Land: The Transformation of Cotton, Tobacco, and Rice Culture since 1880* (Chicago, 1985), xv, 10, 88–90, 168, 174–75, 240–41, 243, 248.

well and pull together. Feed grains, cotton, sugar, tobacco, dairy, poultry, and other interests had to combine forces in order to compete. As chairman of the Senate Agriculture Committee, Ellender tried to keep farm spending under control, curbing excessive and wasteful programs sponsored for selfish reasons.

Like Hubert Humphrey of Minnesota, Ellender had not changed his views on subsidies to agriculture. Critical of spokesmen who advocated subsidies for industry but who wanted to reduce farm spending, Humphrey believed in helping all facets of the economy. He complained that "the same people who are in favor of these industrial and business subsidies are opposed to subsidies to farmers."[7]

Truman had hoped to reduce government farm spending, but his hopes faded when the war in Korea started. Surpluses, once considered wasteful and costly, now became essential reserves for the war in Asia. Invoking national security provisions of the 1949 Agricultural Act, Brannan increased supports in 1951 on every crop except peanuts to 90 percent of parity. When a potato surplus developed, growers dumped tons of low-grade potatoes on the market, which Humphrey blamed on price supports on perishable commodities without acreage or marketing controls.[8]

Ellender's main gripe with the Republicans concerned the farm program. Eisenhower's secretary of agriculture, Ezra Taft Benson, had ties to the Farm Bureau, which favored either price supports on unlimited production or payments equivalent to earnings on full acreage utilization for acres taken out of production. Ellender considered it extravagant and wasteful to let farmers produce alternative crops on land they had been paid to keep out of production and resented pressure from Louisiana Farm Bureau president Larry Lovell, who thought his close association with Benson enhanced his bargaining position with Ellender.[9]

7.   Hubert H. Humphrey to George White, June 16, 1953, in "Leg.: Agriculture Price Supports" Folder, Box 90, Hubert H. Humphrey Papers, Minnesota Historical Society Collection, St. Paul, Minn., hereinafter cited as HHP.

8.   Wayne D. Rasmussen and Gladys L. Baker, "Programs for Agriculture, 1933–1965," in *Agricultural Policy in an Affluent Society,* ed. Vernon W. Ruttan *et al.* (New York, 1969), 81–82; Allen J. Matusow, *Farm Policies and Politics in the Truman Years* (Cambridge, Mass., 1967), 220; Fite, *Richard Russell,* 247; Hubert H. Humphrey, "Dear Friend" letter, n.d., Charles Brannan to Allen Ellender, November 5, 1951, in "Agriculture—Price Supports" Folder, and Charles Stickney to Humphrey, March 7, 1950, in "Agriculture—Wheat Acreage—1951" Folder, all in Box 623, HHP.

9.   "Allen J. Ellender Oral History Interview" by Larry Hackman, August 29, 1967 (John

Ellender and Humphrey worked closely to eliminate flexible supports and achieve 90 percent of parity, but Eisenhower threatened to veto the 1954 farm bill if it contained the rigid 90 percent supports. "We may not have enough votes to override him," Humphrey wrote. He was right. A coalition of Republicans and southern Democrats, demanding compromise, made flexible payments (from 82.5 to 90 percent of parity) part of the Agricultural Act of 1954. Ellender, Young, and Humphrey had lost their fight to keep rigid supports.[10]

The Democrats regained control of Congress in the November, 1954, congressional elections, achieving Senate control by a margin of one. When Ellender assumed his position as chairman of the Agriculture Committee in January, 1955, Lyndon Johnson was Senate Majority Leader, Sam Rayburn, Speaker of the House.[11]

C. J. Bourg of the American Sugar Cane League called Ellender "first friend of the domestic sugar industry." In April, 1951, when raw sugar prices dropped to five cents per pound, Ellender forwarded a letter drafted by Bourg to the USDA asking it to boost raw sugar to six cents per pound. Secretary of Agriculture Charles Brannan agreed to slight increases from time to time.[12]

The sugar program, Ellender realized, was a bounty to producers. "There is no doubt of course that the domestic growers are benefitted by the provisions of the Sugar Act. Without the production payments to domestic sugar producers that are authorized in the Act, our beet and cane sugar farmers could not stay in business," he wrote. Despite sizable payments to farmers, consumers paid a reasonable price for sugar, he believed. Domestic raw sugar producers, competing with refiners bent on keeping raw sugar

F. Kennedy Library, Washington, D.C.; facsimile copy in Nicholls State University Library, Thibodaux, La.), 36–37; Florence LeCompte, interview, August 2, 1979.

10. Hubert Humphrey to Ralph Pickart, December 28, 1954, and Humphrey to C. W. Croes, March 2, 1955, both in "Leg.: Agric. Parity" Folder, Box 115, HHP; New Orleans *Item*, April 20, 1954, various newspaper clippings, May, 1954, all in "1954" Scrapbook, AEP; Edward L. Schapsmeier and Frederick H. Schapsmeier, "Farm Policy from FDR to Eisenhower: Southern Democrats and the Politics of Agriculture," *Agricultural History*, LIII (January, 1979), 367–68; Rasmussen and Baker, "Programs for Agriculture," in *Agricultural Policy*, 82–83.

11. New Orleans *Times-Picayune*, November 2, 1954, in "1954" Scrapbook, AEP; various newspaper clippings, January, 1955, and Baton Rouge *State Times*, February 18, 1955, all in "1955" Scrapbook, AEP.

12. Thomas Becnel, *Labor, Church, and the Sugar Establishment: Louisiana, 1887–1976* (Baton Rouge, 1980), 80.

prices low, refuted the notion refiners could not survive unless the price of refined sugar was 2.25 cents per pound higher than that of raw sugar. Ellender checked with Bourg, who thought a 1.85-cent margin was sufficient for refiners to profit. Splitting the difference between the figures of Bourg and refiners, Ellender said a 2.05-cent differential was reasonable.[13]

In October, 1953, sugarcane workers affiliated with H. L. Mitchell's National Agricultural Workers Union (NAWU) called a strike in Louisiana during the cane-grinding season. Cane growers suggested using imported labor, which Ellender favored. The American Sugar Cane League also sought deferments from military service for sugar workers.[14]

Not directly involved in the controversy, Ellender nonetheless sought Labor Department approval for using British West Indian laborers in south Louisiana during the strike. Paul Chaisson, president of Local 317 of the NAWU, said the Labor Department had "opened the flood gates of foreign labor in an attempt to submarine our union." In a thank-you letter to Ellender at the end of the strike, a corporation spokesman listed ways Ellender's aides had helped. "They used their positions in your office to secure information and to urge approval of the [imported labor] application," he wrote. Ellender also heard from critics of his sugar policies. The Rev. R. A. Auclair, a Catholic priest who worked among rural blacks, asked Ellender to "please do something to give the sugar workers a fair deal." Margaret Smith, an outspoken critic, lashed out at Ellender. "It is time to end this farce. Let the Federal Government get out of the Louisiana sugar business."[15]

In 1955 Humphrey was eager to get a wheat bill with high price supports to the Senate floor. Ellender wanted to conduct grassroots hearings in the grain belt, which Harold Cooley and Humphrey discouraged. "I wish so much that he would abandon the idea," Cooley told Humphrey. Cooley threatened

13. Allen Ellender to Michael Bakalar, July 15, 1950, in "B, 1950" Folder, Box 105, AEP; Becnel, *Labor, Church, and the Sugar Establishment,* 80.

14. "A&F Committee, Farm Workers, Deferment of" Folder, *passim,* Box 392, AEP; Howard Bond to Frank Wurzlow, Jr. (telegram), November 5, 1951, Wurzlow to Bond (telegram), November 5, 1951, Maurice Tobin to Ellender, July 16, 1951, all in "Labor, General, 1951" Folder, Box 637, AEP; Alexander O. Sigur to Ellender, September 26, 1951, Ellender to Sigur, October 20, 1951, both in "Mexican Labor" Folder, Box 392, AEP.

15. J. B. Gremillion to Allen Ellender (telegram), July 28, 1953, and Ellender to Gremillion, July 31, 1953, both in "Legislation, Immigration, 1953" Folder, Box 4, AEP; Becnel, *Labor, Church, and the Sugar Establishment,* 130, 142, 149.

to block extension of the Sugar Act if Ellender did not agree to rigid price supports.

In June Ellender told Humphrey he would conduct field hearings on price supports in Minnesota in the fall. Humphrey feared farmers would reject supports in a field referendum and Congress would not pass a wheat bill. After reminding Ellender he had promised to advocate 90 percent supports, Humphrey told Lyndon Johnson he would press Ellender on wheat legislation.

Ellender had his committee delay passage of the wheat bill because "we might get licked on it." Promising to have a bill ready by the first or second week of January, 1956, Ellender objected to parts of the bill. He hated to see inferior wheat grown only "to sell to Uncle Sam." Protesting, he said, "This wheat is fit only for chicken or hog feed." [16]

Ellender struggled to balance special interests against public interests. Defending pet projects, such as the Sugar Act, due to expire in 1956, forced him to make concessions or to feud with senators normally his allies. Such was the case with J. William Fulbright, the junior senator from Arkansas, with whom Ellender differed sharply over the politics of sugar and rice. Ellender, defending the sugar industry, tried to protect domestic producers from Cuban and other foreign growers. Fulbright, protecting Arkansas farmers who exported rice to Cuba through a reciprocal trade agreement, represented soft drink bottlers who blamed the Sugar Act for raising the price of sugar. In 1949 Fulbright, calling for lower sugar prices and repeal of the Sugar Act, had written a thirteen-page booklet, "Our Sugar Law Is Sour." Labeling sugar the costliest of agricultural programs in 1951, Fulbright called the act "bad legislation" in 1955. Fortunately the feud with Fulbright was limited mainly to agricultural matters.[17]

Although the Agriculture Committee did not handle sugar legislation (it was a tariff matter sent to the Finance Committee), Ellender maintained contact with Finance Committee chairman Harry Byrd of Virginia, who directed sugar legislation and tariffs. Even after a sugar bill got past Byrd's

16. Hubert H. Humphrey to Lyndon Johnson, May 10, 1955, Humphrey to Allen Ellender, May 10, 1955, Humphrey to Harold Cooley, May 12, 1955, Ellender to Humphrey, May 16, 1955, Humphrey to Ellender, May 23, 31, 1955, Cooley to Humphrey, May 31, 1955, all in "Leg.: Agriculture—Price Supports" Folder, Box 115, HHP; various telegrams, n.d. [May, 1955], in "1955" Scrapbook, AEP.

17. Thomas Becnel, "Fulbright of Arkansas v. Ellender of Louisiana: The Politics of Sugar and Rice, 1937–1974," *Arkansas Historical Quarterly*, XLIII (Winter, 1984), 295–96.

committee and the full Senate, Cane League president W. C. Kemper said, "Congressman Cooley must be persuaded to accept the Bill when passed by the Senate." [18]

Confident of his ability and aware of his importance, the senator spoke up freely on many subjects in his rapid Acadian accent. Sometimes he rose on his toes in a rocking motion as he gestured with his hands to make a point. Not particularly articulate in English or French, he had a good memory and command of factual information to bolster his arguments. Faithful in keeping appointments and prompt for meetings and hearings, Ellender was impatient with unreliable or habitually tardy people.

Through the years Ellender had supported the Tennessee Valley Authority and the Rural Electrification Administration against charges of preventing private utility companies from competing in a free market. In 1954 two utility companies on the periphery of the TVA territory negotiated with the Atomic Energy Commission (AEC) to build a plant in Arkansas to provide electricity in the Memphis area, where a power shortage existed. Edgar H. Dixon of Middle South Utilities and Eugene A. Yates of the Southern Company negotiated a contract with the Eisenhower administration over objections by TVA and Congress. The contract would have allowed the AEC to buy power from the Arkansas plant after private investors received a 9- to 11-percent return on their investments. Lister Hill of Alabama and Tennessee's Kefauver claimed "competition and risk" were missing from the contract negotiated with Eisenhower's friends. In July, 1955, the Eisenhower administration, bowing to public pressure, canceled the Dixon-Yates contract.[19]

Ellender's views on many issues were closer to those of conservative Republicans than to those of liberal Democrats. To a Louisianian who shared his fears of labor leaders, Ellender said he hoped that Robert Taft, the conservative Republican from Ohio, would win reelection, and that some Democrats would lose. Milton Young, the North Dakota Republican, became his political and personal friend, often his golfing and (after Helen's death) dinner companion. "Milt is the best 'Democrat' on the Agriculture Committee," Ellender once remarked to Flo LeCompte.[20]

18. W. C. Kemper to Allen Ellender, November 23, 1955, in "Agriculture, Sugar, 1955" Folder, Box 237, AEP.

19. Virginia Van der Veer Hamilton, *Lister Hill: Statesman from the South* (Chapel Hill, 1987), 200; Joseph B. Gorman, *Kefauver: A Political Biography* (New York, 1971), 198–210.

20. Allen Ellender to Percy Saint, November 29, 1950, in "S" Folder, Box 169, AEP; Florence LeCompte, interview, August 2, 1979; George Arceneaux, Jr., interview, December 31, 1979.

Strengthening Taft-Hartley became an issue early in the 1950s. Labor generally opposed any changes; conservative business interests wanted to amend the law. Ellender's mail from conservatives and chambers of commerce ran heavily in favor of strengthening the measure. Knowing amendments could help FEPC provisions find their way into the law, Ellender voted against the proposed changes. Majority Leader Lyndon Johnson thanked him for supporting the Democratic Party line on Taft-Hartley.[21]

For a number of reasons, Ellender opposed granting statehood to Alaska and Hawaii. Neither territory was ready for statehood, he said, without mentioning their sizable non-WASP populations. Because Alaska and Hawaii were separate from the continental mainland, assimilating native populations into the federal union would impose a heavy burden on the American people, Ellender said, masking his "mongrelization" concerns.[22]

Tidelands oil became an emotional issue in oil-rich Louisiana. Both the state and the United States claimed oil found below the continental shelf along the Gulf of Mexico. Determining where state boundaries ended and federal jurisdiction began was the subject of debate in Louisiana, Texas, California—and Washington. Secretary of the Interior Harold Ickes had persuaded President Truman to claim all tidelands areas more than three miles from the coast for the federal government. Because billions of dollars were at stake, states vigorously defended their claims.

Leander Perez, a powerful political dictator in coastal, mineral-rich Plaquemines Parish, became a vocal opponent of Truman's attempt to acquire tidelands oil for the federal government. Equally vociferous on racial matters, Perez considered Truman dangerous to the South. When Estes Kefauver advocated keeping tidelands oil, Perez encouraged an exodus from the Democratic Party. Ellender, refusing to abandon the national party, said he would not run under the rooster, the emblem of the Louisiana Democratic party, captured by Perez and his followers.[23]

Hoping Louisiana could resolve its tidelands interests, Ellender wanted to claim the state's historic boundaries—three miles from the coastline—to

21. Charles C. Savoie and Sabin Savoie to Allen Ellender, April 13, 1954, and Lyndon Johnson to Ellender, May 7, 1954, both in "Legislation, Taft-Hartley Act, 1954" Folder, Box 58, AEP.

22. Allen Ellender to Ethel Olivier, April 11, 1951, in "Hawaii and Alaska" Folder, Box 644, AEP.

23. Robert A. Garson, *The Democratic Party and the Politics of Sectionalism, 1941–1948* (Baton Rouge, 1974), 162, 164; Gorman, *Kefauver,* 168; Glen Jeansonne, *Leander Perez: Boss of the Delta* (Baton Rouge, 1977), 173, 182.

mediate claims tied up in court battles. Governor Robert Kennon, no doubt influenced by Perez, insisted on a line 10.5 miles from the coast. However in 1947 and in 1950 the Supreme Court ruled that "submerged coastal lands beyond the low-tide mark belong to the nation." The senior senator's job might be in jeopardy, some critics suggested, as Louisiana politicians haggled over the tidelands issue.[24]

After Helen died, Ellender reached out to friends and members of his staff to perform chores Helen had done. Although he never chewed gum, when he was under stress, Ellender reverted occasionally to chewing tobacco, a habit that had irritated Helen intensely. More inclined to say "doggoned" than to resort to profanity, the usually mild-mannered senator cussed at times. Intensely loyal, Ellender tended to support friends and dedicated workers, even if they erred or failed to live up to expectations. Reluctant to fire an incompetent worker, Ellender once assigned the unpleasant task of dismissing a staff member to Flo LeCompte.

Ellender's personal appearance and dress were not important to him. He wore suits (his favorite color was blue) that he kept for a number of seasons. In the summer he tended to wear his suits a bit too long before sending them to the dry cleaners. In the winter he seldom ventured outdoors without his dark homburg. His ties did not always match; he kept his shoes clean but not highly polished. He used tonic on his curly hair, which he kept neatly combed. He never propped his feet on his desk, which was usually cluttered with papers. He knew where things were, however, and went through the stack regularly. His six-suite office was lined with photographs covering every square foot of every wall and even part of some door frames. He tried to collect a photograph of every senator he had ever served with. Pictures of presidents and famous world leaders occupied prominent positions about the office. Early in his career he wrote with fountain pens, but he took to using ballpoint pens when they came into vogue. He had a favorite old round chair he preferred to the fancy leather high-back one in his office. He considered his car a means of transportation, not a status symbol, so he did not have it washed regularly. He enjoyed classical and most popular music, but he never developed a tolerance for rock and roll.[25]

Sometimes Ellender had to avoid entanglements with Louisianians who

---

24. Various newspaper clippings, March, 1953, in "1953" Scrapbook, AEP; Hamilton, *Lister Hill*, 181.

25. Florence LeCompte, interview, April 14, 1992.

had run afoul of the law and needed help. In 1952 Lafayette cattleman Alphe Broussard had planned to import from Mexico a herd of French Charolais cattle noted for rapid growth and weight gain. Broussard and several investors purchased the Charolais in Mexico, reportedly paying one million pesos to Mexican authorities for an export quota. Fearing hoof-and-mouth disease could contaminate the entire U.S. herd, the Quarantine Division of the U.S. Department of Agriculture and the National Cattlemen's Association opposed the sale. Convinced the Charolais would revitalize the beef cattle industry of Louisiana, Broussard persisted. In 1953 U.S. authorities indicted him for smuggling the cattle into Texas. Lafayette attorney James Domengeaux, Ellender's opponent in the 1948 election, represented Broussard in his trial before federal judge John Minor Wisdom. Broussard was convicted, despite calling in every political favor he could from friends in the USDA. After the requisite waiting period, Ellender tried to obtain pardons for friends convicted of crimes. For instance, on January 16, 1953, just four days before he left office, President Truman pardoned former governor Richard Leche, who had been convicted in May, 1940, on federal mail fraud charges.[26]

The summer before a gubernatorial election in Louisiana was always soul-searching time for Ellender, who once again agonized about seeking the governor's office, despite his growing influence in the Senate. Discussing the matter with Elward Wright, Ellender concluded, "As far as I am personally concerned I still believe I can do better work here for the people than I can in Louisiana." In mid-July Ellender met with Earl Long and other members of the Regular Louisiana Democratic Organization, who promised to support Ellender if he decided to run for governor. On July 31, Ellender announced he would not seek the governorship.[27] Robert Kennon, a reform Democrat from Minden in north Louisiana, frustrated the Longites by winning the race.

Despite generous subsidies to potato growers, Ellender's farm, now

26. George Arceneaux, Jr., to Allen Ellender, November 10, 1952, in "South American Trip" Folder, Box 1015, AEP; Box 226, *passim,* AEP; Miriam G. Reeves, *The Governors of Louisiana* (Gretna, La., 1980), 106–107.

27. Allen J. Ellender to Elward Wright, June 4, 1951, in Elward Wright Papers, in the possession of Thomas Wright, Houma, La., hereinafter cited as EWP; A. B. Stinson to Allen Ellender, July 31, 1950, and Ellender to Stinson, August 11, 1950, both in "S" Folder, Box 169, AEP; W. C. Feazel to Ellender, June 25, 1953, in "Campaign, Louisiana Politics (1953)" Folder, Box 465, AEP; New Orleans *Times-Picayune,* July 14, 18, 31, 1951, in "1950–1951" Scrapbook, AEP.

leased, was failing. Harris Pitre, the lessee, had fallen behind in rent and loan repayments. Pitre owed the senator five thousand dollars for a carload of seed potatoes, fertilizer, and two years' rent, Ellender told Elward Wright. "It looks as though I will get very little of that," he wrote.[28]

Ellender's wealth over the years had increased steadily if unspectacularly. His taxable income in 1944 was $32,915.59. This was from his Senate salary ($10,000), farm income ($3,666), and his law practice plus rents, royalties, and real estate transactions managed by Wright ($14,878). In 1950, the year he formed an agricultural partnership with his son, Ellender's income dropped to $27,352. In April, 1951, he sent tax forms for Allen Jr. to sign and forward to the IRS. Busy in Washington, Ellender expected to leave in May for a tour of the Pacific. He did not think he would have a chance to visit the family before leaving or on his return trip.[29]

In late May, 1952, Ellender returned unexpectedly to Houma for the funeral of his niece Diane Ellender, Willard and Vi's daughter, who was killed in a motorcycle accident. In April, Diane and her sister Susan, who attended Marymount College in New York, had visited Ellender in Washington. After they had left, he had sent them photographs as mementos of their stay and had talked of getting larger accommodations to entertain his guests. The apartment was lonely since their departure, he wrote. In June he was back in Washington, cooking his Acadian specialties.[30]

When Ellender returned to Louisiana after adjournment, Arceneaux toured the state with him, traveling by automobile at a slow pace. Expecting to leave at six in the morning and travel all day, Ellender visited remote corners of the state. Meals received scant attention, subject to the hospitality of his constituents and the ability and imagination of local cooks. Sometimes they were elaborate; usually they were simple. When Ellender arrived at his destination after dark, he began his many telephone calls. No matter how late he was up the night before, he rose at five the next morning to plan his itinerary. Armed with a detailed list of local public officials, Ellender visited every parish in the state. Presumably to help staffers write follow-up letters,

28. · Allen Ellender to Elward Wright, June 4, 1951, EWP.

29. Allen Ellender to Allen Ellender, Jr., April 23, 1951, and tax returns, various years, all in Box 1, AEP.

30. Susan Ellender to Allen Ellender, February 25, 1953, and Ellender to Susan, May 1, 1953, both in "Misc. Sen. Ellender (Personal)" Folder, Box 1015, AEP; Houma (La.) *Courier,* May 30, 1952, and Jane Eads, Houma (La.) *Courier,* June 6, 1952, both in "1952" Scrapbook, AEP.

Ellender jotted notes to himself: "chatted on street. Met wife and one daughter."

During the holiday recess, Ellender visited friends and family, fished, hunted, and communed with nature, planting trees and looking at farm land. He had time to contemplate the future. After waiting for so long for a propitious opportunity to seek the statehouse, he had forgone the chance to run in 1952 with the backing of Earl Long and his organization. Instead, he would concentrate in 1954 on winning reelection to the only job he wanted. If he won and the Democrats regained control of the Senate, he would be chairman of the Agriculture Committee again, a position he had held only during the Eighty-second Congress. Many details of the farm bill had not been completed, but its basic features seemed to be taking shape.

13

MCCARTHYISM AND THE 1954
SENATE RACE
(1954–55)

$\mathcal{E}$llender's trips abroad seemed perfectly natural in light of his character and philosophy of life. Energetic and curious, he was eager to visit remote corners of the earth. By nature hard-working, he took seriously his fact-finding tours and came to feel reports of his travels reflected his importance and knowledge. Now that Helen was no longer with him, he could assume the task of touring the world when the Senate was not in session. Ostensibly he was saving the taxpayers money, traveling for the Appropriations Committee to investigate how U.S. dollars were being spent abroad.

Ellender had supported the Marshall Plan to aid war-torn Europe after World War II and the Truman Doctrine to keep Greece and Turkey from falling under communist domination. He did not mind aiding Greece, he told an old labor radical, but he had little sympathy for Turkey, which had sold surplus food and chromium to Germany before belatedly joining the Allied cause. Like Richard Russell and Robert Taft, Ellender believed in strong military bases but in holding the line on massive giveaway programs.[1]

In November, 1952, Ellender took Frank Wurzlow, Jr., with him on an

---

1. New Orleans *Times-Picayune,* April 25, 1951, in "1950–1951" Scrapbook, and Allen Ellender to Covington Hall, March 28, 1947, in "Miscellaneous, Senator E. Misc.—1947" Folder, Box 408, both in Allen J. Ellender Papers, Nicholls State University Library, Thibodaux, La., hereinafter cited as AEP; Gilbert C. Fite, *Richard B. Russell, Jr., Senator from Georgia* (Chapel Hill, 1991), 196, 249; James T. Patterson, *Mr. Republican: A Biography of Robert A. Taft* (Boston, 1972), 370–72, 384–85.

inspection tour of South America. Wurzlow sent to the office staff in Washington postcards picturing sunbathers on the famed crescent beaches of Copacabana in Rio de Janeiro, Brazil. As Washingtonians braced for winter, Wurzlow jokingly observed, "You poor fools in the U.S." But he saw the beach only from the car as Ellender speeded from the U.S. embassy to inspect various installations. "Quit envying me," Wurzlow wrote. "We are much too busy to stop for a swim." Nonetheless, Ellender took time for shopping. Among the items he sent back by diplomatic pouch were Indian bows, curios, and a shrunken human skull. Ellender shipped unusual items from abroad to Room 245, Senate Office Building. In the fall of 1954 he waited for a rug from Afghanistan and slingshots from the ruins of Carthage to supplement the unusual items gathered on earlier trips.[2]

As Ellender's travels abroad increased, his self-assurance grew and his observations became frank. On his fifth trip to Europe in 1951 Ellender found "scandalous waste" in American aid programs, especially in France and Germany. High Commissioner John McCloy and his staff in West Germany were "living like princes," Ellender said. When a reporter asked if Ellender planned to air this situation in Congress, he replied, "You're damn right." McCloy, defending his operation, said Ellender had spent just one day in Bonn, and while there he had asked the Army to keep the post exchange open so he could shop. Mutual Security Director W. Averell Harriman asserted, "We are not throwing money away."[3]

Believing economic factors figured strongly in anticommunist posturing, Ellender told a reporter in 1953, "The 'hullabaloo' over communism is largely a result of outsiders who stir up trouble, especially the English and French who spread propaganda in the hope of scaring Congress into giving more economic aid."[4]

In 1952 Ellender wrote, "Frankly, my feeling is that we should cut out all economic aid to Western Europe, except possibly for Austria and Western Germany." He opposed having a U.S. ambassador to the Vatican and voiced his usual opposition to expanding the number of displaced persons allowed to enter the country. Nationally syndicated columnist Drew Pearson gave a

2. Frank Wurzlow, Jr., to office staff, November 17, 1952, George Arceneaux, Jr., to Allen Ellender, November 24, 26, 1952, all in "South American Trip" Folder, Box 1015, AEP; Ellender to Charles Little, November 30, 1954, in "Sen. E's Trip—Middle East" Folder, Box 1022, AEP.

3. New Orleans *Times-Picayune*, December 21, 1951, Washington *Post*, December 21, 22, 1951, all in "1950–1951" Scrapbook, AEP.

4. Houma (La.) *Courier*, October 30, 1953, in "1953" Scrapbook, AEP.

favorable report of Ellender's congressional tour in October, 1953. "Most overseas tours are strictly vacations at the taxpayer's expense," he wrote, "but some are legitimate. For example, Senator Ellender of Louisiana has just returned from a hard-working, two-months, round-the-world mission for the Senate Appropriations Committee." On the other hand, Richard Russell's biographer considered the Georgian's inspection tour a "useless junket" with little influence on subsequent legislation.[5]

Ellender returned from an inspection tour abroad in 1954 with less than surprising findings. Israel would never be self-supporting. If France and Italy wanted to become communist countries after receiving American aid all these years, "let them go," Ellender said. "It would just give Russia a headache to have them behind the Iron Curtain." After three years investigating foreign aid programs, Ellender thought Iraq had the only mission "run . . . as was intended by Congress, as I interpret the law." Continuing his assault on foreign aid spending, Ellender griped about defense costs for Britain, Australia, and New Zealand. Aware costs in the Far East were excessive, Ellender said aid money was "squandered" in Korea and Taiwan. He wanted to use "Voice of America" broadcast monies to send visitors to the Soviet Union.[6]

Defending itself against Ellender's charges of waste, the State Department cited economic, political, and diplomatic reasons why it opposed moving the primary mission in Morocco from Tangier to Rabat as Ellender recommended. An official explained that the move would seem unfriendly to Arab nationalists. Tangier had a favorable exchange rate not available in Rabat; the "Voice of America" had a station in Tangier, where freedom of operation was greater than it would be in Rabat. He closed by informing Ellender, "It would not be desirable to have this situation discussed publicly." The State Department, not recognizing some satellite states, discouraged Ellender from visiting Albania and Bulgaria on his way to the USSR.[7]

5. Allen Ellender to Monroe, Louisiana, League of Women Voters, July 3, 1952, in "Foreign Aid" Folder, and Ellender to Ralph Pons, July 4, 1952, in "Korean Situation" Folder, both in Box 654, AEP; Ellender to James Stirling, February 3, 1953, in "Legislation, General, 1953" Folder, and Ellender to S. J. Bihm, July 3, 1953, in "Legislation, Immigration, 1953" Folder, both in Box 662, AEP; Washington *Post*, October 13, 1953, in "1953" Scrapbook, AEP; Fite, *Richard Russell*, 196.

6. Allen Ellender to Henry Weins, December 10, 1954, George Arceneaux, Jr., to Ellender, January 24, 1955, both in "Sen. E's Trip—Middle East" Folder, Box 1022, AEP; New York *Times*, November 1, 1954, in "1954" Scrapbook, and miscellaneous newspaper clippings, in "1955" Scrapbook, all in AEP.

7. Loy Henderson to Allen Ellender, May 18, 1955, and Memo of Conversation, May 20, 1955, both in State Department File 033.1100-EL/5-1855.

Labor columnist Victor Riesel, concluding that Ellender was naïve about the USSR, thought Ellender overlooked repressive measures in the Soviet Union and foolishly rebuked the American Federation of Labor for refusing to exchange labor delegates with the USSR. If U.S. workers would go there, Ellender suggested, "They might see things in a different light."[8]

Ellender did not hesitate to express his views on other foreign policy issues. He thought Truman had been right to remove Douglas MacArthur from military command in Korea on April 11, 1951.[9]

Local and foreign concerns raised during the 1950s created interest in a constitutional amendment proposed in 1952 by Ohio Republican senator John Bricker to prevent a treaty from altering any rights or statutes guaranteed by the U.S. Constitution. At first the Bricker Amendment stirred little political enthusiasm or momentum, but it resurfaced in 1953. Ellender, along with Eastland and Stennis of Mississippi, Harry Byrd of Virginia, and a number of other southerners, cosponsored it as Senate Joint Resolution 1. President Eisenhower ultimately said it was not needed and would interfere with cooperative efforts among nations.

Incongruous considerations—race, socialized medicine, states' rights— figured in the Bricker Amendment's longevity. Southerners wondered if the United Nations charter could be used to invalidate segregation laws in the South. The American Medical Association, supporting the amendment, questioned whether Article 55(c) of the U.N. charter encouraged socialized medicine. Ellender and Lister Hill of Alabama feared that Article 55 authorized antilynching legislation and a permanent FEPC. Pressure groups lobbied Congress by mail in support of Bricker, but most Americans, polls indicated, either did not understand the issue or did not consider it important.

In February, 1954, President Eisenhower scored a victory in the Senate over the Bricker Amendment by a vote of 50 to 42. The measure to prevent a treaty from altering rights or statutes guaranteed by the U.S. Constitution, introduced in 1952 and again in 1953, had once again failed to pass. Democrats Lyndon Johnson, J. William Fulbright, Albert Gore, Sr., Hubert Humphrey, John Kennedy, Estes Kefauver, and John McClellan all voted against the amendment Eisenhower considered an impediment to foreign relations. Supporters included Ellender, Russell Long, William Jenner, Everett Dirksen,

8. *Inside Labor*, September 2, 1955, in FBI File 62-81810.

9. "MacArthur Dismissal" Folder, *passim*, Box 416, AEP; Fite, *Richard Russell*, 256–57, 262–63.

Joseph McCarthy, Milton Young, Harry Byrd, and most southerners. Although the amendment failed, it influenced Eisenhower to consult Congress before supporting the French in Indo-China later in the year.[10]

In February, 1954, the press, speculating whether Eisenhower would send troops to Indo-China, reported Ho Chi Minh's forces moving toward the French garrison at Dienbienphu, Vietnam. Ellender, who had seen the rugged terrain of Vietnam, hoped the president would not ask to send troops. Unrealistically Ellender recommended that France grant independence to Vietnam, Cambodia, and Laos. When the French garrison at Dienbienphu fell to forces commanded by North Vietnamese general Vo Nguyen Giap in the summer of 1954, Ellender opposed allowing American troops to replace the departing French. Like Kefauver, Ellender favored cooperation with the British, the Australians, and other powers to stop the advance of the Vietnamese communists.[11]

Discussing the widely known but rarely mentioned corruption of Chiang Kai-shek and his Nationalist Chinese government, Ellender bucked the China Lobby in February, 1953. Communists had seized control of China at the end of World War II. Blaming the Democrats for "losing" China to the communists, the China Lobby favored withholding recognition of Red China and defending Nationalist China, headed by Chiang, on the island of Taiwan, or Formosa. Ellender wanted the Nationalist Chinese to get rid of Chiang.[12]

From time to time Ellender had clashed with Wisconsin Republican senator Joseph McCarthy, who used his committee to investigate communist activities in America. Ellender believed McCarthy wasted money on his investigations and trampled on the rights of people he brought before his committee. In 1951 Ellender called McCarthy "a publicity hound" who made foolish statements about communists in the State Department. "They [the communists] are all gone now," Ellender said.[13]

In July, 1953, McCarthy arranged to have klieg lights and television cam-

10.   Duane Tananbaum, *The Bricker Amendment Controversy: A Test of Eisenhower's Political Leadership* (Ithaca, N.Y., 1988), 2–4, 49–50, 52, 69, 71, 118–19, 131, 157–58, 167–68, 200.

11.   New Orleans *Item,* April 20, 1954, in "1954" Scrapbook, AEP; Joseph B. Gorman, *Kefauver: A Political Biography* (New York, 1971), 169, 183, 193; Allen Ellender to Alonzo M. West, June 24, 1954, in "Legislation, Indo-China, 1954" Folder, Box 58, AEP.

12.   Miami *Daily News,* February 12, 1953, in "1953" Scrapbook, AEP.

13.   Thomas Sancton, New Orleans *Item,* January 11, 1951, in "1950–1951" Scrapbook, AEP; Allen Ellender to C. H. Downs, February 3, 1950, in "Appointments" Folder, Box 1004, AEP.

eras set up in the Senate Caucus Room for a meeting of the Appropriations Committee. Before realizing the committee would discuss appropriations for McCarthy's committee, Ellender asked, "Is this to be a show or what will it be?" Daring Ellender and other committee members to conduct the hearing behind closed doors, McCarthy said he needed room to accommodate the public, the press, and television cameramen. Cautious about overzealous efforts to weed out communists in American life, Ellender disliked McCarthy's aggressive tactics and grandstanding style. During a Senate discussion of literature in American libraries in embassies overseas, Ellender questioned Senator Fulbright about books; then he realized McCarthy planned to make an issue of works showing the United States in an unfavorable light. By withdrawing his questions, Ellender prevented McCarthy from saying the State Department aided the communist cause.[14]

Taking "short cuts that would deny to an accused his fundamental constitutional rights would be a first step toward the complete repudiation of all of our civil liberties," Ellender believed. To those eager to ban communists from the motion picture industry, he wrote, "I do not feel that the government should tell the public what it should or can see."[15]

Ellender had tried unsuccessfully to reduce appropriations for Senate investigations. When the Senate appropriated $750,000 in 1953 for McCarthy's committee to study mismanagement of State Department loyalty files, Ellender, claiming the Senate was "going haywire on these investigations," asked to see records of hearings to justify expenditures. Indiana Republican William Jenner, defending McCarthy's request for funds, said there were no records but promised to provide Ellender with all the information he needed.[16]

Ellender suspected the FBI of secretly providing information about suspected communists. He wondered if FBI director J. Edgar Hoover was responsible for security leaks and unfounded charges of communist infiltration of government agencies. In December, 1953, Ellender asked if Hoover had told an investigating committee that suspected communist Harry Dexter White was "unfit" to serve the International Monetary Fund. He asked why Hoover had refused to testify and why he had kept FBI files on White closed. Hoover did not want White transferred from the Treasury Department to

14. New Orleans *Item*, July 24, 1953, in "1953" Scrapbook, AEP; Walter Johnson and Francis Colligan, *The Fulbright Program: A History* (Chicago, 1965), 99–100.
15. Allen Ellender to Emmet Alpha, April 3, 1951, in "Legislation" Folder, Box 644, AEP.
16. Washington *Post*, January 30, 1953, in "1953" Scrapbook, AEP.

the International Monetary Fund because the FBI would have limited access to information about an international body with the status of a foreign embassy. Stories got out anyway, Hoover said. Ellender probably did not believe Hoover, having heard from disgruntled FBI agents about low morale in the bureau because Hoover punished agents who did not shield him from adverse publicity.[17]

Drew Pearson sided with Ellender in his periodic clashes with McCarthy. Ellender, according to Pearson, was modest but had an impressive legislative record; McCarthy had poor legislative and attendance records. Ellender rejected McCarthy's offer of favorable publicity—"Allen, I'm going to make a big man out of you"—in exchange for testimony about communism in Latin America. Ellender declined because the publicity would have hurt U.S. relations with neighbors to the south.[18]

In January, 1954, Ellender was in a familiar setting, on the Senate floor trying to reduce funds for congressional investigations. Unhappy with "headline-hunting" senators, he singled out McCarthy as one who "wasted" funds and "didn't expose any communists." Ellender said, "Unless we check this man he's going to encroach on the prerogatives of every committee in the Senate." The Senate appropriated $214,000 for McCarthy's committee in 1954, one-third of his 1953 allotment. In August, 1954, the Senate began deliberating a motion to censure McCarthy, whose communist-chasing activities had created a frenzy in America and become an embarrassment to the Senate. Ellender, expecting Fulbright and Wayne Morse to bring specific charges against McCarthy, wanted to give him a chance to respond. McCarthy abused witnesses, Ellender thought, but Senator John McClellan of Arkansas and others had relinquished committee investigations to him. "It [the abnegation] gave McCarthy *carte blanche* to do whatever he desired," Ellender wrote Wright.[19]

During his 1954 election campaign, Ellender opposed McCarthy even though his mail ran about ten to one against censuring the controversial senator. Some constituents, however, agreed with Ellender. "Of course it

17.   Allen Ellender to J. Edgar Hoover, December 1, 1953, in "Justice Department" Folder, Box 46, AEP; G. Desmond Hackethal to Ellender, April 25, May 12, 1953, both in "Federal Bureau of Investigation" Folder, Box 222, AEP; Ellender to Hoover, December 1, 1953, Hoover to Ellender, December 3, 1953, both in FBI File 62-81810.

18.   Washington *Post*, April 29, 1954, in "1954" Scrapbook, AEP.

19.   Murrey Marder, Washington *Post*, January 5, 1954, February 3, 1954, Baton Rouge *Morning Advocate*, January 7, 1954, all in "1954" Scrapbook, AEP; Allen Ellender to Elward Wright, August 2, 1954, in "Terrebonne" Folder, Box 1830, AEP.

goes without saying," one constituent wrote, "that McCarthy has never turned up a major communist plot or spy." Another fan, echoing Ellender's view, wrote, "I have become more and more strongly convinced that his use of the Communist issue is phony." Ellender said he would "try to keep an open mind until I hear Joe." Out of the country during subcommittee hearings on McCarthy, Ellender listened to debate on the floor to get the facts, "both pro and con." Richard Russell considered McCarthy more of a problem for the Republican Party than for the country. He and Ellender voted to censure McCarthy. The vote on December 2, 1954, was 67 to 22.[20]

Getting an early start in his reelection campaign, Ellender worked as though he were an underdog fighting uphill. His opponent, Frank Ellis, had little name recognition, even though he was a member of the upper house of the state legislature. Ellis was from Covington in St. Tammany Parish, a rural piney-woods area north of New Orleans across Lake Pontchartrain.[21]

Ellender's fourth Senate election campaign was similar to those in 1936, 1942, and 1948. Elward Wright and Wurzlow, both totally loyal and eminently knowledgeable about Louisiana politics, directed operations from Houma and Washington, respectively. George Arceneaux, Jr., and Flo LeCompte also had campaign experience. Ellender expected a substantial campaign chest. He had lists of many kinds: mailing, campaign workers, polling commissioners, and political "experts" in all corners of the state who would provide him inside information and advice. Ellis had little chance of winning and knew it, Wurzlow told Ellender. He was in the race "to make a little money for himself." Even an unsuccessful race could produce revenue a candidate could pocket if he solicited vigorously and spent sparingly, Ellender and Wurzlow knew.[22]

Ellender took all competition seriously. An April, 1954, poll showed Ellis with only 8 percent of voter support, a New Orleans legislator reported. New Orleans mayor deLesseps S. Morrison, he said, would remain neutral

20. Many letters to Allen Ellender, January–December, 1954, Allen Prassel to Ellender, November 29, 1954, Harold Lee to Ellender, December 4, 1954, all in "McCarthy Censure, 1954" Folder, Box 683, AEP; Ellender to Charles Little, November 30, 1954, in "Sen. E's Trip—Middle East" Folder, Box 1022, AEP; New York *Times,* November 1, 1954, in "1954" Scrapbook, AEP; Fite, *Richard Russell,* 308–309; Stephen E. Ambrose, *Nixon* (3 vols.; New York, 1987), I, 340.

21. Allen Ellender to Frank Wurzlow, Jr., December 15, 1953, in "Washington Office" Folder, Box 46, and summary note prepared by Florence LeCompte in Box 1830, both in AEP.

22. Frank Wurzlow, Jr., to Allen Ellender, April 28, 1954, Box 1824, AEP.

in the campaign but not "do anything to hurt you." New Orleans congress-man F. Edward Hebert believed *Times-Picayune* publisher John Tims would endorse Ellender. Governor Kennon's support for Ellis and Mayor Morrison's inactivity worried him, Ellender told Tims.[23]

Ellender was unlikely to receive support from organized labor or from blacks. An old friend hinted that Ellis was picking up black support and warned Ellender he might be asked to state his views on right-to-work legislation. The Louisiana legislature would probably consider in the summer session the controversial labor measure organized labor opposed. Congressman Otto Passman of Monroe, promising to encourage his friends to support Ellender, sent a check for two hundred dollars. "On account of the position of labor and the colored people, we must not take any chances," he said. If Ellender could downplay his views on Taft-Hartley, he would receive a fair share of the labor vote, a fan suggested, knowing labor considered Ellis to be less than an ideal candidate. Spurred into action, Ellender met with union representatives at the Standard Oil refinery in Baton Rouge on July 10 to neutralize the Ellis vote. Woody Dumas, a union leader at the plant, supported Ellender in the Second Ward in Baton Rouge.[24]

By July reports from around the state indicated a comfortable Ellender lead. "Generally, too, the country parishes seem to believe that the colored vote will go along with the parish leadership, which means for you," an office report stated. "Where there is no large labor vote, there is no concern whatsoever."[25]

The Ellender campaign had ample funds. Old friends, lobby groups, old Longites, the business community—all contributed to the cause. To comply with campaign-funding rules, Wright had to file forms provided by the secretary of the Senate. Admitting that the bookkeeping was casual and there was no voucher system to account for exact campaign spending, Wright told Arceneaux, "We sometimes think it best not to keep too accurate a record."[26]

Loopholes in campaign-financing laws permitted Wright considerable

23. Frank Wurzlow, Jr., to Allen Ellender, April 9, 1954, Box 1824, AEP; F. Edward Hebert to Frank Wurzlow, Jr., (telephone report), June 14, 1954, Allen Ellender to John Tims, August 7, 1954, both in Box 1829, AEP; deLesseps Morrison to Ellender, May 14, 1954, Ellender to Morrison, April 3, 1954, both in "C.A.B." Folder, Box 77, AEP.

24. L. Austin Fontenot to Elward Wright, May 15, July 1, 1954, both in "St. Landry" Folder, Box 1830, AEP; Otto Passman to Allen Ellender, July 14, 1954, Box 1823, AEP; A. Stewart Wallace, Jr., to Elward Wright, July 21, 1954, Box 1824, AEP.

25. Office report to Allen Ellender, July 2, 1954, Box 1832, AEP.

26. Elward Wright to George Arceneaux, Jr., August 2, 1954, *ibid.*

leeway in reporting receipts and expenditures. Some forms applied only to general elections. Consequently, Ellender's primary campaign in July, 1954, for instance, showed "no contributions and no expenditures," Wright informed Wurzlow. Longites convicted in the scandals sent money to Wright. Ellender received a letter from Abe Shushan, who apologized for failing to send a check. "I hope he sends us a nice sum," Ellender told Wright. Old foe Jimmy Noe, now a supporter and fund-raiser, sent one thousand dollars to Ellender's campaign by Weiss. "It appears now that we will have a surplus of around $1,000," Wright told Wurzlow after the campaign. Tightfisted senator Richard Russell returned unused campaign contributions to his Georgia supporters on a pro-rata basis. Ellender, transferring unused funds to other accounts, kept the surplus for future campaigns.[27]

Leander Perez, contributing one thousand dollars and soliciting funds from his friends, dropped hints to Ellender of favors he wanted. Promising to visit Perez at his hunting camp, Ellender said he would cook a meal for him. Robert Maestri, who had contributed generously to Huey Long's campaigns, provided names and phone numbers of prospective contributors Ellender should contact.[28]

Clarence Savoie, the crusty sugar planter, contributed five hundred dollars to the Ellis campaign. Insisting that he was not campaigning for Ellis or supporting him, Savoie also raised four thousand dollars for Ellender's campaign. "The only thanks we want is ACTION," he wrote in August, 1954. "Therefore, I am hoping to hear from you soon, and read of some action on your part in behalf of the Sugar farmers." Ellender, slow in responding to hostile mail, was in Europe when Wurzlow replied in October, 1954.[29]

"I don't like the idea of trying to collect funds after the election," Ellender wrote, "except from those who actually promised to contribute." In August, Wright asked Noe to send the second thousand dollars he had prom-

27.   Elward Wright to Frank Wurzlow, Jr., September 24, 1954, *ibid.;* Allen Ellender to Wright, August 4, in "Terrebonne" Folder, Box 1830, Ellender to Abraham Shushan, August 4, 1954, Box 1829, both in AEP; Fite, *Richard Russell,* 205, 209.

28.   Leander Perez to Allen Ellender, February 17, 1954, Robert Maestri to Ellender, May 17, 1954, both in Box 1829, Ellender to Perez, August 9, 1954, in "Plaquemines" Folder, Box 1830, all in AEP.

29.   A list of contributors in Box 1838, AEP, provided the figure cited. Unidentified newspaper clipping, n.d., Box 1829, AEP; Clarence Savoie to Allen Ellender, August 17, October 5, 1954, Frank Wurzlow, Jr., to Savoie, October 14, 1954, all in "Agriculture, Sugar, 1954" Folder, Box 202, AEP.

ised, but to disregard the request if he had given the money to Ellender personally. Wright told Wurzlow, "I also expected a check of $1000.00 from Jimmy Noe. This hasn't arrived either." Noe, ignoring the request, sent no check.[30]

During an election campaign Ellender always contributed to black Protestant churches soliciting funds. Usually he sent a check for $10, sometimes $25, and a note saying he wished that he could give more. Meanwhile, campaign funds came in from all corners of the state. At the end of July, 1954, the campaign checking account at the Whitney National Bank in New Orleans showed a balance of $5,424.67.[31]

Every detail of the campaign received Ellender's careful attention. When his opponent, using a 1940 thank-you letter from Ellender, tried to confuse voters into thinking Ellender had something good to say about Ellis, Ellender complained. When two factions in rural Avoyelles Parish supporting Ellender began to feud in June, Flo informed Ellender he might have to go to central Louisiana to make peace between the rivals.[32]

Ellender trounced Ellis in the Democratic primary on July 27, 1954, carrying every parish except Orleans and St. Tammany. New Orleans, which Ellender had carried by a margin of nearly 75 percent in 1948, Ellis took by a four-thousand-vote margin. Ellender, attributing the loss to the Negro and labor vote and the failure of Mayor Morrison and Governor Kennon to support him, explained to Thibodaux attorney Harvey Peltier, "Morrison did not come through." He added, "As a result of his inactivity the burden of furnishing as much as $60 per precinct fell on me, and believe me, it cost plenty."[33]

In August, 1954, Ellender, weary from his reelection campaign and repulsed by McCarthyism, left for an inspection tour of Europe and the Near East. "I was a little surprised at Allen leaving before Congress actually adjourned," Wright wrote Wurzlow. "I have had two or three people say to

30. Allen Ellender to Elward Wright, July 29, 1954, Box 1832, Wright to James A. Noe, August 9, 1954, Box 1823, Wright to Frank Wurzlow, Jr., August 21, 1954, in "Terrebonne" Folder, Box 1830, all in AEP.

31. "Contributions" Folder, and Robert L. James to Allen Ellender, October 18, 1954, in "1954 Campaign" Folder, both in Box 1022, AEP; Florence LeCompte to Elward Wright, September 10, 1954, Box 1823, and Box 1832, *passim,* AEP.

32. "Ellis Campaign Materials" Folder, *passim,* Box 1832, and Florence LeCompte to Allen Ellender, June 14, 1954, Box 1829, all in AEP.

33. Allen Ellender to Cleburne Edmundson, August 17, 1954, and Ellender to Harvey Peltier, August 4, 1954, both in Box 1829, AEP.

me, 'I see *Marco Polo* started off again.' " Wurzlow, thinking Ellender should have waited for the session to end before leaving, informed him of constituent complaints. He recommended Ellender return to tour Louisiana before the November elections.[34]

A prophetic Ellender supporter, A. Stewart Wallace, Jr., scrutinizing predominantly black and labor precincts in Baton Rouge, predicted that more blacks would be voting in the future. He considered Ellender's assertion that blacks did not really want to end racial segregation pure fantasy. "If we believe this we shall be living in a fool's paradise," he said. Television, he predicted, would play an increasing role in determining the outcome of political campaigns.[35]

Race interfered with Ellender's farm policy. Ellender's relationship with Hubert Humphrey of Minnesota suffered because of racial differences. Civil rights in the 1950s, like the slavery issue of the 1850s, dichotomized congressmen and caused emotional responses to political issues.

Like Richard Russell, Ellender thought the Warren Court was making law, not interpreting it. He sent his staff to the Senate Library for materials about Jefferson, Calhoun, Jefferson Davis, Tom Paine, and Tocqueville to corroborate his states' rights position. "He read history, but you seldom caught him at it," George Arceneaux, Jr., observed. Noted for a good memory, Ellender reached conclusions by listening and discussing, not by interpreting the ideas of great political thinkers.

Although Ellender thought the court had erred, he did not advocate physical resistance. With aides Wurzlow and Arceneaux, he discussed philosophies of government and responsibilities of public servants. Believing a senator had to uphold the Constitution, Ellender obeyed the law, even when he disagreed with it. Defying the Supreme Court was out of the question. The South, in a futile nineteenth-century attempt at resistance, had failed in a bloody civil war. Southwestern Louisiana Institute, a state college in Lafayette, would have to admit forty black students as a result of a suit filed by NAACP attorney A. P. Tureaud, Arceneaux informed Ellender in September, 1954.[36]

34.   Elward Wright to Frank Wurzlow, Jr., August 21, 1954, in "Terrebonne" Folder, Box 1830, AEP; Wurzlow to Allen Ellender, August 24, October 12, 1954, in "Sen. E's Trip—Middle East" Folder, Box 1022, AEP.

35.   A. Stewart Wallace, Jr., to Allen Ellender, July 28, 1954, Box 1824, AEP.

36.   George Arceneaux, Jr., interview, December 31, 1979; Claude Duval, interview, December 18, 1979; Arceneaux to Allen Ellender, September 20, 1954, in "Sen. E's Trip—Middle East" Folder, Box 1022, AEP; Fite, *Richard Russell,* 150–51, 331.

Believing laws designed to protect the rights of black Americans could be used for sinister ends, Ellender sanctioned conspiracy theories and myths of Reconstruction in Louisiana. Embracing the myth of black rule in the South, he blamed outsiders, not uneducated blacks, for the corruption and bloodshed.[37] Although Ellender considered himself a practical man and a flexible politician, his views on race had changed little over the years. Unyielding on racial matters, he had not adjusted like southerners with presidential aspirations. Senator Estes Kefauver of Tennessee, for instance, setting his sights on the White House in the 1950s, dropped his tough segregationist line and refused to sign the "Southern Manifesto," which Ellender and most other Deep-South Democrats endorsed.[38]

A senator is generally ranked on legislative accomplishments (the significance of bills enacted into law), but he is judged also on how honestly and impartially he represents his constituents. On the first count, Ellender succeeded with bills on housing, agriculture, and education. On the second count, he failed. For his treatment of black Americans alone, he fell short, even if one makes a scrupulous effort to judge him by the standards of his times. During Ellender's tenure in office, significant racial changes occurred. Many Americans came to favor racial integration and black enfranchisement. But Ellender could not or would not accept major racial adjustments. By this measurement alone, Ellender could never be considered a great senator.

When he was free from legislative and administrative chores, Ellender expanded his Louisiana social connections. Over the years he had increased his cordial contacts with family and political friends. His Christmas card list had grown to 450, and his family gift list was three pages long. He purchased many gifts abroad, such as a "sapphire bracelet, sapphire ring, blue silk nightgown, cigars." In January, 1955, he gave a party at Apartment 306-G, 3900 Connecticut Avenue, and sent printed invitations, complete with menu. Besides serving a variety of drinks, Ellender cooked shrimp-okra gumbo, Canada goose, and wild duck with oyster dressing.[39]

When the Bank of Terrebonne sold its building in 1955, Ellender had to move the satellite office he maintained in Houma. Flo LeCompte, who su-

37.　George Arceneaux, Jr., interview, December 31, 1979. See C. Vann Woodward, *New Republic,* March 14, 1988, p. 40, for a precise analysis of how both North and South found it convenient to believe that Reconstruction had brought no positive good to the country.

38.　Gorman, *Kefauver,* 236.

39.　"Sen. Ellender—Personal" Folder, *passim,* Box 1031, AEP.

pervised the office when she was in Houma, moved to an office in Elward Wright's building on Barrow Street; it rented for seventy dollars per month. Continuing to handle Ellender's personal affairs, Flo deposited checks in his Houma account and maintained close ties to the Washington office. She told Ellender he would probably have to sue a delinquent renter if he expected to collect money owed him.[40]

Drew Pearson criticized Ellender for negotiating a sweetheart land deal with Southdown Sugar Company in 1955. Pearson claimed Southdown sold land in Houma to Ellender for $2,500 per acre. Despite the carping, Ellender's purchase was like most of his other transactions—an honest business deal.[41]

When Congress recessed, Ellender returned to Louisiana for a welcome rest. Unless the Democrats could find a viable challenger to Eisenhower in 1956, he would face four more years of Republican administration. Accomplishing his legislative agenda would be easier with a Democrat in the White House.

40. Allen Ellender to Joe Duke, November 10, 1955, Florence LeCompte to Ellender, November 2, 22, 1955, all in "Sen. Ellender—Personal" Folder, Box 1031, AEP.

41. Albuquerque *Tribune,* November 4, 1955, in "1955" Scrapbook, AEP; Washington *Post,* August 25, 1955, FBI File 62-81810; Terrebonne Parish Conveyance Book 218, Folio 523, April 30, 1955, in Terrebonne Parish Courthouse, Houma, La.

DEEDS

NOT

PROMISES

WILL

RE-ELECT

ALLEN J. ELLENDER

TO THE UNITED STATES

SENATE

For the best interests of Your Country at War, let's give Senator Ellender an overwhelming vote of confidence September 8.

TUNE IN ON THESE RADIO ADDRESSES MONDAY, SEPT. 7
9:00 TO 9:30 P. M.

UNITED STATES SENATOR
ALLEN J. ELLENDER
Over Stations KWKH, WDSU, WJBO, WMIS, KVOL, WNOE.

Typical Ellender ad used in his 1942 reelection campaign.

Allen J. Ellender Collection, Allen J. Ellender Archives, Nicholls State University

Allen and Helen greet Allen Jr. in 1937, shortly after he registers at Virginia Military Institute.

Allen J. Ellender Collection, Allen J. Ellender Archives, Nicholls State University

Ellender (second from left) with some close friends and advisers: Frank Wurzlow, Jr., Elward Wright, and George Arceneaux, Jr.

Allen J. Ellender Collection, Allen J. Ellender Archives, Nicholls State University

On June 4, 1946, President Truman signs the National School Lunch Act, coauthored by Ellender (standing behind Truman's chair).

Courtesy Southdown Museum in Houma

Ellender (second row, second from left) and other Democrats pose with President Eisenhower on February 19, 1953.

Courtesy Southdown Museum in Houma

President Kennedy hands Ellender the first pen used to sign the 1962 Farm Bill.
Courtesy Southdown Museum in Houma

Ellender presents President Nixon reports of his travels; they sometimes were printed as Senate documents.
Allen J. Ellender Collection, Allen J. Ellender Archives, Nicholls State University

Ellender and President Lyndon Johnson share a laugh.
Allen J. Ellender Collection, Allen J. Ellender Archives, Nicholls State University

Ellender receives a birthday cake from Ladybird Johnson, probably in 1967 on his seventy-seventh birthday.
Allen J. Ellender Collection, Allen J. Ellender Archives, Nicholls State University

The senator tastes his famous gumbo, a dish he served to several presidents.

Allen J. Ellender Collection, Allen J. Ellender Archives, Nicholls State University

Ellender works out in the Senate gym in 1937.

Allen J. Ellender Collection, Allen J. Ellender Archives, Nicholls State University

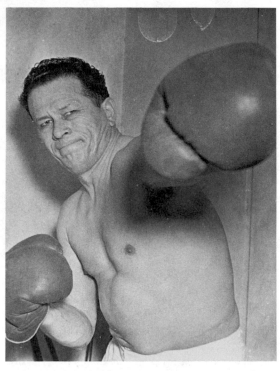

14

TRYING TO DEFROST THE
COLD WAR
(1956–63)

*B*y the beginning of the second Eisenhower administration, Ellender's life was dominated by four major interests: agriculture, foreign policy, race, and family. He continued to stress economic factors as he grew in seniority and power on the Appropriations Committee, but the politics of race influenced his thinking about agriculture and foreign policy. Family and Louisiana matters always occupied an important part of his life.

On his early travels abroad, Ellender carried a diary and scribbled bits of information for a report to Congress. On his return, he threw the diary on the desk of George Arceneaux, Jr., or Frank Wurzlow, Jr., and asked for a rough draft of a report. When the aides grew weary of deciphering the senator's bold scribbling and parsing his Cajun syntax, they persuaded him to use a tape recorder. In time, the recorder gave way to an audio movie camera.[1]

Ellender's trips grew longer in distance and duration, and his shopping interests expanded exponentially. Sometimes he had to obtain a special passport to visit an Iron Curtain country unrecognized by the United States. Ellender's calls for reducing foreign aid seemed less than genuine in January, 1957, after *Time* publicized the junket of his occasional escort, Grace Johnson, to France with fellow Appropriations Committee investigator Frances Holloway of Mississippi. Using counterpart funds (local currencies accruing to

1. George Arceneaux, Jr., interview, December 31, 1979.

the United States in exchange for U.S. dollars spent on foreign aid programs) the women lived extravagantly during their twenty-day French excursion in the fall of 1956. The women embarrassed embassy personnel and created an image of the wasteful ugly American, something Ellender had tried to eradicate. "These two women are the worst we've ever known," an unidentified diplomat said, fearful of offending members of the Senate Appropriations Committee.[2]

Although Ellender regarded communism as no major threat to the United States, he nonetheless provided background security information on suspected communists from time to time. In February, 1956, an attorney representing a medical foundation asked Ellender for information on two doctors at Touro Infirmary in New Orleans. Ellender forwarded his request to the House Un-American Activities Committee for loyalty checks on the doctors. According to Ellender's report, Touro had nothing to fear concerning the doctors.[3]

United States policies for dealing with the Soviet Union were wrong, ineffective, and tremendously costly, Ellender believed. The Soviets rejected inspection of military facilities in arms-reduction agreements, he thought, because they did not have the armaments U.S. experts claimed they had; consequently, "we have been expanding our military might on a somewhat false assumption." The United States bore the burden of defending Europe in "this mutual security fable," Ellender wrote. Because of misleading military advice, he said, "Congress has absolutely and positively lost the purse strings."[4]

Ellender believed a sincere exchange of ideas, students, trade goods, and information would do more to weaken communism than hard-line U.S. propaganda statements. Considering him naïve and an amateur in dealing with communist regimes, FBI and State Department experts sometimes denied him access to information. Critics accused him of being "soft" on communism. George Sokolsky, the nationally syndicated columnist, believed he had been duped by the communists. Dr. Alexander Sas-Joworsky, a veteri-

2. Passport application letters and information, 1946–1971, State Department File 033.1100-EL/9-1758; *Time,* January 7, 1957, pp. 15–16.

3. Charles McClaskey to Allen Ellender, February 25, 1956, Ellender to Francis Walter, March 2, 1956, Walter to Ellender, March 5, 1956, Ellender to McClaskey, March 12, 1956, all in "1956 Un-American Activities Committee" Folder, Box 687, Allen J. Ellender Papers, Nicholls State University Library, Thibodaux, La., hereinafter cited as AEP.

4. Allen Ellender 1956 Field Notes, Vol. 2, pp. 247, 255, 274, 276, Box 1527, AEP.

narian from Abbeville, Louisiana, who became a celebrity of sorts answering questions about American history on a nationally televised quiz show, made similar accusations. Propelled to fame as a patriotic naturalized Pole, Sas-Joworsky lost favor when the American public discovered later that the quiz show had been rigged. An Ellender political supporter, calling Sas-Jaworsky "the horse doctor," warned, "Dr. Sas went out of his way to make it appear that you were some sort of spokesman for the Russian Communist."[5]

Ellender frequently explained his views on communism and the Cold War to constituents. "The Russian people are better off today under Communism than they ever have been," he wrote. "As much as I abhor Communism, and as much as I dislike to admit that, it is the truth." The year after the USSR launched Sputnik, he told Richard Russell, "I feel very strongly that we should not hide our heads in the sand about Russian progress in various fields, simply because we do not like the system which has brought about these changes."[6]

Ellender believed in détente with the USSR and encouraged a broader exchange program between the two world powers. Having Russian students observe life in the United States was a better alternative to the ideological clash than the arms race, he thought. Opposed to massive foreign aid programs enriching anticommunist dictators, Ellender wanted to sell surplus wheat directly to the Soviet Union. "We shouldn't allow the countries of western Europe to act as brokers for us," he complained. European nations sold flour produced from U.S. wheat to countries behind the Iron Curtain, Ellender discovered.

He accused the State Department and the CIA of deliberately stirring up geopolitical animosity against the Soviets. "I hope I am in error but I have a hunch that our Defense Department is prone to keep the international situation boiling over so as to obtain all it asks for at the Washington level," he noted on a visit to Europe.[7]

5. New Orleans *Times-Picayune*, June 2, 4, 1958, in "1958" Scrapbook, AEP; L. Austin Fontenot to Allen Ellender, January 25, February 15, 23, 1959, all in "Allen J. Ellender" Folder, Box 10, John Fournet Papers, Louisiana and Lower Mississippi Valley Collections, Louisiana State University, Baton Rouge, La.

6. Allen Ellender to Norman Bauer, March 25, 1959, in "Communism, 1959" Folder, Box 731, and Ellender to Richard Russell, Jr., July 29, 1958, in "Sen. Ellender's Report, 1958" Folder, Box 1056, both in AEP.

7. "Allen J. Ellender Oral History Interview," by Larry Hackman, August 29, 1967 (John F. Kennedy Library, Washington, D.C.; facsimile copy in Nicholls State University Library, Thibodaux, La.), 3–7, 39–40, hereinafter cited as Ellender interview for JFK Library; Allen

Sometimes Ellender admitted making premature judgments and inaccurate appraisals of foreign policy. Apologizing to the U.S. ambassador to Peru, he wrote, "It was only after the report had gone to printers and was actually completed that I realized I was a little harsh in my comments about you. I meant no harm." The CIA's legislative counsel claimed Guatemala president Ydigoras Fuentes denied telling Ellender that the University of Guatemala was a "hotbed of Communists," as Ellender claimed in a report. Ellender had an exaggerated view of the importance of his travels. Offering to share firsthand information with President Eisenhower in 1956, he received evasive responses from the president's chief assistant, Sherman Adams.[8]

Back home after Congress recessed in 1959, Ellender announced his 1960 presidential race predictions: Nelson Rockefeller to edge out Richard Nixon for the Republican nomination, Stuart Symington of Missouri to win the Democratic nomination over Lyndon Johnson.[9] His dismal record as a predictor of presidential sweepstakes winners had not deterred him from speaking up. He did not mention John Kennedy, not even as a long-shot. As usual he was wrong.

Although Ellender usually supported presidential appointees, he was disappointed when President Kennedy reappointed Allen Dulles to head the Central Intelligence Agency. Dulles could not find a "black elephant in a snowstorm," Ellender said. From time to time, Ellender had received secret correspondence about attempts by Dulles to hide information from him. The budget of the U.S. Information Service was hidden, one source reported, quoting Dulles' 1957 justification for deceiving Ellender: "Do it in such a way that this Louisiana donkey can not do us any harm even if he does notice something."[10]

Ellender favored a complete overhaul of the Central Intelligence Agency. He called the Bay of Pigs invasion the "fiasco in Cuba," and urged caution in July, 1961, when the Berlin Wall went up. Ellender did not want the

---

Ellender 1960 Field Notes, in "France" Folder, p. 20, and "Syria, Jordan, and Israel" Folder, p. 1812, both in Box 1549, AEP.

8. Allen Ellender to Theodore Achille, April 9, 1959, and John Warner to Ellender, April 20, 1959, both in "South American Tour, 1959" Folder, Box 1065, AEP; Allen Ellender to Sherman Adams, November 5, 1956, and Adams to Ellender, November 12, 1956, both in "Personal—1956 World Tour" Folder, Box 1843, and Box 1064, *passim*, AEP.

9. Miscellaneous newspaper clippings, December, 1959, in "1959" Scrapbook, AEP.

10. Ellender interview for JFK Library, 19–20, 21; [?] to Ellender, April 11, 1961, and Mario Fellom to Ellender, December 4, 1961, both in "Ellender, Personal" Folder, Box 1106, AEP.

president to call out the Louisiana National Guard, saying some people might overreact when Nikita Khrushchev "pops off," but the crisis was not nearly as serious as some claimed. Every year when funding for foreign aid came up, Ellender observed, "a new crisis looms." In August, 1961, Ellender introduced an amendment to an appropriations bill to reduce total foreign aid spending from $1.8 billion to $1.3 billion. Eventually he succeeded in reducing the upper limit substantially, but Congress restored some cuts he had made. "Why should we give prosperous Japan any money is something I cannot understand," he lamented in convoluted syntax.[11]

Veteran foreign service personnel considered Ellender naïve and unrealistic in dealing with communist nations, but Ellender thought his Latin American reports helped shape Kennedy's thinking about the Alliance for Progress. State Department and FBI records obtained through the Freedom of Information Act indicate concern over Ellender's visits, especially to Iron Curtain countries. Soviet leaders granted him permission to visit restricted areas of the Soviet Union in August, 1957. Unimpressed, State Department personnel knew they would have to grant reciprocal permission to members of the Soviet embassy in Washington to visit "equivalent closed areas of the U.S."[12]

The FBI maintained a rather extensive newspaper clipping file on Ellender's observations about waste and duplication. Hoover may have leaked information about Ellender's golfing or shopping excursions at army post exchanges to Sokolsky and Drew Pearson. An internal FBI memo in the summer of 1960 provided agents abroad a sample response to Ellender's queries. Staffers should answer basic questions about the number of agents, automobiles, and the like, the memo suggested, but when asked about cost figures, agents were encouraged to say, "we are not in possession of complete figures."[13] The State Department and the FBI resented Ellender's probes into the cost of maintaining embassies, but as Ellender's seniority on the Appro-

11. Allen Ellender to many constituents, August, 1961, in "Legislation, Berlin Crisis" Folder, Box 771, AEP; New Orleans *Times-Picayune,* April 30, 1961, Edgar Poe, New Orleans *Times-Picayune,* July 23, 1961, both in "1961" Scrapbook, AEP; Houma (La.) *Press,* August 22, 1961, in "1961" Scrapbook, AEP.

12. Ellender to Eula Breidenbach, November 1, 1962, in "United Nations, Admission of Red China" Folder, Box 815, AEP; Ellender interview for JFK Library, 6–7, 25–26; Warren Harang, Jr., interview, June 6, 1980; Irving Legendre, Jr., interview, June 18, 1980; Moscow to Secretary of State (telegram), August 31, 1957, State Department File F0001.

13. FBI Memo, July 20, 1960, FBI File 62-81810.

priations Committee grew, governmental agencies found it increasingly difficult to brush aside his inquiries.

Both the FBI and the State Department briefed American embassy personnel prior to a visit by Ellender. Concerned that Ellender would discover clandestine intelligence operations in Mexico, one embassy staffer sought advice from his superiors. "My understanding is that Senator Ellender has visited many embassies throughout the world and has [a] reputation for conducting rather searching interviews. He will ask for embassy organization charts and would probably note fact that we occupy entire floor of embassy and yet did not appear before him," he wrote. Hoover instructed the agent to be cautious of statements to Ellender. "Avoid participation in briefing session if you can do so without embarrassment," Hoover wrote.

Without mentioning investigations of communist activities south of the border, an FBI agent in Mexico told Ellender the FBI had thirteen agents in Mexico for "criminal liaison functions" regarding car theft and swindling schemes. "Well, are you here for the benefit of the Mexicans or for the United States?" Ellender inquired. The agent said he was there to protect U.S. interests. Penciled at the bottom of the communiqué, possibly by Hoover himself, was the observation: "We can expect some trouble from this 'blabber mouth.' "[14]

During a 1955 visit to the Soviet Union, Deputy Premier A. I. Mikoyan, impressed with Ellender's genuine curiosity and his atypical, nonbelligerent attitude toward the USSR, invited him for a return visit. Ellender made his second trip to the Soviet Union in July, 1956, armed with a 16-millimeter Bell and Howell model 200 EE sound camera. Nikita Khrushchev granted him a two-hour-and-thirty-eight-minute interview. Ellender discussed the Egyptian takeover of the Suez Canal and inspected agricultural operations in the Ukraine, the Caucasus region, and Siberia. He returned on October 31 with reams of field notes and cans of film footage.[15]

Ellender wrote a six-page letter to Khrushchev when he returned home. It was blunt and to the point. The Soviet invasion of Hungary, he said, shocked the Western world. Agricultural operations needed weed control,

14. Department of State Instruction 1375 to various cities, September 17, 1958, State Department File 033.1100-EL/9-1758; Hoover to [?], September 30, 1958, [?] memo to Bureau, September 26, 1958, [?] to [?], October 31, 1958, all in FBI File 62-81810.

15. Washington (D.C.) *Star,* August 6, 1956, FBI File 62-81810; C. H. Percy to Allen Ellender, September 7, 1956, in "1956 Trip" Folder, Box 1527, AEP.

fertilization, land preparation, irrigation, mechanization, dissemination of agricultural information, and proper crop selection. He cautioned the Soviets about the dangers of a dust bowl.[16]

Claiming he planned his own itinerary, Ellender said he went wherever he wanted to go in the Soviet Union, not merely where the Soviets wanted him to go. He wanted Hoover, who had received some favorable critical reviews for *Masters of Deceit,* to say Ellender's reports from abroad were useful. J. P. Mohr, claiming that FBI policy prohibited the director from making observations, said the FBI had also turned down Ellender's critics who wanted Hoover to demean Ellender's reports.[17]

To the chagrin of the State Department, Ellender traveled extensively in 1962. Cablegrams he sent to President Kennedy about an exchange program with the Soviet Union had not been forwarded to the president, he complained early in the year. Blaming the State Department for deceiving the president about U.S. failure to live up to provisions of the program, Ellender said, "Evidently there is someone in the State Department who is holding things back and trying to make things as difficult as possible in respect to the exchange program."[18]

Uncharacteristically, Ellender seemed eager to publicize his trips to the USSR. Usually content to work unobtrusively within the party and committee system to achieve legislative goals, he abandoned his unassuming approach when discussing his travels. He sent printed reports of the trips to state and local politicians, schools, judges, law enforcement personnel, and anyone who requested them. He scheduled showings of his films in the auditorium of the New Senate Office Building on different dates and invited bureaucrats, elected officials, and department heads in Washington to attend.[19]

In a subtle way Ellender served as a check on managers of U.S. foreign policy during the first decades of the Cold War. He had demonstrated a stubborn streak and continued to challenge U.S. Cold War strategy even though he came from a conservative section of the country and most of his constituents did not agree with him. Although his predictions about the economic collapse of communism seem prophetic in retrospect, it is debatable whether he influenced cold warriors of the 1950s and 1960s.

16. Allen Ellender to Nikita S. Khrushchev, November 20, 1956, Box 1527, AEP.

17. Unidentified newspaper clipping, June 12, 1958, and J. P. Mohr to Clyde Tolson, August 12, 1958, both in FBI File 62-81810.

18. New Orleans *Times-Picayune,* February 6, 1962, in "1962" Scrapbook, AEP.

19. "Ellender's Film" Folder, *passim,* Box 1123, AEP.

At any rate, Ellender's travels filled his need to be a world ambassador, meeting international leaders, devising policies, advising presidents. The trips flattered his ego, creating the impression he was energetic and important. In a way his trips replaced Louisiana as a refuge during stressful times. He may have used travel as an escape from a busy, troubled world. He may have been running away from himself, hiding his loneliness in continent-hopping schedules that took up much of his spare time.

Ellender visited other Iron Curtain countries as well. In April, 1957, he attended a reception in the Hungarian legation in Washington. Anticommunist Hungarians in Washington picketed Ellender's apartment to protest. Ellender, thinking the State Department was "short-sighted and stupid" to boycott the reception, ignored the pickets. "Let them come—they can show up with a camera for all I care."[20]

Ellender's visit to Hungary in October and November concerned the State Department and the FBI. Chargé d'Affaires Garret G. Ackerson, Jr., wrote a six-page letter outlining his frustrations concerning Ellender, who wanted to know what plans had been made for him to visit the "big boys" in the government so he could learn "what makes them tick." The United States did not recognize Hungary, Ackerson explained, and Ellender should not have come in the first place. Ellender understood Ackerson's position but disagreed, as he had about attending the Hungarian celebration earlier in the year. Ellender made his own arrangements, also to Ackerson's dismay. Calling on Hungarian officials implied recognition of sorts by the United States. Ellender visited Hungarian leader János Kádár and Joseph Cardinal Mindszenty during his visit.

Ackerson's report had only one positive comment about his guest: "The Senator was perfectly sincere in his expressed wish that social engagements should be kept to a minimum." When Ellender openly discussed confidential information he had gathered in the USSR, embassy personnel suggested he remain silent in the presence of Hungarian butlers serving coffee. Ellender seemed unconcerned, even when officers referred to buildings "which may have ears."[21]

Thinking Ellender had been "completely duped by the propaganda of communist officials," Ackerson wanted a "clear disassociation of the Administration from the Senator's visit here and his misstatements on Hungarian

20. Miscellaneous newspaper clippings, April 5, 1957, and Washington *Post,* April 21, 1957, all in "1957" Scrapbook, AEP.
21. Ackerson to State Department, November 1, 1957, FBI File 62-81810.

developments." When asked if he had read the State Department version of the Hungarian uprising "uncolored by Soviet propaganda," Ellender said he did not trust official reports and preferred to gather information firsthand. According to FBI files, some information on Ellender's visit came from Col. U. P. Williams of army intelligence, whose report had exceeded his jurisdiction. "He and the Army could be in serious trouble since such reporting is outside the scope of the Military Attaché's authority," an FBI report indicated.[22]

Ellender's impressions of Vietnam and Japan were equally critical. Vietnam was rife with corruption, he said in 1956. The United States paid "$1000 American per month" rent for a library and a film center owned by bankers. "I boiled over when I saw that plant," he said. "Rents are exorbitant and it is maddening that the local government will not force these highjackers to pay taxes." On September 20, 1956, Ellender wrote: "The Japs need no help. To begin with, the Japanese are competent people." He visited schools, universities, and agricultural facilities. "Japan is not a backward country," he said, hoping to eliminate U.S. Technical Aid Program personnel in Japan. "I believe this is a shameful expenditure of public funds," he concluded.[23]

In Cuba in December, 1958, Ellender played golf and held a press conference to explain how he had been able to ride in a Soviet naval vessel and later describe the vessel to the U.S. Navy. He had accomplished this feat by demonstrating the right attitude toward the Soviet Union. Unimpressed, the legal attaché sarcastically suggested to Hoover a role for Ellender in the Central Intelligence Agency: "It is a pity Allan Dulles dont [*sic*] hire him in view of his great intelligence ability."[24]

Ellender's most controversial trip came late in 1962 when he visited Africa and made disparaging remarks about African self-government. "I have yet to meet any Africans who have the capability to run their own affairs," Ellender stated on December 2. Appalled, the State Department scurried to rectify the diplomatic blunder. Democratic senator Vance Hartke of Indiana retraced Ellender's route in an attempt to undo the damage Ellender had done.

On December 4, Uganda, Tanganyika, and the Congo announced that

22. Ackerson to Secretary of State, November 13, 1957, State Department File F0008; R. R. Roach memo to A. H. Belmont, November 18, 1957, FBI File 9-2629.

23. Allen Ellender 1956 Field Notes, Vol. 2, pp. 176, 177, 150, 154, Box 1527, AEP.

24. Legal Attaché to Hoover, December 15, 1958, FBI File 62-81810.

Ellender was unwelcome in their countries. Landing at Dar-es-Salaam, Tanganyika, on December 5, Ellender received a curt directive: "You are hereby ordered to leave the country immediately." He remained aboard his Air Force C-47 plane for several hours. Finally, in Djibouti, French Somaliland, a French colonel told Ellender he was welcome. "It's great to breathe free air," Ellender responded. "I've been a virtual prisoner for two days." In Mogadishu, Somalia, he was allowed to spend one night at the embassy, but he had to leave by six o'clock the next morning. Ellender tried to impress the people of Mali with his ability to speak French, columnist Jack Anderson reported. "Proud of his Cajun and uses it every chance he gets," Anderson said, but he quoted a confidential State Department source as having said, "the Senator speaks an adequate but at times impenetrable French."

The whole affair was widely publicized in Africa, Europe, and the United States. *Time* in mid-December featured photographs and quotes. In typical fashion, Ellender's staff gathered newspaper clippings—both critical and favorable—and arranged them in a special scrapbook.

Ellender offered neither apologies nor retractions. Back home with his son and his grandchildren several days before Christmas, he labeled his country's Africa policy "tip-toe diplomacy." He told the *Times-Picayune* he was "disappointed" with the critical responses to his truthful and painful observations. In the "favorable editorials" section of his African trip scrapbook were several clippings from segregationist newspapers in the South. On Christmas day, William Buckley's *National Review* alluded to "sensitive truths" Ellender had publicized. Critics had not discussed the merits of Ellender's statements, the editor suggested.[25]

The racial controversy Ellender's African trip engendered dramatized how the politics of race intruded into other facets of his political career.

The civil rights movement, Ellender thought, was getting out of hand. The Montgomery bus boycott in 1955 prompted Ellender to join one hundred other southern congressmen in signing the so-called Southern Manifesto of 1956—the "Declaration of Constitutional Principles"—which called the 1954 *Brown* decision an abuse of judicial power. In 1956 Ellender had mulled over the list of candidates who might win the Democratic nomination and challenge Eisenhower in November. Judging Estes Kefauver and

25. Jack Anderson, Washington *Post*, August 6, 1963, in "1963" Scrapbook, AEP; Drew Pearson, Washington *Post*, December 29, 1962, FBI File 62-81810. The complete controversy is covered by newspaper clippings in a large volume called the "1962 African Trip" Scrapbook, AEP.

Averell Harriman as not "right" on civil rights, Ellender favored A. B. "Happy" Chandler of Kentucky as the Democratic standard bearer.[26]

Ellender was surprised by racial changes sweeping the country. In July, 1957, he accused President Eisenhower of "downright hypocrisy" in talking about states' rights while urging passage of civil rights legislation. The administration bill "cuts the heart out of states' rights," Ellender said. Yet Eisenhower's biographer faults the president for failing to provide moral or political leadership on racial matters.[27]

In November, 1957, Eisenhower sent federal troops into Little Rock, Arkansas, when Governor Orval Faubus tried to use National Guard troops to prevent black students from integrating a white high school. That same year Martin Luther King, Jr., and other black leaders formed the Southern Christian Leadership Conference, and Congress passed a watered-down civil rights bill, mainly through the efforts of Senate majority leader Lyndon Johnson. Ellender voted against the measure, which created a civil rights commission in the Justice Department.

While the troops were in Little Rock, Ellender responded from Houma with a letter for distribution to constituents. Flo LeCompte, who had accompanied Ellender to Louisiana, apologized for sending Arceneaux a rough draft of Ellender's letter on the matter, but she had a good excuse: "I'm chauffeur again today and the boss is going fishing." Ellender, who was touring the state, had voted against all civil rights bills, LeCompte explained to correspondents.[28]

Starting in the 1950s, racial considerations increasingly became an issue in education and housing legislation. In 1959 Ellender, a member of the so-called southern caucus, voted for the National Defense Education Act with some misgivings. Senator Lister Hill of Alabama supported NDEA, but Russell of Georgia opposed the measure because it implied that racial guidelines would influence grant applications.[29]

26. Allen Ellender to Francis Walter, April 9, 1956, in "Civil Rights Data" Folder, Box 688, Associated Press release, March 25, 1956, in "1955–1956" Scrapbook, both in AEP; New York *Daily News,* May 6, 1956, FBI File 62-81810.

27. Washington *Post* and Washington (D.C.) *Times Herald,* July 1, 1957, FBI File 62-81810; Stephen E. Ambrose, *Eisenhower: Soldier and President* (New York, 1990), 368, 409, 445.

28. Florence LeCompte to George Arceneaux, Jr., November 18, 1957, and LeCompte to George Dykes, November 22, 1957, both in "Civil Rights—Little Rock Situation" Folder, Box 706, AEP.

29. Gilbert C. Fite, *Richard B. Russell, Jr., Senator from Georgia* (Chapel Hill, 1991), 346; Virginia Van der Veer Hamilton, *Lister Hill: Statesman from the South* (Chapel Hill, 1987), 230–31, 233.

An early supporter of federal education programs, Ellender stopped voting for education bills which now included racial guidelines to be met if states and cities expected to qualify for funds. Ellender's attempts to curtail foreign spending and improve relations with the Soviet Union suffered from his remarks about the inability of African nations to govern themselves.

Senate majority leader Lyndon Johnson predicted Congress would pass a civil rights bill in the 1960 session. He anticipated having late-night sessions in order to hammer out a measure, which Richard Russell of Georgia hoped to block with parliamentary maneuvers. Ellender insisted on a quorum at every regular subcommittee meeting during the civil rights discussion. He canceled Agriculture Committee wheat hearings and said he would filibuster if necessary to block civil rights legislation.[30]

Ellender was an important part of the southern Senate team determined to block the Civil Rights Bill of 1960. As captain of one of three Senate teams organized to talk the measure to death, Ellender assigned the speaking order and made sure a floor watcher was present while a team member spoke. Prominent members of Ellender's losing team included J. William Fulbright of Arkansas, Sam Ervin, Jr., of North Carolina, James Eastland of Mississippi, and Harry Byrd of Virginia. George Arceneaux, Jr., dispatched memos from Ellender's office to various team members.

In March the southern teams talked around the clock. Periodically, team members demanded quorum calls. Unless fifty-one members were present the Senate could not conduct business. Ellender's nearby office, equipped with a cot and kitchen facilities, gave him an advantage in meeting quorum calls. From mid-February until mid-April the debate raged. Finally the bill was passed on April 17, despite the efforts of Ellender and his colleagues, who nonetheless had succeeded in divesting the bill of restrictions aimed exclusively at the South.[31]

Racial segregation of schools would end, Ellender realized, but he hoped change would be gradual and people would act responsibly. Convinced that leaders like Martin Luther King, Jr., were unreasonable to demand rapid change, Ellender spoke of integration as a great imposition on whites. He somehow persuaded himself that President Kennedy agreed with him. Attorney General Robert Kennedy pushed civil rights legislation, Ellender said,

30. Miscellaneous newspaper clippings, January–February 1960, in "1960" Scrapbook, AEP.

31. Allen Ellender to Guy Miller, April 13, 1960, Box 1083, New Orleans *Times-Picayune,* April 18, 1960, in "1960" Scrapbook, both in AEP.

because it increased JFK's reelection prospects for 1964. Only reluctantly, Ellender thought, did the president go along.[32]

In June, 1963, Ellender rekindled the racial animosity he had created during his African trip when he criticized black leaders in Washington, D.C. Calling the city "a mess," Ellender again said blacks could not govern themselves. Angry responses from the diplomatic corps were soon forthcoming. Officials staffing the embassies of Haiti, Liberia, and Ethiopia seemed to be the most offended. Ellender did not speak for the government or for the majority of American people, Secretary of State Dean Rusk insisted. But Ellender's refusal to apologize or soften his views made Rusk's attempt to appease African ambassadors difficult. "I'll be damned if I believe it," Ellender said. "I think I speak for the bulk of the American people." On ABC's "Issues and Answers" program, Ellender insisted, "All I did was tell the truth." Jack Anderson said Ellender's African trip cost taxpayers thirty thousand dollars for planes and expenses, not just six hundred dollars as Ellender claimed.[33]

Southerners had defeated attempts by "liberals" to ease the rules on cloture, the process by which the Senate limited debate and ended a filibuster of racial legislation, Ellender told Frank Wurzlow, Jr., in February, 1963. The senator expected more dogfights throughout the session. The physically taxing confrontations prompted Ellender's doctors to suggest rest and a reduction in his food consumption. Ellender did not think the southerners would win.[34]

For good reason Ellender expected setbacks in the civil rights struggle. As early as 1957, he had observed, "Unfortunately, our forces are dwindling with each session and it becomes more difficult to combat these nefarious proposals." Richard Russell's influence was declining as his health deteriorated, and liberal senators Hubert Humphrey, George Muskie, Eugene McCarthy, and Philip Hart were growing in prestige. With only eighteen other senators who felt as he did, Ellender told a constituent, there was nothing to do but filibuster. In 1962 he voted against the confirmation of Thurgood Marshall's nomination for the Supreme Court, but the Senate confirmed him by a vote of fifty-four to sixteen.[35]

32. Ellender interview for JFK Library, 40–42, 43, 49.

33. Miscellaneous newspaper clippings, June 17, 1963, in "1963" Scrapbook, AEP. FBI File 62-81810 contains the information on Rusk, Anderson, and the ABC program.

34. Allen Ellender to Frank Wurzlow, Jr., February 8, 1963, and Florence LeCompte to Wurzlow, June 18, 1963, both in the Elward Wright Papers, in possession of Thomas Wright, Houma, La.

35. Allen Ellender to R. W. Wasson, March 5, 1957, in "Education, 1957" Folder, Box

In August, 1963, Ellender asked J. Edgar Hoover to check into complaints from officials in Clinton, Louisiana, about FBI pressure on the registrar of voters in East Feliciana Parish. Hoover's version of voter registration in East Feliciana was entirely different from the one Ellender had received. When blacks attempted to register to vote, Hoover reported, they were intimidated by officials in the district attorney's office and by sheriff's personnel. The bureau had evidence to corroborate its findings, Hoover wrote.[36]

Ellender faced other problems closer to home. In 1955 his brother Claude became ill with a fast-growing form of melanoma. Ellender was deeply saddened by Claude's bleak prospect for survival. The illness indirectly caused the loss of Frank Wurzlow, Jr., who had graduated from American University in 1955 with plans to join the firm of Ellender and Wright in Houma after he passed the Louisiana bar examination. Wurzlow had hoped to take six months to study, and then begin his practice with Claude and Elward. Claude's illness accelerated the process. Fortunately for Ellender, George Arceneaux, Jr., was ready to step in and take Wurzlow's place in Washington. Claude worked nearly to the end, even though he suffered considerable pain. He died on May 6, 1956. Allen, a pall bearer, helped to place Claude's body in its final resting place in Houma's Magnolia Cemetery. Claude's death left a void in the senator's life. "My life, as you know, has been lonely since the death of my wife in 1949," he wrote, "and Claude's passing makes me feel even more alone."[37]

In the eyes of his grandchildren and his nieces and nephews who congregated at Wallace Jr.'s house for Christmas dinner, Ellender qualified as an expert on international affairs. Irving Legendre, Jr., of Thibodaux, who married Willard's daughter Byrne in 1956, met Ellender for the first time that Christmas. The atmosphere was almost like a press conference, he remembered, with thirty or forty family members asking questions about the USSR and taking only minor exceptions to Uncle Allen's more daring opinions.[38]

706, AEP; Ellender to William Romans, May 23, 1963, in "Segregation-Integration" Folder, Box 841, AEP; Ellender to Lyall Shiell, Jr., March 19, 1962, in "Education, Federal Aid to" Folder, Box 802, AEP; Ellender to Carl Knotts, September 19, 1962, in "Ellender's Film" Folder, Box 1123, AEP; Fite, *Richard Russell,* 371–72.

36.   FBI to Allen Ellender, August 30, 1963, FBI File 62-81810.

37.   Frank Wurzlow, Jr., interview, April 9, 1980; George Arceneaux, Jr., interview, December 31, 1979; Thelma Ellender, interview, June 20, 1991; Allen Ellender to Harry Byrd, May 19, 1958, in "Ellender—Personal" Folder, Box 1056, AEP.

38.   Irving Legendre, Jr., interview, June 18, 1980.

Hunting, fishing, and cooking continued to dominate Ellender's holiday recreation. His fishing trips now took on added importance, providing raw materials for his gumbos and the other Cajun delicacies he was becoming famous for in Washington. His cookouts became bigger and bigger, and more frequent than those in his early career. He needed a large and ready supply of seafood on hand at all times. After a successful fishing trip, Willard always contributed his share of the catch to Allen for his freezers in Washington. Willard could not, however, give away another fisherman's share, he reminded his brother, even if presidents and important political leaders would be the beneficiaries.[39]

Meanwhile Ellender's thoughts were never far from the problem of drafting farm legislation. While dealing with racial matters and foreign affairs, he had struggled also with the politics of agriculture. Critics of farm policy complained about waste and searched for ways to cut government spending. For the agricultural establishment the biggest problem was getting various entities to agree on and support a sensible program.

39. Noble Rogers, interview, June 30, 1980.

15

SHAPING FARM POLICY
(1956–64)

$\mathcal{E}$llender's thoughts were never far from the politics of agriculture, even during controversies over civil rights and foreign policy. As chairman of the Senate Committee on Agriculture he was an acknowledged expert on farm legislation. Though considered a defender of farmers, he nevertheless realized that they received handsome subsidies from the government. As a member also of the Appropriations Committee, Ellender had for years called for cuts in foreign aid and other forms of waste. He could not afford to advocate giving farmers all that they could get from Uncle Sam. When his constituents criticized him for not supporting their selfish schemes, he was quick to point out the bounties they already enjoyed.

Rejected by the Eisenhower administration and frustrated by the agricultural establishment, Ellender struggled to establish a sensible farm policy. Early in the 1956 session the Republicans wrote a farm bill to replace the 1954 Agricultural Act. It retained the flexible price support concept and the Soil Bank from the 1949 act. The Senate Agriculture Committee hammered out a compromise measure, which both houses of Congress passed and sent to the president early in April. To the dismay of Ellender and influential farm Republicans, Eisenhower vetoed the compromise measure on April 16. Republican senator Milton Young of North Dakota, Ellender's close friend on the Agriculture Committee, was furious at Eisenhower for denying farmers an opportunity to improve wheat prices before the election. Late in 1956, Senator Hubert Humphrey of Minnesota, unhappy with the helter-skelter Republican Soil Bank, gathered evidence of its shortcomings.[1]

1. Various newspaper clippings, April, 1956, in "1955–1956" Scrapbook, Allen J. Ellender Papers, Nicholls State University Library, Thibodaux, La., hereinafter cited as AEP; Hubert

When the Eighty-fifth Congress convened in January, 1957, Democrats controlled both houses of Congress, despite Eisenhower's impressive reelection victory in November, 1956. The farm budget had increased from about $1 billion per year in 1950 to about $10 billion by the late 1950s. As usual, writing a farm bill involved a balancing act, raising the ante for one commodity, lowering it for another, all with just consideration for the voting strengths of the areas represented and the clout of committee chairmen bent on sheltering various special interests. No farm commodity, Ellender asserted, had received more favorable treatment over the years than corn, which in 1957 cost taxpayers about $300 million.[2]

Ellender balked at continuing the Soil Bank and the flexible price supports. He wanted to write a new comprehensive farm bill, not develop a piecemeal approach for various commodities. Passing a farm bill in 1958 would be difficult, he knew, for discontented cotton interests could block passage of an omnibus bill. Unless the various cotton interests and farm groups came together, his committee could not devise a comprehensive farm bill acceptable to the secretary of agriculture and the president.[3]

In late July the Senate passed a condensed bill Ellender had been pushing; it provided lower price supports but larger production levels for cotton, rice, corn, and other feed grains. In mid-August the House passed its version; early in September the final bill passed both houses. Its passage surprised Ellender because Congress had failed to address the wheat problem. "We are producing twice as much wheat as we can consume," Ellender said. Nonetheless, the Agricultural Act of 1958 included several innovative cotton and corn programs.[4]

Humphrey to Allen Ellender, December 3, 1956, and Ellender to Humphrey, December 8, 1956, both in "Leg., Agriculture: Soil Bank" Folder, Box 134, Hubert H. Humphrey Papers, Minnesota Historical Society Collection, St. Paul, Minn.

2. Robert H. Ferrell, *Harry S. Truman and the Modern American Presidency* (Boston, 1983), 105–106; United Press International wire copy, April 10, 1957, in "1957" Scrapbook, AEP.

3. New Orleans *Times-Picayune*, January 10, 1959, various newspaper clippings, January, 1958, all in "1958" Scrapbook, AEP; Allen Ellender to Dan P. Logan, January 30, 1958, and Ellender to J. P. Henican, Jr., March 17, 1958, both in "Agriculture, Cotton, 1958" Folder, Box 264, AEP.

4. Various newspaper clippings, March–June, 1958, New Orleans *Times-Picayune*, July 26, 1958, New Orleans *States*, September 9, 1958, all in "1958" Scrapbook, AEP; Wayne D. Rasmussen and Gladys L. Baker, "Programs for Agriculture, 1933–1965," in *Agricultural Policy in an Affluent Society*, ed. Vernon W. Ruttan *et al.* (New York, 1969), 83–84; Edward L. Schapsmeier and Frederick H. Schapsmeier, "Farm Policy from FDR to Eisenhower: Southern Democrats and the Politics of Agriculture," *Agricultural History*, LIII (January, 1979), 370–71.

In 1959 Congress again debated placing a limit on farm benefit payments. The House came up with a fifty-thousand-dollar limit on CCC (Community Credit Corporation) loans, but Senator John Stennis of Mississippi introduced several amendments designed to circumvent the limit. As usual, Ellender disagreed with the idea of limiting payments, which he believed would do little to solve the problem of rural poverty. During debate on the bill, Ellender explained his opposition to limiting farm payments. He posed a number of rhetorical questions designed to compare farm subsidies to industrial subsidies: Why not limit the post office to fifty thousand dollars per year for delivery of *Life*? Why not restrict airlines and defense contractors to a fifty-thousand-dollar limit? The bill, stripped of its bite, was passed on June 3, 1959.[5]

Historian Pete Daniel, noting the reluctance of southern politicians to deal with rural poverty, thought that USDA payments to farmers reflected intentions of federal policymakers. A study of benefit payments, he thought, would contribute to understanding the economic history of U.S. farm policy.[6]

Ellender's fourth reelection campaign in 1960 was almost no contest at all. A. Roswell Thompson, a New Orleans taxi driver, entered the Democratic primary against Ellender but withdrew at the urging of Governor Earl Long. Mayor Morrison did not enter the race as predicted, and the Republican candidate, George Reese, was a political unknown. In November, Ellender sent out letters telling constituents he was neither soliciting campaign contributions nor campaigning strenuously. He was supporting John F. Kennedy and the Democratic ticket in the presidential election. As expected, Ellender carried every parish in the election.[7]

Even though Ellender supported Kennedy, he disagreed with many of his liberal views on labor and race. When Kennedy supporter Camille Gravel advocated a liberal racial stand, Ellender joined other Democrats to oust him

5. *Congressional Record*, 86th Cong., 1st Sess., Vol. 105, Pt. 3, March 5, 1959, pp. 3427–28; see Joyce Appleby, "Commercial Farming and the 'Agrarian Myth' in the Early Republic," *Journal of American History*, LXVIII (March, 1982), 833–49; Theodore Saloutos, "New Deal Agricultural Policy: An Evaluation," *Journal of American History*, LXI (September, 1974), 404–405; the entire legislative debate can be found in *Congressional Record*, 86th Cong., 1st Sess., Vol. 105, Pt. 6, May 18, 1959, pp. 8337–40, Pt. 7, May 20, 1959, p. 8635, May 28, 1959, p. 9318, June 2, 1959, pp. 9550, 9555–58, June 3, 1959, pp. 9667–68; New York *Times*, August 5, 1959.

6. Pete Daniel, *Breaking the Land: The Transformation of Cotton, Tobacco, and Rice Culture since 1880* (Chicago, 1985), xv, 173.

7. Box 1083, *passim*, AEP.

as a Louisiana Democratic committeeman. Nonetheless, Kennedy had impressed Ellender. In the Senate, Kennedy had said little, except on labor matters, but people listened when the handsome Harvard graduate spoke, Ellender remembered. Ellender had been charmed and overwhelmed by the articulate Kennedy, much as he had succumbed to the charm of Huey Long.

Ellender did not consider Republican candidate Richard Nixon "presidential caliber by any means," but he convinced himself that Kennedy would have voted like southerners on racial matters except for strong pressure from his New England constituents. At any rate, Ellender became a Kennedy supporter after the Kennedy-Nixon debates. On one occasion he cooked an oyster jambalaya for Kennedy and spoke favorably in his behalf.[8]

Republican members of Congress had been particularly unhappy with Eisenhower and Agriculture Secretary Ezra Taft Benson for having reduced wheat price supports from $1.77 per bushel to $1.30. Presidential candidate Richard Nixon, distancing himself from Ike's farm policies, suggested he would dump Benson.[9] In November, Kennedy defeated Nixon in one of the closest presidential races in U.S. history.

Ellender had a good working relationship with Orville Freeman, Kennedy's secretary of agriculture. Only one slight altercation early on temporarily marred their normally harmonious relationship. After being named secretary, Freeman asked Ellender's advice about an appointee for undersecretary. Ellender read off a list of people he considered knowledgeable; Freeman then admitted having already promised the job to someone unlisted by Ellender. "Why in hell did you come to see me if you already had made up your mind?" Ellender inquired angrily. Once that incident was behind them, they dealt more honestly and directly with each other and became friends. On several occasions Ellender took Freeman to south Louisiana on fishing trips.[10]

Ellender had to maintain a delicate balance among the various farm interests, the administration, and his own constituents, among whom were commercial farmers and agribusiness giants. By 1960 tenant farmers and

8. "Allen J. Ellender Oral History Interview," by Larry Hackman, August 29, 1967 (John F. Kennedy Library, Washington, D.C., facsimile copy in Nicholls State University Library, Thibodaux, La.), 2, 3, 7–8, 9, 11, 12, 14, hereinafter cited as Ellender interview for JFK Library.

9. Allen Ellender, "Agriculture, Rice, 1961" Folder, Box 309, AEP; William M. Blair, New York *Times,* February 5, July 2, 1960, and miscellaneous newspaper clippings, May, 1960, in "1960" Scrapbook, all in AEP.

10. Ellender interview for JFK Library, 13, 16–17; Gerald Voisin and Kirby Brunet, interview, July 7, 1980.

small farmers had for the most part been driven from the land. Ellender agreed with Kennedy and Freeman on the need to control the cost of storing surplus grain. But he did not like a Kennedy bill that would have given the secretary of agriculture great latitude in writing farm programs.

Even racial matters sometimes popped up to block farm legislation. John Stennis of Mississippi, suspecting Freeman of trying to desegregate the Agricultural Extension Service, complained to Ellender, who agreed with Stennis. As a result Freeman backed down on his integration plans for the time being. When Freeman suggested a farm measure Ellender did not like, the senator either told him it would not pass or modified the bill when it got to the Agriculture Committee. "When it came to the Senate, when it came to me, I just changed it," Ellender stated.[11]

The Kennedy farm bill surfaced in March, 1961, to mixed reviews. The administration would go along with some changes, Freeman told Ellender, as long as they followed guidelines suggested in the original bill. "I don't want to vote out a bill giving farmers less than they are now getting," Ellender said. In June the Senate passed a $7-billion farm bill, which cut the cost of storing surplus grains and raised price supports. A House version of the bill restored some of the cuts. President Kennedy signed the compromise farm measure on August 8 with senators Ellender and Humphrey, Secretary Freeman, and Vice-president Lyndon Johnson looking on. The group had a good laugh when Ellender leaned over and told the president, "I've got five grandsons. I need five pens." A smiling Kennedy handed over five souvenir pens.[12]

Because compromise farm measures frequently contained temporary provisions, farm legislation was once again a hot political issue early in 1962. Although Ellender complained frequently of the costs of storing and handling wheat and feed grains, Freeman considered him sympathetic to the Kennedy farm program and wrote confidentially to him of threats to "our" bill. Hoping to pass the farm bill before the Easter recess, Freeman knew the Farm Bureau stood in his path. "I'd appreciate it if you would keep this strictly confidential for I don't want to tip off the opposition." Directing passage of the administration bill in May, Ellender pinpointed corn as a

11. John Stennis to Allen Ellender, March 28, 1961, and Ellender to Stennis, March 29, 1961, both in "Agriculture, General—1961" Folder, Box 304, AEP; Ellender interview for JFK Library, 36.

12. New York *Times,* March 17, June 28, July 25, July 27, 1961; Louis Panos, New Orleans *Times-Picayune,* August 9, 1961, in "1961" Scrapbook, AEP.

particularly costly feed grain program. The USDA could cut farm spending by $2 billion in storage costs alone if Congress passed the bill with stiff controls, Ellender said. The Senate passed the Kennedy farm bill, forty-two to thirty-eight, on May 25. But in the House, Ellender said, feed grain producers stripped the bill of its controls. "People won't stand for these surpluses forever," he added.[13]

In September, 1962, conferees from the House and Senate met to smooth out slightly different versions of the compromise omnibus farm bill. Although Ellender chaired the Senate conferees, he could not retain all the strict controls Kennedy and Freeman sought. In 1963 wheat and corn growers would receive high supports and payments on land taken out of production. Price supports on corn and other feed grains would not be lowered until 1964.[14]

While both sides were debating feed grain proposals, Billie Sol Estes, a promoter of grain-storage facilities in the West, was indicted for fraud. Estes had received no special favors from the USDA, Ellender claimed, but he had hoodwinked a number of farmers and bankers with his storage scams. Asked if he knew Estes, Ellender replied, "No indeed. I don't know Billie Sol Estes from Adam's off-ox. I never saw him." Estes was tried and convicted in a courtroom before twelve television cameras. Later his conviction was overturned on appeal to the U.S. Supreme Court.[15]

President Kennedy and Secretary Freeman considered Ellender a key member of their agricultural team. Freeman sent confidential memos to the president on the progress of various farm measures and indicated how Ellender felt about their prospects for passage. He had correctly predicted agricultural failure and starvation in Ethiopia, Freeman told Kennedy. Freeman reminded the president, "He has fought hard for the Administration farm program. Some expression of approval by you would make him very happy."

Freeman disclosed to Kennedy his personal liking for Ellender:

13. New York *Times,* March 25, 1962; William M. Blair, New York *Times,* March 26, June 23, June 24, 1962; Orville Freeman to Allen Ellender, March 26, 1962, in "Department, Agriculture, General, 1962" Folder, Box 327, AEP; *Congressional Record,* 87th Cong., 2d Sess., Vol. 108, Pt. 7, May 24, 1962, pp. 9210–11; *New Republic,* October 27, 1962, p. 16; New York *Times,* May 26, 1962.

14. *Congressional Record,* 87th Cong., 2d Sess., Vol. 108, Pt. 9, June 23, 1962, pp. 11451–54; New York *Times,* September 13, 1962.

15. New Orleans *Times-Picayune,* June 5, 1962, in "1962" Scrapbook, AEP; James J. Kilpatrick, New Orleans *Times-Picayune,* September 3, 1990.

I've come to feel real personal affection for Senator Ellender. He is a man of strong feeling, a hard fighter. In many, many areas I do not share his philosophy. Yet he has been fair and even kind to me. He is really a warm hearted and sensitive person. He is tough minded and courageous and honest. Once he tells you what he will do, you can rely on his standing with that position. He does not give assurances and then slip sideways and finally backwards like many I could name. I recall very vividly the occasion when Charley Shuman referred contemptuously to the Cochrane-Freeman-Kennedy bill in 1961, and Ellender leaned over the Senate table, shook his finger at him, and said, "Mr. Shuman, I'll have you know that's the Cochrane-Freeman-Kennedy-Ellender bill."[16]

In April, 1963, Ellender criticized the Rural Electrification Administration, a part of the USDA which he had for years defended. Professing not to have turned against REA but rather against its expanding role—producing power in competition with private utility companies—Ellender wondered if REA generating and transmitting plants, financed by 2-percent loans, were "trying to build an empire at public expense."[17]

Frequently Freeman discussed strategy with Ellender. In March, 1963, the dairy interests planned to call for 75 percent of parity as their line in milk hearings before the Senate Agriculture Committee. Freeman hoped Ellender would open the hearings with a lower figure.

By midsummer both Harold Cooley of North Carolina and Herman Talmadge of Georgia had introduced cotton proposals. Calling the Cooley bill "a subsidy of a subsidy," Freeman told the president he hoped the Talmadge bill in the Senate would prevail. "I haven't pushed Ellender on this yet. His reservation is: 'Will it cost more?' It will," Freeman admitted.[18]

Ellender returned to Louisiana in October, 1963, to visit friends and relatives and to fish. Although he welcomed a break from the politics of agriculture, he could hardly forget pending farm bills. Orville Freeman

16. Orville Freeman, January 9, 1963 (memo), in "USDA Notebook, 1963 (5)" Folder, and Freeman to John F. Kennedy (memo), March 4, 1963, in "USDA Notebook, 1963 (2)" Folder, both in Box 10, Orville Freeman Papers, Minnesota Historical Society Collection, St. Paul, Minn., hereinafter cited as OFP.

17. New Orleans *States-Item*, April 3, 1963, Houma (La.) *Press*, May 7, 1963, both in "1963" Scrapbook, AEP.

18. Orville Freeman to Allen Ellender, March 5, 1963, in "USDA Notebook, 1963 (5)" Folder, Freeman to John Duncan, March 4, 6, 1963, in "USDA Notebook, 1963 (6)" Folder, and Freeman to John F. Kennedy, July 5, 1963, in "USDA Notebook, 1963 (1)" Folder, all in Box 10, OFP.

joined him for a fishing trip in Louisiana. Freeman met Ellender's grand-children and other members of the family. Undoubtedly they discussed agricultural legislation during their respite from the clamor of the nation's capital.[19]

Ellender was on the Senate floor for discussion of a library bill on November 22, 1963, when John Kennedy suffered his fatal wounds at Dealey Plaza in Dallas. Like other ranking congressional leaders, Ellender pledged support to Lyndon Johnson, who soon realized how demanding the life of a president could be. Like many Americans, Ellender wondered if the assassination was part of a plot against the United States.

The farm program was only one of many problems Johnson faced. When he first assumed office, he jokingly threatened to have Agriculture Secretary Orville Freeman arrested if he tried to resign. Freeman stayed and provided the president a quick summary of the cotton problem. Overproduction was the culprit. In 1961 farmers produced 14.2 million bales on 18.5 million acres of land; in 1963 they produced 15.1 million bales on 16 million acres. The textile industry hated the two-price cotton arrangement, which cost domestic mills 8.5 cents more per pound for cotton than their foreign competitors.

Johnson hoped to balance the budget and reduce spending before the 1964 election. Lowering benefit payments on cotton was one economy move he considered, but Freeman said "this was the real handicap and block in getting any cotton legislation passed." Ellender's help was essential, he reminded the president.[20]

Before the Senate adjourned in 1963, Freeman had a lengthy conference with Ellender. "He is busy, does not want to hold hearings, and is generally frustrated at this point," Freeman told Johnson. "He is deeply concerned about government spending, as you well know." Ellender wanted to reduce supports on cotton from thirty-two cents to thirty cents per pound and increase acreage, which he calculated would save taxpayers $168 million.

Other complicated cotton plans competed with Ellender's. Harold Cooley of North Carolina had a three-price plan. Hubert Humphrey of Minnesota wanted to add a mill subsidy to make U.S. textile manufacturers

19. Orville Freeman to Allen Ellender, October 3, 1963, in "USDA Notebook, 1963 (5)" Folder, Box 10, OFP.

20. Orville Freeman to Lyndon Johnson (memo), December 2, 1963, in "USDA Notebook, 1963 (2)" Folder, and Freeman memo for files, December 4, 1963, in "USDA Notebook, 1963 (5)" Folder, both in Box 10, OFP.

competitive with foreign mills. Eugene Talmadge of Georgia favored sliding price supports and having some restrictions on production. A Talmadge-Humphrey compromise bill combining features favored by both men received some Senate support.

Freeman hoped Ellender would support the Talmadge cotton plan and a new wheat proposal before the fall elections. He became discouraged when Ellender said Talmadge-Humphrey would not pass. "If we can get Senator Ellender to support it I am confident we can pass it," Freeman wrote Talmadge. Farm legislation, Ellender realized, had little chance of passing this late in the session.[21] He was right. Congress adjourned without passing a farm bill.

Early in 1964 President Johnson called for voluntary acreage cutbacks and lower price supports. In February Freeman told Johnson, "Senator Ellender is driving hard. He plans to join wheat and cotton." By mid-February both Ellender and the president had decided to try to pass a wheat and cotton bill before Congress considered the Civil Rights Bill. Ellender, however, could not convince members of his Senate Agriculture Committee to go along with his cotton proposals.[22]

In March a coalition of wheat and cotton senators finally defeated Ellender's proposals and passed a wheat and cotton bill, but the measure died in the House. Congress passed no permanent cotton or wheat package in election year 1964; it compromised and drafted short-term bills or granted extensions to existing measures. The whole farm program was a patchwork quilt, badly in need of guidelines.[23]

Something of a personality in Washington, Ellender was featured in a New York *Times* sketch in February, 1959. It described him as five-feet-four-inches

21.   William Blair, New York *Times,* December 11, 1963; Orville Freeman memo to Lyndon Johnson, December 6, 1963, in "USDA Notebook, 1963 (2)" Folder, Box 10, OFP; mimeographed text of radio report, October 19, 1963, Box 1487, mimeographed text of radio report, May 25, 1963, Box 1486, both in AEP; Freeman, December 20, 1963 (memo), Freeman, December 24, 1963 (memo for files), and Freeman to Herman Talmadge, December 30, 1963, all in "USDA Notebook, 1963 (5)" Folder, Box 10, OFP; mimeographed text of radio report, November 30, 1963, Box 1487, AEP.

22.   Freeman to Lyndon Johnson, February 10, 1964, in "USDA Notebook, 1964 (1)" Folder, Box 10, OFP; Mike Manatos to Larry O'Brien (memo), February 15, 1964, in Allen Ellender Name File, Box 60, White House Central Files, Lyndon Baines Johnson Library, Austin, Tex., hereinafter cited as LBJ; William Blair, New York *Times,* February 19, 1964; mimeographed text of radio report, February 22, 1964, Box 1487, AEP.

23.   *Congressional Record,* 88th Cong., 2d Sess., Vol. 110, Pt. 3, March 3, 1964, p. 4159; William Blair, New York *Times,* March 3, 7, 1964.

tall and eager to visit every country in the world. It made other points: Once a year Ellender played host at a seafood dinner for newsmen and then at a separate one for the women, his office suite being too small to accommodate more than a small group at one time. However, Ellender told the male journalists he was keeping the women away from "you handsome fellas." He had announced his availability to escort the queen of the Washington Mardi Gras ball, and jokingly eliminated congressmen he considered ineligible. He had voted against antilynching legislation and had written detailed reports of his junkets to justify their costs.[24]

When Senator Matthew Neely of West Virginia died on January 18, 1958, Ellender received his historic old office, Room G44, high in the Capitol dome, with a great view down the Mall to the Washington Monument. The hard-to-find office, called the Hideaway, or Hideout, had been used before the Civil War by both Henry Clay and Daniel Webster. The charming old office had high ceilings and a fireplace.[25] It was an ideal place for Ellender to host luncheons for congressional and administrative leaders.

In November, 1960, *This Week,* a national Sunday newspaper supplement, featured Ellender prominently in an article accenting wasteful congressional studies and phony investigations, many conducted by professional investigators promising headlines to senators. Ellender claimed his investigations were legitimate, as were those by Senator McClellan of Arkansas on labor and Senator Robert S. Kerr of Oklahoma on water use. One senator, the article alleged, formed a committee to give a job to his ghostwriter; another tried to find ways to pay for his trips back to his home state.[26]

Ellender relied on his faithful staff to perform many personal chores for him, including helping to select a new car. The black 1957 Buick with the features Ellender wanted listed for $4,698 minus $1,357 in trade for his old car whose blue-book value was only $375. He bought the car. Later, on a cold night in January, 1958, Ellender offered journalist Kay Ray of New Orleans a ride home after a national Women's Press Club dinner in Washington. Ray stood shivering in the parking lot as Ellender searched frantically for his 1951 Buick before finally remembering he had purchased a new car.[27]

24. New York *Times,* February 17, 1959.

25. Betty Beale, Washington (D.C.) *Evening Star,* January 26, 1959, in "1959" Scrapbook, AEP; Elinor Lee, unidentified clipping, in "1962" Scrapbook, AEP.

26. Charles Sopkin, "It's Time to Investigate the Investigators," November 13, 1960, pp. 6–7, 9, in FBI File 62-81810.

27. Unidentified George Dixon column, n.d., n.p., in "1958" Scrapbook, AEP.

Even though Ellender was sixty-eight in 1958, his competitive nature remained, especially on the golf course, where he battled fiercely. On one occasion Ellender was paired in match play against Houma attorney Claude Duval, one of the best club golfers in town. As he peered at the green in the distance, Ellender asked Duval what club to use. Duval suggested one. But when his shot fell far short, Ellender protested indignantly, "You told me the wrong club!" Later when Duval realized Ellender was just one shot off the pace, he jokingly told him to select his own clubs.[28]

On September 2, 1960, doctors at Bethesda Naval Hospital in Washington removed a bone from Ellender's ear that had impaired his hearing. The minor surgical procedure, described by Ellender as "nothing serious," caused few inconveniences. Doctors did not want him to travel by air for a while, but Ellender told Milton Young of North Dakota they could resume their usual golf game in January. When Congress recessed, Ellender drove to Louisiana to observe the presidential election from his home base. In January, 1963, Ellender entered Bethesda Naval Hospital for a checkup and a rest. Insisting he did not feel ill, he said, "The doctors seemed to think I needed a little rest. I suppose they were right, because I did almost nothing but sleep and eat for a week." He left the hospital with a clean bill of health. In March he was involved in a minor auto collision, a fender-bender, at Connecticut and Florida avenues. The accident caused no injuries and only $25 in damage to Ellender's car and $125 to the other vehicle.[29]

Ellender was seventy-three years old in 1963 and in good health, but he maintained a grueling schedule. He himself sometimes wondered why he worked so hard. "I suppose," he told a relative, "the answer is that I am always happiest when I am busiest." Regular visits to Dr. George W. Calver, the Capitol physician, reaffirmed his good health. Ellender's pulse was usually about 65 beats per minute. His weight fluctuated from 155 to nearly 170 pounds. His blood pressure usually registered 116 over 72 or 114 over 68. His electrocardiogram results may have prompted Calver to persuade the senator to slow down a bit.[30]

28. Claude Duval, interview, December 18, 1979.

29. Allen Ellender to Clinton Anderson, September 2, 1960, and Ellender to Milton Young, September 6, 1960, both in "Ellender Film" Folder, Box 1085, AEP; New Orleans *Times-Picayune,* September 6, 1960, in "1960" Scrapbook, AEP; Allen Ellender to J. A. Llompart, January 24, 1963, in "Ellender Personal" Folder, Box 1145, AEP; New Orleans *Times-Picayune,* January 22, 1963, Washington *Post,* March 8, 1963, both in "1963" Scrapbook, AEP.

30. Allen Ellender to Emily Ellender, August 12, 1958, in "Ellender—Personal" Folder, Box 1056, and health records, 1943–1964, in Box 1843, both in AEP.

Ellender had not changed his life-style over the years, his income tax returns reveal. In 1958 he paid $13,481 in federal taxes on an income of $32,634. Of that amount, $12,500 came from his Senate salary, about $10,000 from his partnership with his son, about $10,000 in rents and royalties. Flo LeCompte continued to handle Ellender's personal correspondence and even worked on his income tax returns. In March, 1959, she sent him a corrected copy of his returns with a note: "I refigured the entire return, to show that it should have been $292 less than originally figured. I believe you will find everything correct now." [31]

Political infighting over foreign aid and the farm bill had caused no visible diminution in Ellender's popularity with the administration. In December, Freeman delivered a speech on Ellender's behalf at a testimonial dinner in Alexandria, Louisiana. Defending Ellender as "a hard man with a buck, but a man with a warm heart for the family farmer," Freeman cited Ellender as a major architect of the Feed Grain Program. [32]

Ellender's involvement with political and national issues never ceased. He had disapproved of President Kennedy's nomination of his brother Robert for attorney general in January, 1961. He was even more vocal in opposing Robert Weaver, a fifty-three-year-old Negro, to head the Housing and Home Administration. Claiming to have seen evidence of Weaver's "activities with communists," Ellender was probably more concerned about Weaver's NAACP involvement than his ties to radicals. For years an advocate of détente and a critic of communist-chasing fanatics like Joe McCarthy, Ellender used the same tactic as his old opponent to discredit Weaver. [33]

Although he was in good health, Ellender began to look into ways to transfer his property to his only child without having to pay steep gift and estate taxes. Elward Wright and Wurzlow, now law partners in Houma, prepared legal instruments for him on the advice of E. R. T. Marquette of Houma, a certified public accountant with detailed knowledge of estate planning and tax law. Flo LeCompte provided Wurzlow with details of Ellender's rental income from a laundry, a service station, a taxi company, a supermarket, and a realty company. Ellender also received oil royalty checks from Texaco, Union Oil, Prentice Drilling Company, and a number of others.

31. Florence LeCompte to Allen Ellender, March 27, 1959, and tax records, both in Box 2, AEP; George Arceneaux, Jr., to Ellender, March 4, 1957, in "Ellender—Personal" Folder, Box 1046, AEP.

32. Orville Freeman speech (mimeographed), December 14, 1961, in "Agriculture, General, 1961" Folder, Box 304, AEP.

33. New Orleans *Times-Picayune,* January 23, 1961, in "1961" Scrapbook, AEP.

Ellender's most valuable assets were tracts of land in Terrebonne Parish: the family sugarcane lands on Bayou Terrebonne, his Coteau farm, a small tract at Mechanicville, and city lots and parcels bought with Elward Wright over the years. Marquette recommended changing the partnership Ellender and his son had formed some years earlier to a corporation "in a tax free exchange." To provide Ellender with controlling interest and a way of reducing his estate to a minimum, Marquette suggested having two classes of stock, voting and nonvoting. Ellender could retain 51 percent of the voting stock; he could donate the nonvoting stock to Allen Jr. and his children. "After your passing," Marquette wrote, "your son Allen would have controlling interest in the corporation." Paying gift taxes now, he explained, was better than huge estate taxes later. "It is often overlooked that gifts subject to gift taxes serve to reduce the estate tax at its highest bracket while the gift tax is paid at its lowest rates," he explained.

Ellender and his son established two corporations, Willowwood, Inc., and Briarpatch, Inc. Ellender was president of both corporations, LeCompte was treasurer, Allen Jr. was vice-president. The voting stock of the two corporations, Marquette explained, should receive dividends; "otherwise the IRS might consider it worthless and a mere tax dodge." Ellender's grandchildren, he reminded Wurzlow, would pay no taxes on dividends of less than six hundred dollars per year.[34] Wurzlow may have communicated to Ellender only the broad outline of Marquette's proposals.

Ellender had notions of how he wanted to dispose of his property, but he worried about their legality. Asking Wurzlow and Wright to point out any problems with his proposals, Ellender wrote, "To be frank with you, I have not looked into a law book since I came to the Senate." He wondered if he could transfer three thousand dollars in stock to his grandchildren each year without having to pay taxes. He wondered, too, if there was a limit to the total amount he could give the youngsters over the years. He also sought ideas for disposing of his rental properties, his thirteen lots in the Connally Subdivision, and his property at Mechanicville. In 1962 he sold 9.7 acres of the Mechanicville farm to the Terrebonne Parish School Board for fifty-eight thousand dollars. Today the East Street School occupies the site.[35]

34. E. R. T. Marquette to Allen Ellender, March 1, 1963, Florence LeCompte to Frank Wurzlow, Jr., July 9, 1963, Marquette to Wurzlow, November 19, 1963, all in the Elward Wright Papers, in possession of Thomas Wright, Houma, La.; Terrebonne Parish Conveyance Book 366, Folio 99 (Briarpatch), Folio 107 (Willowood), December 31, 1963, in Terrebonne Parish Courthouse, Houma, La.

35. Allen Ellender to Frank Wurzlow, Jr., November 26, 1963, in Wright Papers.

Thus Ellender settled his physical possessions. He could relax about that aspect of his life and concentrate on his political career. He had been re-elected for another term in 1960. His influence in the Senate had grown over the years as he gained in seniority. After being ignored by the Eisenhower administration, he could look forward to working further with Lyndon Johnson, his old Senate colleague, who was now the president of the United States. Both men had become important national leaders.

PART FOUR

Senate Leader

16

WORKING WITH LBJ
(1963–68)

$\mathcal{L}$yndon Johnson seemed more compatible with Ellender's southern background than Kennedy had been. Yet Ellender sensed an urgency, a momentum to complete programs Kennedy had only envisioned. Would this impetus, combined with Johnson's efforts to rally and unify the nation, create a push for civil rights legislation stronger than the Kennedy administration ever imagined? Although he had gotten along with Johnson over the years, Ellender knew the Texan was tougher and more aggressive than Kennedy had been. He had seen Johnson cultivate Senate leaders and had noted his meteoric rise to the post of senate majority leader.[1] Ellender would have to see what kind of arrangement he could work out with his old Senate sidekick.

Kennedy had visited Ellender's office for gumbo and given Ellender commemorative pens for his grandchildren after signing farm legislation. In New Orleans in 1961 at the swearing-in ceremony of deLesseps Morrison as ambassador to the Organization of American States, Kennedy recognized Ellender publicly by asking him to stand momentarily. At the dedication of a dock terminal in New Orleans the next year, he again recognized Ellender publicly.[2]

1. Florence LeCompte, interview, July 28, 1991; Virginia Van der Veer Hamilton, *Lister Hill: Statesman from the South* (Chapel Hill, 1987), 209; "Allen J. Ellender Oral History Interview," by Larry Hackman, August 29, 1967 (John F. Kennedy Library, Washington, D.C.; facsimile copy in Nicholls State University Library, Thibodaux, La.), 12, 14; Ronnie Dugger, *The Politician: The Life and Times of Lyndon Johnson: The Drive for Power, from the Frontier to Master of the Senate* (New York, 1982), 343; Robert A. Caro, *The Years of Lyndon Johnson: Means of Ascent* (New York, 1990), 412.

2. *Public Papers of President John F. Kennedy* (3 vols.; Washington, D.C., 1963), I, 510, II, 357.

No one, however, made Ellender feel indispensable the way Lyndon Johnson did. First elected to the House in 1937 as a New Dealer, Johnson became a protégé of Sam Rayburn. In 1948 Johnson moved to the Senate where he cultivated important leaders, such as Richard Russell, Jr., of Georgia and John McClellan of Arkansas. He consulted Ellender about public works and farm legislation. Johnson studied legislation—and human nature—and knew what the people capable of passing it wanted. When Ellender won reelection in 1954, Johnson sent a friendly note: "We will have six more years of mutual service in the Senate." He gave Ellender a standing invitation to visit his ranch, and he never missed an opportunity to brag about the Cajun's gumbo.

By 1958 Ellender and the Senate majority leader had become strong admirers of each other. Each credited the other with legislative leadership against difficulties imposed by the Eisenhower administration. Ike may have ignored Ellender's foreign travels, but Johnson, deciphering Ellender's scribbled postcards from abroad, proclaimed an interest in seeing his filmed reports, "possibly between sips of that excellent Ellender gumbo." Ellender kept the majority leader posted on farm bills.[3]

Although they agreed on a surprising number of issues, Ellender and Johnson differed sharply on race. Like other southerners with national ambition, Johnson had broken with his racial past to become a liberal on civil rights legislation. Ellender knew southerners—especially those who remained segregationists—had little chance of winning outside the South. Richard Russell, he thought, would have been a good president, but his efforts to seek office in the late 1940s and early 1950s never generated much interest.[4]

Times were propitious for civil rights legislation after the Kennedy assassination. Polls indicated that most Americans wanted significant change. Ellender and his colleagues planned to employ their usual tactics to obstruct the measure, but now, for the first time, they feared they might lose. Their

3. Allen Ellender, interview by T. Harrison Baker, July 30, 1969, in Oral History Collection, Lyndon Baines Johnson Library, Austin, Tex., 2, 3–5, hereinafter cited as Ellender interview for LBJ Library; Lyndon Johnson to Allen Ellender, July 28, 1954, Ellender to Johnson, October 20, 1955, Johnson to Ellender, October 22, 1955, Ellender to Johnson, November 2, 1957, Johnson to Ellender, November 13, 1957, Ellender to Johnson, September 5, 1958, and Johnson to Ellender, September 16, 1958, all in Congressional File, "Ellender, Allen J., Sr.," Box 43, and Arthur Perry to Walter Jenkins (memo), n.d. [February, 1958], Ellender to Johnson, July 14, 1958, both in Senate Papers, "Ellender," Box 366, all in Lyndon Baines Johnson Library, Austin, Tex., hereinafter cited as LBJ.

4. Ellender interview for LBJ Library, 7, 10, 12.

strength had diminished. From April until June, Ellender and Deep South senators conducted a filibuster. Ellender refused to conduct hearings on food stamps, Freeman told Johnson in April, until the civil rights discussions had ended. "He is tired and getting cranky," Freeman observed. On June 10 the Senate, invoking cloture for the first time on civil rights, imposed a one-hour time limit on each senator. This effectively ended the filibuster and cleared the way for passage of the milestone legislation. A coalition of northern Democrats and Republicans finally combined forces to end debate. The House passed the measure quickly; Johnson signed the bill on July 2.[5]

Although Ellender had suffered a legislative setback, he still maintained cordial relations with the Johnson administration. In May, before the civil rights struggle had been decided, he prepared one of his Cajun feasts at the Hideaway, serving LBJ gumbo, green salad, raspberry sherbet, and pralines. After Johnson signed the civil rights bill, Ellender took defeat sensibly. Resistance, he asserted, "must be within the framework of the orderly process established by law."

Johnson appreciated Ellender's magnanimous stand and told him so. "Your leadership as the first southern Senator to call for compliance with the Civil Rights Act was truly an illustration of statesmanship at its best," he wrote. "I can fully appreciate the courage required to be the first to take such a stand, and I want you to know that, in my view, your action may well prove to be the difference between peace and violence in many areas of the country." When Johnson campaigned in New Orleans against Republican Barry Goldwater in October, Ellender, Russell Long, and other party regulars were there to support him.[6]

Demonstrating his persuasive charm in New Orleans at a fund-raiser, Johnson told an audience, "Senator Ellender gets me to do nearly everything

5. Gilbert C. Fite, *Richard B. Russell, Jr., Senator from Georgia* (Chapel Hill, 1991), 407–410; *Congressional Quarterly Weekly Report*, July 22, 1966, p. 1538, July 29, 1972, p. 1853; Orville Freeman to Lyndon Johnson, April 17, 1964, in "USDA Notebook, 1964 (1)" Folder, Box 10, Orville Freeman Papers, Minnesota Historical Society Collection, St. Paul, Minn., hereinafter cited as OFP; Michael I. Sovern, *Legal Restraints on Racial Discrimination in Employment* (New York, 1966), 61–62.

6. Lyndon Johnson to Allen Ellender, July 23, 1964, and Marvin Watson to Johnson (memo), June 1, 1965, both in Allen Ellender Name File, Box 60, White House Central Files, LBJ; Betty Beale, Los Angeles *Times*, May 24, 1964, and unidentified clipping, July 5, 1964, both in "1964" Scrapbook, Allen J. Ellender Papers, Nicholls State University Library, Thibodaux, La., hereinafter cited as AEP; Glen Jeansonne, *Leander Perez: Boss of the Delta* (Baton Rouge, 1977), 319.

he wants me to without . . . lagniappe." Johnson said he searched the White House for Ladybird one day, only to hear, "She is up eating with Senator Ellender." Continuing, Johnson said, "So I put on my hat and invited myself. I went up there and I was the only man there except Ellender, and he had all the pretty women in Washington up there in the room eating with him!" Ellender had cooked for the Johnsons and others on May 14 and August 21. On October 9, Johnson had visited Ellender in his Jung Hotel suite in New Orleans.[7]

When Johnson presented his Voting Rights Bill in March, 1965, Ellender once again voiced opposition, even though there was little chance of preventing passage. No teams of filibusterers queued up this time; only Ellender threatened to filibuster against the measure, which called for federal voter registrars to enroll blacks in areas where traditionally they had been denied the right to register and to vote. In the midst of the controversy, Oklahoma City University planned to present Ellender an honorary degree at a convocation. A protest by the National Association for the Advancement of Colored People caused university officials to cancel the formal presentation and confer Ellender's degree in his hotel room instead.[8]

Several days after the president signed the Voting Rights Act in August, 1965, riots erupted in the Watts area of Los Angeles and spread to other American cities. Johnson viewed the disturbances as a personal rejection by blacks; Ellender, thinking they confirmed his long-standing racial notions, called for law and order.[9]

Ellender had come into his own as an agricultural leader during the Kennedy years. Eisenhower, who never seemed to understand farm policy, had advocated measures unpopular with Ellender, and he had rebuffed Ellender's offer to share knowledge acquired in his travels abroad. Kennedy, on the other hand, had deferred to Secretary of Agriculture Orville Freeman, who appreciated Ellender's talents.

Johnson and Freeman knew Ellender was not in step with the civil rights

7. Diary Cards, May 14, August 21, October 9, 1964, in Appointment Files, Box 24, LBJ; *Public Papers of the Presidents of the United States: Lyndon B. Johnson* (10 vols.; Washington, D.C., 1965), II, 1281.

8. FBI File 62-81810; New Orleans *Times-Picayune*, March 18, 1965, in "1965" Scrapbook, AEP.

9. Joseph Califano to Lyndon Johnson (memo), September 29, 1965, in Allen Ellender Name File, Box 60, White House Central Files, LBJ.

movement, but they needed him if they hoped to draft a sensible farm program. On the one hand, Ellender favored reducing the federal debt and
balancing the budget; on the other, he wanted to protect his agricultural
constituents.

Ellender opposed some of Johnson's antipoverty programs, but he had
taken an interest in a 1961 pilot food stamp program, which allowed welfare
clients to purchase about ten dollars' worth of food for about six dollars. He
hoped the experimental concept would increase consumption of foodstuffs
and improve nutrition for impoverished Americans the way the Food for
Freedom program had provided surplus food for shipment abroad. During
the latter stages of the New Deal the USDA had experimented with a limited
program. In the mid-1950s Congress revived the food subsidy concept, but
Secretary of Agriculture Ezra Taft Benson blocked its implementation. While
campaigning for president, John Kennedy promised to start a food stamp
program if he were elected.[10]

Ellender was "warming up" to the food stamp program, the White
House learned in April. If the president requested hearings immediately,
Ellender would oblige, a Johnson aide told him. The House passed the food
stamp bill, H.R. 10222, on April 9, 1964. In May, Johnson informed Larry
O'Brien, "I have called Ellender about hearings." Ellender introduced S. 1387,
the measure to make food stamps a permanent part of farm legislation. As
expected, food stamp legislation sailed through easily.[11]

Johnson's War on Poverty included other programs to deal with rural
poverty, but the agricultural establishment ignored them. Title III of the
Economic Opportunity Act of 1964 had called for direct grants to poor
farmers. However, this part was cut from the final version of the bill. Johnson's efforts to help poor farmers came to naught; instead they left the land
to become part of the urban masses in need of food stamps, welfare, and
other forms of relief.[12]

10. Julius Duscha, "Is the Food Stamp Plan Working?" *Reporter,* March 1, 1962, p. 38;
Wall Street Journal, July 3, 1961, February 5, 1964, March 5, 1964.

11. H.R. 10222, 88th Cong., 2d Sess., copy in "Food Stamp Act" Folder, Box 850, AEP;
Mike Manatos to Larry O'Brien (memo), April 23, 1964, and Lyndon Johnson to O'Brien, May
13, 1964, both in Office Files of Larry O'Brien, Box 27, LBJ; Allen Ellender and Russell Long
to Clifton Dolese, June 18, 1964, and Ellender and Long to R. L. Savoy, September 22, 1964,
both in "Agriculture, Dept. of—Food Stamp Program" Folder, Departmental Files and Independent Agencies Materials, Russell B. Long Papers, Louisiana and Lower Mississippi Valley
Collections, Louisiana State University, Baton Rouge, La.

12. Gilbert Fite, *Cotton Fields No More: Southern Agriculture, 1865–1980* (Lexington, Ky.,
1984), 220–22.

From time to time Ellender felt neglected by the White House, Vice-president Hubert Humphrey told Johnson in August, 1965. Reminding presidential advisers of Ellender's role in passing the food stamp bill, Humphrey said passing cotton and wheat legislation was impossible without the Cajun senator's help. His recommendation to LBJ: stroke and flatter the Cajun senator. "The President's seeing Allen Ellender and it being well publicized in Louisiana could be helpful for the ticket in November," Humphrey continued. "Anyway, Ellender has some views on the Soviet Union which the President may want to hear. He is an interesting man, and he can be very helpful." The vice-president concluded: "What he decides will depend in a large measure upon how much attention he receives." Shortly afterward, Johnson bragged publicly about Ellender's cooking.[13]

Accepting Humphrey's advice, Freeman wrote Johnson in September, "I may be calling on you for a little help with the Senior Senator from Louisiana." Freeman said, "As you know, he is deeply concerned about the national debt." Late in the year Freeman reported, "I am keeping in touch with him and plan to do a good deal of listening and little talking. I hope that this will work as well this time as it has in the past."[14]

In 1965 Budget Director Kermit Gordon said the domestic sugar industry was "inefficient, uneconomical, and should be eliminated." Unperturbed, Ellender relied on the American Sugar Cane League and the Louisiana Farm Bureau Federation to defend the industry. Congress renewed the Sugar Act in 1965 after stormy debate. Although the press labeled the sugar program a costly bonanza, the extension passed with the blessing of LBJ. Meanwhile, Louisiana rice farmers threatened political reprisal against Ellender unless he did more for them. In March a banker from Crowley, in the heart of Louisiana rice country, sent Ellender a telegram saying his political future was on the line unless he came up with a good rice bill. The White House realized Ellender's predicament but knew Freeman hoped to write a new rice program. Raising rice supports, Freeman feared, would cause a clamor to raise others as well: "We must automatically increase cotton supports and the race will be on."[15]

13.   Hubert Humphrey to Jack Valenti (memo), August 4, 1964, in Allen Ellender Name File, Box 60, White House Central Files, LBJ; Diary Cards, August 21, 1964, in Appointment Files, Box 24, LBJ.

14.   Orville Freeman to Lyndon Johnson, September 4, November 16, 1964, both in "USDA Notebook, 1964 (1)" Folder, Box 10, OFP.

15.   Fernand Falgout, Jr., to Lyndon Johnson, March 30, 1965, in "Department, Agriculture, Sugar, 1965" Folder, Box 393, AEP; New York *Times,* editorial, October 6, 1965; New York *Times,* October 21, 1965; E. W. Kenworthy, New York *Times,* October 23, 1965; Ellender

Using administration figures and some of his own, Ellender responded forcefully to rice interests, especially since he would face a reelection campaign in the next year. Pointing out benefits rice farmers enjoyed, he challenged their suggestion that he had done little for them. "I cannot do the impossible, and if you and others desire to try to punish me politically for doing the best I can, that is your privilege," he wrote. The Budget Bureau calculated rice to be the most expensive of all commodities on a per unit basis, he said.[16]

Solving wheat and cotton problems would be complicated, Ellender realized, as Congress in 1964 had come up with only a patchwork farm program. Unless various farm organizations presented a unified front to support LBJ's farm package, Freeman hinted in April, 1965, Congress would not pass an extension to a single commodity program. All the while, Ellender studied financial reports projecting a farm deficit of $8.5 billion at the end of May.[17] LBJ's promised cuts, Ellender knew, were unrealistic.

The fight over a cotton bill in 1965 brought out the biggest weapons of agricultural spokesmen. The struggle dragged on through the summer of 1965 and into the fall. It produced furious debate in both the House and in the Senate. Before the bill was finally passed, Congress once again debated limiting benefit payments to individual farmers.

Ellender continued to advocate his two-price cotton policy, which called for direct payments to farmers who abided by acreage restrictions and subsidies to textile mills for increasing domestic cotton consumption. Stocks of cotton in storage had soared from 7.7 million bales in 1962 to 14.2 million bales in 1965, Ellender noted. At the current rate, the total would be 15 million bales in 1966, he wrote. "I will continue to rack my brain, to talk, drink, eat, and sleep cotton," Freeman wrote, "and if I have any brainstorms I'll drop you a note."[18]

---

press release (mimeographed), March 5, 1965, and Barton Freeland to Ellender (telegram), March 30, 1965, both in "Department, Agriculture, Rice, 1965" Folder, Box 393, AEP; C. R. Eskildsen to Jack Valenti (memo), December 9, 1964, and Valenti to Lyndon Johnson (memo), March 1, 1965, both in Allen Ellender Name File, Box 60, White House Central Files, LBJ.

16. Allen Ellender to Barton Freeland, April 21, 1965, in "Department, Agriculture, Rice, 1965" Folder, Box 393, AEP.

17. New York *Times,* April 14, 1965; Gordon Roth to Herbert Waters, April 3, 1965, in "Leg.: Agriculture Farmers Union" Folder, Box 125, Hubert H. Humphrey Papers, Minnesota Historical Society Collection, St. Paul, Minn.

18. Allen Ellender "Personal and Confidential" to Stuart Symington, August 9, 1965, and Orville Freeman to Ellender, August 11, 1965, both in "1965 Legislation Agriculture" Folder, Box 871, AEP.

Harold Cooley and a few insiders on the House Agricultural Committee drafted H.R. 9811, which became the 1965 farm bill. They added a safety valve for cotton called the snapback. Section 103 (d) (12) specified that if Congress imposed a limit on payments to farmers, a modified form of price support loans would automatically "snap back" into operation.[19]

Fighting over the snapback in the House was bitter, but Cooley won by a vote of 221 to 172 on August 20. Ellender told constituents he considered it too costly, and unlikely to reduce cotton output. Ellender amended it in committee to include a domestic allotment on cotton with effective production controls. In September the full Senate took up the cotton measure. Herman Talmadge introduced an amendment to replace Ellender's two-price cotton with a one-price system. The Talmadge amendment included the snapback provision, which no senator mentioned. At the urging of the textile lobby and the administration, the full Senate "undid our handiwork," Ellender said. On September 10, the Senate voted in favor of Talmadge's plan over Ellender's.[20]

The big debate in the Senate was over the limit on benefit payments to farmers. On this point Ellender and Talmadge were in full agreement; they did not favor a limit on the maximum payment any farmer received. In September the Senate passed the farm bill and sent it to a conference committee to iron out differences with the House version passed earlier. The final version of the bill provided direct support payments of twenty-one cents per pound for cotton to growers who did not use their entire acreage allotments. President Johnson signed the bill into law on November 3, 1965.[21]

The controversy over limiting the size of benefit payments to American farmers flared up again in June, 1966, when the Senate discussed agricultural

19. *Congressional Record,* 89th Cong., 1st Sess., Vol. III, Pt. 15, August 17, 1965, p. 20726; *House Reports,* 89th Cong., 1st Sess., No. 631, "Food and Agriculture Act of 1965," 40.

20. Marjorie Hunter, New York *Times,* August 19, 20, 1965; Ellender to J. E. Ebrecht, August 20, 1965, in "1965 Legislation Agriculture" Folder, Box 871, and mimeographed "Farm Talk" newsletter, August 28, September 18, 1965, Box 1488, all in AEP; New York *Times,* September 3, 1965; Harlow Sanders to J. William Fulbright, September 4, 1965, Folder 4, Box 10, Series 41.1, in J. William Fulbright Papers, Special Collections, University of Arkansas Library, Fayetteville, Ark., hereinafter cited as JWFP; *Congressional Record,* 89th Cong., 1st Sess., Vol. III, Pt. 17, September 10, 1965, pp. 23425–26.

21. *Congressional Record,* 89th Cong., 1st Sess., Vol. III, Pt. 18, September 14, 1965, pp. 23726, 23733, 23728, 23736; New York *Times,* September 27, November 4, 1965; Allen Ellender to C. E. Hester, October 9, 1965, in "1965 Legislation Agriculture" Folder, Box 871, and mimeographed "Farm Talk" newsletter, October 16, 1965, Box 1488, both in AEP.

appropriations for 1967. With strong opposition from textile interests—and the usual farm coalition—the limit measure went down to defeat by a vote of fifty-three to twenty-eight on July 15.[22]

Many farmers and politicians understood the real impact of the limit on farm legislation. "Almost nothing could adversely affect Arkansas's economy as much as a limitation on farm payments," wrote Frank Hyneman, president of the Agricultural Council of Arkansas, to Senator Fulbright in 1967. After intense debate on July 13, 1967, the Senate overwhelmingly rejected the limitation amendment, just as it had for eight years. In October, President Johnson and Orville Freeman met with Ellender and other southern cotton leaders in an off-the-record discussion of cotton legislation. Freeman thanked Ellender for coming to his defense against Jamie Whitten, the Mississippi congressman who had screamed at Freeman several times about cotton exports hurting U.S. producers. Ellender had finally jumped in asking, "How, how, how?" An appreciative Freeman said, "That shut him up quick."[23]

By January, 1968, advocates of a limit on payments seemed to be gaining public support for some kind of control on runaway benefit payments. Ellender held firm in opposition. In August, Freeman told Johnson he hoped to eliminate a twenty-thousand-dollar limit on the farm bill when it got to the conference committee. Using parliamentary maneuvers to frustrate reformers in late September, Ellender and his colleagues deleted the twenty-thousand-dollar limit.[24]

The acrimonious dispute spilled over into discussion of sugar legislation. In September, 1968, Ellender asked to see the president with Louisiana congressman Edwin Willis about proposed cuts in sugarcane acreage allotments

22. *Congressional Record,* 89th Cong., 2d Sess., Vol. 112, Pt. 10, June 8, 1966, pp. 12690–92, Pt. 12, July 15, 1966, pp. 15823–39.

23. Frank Hyneman to J. William Fulbright, July 19, 1967, Folder 1, Box 4, Fulbright to Wilson, May 22, 1966, Folder 2, Box 4, both in Series 42.2, JWFP; *Congressional Record,* 90th Cong., 1st Sess., Vol. 113, Pt. 14, July 13, 1967, pp. 18848–80; New York *Times,* June 20, July 12, July 13, August 5, 1967; Mike Manatos to West Lobby (memo), October 9, 1967, in Allen Ellender Name File, Box 60, White House Central Files, LBJ; Diary Cards, October 9, 1967, in Appointments File, Box 24, LBJ; Orville Freeman to Allen Ellender, October 13, 1967, in "Cotton, Dept. Agriculture—1967" Folder, Box 417, AEP.

24. *Congressional Record,* 90th Cong., 2d Sess., Vol. 114, Pt. 9, May 1, 1968, pp. 11286–90, Pt. 11, May 23, 1968, p. 14683, Pt. 12, May 29, 1968, pp. 15546–55, Pt. 19, July 31, 1968, pp. 24393–402, Pt. 20, September 5, 1968, pp. 25852–53, September 12, 1968, p. 26750, Pt. 21, September 25, 1968, p. 27981; New York *Times,* August 1, 1968; Orville Freeman to Lyndon Johnson (memo), August 2, 1968, in Allen Ellender Name File, Box 60, White House Central Files, LBJ.

for the 1969 season. After meeting with Ellender and Willis, the administration reduced the size of acreage cuts and approved the Sugar Act extension. In the midst of the 1968 agricultural spending controversy, Ellender celebrated his seventy-eighth birthday on September 24 by cooking gumbo and inviting a number of dignitaries. The president, eager to flatter Ellender, showed up with Lady Bird, their daughter Lynda Robb, and a birthday cake.[25]

Drew Pearson suggested that Ellender was politically vulnerable in 1966 because of his diplomatic blunders in Africa, his opposition to minimum wage legislation, and his record on civil rights. Camille Gravel, a liberal Louisiana Democrat, could defeat Ellender if blacks in Louisiana registered and voted, Pearson thought. The journalist acknowledged Ellender's support for education, school lunches, public housing, and his vocal opposition to Joseph McCarthy before most congressmen had dared to speak out. Louisiana newspapers speculated about potential opponents for Ellender in 1966. One possible foe, New Orleans district attorney Jim Garrison, had decided to seek reelection as DA rather than challenge Ellender. Governor John McKeithen, citing a recent poll, claimed he could defeat Ellender in a Senate race. McKeithen planned to run only if he failed to pass a constitutional amendment to allow himself to succeed himself as governor. And still a third challenger, state legislator John Garrett of Haynesville, had announced plans to oppose Ellender. Because these preliminary announcements often did not produce a candidate, Ellender ignored them.[26]

In November Ellender voted by absentee ballot in the general election for Amendment Number 1 to the Louisiana Constitution to allow Governor McKeithen and future governors to succeed themselves in office. He also voted for Amendment No. 10, a proposal to build a domed stadium in New Orleans with public funds.[27] Both amendments were passed.

25. *Congressional Record*, 90th Cong., 2d Sess., Vol. 114, Pt. 22, October 8, 1968, pp. 30060–66; Mike Manatos to Lyndon Johnson (memo), September 4, 6, 1968, Thomas Hughes to Orville Freeman, September 4, 1968, all in Allen Ellender Name File, Box 60, White House Central Files, LBJ; Diary Cards, September 9, 1968, in Appointment File, Box 24, LBJ; "Weekly Report from Congress," May 16, 1964, Box 1487, AEP; "Weekly Report from Congress," September 14, 21, 1968, Box 1494, AEP; Betty Beale, Washington (D.C.) *Evening-Star,* September 25, 1968, and United Press International wire copy, September 24, 1968, both in "1968" Scrapbook, AEP.

26. Bureau memo, September 10, 1965, FBI File 62-81810; Drew Pearson, Washington *Post,* September 10, 1965, and unidentified newspaper clippings, January, 1965, all in "1965" Scrapbook, AEP.

27. New Orleans *Times-Picayune,* November 4, 1966, in "1966" Scrapbook, AEP.

In its rating of the Eighty-eighth Congress, the liberal weekly *New Republic* gave Ellender good marks on only two roll call votes, wheat sales to the USSR and the Test Ban Treaty. He got bad marks for everything else. He voted against Medicare, the antipoverty program, and formation of the Youth Conservation Corps. Medicare, Ellender thought, would have taxed all Americans to pay for medical services in other states, rejecting an argument he had used earlier in his career to justify federal aid to education.[28] The periodical had failed to note a significant Ellender contribution, not even his support for the food stamp measure, an important part of the antipoverty program.

Returning to Louisiana late in September, 1965, after Congress had passed the farm bill, Ellender visited his son, who had suffered a nasty cut on his hand while cleaning up after Hurricane Betsy. The injury prevented Allen Jr. from performing surgery for a time. In a letter to President Johnson asking for emergency aid for hurricane victims, Ellender mentioned Allen Jr.'s injury and his hope for a full recovery. Promising emergency aid to storm victims, Johnson wrote, "The news of your son's accident is very distressing. Please keep me informed of his progress."[29]

By mid-December, Ellender was conducting his annual rounds in Louisiana to maintain personal political contacts. He told supporters he hoped to win reelection in 1966. He had blocked efforts to limit the size of benefit payments and had taken care of his sugar and rice constituents. He had helped pass the food stamp measure.

When Harry Byrd of Virginia died in 1966, Ellender became the third-ranking senator, exceeded in seniority only by Carl Hayden of Arizona and Richard Russell. Even though he was seventy-five, he campaigned and vacationed in his usual energetic style. He seemed eager to return to the U.S. Senate. Proficient in the game of broker politics, he thought he deserved a chance to serve Louisiana six more years.

28. *New Republic,* October 17, 1964, pp. 14–15; mimeographed text of radio report, August 17, 1963, Box 1486, February 27, 1965, Box 1487, both in AEP.

29. Allen Ellender to Susan Stall, September 29, 1965, in "Ellender Personal" Folder, Box 1178, AEP; Lyndon Johnson to Allen Ellender, September 15, 1965, in Allen Ellender Name File, Box 60, White House Central Files, LBJ.

17

THE GREAT SOCIETY
UNDER SIEGE
(1966–68)

*I*n the midst of political battles over civil rights and agriculture, Ellender prepared for his sixth election campaign. He had completed nearly five full terms in Washington and felt confident about his reelection chances. The new civil rights legislation affected registration and voting patterns in Louisiana, but no apparent champion of black or liberal causes had emerged to challenge him. His position on sugar, rice, and cotton legislation had strengthened his hand with his constituents. He was seventy-five years old, but his active schedule and energetic ways led people to assume that he was much younger.

Ellender's team of veteran campaigners was in place for his reelection bid. Elward Wright managed the Louisiana front from his law office in Houma. Wright had extensive lists of past contributors, campaign workers, and "friends" and contacts throughout the state. Next to the names on one list were such comments as "has written a number of times and seems anxious to help," "may want to be paid," "the Sen. is a little skeptical about him, because he runs down so many people," or "old friend of the Senator's."[1]

Not until April did Ellender finally learn who his opponents would be in the Democratic primary scheduled for August 13. Camille Gravel, a liberal attorney from Alexandria, announced rather late. A Roman Catholic and the

---

1. Box 1838, Allen J. Ellender Papers, Nicholls State University Library, Thibodaux, La., hereinafter cited as AEP.

father of ten children, the fifty-year-old Gravel, a former assistant district attorney and a member of the Knights of Columbus, had been a strong backer of John Kennedy in 1960. He and Ellender had clashed then over civil rights programs of the Democratic Party. The winner would face the Republican opponent, if there was one, in the November general election.

Labeling Ellender a tool of special interests, Gravel called him a senator *from* Louisiana, not a senator *for* Louisiana. A servant of big farmers and an opponent of Medicare, Ellender served big business and opposed benefits for workers, Gravel said, more candidly than the Ellender camp would have admitted. Calling himself a "progressive" moderate Democrat, Gravel said Ellender's "sorry voting record" showed he had voted against every minimum wage increase and against every Social Security extension.[2]

In some ways Ellender had become a political hybrid. Although he had a typical white southerner's attitude toward race and labor, he did not always support the southern line on presidential appointments or on foreign policy and the Cold War. Conservative congressional-rating organizations, which gave liberal Jacob Javits of New York a zero and conservative Richard Russell of Georgia an eighty-three, rated Ellender in the high forties or low fifties. Liberal rating groups, which usually gave Javits high scores, gave Ellender ratings in the low to midtwenties, whereas conservatives like Milton Young of North Dakota and James Eastland of Mississippi scored five or less. In other words, Ellender did not fall into a neat category for classification. On most issues he was conservative; on others surprisingly liberal. The liberal *New Republic* on twelve roll call votes in the Eighty-ninth Congress gave Javits and Walter Mondale of Minnesota scores of eleven, Young a two, and Eastland a zero. Ellender scored a four. In 1965 he had voted to support Lyndon Johnson's position 44 percent of the time. He supported the Democratic Party position only 35 percent of the time. But 77 percent of the time he supported positions endorsed by a conservative coalition of Republicans and southern Democrats.[3]

In an urban industrial area Gravel's charges might have swayed voters, but in conservative Louisiana, Ellender's voting record enhanced his popular appeal. He had voted against repeal of the Tonkin Gulf Resolution, for delaying implementation of the $1.60 minimum wage law until 1969, and for Everett Dirksen's constitutional amendment to circumvent one-man,

2. Random newspaper clippings gathered by Ellender's clipping service, Box 1838, AEP.

3. *Congressional Quarterly Weekly Report*, July 22, 1955, p. 1538, November 4, 1966, p. 2766; *New Republic*, October 22, 1966, p. 19.

one-vote guidelines by allowing one house of the state legislature to be apportioned on a geographical basis. Demonstrating a knack for turning negative criticism into positive campaign strategy, Ellender claimed that a 1966 political coup in Ghana proved his widely criticized statement about the inability of African nations to govern themselves without outside help to be true. To think, Ellender said, he had been declared unwelcome in some parts of Africa three years earlier for voicing an obviously sensible view.[4]

Two other opponents entered the Senate race against Ellender, state senator W. J. DeBlieux of Baton Rouge and Troyce Guice, thirty-three, an automobile dealer from Ferriday. Staffers in Ellender's office said Crowley congressman Edwin Edwards would back his opponents. As the filing deadline approached in late June, Wright hoped Ellender would face token opposition and would require only a token campaign. This seemed likely after his most serious opponent, Gravel, withdrew from the race, apparently because he failed to generate much support. Ellender would not be popular with black registered voters, his campaign team realized, but white Democrats still comprised the largest bloc of potential supporters. When campaigning for black support, Ellender and Wright used friendly sheriffs in the various parishes to court the black vote in subtle ways. Through the sheriffs they found small political jobs for part-time black preachers in exchange for a few favorable comments about Ellender. They also bought advertisements in black newspapers and contributed money to black churches.[5]

As usual Ellender had little difficulty financing his election campaign. In August he thanked New Orleans businessman Louis Roussell and former Huey Long financier Seymour Weiss for contributions made to his campaign fund.[6] Once television became an important part of American life, and media exposure vital in shaping political thinking, Ellender hired professionals to conduct polls and prepare television, radio, and newspaper advertisements. These innovations added considerably to the cost of campaigning.

The company Ellender and Wright chose to manage the 1966 campaign, Bauerlein, of New Orleans, proposed a budget exceeding $100,000, most of

4. *New Republic*, October 22, 1966, pp. 16–17; Alexandria (La.) *Town Talk*, March 8, 1966, Box 1838, AEP.

5. Random 1966 newspaper clippings, and office note to Allen Ellender, April 22, 1966, all in Box 1838, Elward Wright to C. R. Morrison, June 6, 1966, Box 1836, and figures from Board of Registration, East Baton Rouge Parish, Box 1834, all in AEP; Elward Wright, interview, November 8, 1979.

6. Allen Ellender to Seymour Weiss, August 1, 1966, and Ellender to Louis Roussell, August 4, 1966, both in Box 1834, AEP.

which would go to media time and lineage in major urban areas. A slightly reduced alternative budget called for spending only $92,000; another budget called for spending nearly $260,000. Between June 17 and August 15, Wright wrote seven checks to Ken Gormin of Bauerlein for a total of about $86,000. Ellender planned a radio and television blitz during the last two weeks of the campaign.[7]

Flo LeCompte regularly forwarded funds received in Ellender's Washington office to Wright in Houma. After receiving a cash contribution, LeCompte said, "At the Senator's suggestion, I deposited the cash to my personal account and then wrote a check to Allen J. Ellender Campaign Fund." Medical doctors contributed to the fund "for a friend of organized medicine." The Democratic Senatorial Campaign Committee sent Ellender a check for seven thousand dollars. Campaign headquarters received more than thirteen thousand dollars in contributions and loans from New Orleans and funneled most of it back to the Crescent City Democratic Association through its agent, Pete Gagliano.[8]

Ellender's lopsided victory on August 13 represented more than 74 percent of the total votes cast in the statewide primary. In some parishes he received 85 percent of the vote. In a handwritten note to Ellender marked "personal & confidential," Wright told his old friend, "You got plenty of votes and cash, too." Total receipts came to $126,524, Wright said; expenditures totaled $114,955—newspapers $50,287, television $31,626, radio $23,565, the Houma office $1,382, and other $8,095. The balance came to $11,569, which could be carried over for future campaigns or used as personal funds. In September, Ellender told a New Orleans fund-raiser to send any surplus funds to Wright in Houma. "As you may know, any surplus there will be transferred to my 'Reports from Congress' account, which I use for public service purposes."[9]

Because Ellender faced no Republican opposition, his successful campaign was behind him long before the November elections. In the meantime, he could plan a few fishing trips in Louisiana with Willard and his old

7. Boxes 1837 and 1838, AEP, contain detailed correspondence and financial records pertaining to the 1966 election.

8. Florence LeCompte to Elward Wright, July 19, 23, August 19, 1966, Ellender to Wright, July 26, 1966, all in Box 1838, AEP; Box 1834, *passim,* AEP.

9. Elward Wright to Allen Ellender, August 27, 1966, Ellender to Albert V. LaBiche, September 13, 1966, both in Box 1834, AEP; random newspaper clippings in Elward Wright Papers, in the possession of Thomas Wright, Houma, La., hereinafter cited as EWP.

friends. Ellender spent the weekend after his victory in Houma with his family. On Monday Allen Jr. and two of the grandchildren drove him to the airport in New Orleans. Before the day was over, he was on Capitol Hill considering minimum wage increases and legislation for rent supplements.[10]

The United States by then had become more deeply involved in Vietnam. "Personally, I went on record as far back as 1954 against the involvement of U.S. forces in Viet Nam, and advised President Eisenhower against it," he wrote in 1965. "We have almost no commercial ties there, and no historical ties," he said in 1963. "On the other hand, we stand to lose a great deal, including men, materiel, money, and a large amount of national prestige."[11]

When the Tonkin Gulf Resolution first came up for discussion in 1964, Ellender posed pointed questions to J. William Fulbright, chairman of the Senate Foreign Relations Committee, who was pushing the resolution. Demanding specific details of the PT boat attacks on the *Maddox* in the Gulf of Tonkin, Ellender tried to determine whether the U.S. Navy had provoked an attack. At one point in the discussion he introduced a resolution to limit the president's war-making powers, but he withdrew it later on the advice of Fulbright, who assured him the Tonkin Gulf Resolution applied to defensive operations at sea, not to land operations. In the end, Ellender joined all but two senators in voting for the resolution.[12]

By May, 1965, Ellender realized, the United States was engaged in a major war. Whenever Johnson sought additional funding and manpower, he invited Ellender and about thirty other members of Congress to the White House for briefings on Vietnam. By July, Ellender was saying he had no choice but to support the president, who had taken a gamble in Vietnam. Ellender disliked antiwar demonstrations and believed they were encouraged by a small minority of Americans. He supported the bombing north along the seventeenth parallel, sending more men into combat, and increasing the draft.[13]

10. Patricia Gorman, New Orleans *States-Item*, August 15, 1966, in "1966" Scrapbook, AEP.

11. Mimeographed text of radio reports, September 7, 1963, May 8, 1965, both in Box 1486, AEP.

12. Allen Ellender, interview by T. Harrison Baker, July 30, 1969, in Oral History Collection, Lyndon Baines Johnson Library, Austin, Tex., 16–17.

13. *Ibid.*, 16; mimeographed text of radio report, May 8, May 15, May 29, July 17, July 31, 1965, January 15, February 15, 1966, all in Box 1488, AEP.

Ellender had no plan for ending the war. When Senator Wayne Morse of Oregon called for a U.S. withdrawal from Vietnam, Ellender seemed to concur, as though he had favored such a move for some time. Nevertheless, Ellender voted against all end-the-war amendments. Although Vietnam was not the logical place to fight communism, Ellender and Richard Russell thought, once U.S. land forces had been committed to the area, they should have a chance to finish the job. Ellender felt the United States should fight to win or get out completely.[14]

Ellender favored using air strikes against North Vietnam to improve American chances for success. "We can't possibly win in North Vietnam without air power," he said. Late in the year, he labeled the struggle a war the United States "cannot afford to fight and cannot afford to quit." American aid money, he complained, "is being used to fill the coffers of the Vietnamese government." Ellender favored continuing the bombing until the North Vietnamese agreed to talks. Meanwhile, Ellender received his share of favors, according to the president's "Congressional Favors File."[15]

On the home front, the war in Vietnam erupted into a major confrontation involving civil rights and law and order. Attracting world attention and dominating domestic concerns, the war overshadowed other areas of foreign policy. Ellender gradually acquiesced to escalation, criticizing instead riots, demonstrations, and unrest at home.

During his reelection campaign, Ellender had prepared a forceful speech supporting LBJ's hard line against Ho Chi Minh, possibly for later use in the campaign. But he never delivered it. Immediate decisive action was the way to prevent major disaster in the future, he asserted. Claiming the time for debate was over, he said the United States should "go all out or get out." Ellender criticized European allies who did not support American efforts in southeast Asia. By the summer of 1967 Ellender had become more vocal,

14. *Congressional Quarterly Weekly Report,* July 29, 1972, p. 1853; Tristan Coffin, *Senator Fulbright: Portrait of a Public Philosopher* (New York, 1966), 217–18; miscellaneous newspaper clippings, February, 1964, in "1964" Scrapbook, AEP; Gilbert C. Fite, *Richard B. Russell, Jr., Senator from Georgia* (Chapel Hill, 1991), 437, 440, 448; "Allen J. Ellender Oral History Interview," by Larry Hackman, August 29, 1967 (John F. Kennedy Library, Washington, D.C.; facsimile copy in Nicholls State University Library, Thibodaux, La.), 29.

15. Miscellaneous newspaper clippings, January, 1965, in "1965" Scrapbook, AEP; mimeographed text of radio report, January 15, 1966, Box 1488, AEP; Diary Cards, December 9, 1964, February 20, July 28, 1965, in Appointment Files, Box 24, and "Ellender, Allen J.," Congressional Favors File, various dates, Box 9, all in Lyndon Baines Johnson Library, Austin, Tex., hereinafter cited as LBJ.

more specific regarding Vietnam. "We've paid until it hurts," he said, lamenting the cost of sending two Korean divisions to Vietnam. "We must not only pay for their logistics, but also the support of their widows and children," he said. Predicting a cease-fire by the end of 1967, Ellender said, "We should get our men home through an honorable solution in Vietnam." [16]

Senate Armed Services Committee chairman Richard Russell influenced Ellender's thinking on Vietnam more than did Foreign Relations Committee chairman J. William Fulbright. Russell favored bombing North Vietnam and blockading Haiphong harbor and the Vietnam coast. Ellender's mail included emotional observations about war casualties. A New Orleans correspondent wrote dramatically: "Die, lads, 337 of you die now, this week, it's for us." The president and military leaders were doing everything possible to win the war, Ellender told him.[17]

Despite growing skepticism about foreign affairs in general, Ellender usually defended President Johnson. Explaining in March why he did not support a move to rescind the Tonkin Gulf Resolution, he said, "It may well be that those in opposition to our course in Vietnam are attempting to use the confusion which existed at the time, to reinforce their attacks on current policy." [18]

At the opening of the Ninetieth Congress on January 7, 1967, Ellender was exceeded in seniority only by Carl Hayden of Arizona and Richard Russell of Georgia. Hayden was ninety and planning to retire at the end of the session; Russell's emphysema was becoming more incapacitating. When Hayden and Russell were indisposed, Ellender directed Appropriations Committee hearings. Starting in 1967, Ellender spent most of his time working with the Appropriations Committee. Because the 1965 Agricultural Act was working well, he and Freeman agreed there was no need for a new farm

16. Speech, February 24, 1966, Box 1841, AEP; New Orleans *States-Item,* February 10, 28, 1966, both in "1966" Scrapbook, AEP; New Orleans *Times-Picayune,* June 7, 1967, New Orleans *Item,* June 7, 1967, both in "1967" Scrapbook, AEP.

17. Fite, *Richard Russell,* 454; Path Miller to Allen Ellender, May 26, 1967, and Ellender to many constituents, March 1967, all in "Foreign Relations (Vietnam) Legislation" Folder, Box 901, AEP.

18. Allen Ellender to Claribel H. Weaver, February 8, 1968, and Ellender to Henry O. Williams, Sr., March 4, 1968, both in "Foreign Relations, Vietnam" Folder, and Ellender to Ernest Meredith, April 24, 1968, in "1968 France Legislation" Folder, all in Box 919, AEP; "Weekly Report from Congress," February 3, 1968, Box 1494, AEP.

bill. Ellender focused on the president's greatest burden—Vietnam. In exchange for support from Ellender, Johnson granted many favors. Convinced the budget was getting out of control when LBJ asked for $9.4 billion in January, Ellender nonetheless acquiesced, figuring the admirals and generals would get what they wanted. In June, Congress voted for an additional $70.3 billion in defense, mostly for Vietnam.[19]

Ellender's statements of opposition to the war in Vietnam were inconsistent with his votes to finance and expand the war. Undoubtedly, Johnson flattered him; he also agreed to his farm proposals and granted many favors asked for his constituents. Perhaps Ellender, thinking Johnson's antiwar opponents responsible for political chaos at home, believed the president's only hope for domestic tranquillity was victory in Southeast Asia.

White House files from 1966 to 1968 indicate extensive political and social meetings between the president and Ellender. For instance, on October 16, 1967, a White House aide told another aide of Ellender's eagerness to cook shrimp curry for the president. The next day he handed the president Ellender's luncheon list with two open spots he could fill with whomever he wanted. Unlike Richard Russell, who distanced himself from Johnson during the civil rights struggles, Ellender maintained close ties to his old Senate sidekick, who happened to be the most powerful political leader in the world.[20]

In January, 1968, Ellender approved LBJ's plan to halt the bombing of North Vietnam if prospects for meaningful talks improved. In February, Johnson promised to increase rice production allotments, which would benefit Louisiana farmers. In March, Johnson announced his support for Ellender's rural economic development bill, which had failed in two previous attempts. In September, Johnson invited Ellender to accompany him on Air Force One to New Orleans for a presidential address to an American Legion

19. New Orleans *States-Item*, April 29, 1968, Edgar Poe, New Orleans *Times-Picayune*, May 5, 1968, both in "1968" Scrapbook, AEP; "Weekly Report from Congress," April 27, May 4, 1968, Box 1494; "Weekly Report from Congress," January 21, 28, February 11, March 4, June 3, 17, 1967, all in Box 1493, AEP; Mike Manatos to Lyndon Johnson (memo), June 21, 1967, in Allen Ellender Name File, Box 60, White House Central Files, LBJ.

20. Diary Cards, February 3, 24, March 11, May 18, July 19, 1966, January 9, March 1, July 25, October 9, 11, 18, 1967, January 31, March 13, September 9, 10, 1968, in Appointments File, Box 24, LBJ; Mike Manatos to Lyndon Johnson (memo), April 22, 1966, Marvin Watson to Johnson (memo), February 16, 1967, Johnson to Allen Ellender, February 22, 1967, Manatos to Johnson, October 16, 17, 1967, all in Allen Ellender Name File, Box 60, White House Central Files, LBJ.

convention. Ellender approved LBJ's hard-hitting speech and, later in the month, got the president to reduce sugarcane acreage cuts for Louisiana.[21]

Meanwhile, the country, torn by rioting and political dissension, prepared for the presidential election. Johnson, under increasing pressure from opponents of the war in Vietnam, announced in March, 1968, he would not seek reelection in November. Calling him a "patriot" for stepping aside in order to achieve peace, Ellender said Johnson was not to blame for the war in Vietnam. In April the assassination of Martin Luther King, Jr., touched off racial riots in a number of U.S. cities. Hubert Humphrey, once considered the favorite of liberals and Johnson's likely successor, faced challengers who disliked the administration's war policy. Robert Kennedy and George Wallace vied for leadership among Democrats. In June, Kennedy was assassinated just as his challenge to Humphrey for the nomination had been enhanced by primary victories, notably in California.

In July, Humphrey won the nomination at the Democratic convention while police and demonstrators engaged in violent confrontation. George Wallace and Curtis LeMay promptly formed a splinter independent party. Meanwhile, Republicans nominated Richard Nixon and Spiro Agnew to lead their party in the election.[22]

All the while Ellender criticized antiwar demonstrations, marches, and protests, equating them with civil rights activities. He fumed when boxer Cassius Clay refused to be drafted and black militant Stokley Carmichael encouraged rebellion from exile in Havana. He supported a bill to ban flag burning. Calling black activist Rap Brown "that racial troublemaker," Ellender said, "I would not put him in the jailhouse, I would put him under it." Ellender refused to vote for funds for the War on Poverty because of demonstrations in Washington, D.C., demonstrations that, he thought, should not receive extensive television coverage. Giving money to cities, Ellender said in March, 1969, would not stop violence, which he attributed to an atmosphere of lawlessness associated with racial sit-ins and marches.[23]

Ellender viewed the 1968 presidential race with little or no enthusiasm. Hubert Humphrey, like Adlai Stevenson in the 1950s, was too closely asso-

21. "Weekly Report from Congress," January 27, February 3, March 2, 16, September 14, 21, 1968, all in Box 1494, AEP.

22. "Weekly Report from Congress," April 6, 1968, *ibid.*

23. "Weekly Report from Congress," June 11, 1966, Box 1838, May 13, 19, June 24, August 26, September 2, 16, 1967, Box 1493, March 2, 9, June 29, 1968, Box 1494, all in AEP; *New Republic,* October 22, 1966, p. 17.

ciated with civil rights for his liking. In addition, Humphrey had endorsed Johnson's Vietnam policy, which was becoming increasingly untenable. Third-party candidates George Wallace and Curtis LeMay were not a viable alternative in the view of Ellender, who scheduled an extensive fall and winter tour of the Far East. Weary of the chaos, rioting, and political turmoil, Ellender turned his back on the counterculture tearing the country apart.

As he grew in seniority, Ellender took more seriously his inspection tours of foreign lands. After five visits to the Soviet Union, his surprisingly liberal view of détente with the USSR had become more pronounced. At first Ellender considered Nikita Khrushchev a clown, but later changed his mind and viewed him instead as a diamond in the rough. "It seems to me that we have as much to fear from ignorance, prejudice, selfishness and bias in our own nation," Ellender observed, "as we have from a similar condition on the part of the Russian leadership." On another occasion he stated in his Acadian style: "I often wondered why in hell we don't get together with the Russians?"[24]

American taxpayers were financing Ellender's home movies of his travels abroad, Drew Pearson and Jack Anderson claimed in 1967. Ellender used his own camera, but the Senate Recording Studio handled film processing for him: it sent film for processing and splicing to the USDA; then it added Ellender's voice narration to film for Louisiana television stations. The USDA sent a bill to the recording studio for processing the film.

After "Washington Merry-Go-Round" criticized the policy, Ellender paid the recording studio with a check for $6,165, explaining that it was "only because I desire to have all the charges at hand so that full payment could be rendered at one time." Extant records do not indicate clearly when Ellender began to pay for processing film. As early as 1956, he had paid for film from his "Reports from Congress" account. While answering charges by Pearson and Anderson in the summer of 1967, Ellender voted to censure Senator Thomas Dodd of Connecticut for spending political contributions on personal items.[25]

24. "Allen J. Ellender Oral History Interview," by Larry Hackman, August 29, 1967 (John F. Kennedy Library, Washington, D.C.; facsimile copy in Nicholls State University Library, Thibodaux, La.), 26–28, 29; quotations are from *Congressional Quarterly Weekly Report*, July 29, 1972, p. 1853.

25. *Congressional Record*, 90th Cong., 2d Sess., Vol. 114, Pt. 22, September 26, 1968, pp. 28285–88; New Orleans *Times-Picayune*, June 24, 1967, Charleston (W.Va.) *Gazette*, July 23, 1967, both in "1967" Scrapbook, AEP; George Arceneaux, Jr., to Florence LeCompte, October 10, 1956, in "Personal—1956 World Tour" Folder, Box 1843, AEP.

Ellender had voiced opposition to the war but voted to sustain it. Rather than take the lead in resistance to the war, he acquiesced to the charms of LBJ and convinced himself that antiwar demonstrators were really civil rights protesters committed to a new cause. Many of his constituents resisted civil rights legislation, supported the war, and opposed gun control. Thus, he took a safe political stance, maintained the friendship of Johnson, and garnered many government programs for his home state, although he stressed cutting waste and reducing government spending. He had not varied much from his position of support for Huey Long, Franklin Roosevelt, or Harry Truman.

Ellender continued to oppose gun control legislation, even when the measure received renewed support after the assassinations of Martin Luther King, Jr., on April 4 and Robert Kennedy on June 6. Russell Long and Wayne Morse in the Senate agreed with Ellender; Lyndon Johnson, Eugene McCarthy, and Attorney General Ramsey Clark all favored gun control. Ellender told constituents he considered gun control a local issue, but he favored curbs on mail-order purchases of weapons.

Ellender explained to critics how he decided issues. "I try to think problems through and then act accordingly," he wrote, explaining his opposition to Medicare, the antipoverty program, and gun control. In opposing the antipoverty program Ellender was refusing aid to some of the rural poor who had received few farm benefits and had been driven from the land. Many now resided in urban slums. He seemed no more sympathetic or inclined to help them now. He would vote to confirm the nomination of Abe Fortas to the Supreme Court as he had voted to confirm every other nominee except Thurgood Marshall.[26]

From time to time Ellender received hate mail and death threats, which the FBI investigated. In July and again in August, 1966, a former mental patient wrote intimidating letters. One letter threatened to "decimate by torture your entire family."[27] If Ellender worried about the threats from the deranged antagonist, whose name was deleted in the FBI files released to the author, he kept his concerns to himself.

---

26. *Congressional Quarterly Weekly Report,* June 21, 1968, p. 1558; Allen Ellender to Lloyd Gaubert, August 13, 1968, and Ellender to many constituents, September 20, 1968, both in "1968 Firearm Legislation" Folder, Box 919, AEP; "Weekly Report from Congress," June 15, 1968, Box 1494, AEP.

27. FBI File 9-45583.

Ellender's only sister, Walterine, died at Terrebonne General Hospital on February 21, 1967. She was seventy and had lived in Houston until 1959, when her husband, Charles Caillouette, retired. Walterine and Charles had moved into the family home Wallace had built on Hope Farm Plantation. Ellender flew in from Washington to attend the funeral at St. Ann's Church in Bourg, a short distance above the Ellender lands along the banks of Bayou Terrebonne. Lyndon Johnson sent Ellender a sympathy note.[28]

Several months later, on May 20, while Ellender was in Ruston to deliver the graduation address at Louisiana Tech University, his brother Willard died suddenly of a heart attack at home. Willard, sixty-one, had recovered from a mild attack in 1961. He and his cousin Dr. Ernest Ellender, Jr., had established the Ellender Memorial Hospital. Allen and Willard had remained close through the years. The brothers had often hunted and fished together, enjoying long conversations while cleaning and cooking their fish and game. "His sudden death was a great shock to the family and is a loss that will be deeply felt for a very long time to come," he wrote. "He was more like a son to me than a brother, and his sudden death comes as quite a shock," he told another. "I cannot yet realize he is gone."[29]

Although Ellender was nearly seventy-seven when Walterine and Willard died, he contemplated his own mortality only briefly. He had already made provisions for disposing of his property; his life-style continued unchanged. Occasionally he seemed tired and complained of not feeling well, Flo Le-Compte noticed. He blamed periodic bouts of indigestion on unwise eating habits or on straying from his simple diet to indulge in Mexican food or other exotic culinary delights. Ellender visited Bethesda Naval Hospital on May 11, 1967, at 8:30 P.M., according to a memo President Johnson received and which provided no other information. Perhaps he experienced indigestion.[30]

After serving twenty-five years in the nation's capital in Ellender's office, Flo LeCompte returned to Louisiana in 1967 to help care for her ailing sisters

28.   Houma (La.) *Courier,* February 24, 1967; Charles Caillouette, interview, November 23, 1979; Lyndon Johnson to Allen Ellender, February 22, 1967, in Allen Ellender Name File, Box 60, White House Central Files, LBJ.

29.   Ellender to R. E. Thompson, June 26, 1967, in "Fire Ants, Dept. Agriculture, 1967" Folder, Box 418, AEP; Ellender to Julian C. Miller, June 26, 1967, in "Sweet Potatoes, Dept. Agriculture, 1967" Folder, Box 419, AEP; Shreveport *Times,* May 30, 1967, Houma (La.) *Courier,* June 2, 1967, both in "1967" Scrapbook, AEP.

30.   James Cross to Juanita Roberts (memo), May 12, 1967, in Allen Ellender Name File, Box 60, White House Central Files, LBJ.

and her ninety-three-year-old father. LeCompte did not terminate her employment with "the Senator" (as she always called him); instead she ran his Houma office. Home at night to help care for her family, LeCompte spoke to Ellender on the telephone every day when he was in Washington. When he was in Louisiana, she drove him around and performed secretarial chores in the office. She returned to Washington occasionally for visits.[31]

Ellender had lost Claude, Willard, and Walterine. Wallace Jr. was his only remaining sibling. After Helen died in 1949, Ellender had turned to Claude and Thelma; after Claude died in 1956, he had visited with and engaged in outdoor activities with Willard. He conferred often with Wallace Jr. about farm operations, but he had a much closer personal relationship with Willard. After Willard's death, Ellender sometimes asked Irving Legendre, Jr., who had married Willard's daughter Byrne, to take him fishing. The relationship was good for Ellender; Irving deferred to the senator and took him to new fishing spots in neighboring Lafourche Parish where the Legendres lived. Ellender liked to spend time at the Legendre summer home on Grand Isle where the atmosphere was informal and the fishing was good.

The Legendre "camp" was large and usually filled with visitors, family, and young people. Ellender enjoyed cooking for them and lecturing them on world affairs. His nieces and nephews sat around attentively, but they disliked having their uncle quiz them on geography or world politics. Ellender amazed the young people who gathered about him with his energy. He often stayed up late at night talking or reading, but rose early the next morning to begin the day's fishing. He never asked to come in early as long as the fish were biting. His typical fishing attire was a long-sleeved white shirt buttoned at the neck, cotton gloves, and an old hat purchased in Europe in the 1930s and worn because it was "too good to throw away." His expertise in fishing had not improved over the years, but he made up for the shortcoming with enthusiasm.[32]

From time to time Ellender wrote friendly letters to former president Harry Truman. After returning from the Far East, he told Truman that the North Koreans and Chinese were "arrogant." Had Douglas MacArthur followed Truman's advice in Korea in 1950, the situation would be better today, he suggested. As usual, the FBI received reports of Ellender's jaunts, especially his fifty-three days touring and filming in the Soviet Union. An agent

31. Florence LeCompte to Mona Jennings, January 11, 1967, in "Ellender Personal" Folder, Box 1197, AEP; Florence LeCompte, interview, June 20, 1991.

32. Irving Legendre, Jr., interviews, June 18, July 10, 1980.

in Hong Kong described Ellender's knowledge of the Soviet Union as "superficial at best." Furthermore, Ellender was "naïve in matters of relationships between countries," had become "very senile," and showed a "strong hostility toward the Bureau and the Director." Hoover may have been gathering information to counter Ellender's report of FBI operations abroad.[33] Ellender may have been naïve or wrong, but he was not senile.

The Ellender clan gathered for the Christmas of 1968 at Wallace Jr.'s.[34] As usual, Ellender's hectic schedule allowed insufficient time for visiting with family. Before long he had to depart for Washington for the opening of the Ninety-first Congress in January, 1969. He would have to contend with a new president, Richard Nixon, who had inherited a multitude of problems.

33. Allen Ellender to Harry Truman, December 29, 1968, "General—Ell–Ellery" Folder, Box 87, Truman Library, Independence, Mo.; [?] to Director, December 5, 1968, FBI File 62-81810; Allen Ellender "Press Releases" Folder, Box 1498, AEP. See Kenneth O'Reilly, "The FBI and the Politics of the Riots, 1964–1968," *Journal of American History,* LXXV (June, 1988), 91–114, and Athan G. Theoharis and John Stuart Cox, *The Boss: J. Edgar Hoover and the Great American Inquisition* (Philadelphia, 1988), for examples of how the crafty Hoover survived the wrath of several U.S. presidents.

34. Charles Caillouette, interview, November 23, 1979.

18

LEADER OF THE SENATE
(1969–71)

$\mathcal{B}$efore he left office Lyndon Johnson thanked Ellender. "I recall the many good days we have shared, working together on the Nation's business. The Senate will always remain one of the cornerstones of my life. Thank you for your devotion to an institution we both cherish and for helping to sustain me over these years." Departing secretary of agriculture Orville Freeman also wrote Ellender, calling him "a great agricultural statesman." Terming Freeman one of the greatest secretaries who ever served, Ellender replied, "It is you and not I to whom the phrase 'great agricultural statesman' should apply."[1]

The retirement of Carl Hayden of Arizona at the end of the Ninetieth Congress left only Richard Russell of Georgia with more years of service than the Louisianian when the Ninety-first Congress convened in January, 1969. However, Russell died from emphysema on Thursday, January 21, 1971. "I share this loss," Ellender said, "with a deep sense of personal sorrow for my longtime friend." President Nixon and Vice-president Agnew, along with Ellender and fifty-four other senators, attended Russell's funeral in Winder, Georgia.[2]

---

1. Lyndon Johnson to Allen Ellender, January 17, 1969, in Allen Ellender Name File, Box 60, White House Central Files, Lyndon Baines Johnson Library, Austin, Tex., hereinafter cited as LBJ; Orville Freeman to Allen Ellender, January 9, 1969, and Ellender to Freeman, January 13, 1969, both in "General, Department Agriculture" Folder, Box 464, Allen J. Ellender Papers, Nicholls State University Library, Thibodaux, La., hereinafter cited as AEP.

2. Gilbert C. Fite, *Richard B. Russell, Jr., Senator from Georgia* (Chapel Hill, 1991), 491; Allen Ellender "Press Releases" Folder, Box 1498, AEP.

Ellender now advanced to the zenith of his influence in the U.S. Senate: president pro tempore. He presided over the Senate in the absence of the vice-president and was third in line of succession to the presidency. Ellender also became chairman of the powerful Appropriations Committee, which oversaw all spending bills considered in the upper house. He moved into Russell's suite of offices in the new Senate office building and soon adjusted to having a press secretary and a chauffeur to drive him around in a black Lincoln Continental reserved for the president pro tem. He had more spacious accommodations for his Acadian dinners. People recognized him in the Senate restaurant; staffers at the USDA stood up when he walked into their offices. Florence LeCompte and her sister Anna came to visit him when he became president pro tem. They stayed several days at his apartment, but Ellender usually did not return from his office until late at night. One night he returned early, and they listened to classical music from his large collection.[3]

In 1971 Ellender's alma mater, Tulane University, honored its most influential alumni serving in public office—Ellender and New Orleans congressmen F. Edward Hebert and Hale Boggs. Ellender was president pro tem of the Senate, Boggs was majority leader in the House, and Hebert was chairman of the House Armed Service Committee. Nixon, no doubt eager to court favor from the influential Louisianians, dropped in on the social gathering.[4]

Ellender's prestige did not change his philosophy or alter his work habits, but he may have taken himself a bit more seriously than he had in the past. His overseas inspection tours took on more importance; his written reports on them now became Senate documents.[5] Ellender exercised considerable control over budgetary matters. His approach to agricultural policy, the Rural Electrification Administration, and the war in Vietnam reveals how he functioned in the national arena.

Even though Nixon took office talking of peace, he requested funds for two projects Ellender opposed: an antiballistic missile system (ABM) and

---

3. *Newsweek,* February 8, 1971, p. 21; Florence LeCompte, interviews, November 1, 1979, June 11, 1980; Irving Legendre, Jr., interview, June 18, 1980.

4. F. Edward Hebert, *Last of the Titans: The Life and Times of Congressman F. Edward Hebert of Louisiana* (Lafayette, La., 1976), 36; New Orleans *Times-Picayune,* May 21, 1971, in "1969" Scrapbook, AEP.

5. "Allen Ellender, Oral History No. 149," April 30, 1971, by Hugh Cates, in the Richard B. Russell Collection, Richard B. Russell Memorial Library, University of Georgia, Athens, 11.

renewal of the NATO alliance. Not surprisingly, Ellender asked to reduce troop strength in Europe and criticized the antiballistic missile program. On August 6, 1969, the Senate voted fifty to fifty on an antiballistic missile bill. Vice-president Spiro Agnew broke the tie in favor of the ABM appropriation.[6]

In September, *New Republic* published a feature story on Ellender called "The Travels of Allen Ellender," a critical but fair report of his simple ways and energetic pursuit of a more viable but less expensive foreign policy. The article focused on his concerns about spending programs feeding on themselves. In many instances politicians abroad used "communism to pull our leg," Ellender said. When U.S. embassy personnel in the Soviet Union accused him of being naïve about dealing with the Soviets, Ellender replied, "The trouble with you goddam diplomats is you have a chip on your shoulder."[7]

In 1969 Ellender completed his two-reel, sixty-two-minute audio-color film on the USSR called *Faces of Russia,* which was based on his fifty-three-day tour of the country in the fall and winter of 1968. Once again, Dr. Alexander Sas-Joworsky, the Abbeville veterinarian, accused him of being soft on communism. "As you have done with great regularity over the past ten or twelve years," Ellender wrote his critic, "you again gave a completely erroneous interpretation to remarks I made regarding relations between the U.S. and the U.S.S.R."[8]

Meanwhile, the unpopular war in Vietnam had caused significant problems in America. Lyndon Johnson's career had been cut short by it; Hubert Humphrey had lost the presidency to Richard Nixon largely because of it. Ellender had voted to appropriate funds to escalate the struggle. Now, as chairman of the Appropriations Committee, he was being courted by Nixon, just as Johnson had sought his support.

Nixon planned secret bombings of Cambodia in 1969, hoping to find and destroy the Central Office for South Vietnam (COSVN), the joint head-

6. New Orleans *Times-Picayune,* February 3, March 24, 1969, Miami *News,* April 14, 1969, all in "1969" Scrapbook, AEP.

7. Stephen S. Rosenfeld, "The Travels of Allen Ellender," *New Republic,* September 27, 1969, pp. 25–30, in "1969" Scrapbook, AEP.

8. Allen Ellender to Alexander Sas-Jaworsky, February 25, 1969, in "Foreign Relations—Vietnam Legislation" Folder, Box 937, and "Press Releases" Folder, *passim,* Box 1498, both in AEP.

quarters of the Viet Cong and the North Vietnamese in South Vietnam. Raids in April and May failed to find COSVN; by May, 1970, Congress had learned about the secret bombing of Cambodia. Nixon should have consulted Congress, Ellender felt. U.S. attacks on Cambodia, Ellender realized, had weakened chances of success for the Vietnamization program—the plan to turn the war over to the Vietnamese people. Ellender knew political pressure on the president would mount. "If they don't find that headquarters pretty soon, there's going to be a hell of a stink here in Congress," Ellender said, "and hell to pay for Nixon politically."[9]

Ellender considered Nixon's talk of gradually withdrawing U.S. troops a positive sign, but "I am opposed to our ending the war in a way that may make it appear that we have been defeated," he added. "I do not believe we can just withdraw." He noted, "The search for peace is spreading in this country"; anti-war advocates "are gaining in strength."[10]

The slain villagers at My Lai "got just what they deserved," Ellender concluded in January, 1970, after he heard reports about South Vietnamese citizens aiding the Viet Cong. However, most Americans, he knew, were growing weary of the war. On April 10, 1970, the Senate Foreign Relations Committee voted unanimously to rescind the 1964 Tonkin Gulf Resolution, which both Johnson and Nixon had used to justify expansion of military activities in the Far East. Nixon said he did not need the Tonkin Gulf Resolution to pursue American interests there.[11]

On May 11, the Foreign Relations Committee voted nine to one for the Cooper-Church amendment to an appropriations bill. Named after Republican senator John Sherman Cooper of Kentucky and Democratic senator Frank Church of Idaho, the measure would have prohibited use of military funds for action in Cambodia and Laos and removed all U.S. troops from Vietnam by June 30, 1971. Nixon claimed Cooper-Church and another end-the-war measure, McGovern-Hatfield, were unconstitutional, but clearly the

9.   Stephen E. Ambrose, *Nixon* (3 vols.; New York, 1989), II, 256–57, 272, 347; "Weekly Report from Congress," April 18, 1970, Box 1508, AEP; Washington *Post*, May 5, 1970, in "1970" Scrapbook, AEP.

10.   "Weekly Report from Congress," June 14, July 19, August 9, 1969, all in Box 1495, AEP; Allen Ellender to Katherine Haspel, November 17, 1969, Ellender to Gary Caldwell, November 18, 1969, Ellender to J. E. Van Valendurg, November 18, 1969, Ellender to many constituents, November, 1969, and Ellender to D. F. Overdyke, Jr., December 12, 1969, all in "Foreign Relations—Vietnam Legislation" Folder, Box 937, AEP.

11.   United Press International wire copy, January 16, 1970, in "1970" Scrapbook, AEP; Ambrose, *Nixon*, II, 338–39.

Senate was standing up to the president. Ellender voted against Cooper-Church. Even though he had become a critic of the war, Ellender also voted in September, 1970, against the McGovern-Hatfield resolution to remove all troops from Vietnam by December 31, 1971. Thirty-nine senators voted for the measure. Noting a significant shift in public opinion, Ellender had summarized the public view in 1966 as "win or get out." Now the prevailing notion was "the price is too high to stay any longer." Resolutions mandating a troop withdrawal by a specific deadline, Ellender felt, tied the hands of the commander-in-chief. He had supported Truman in 1951 when he removed Douglas MacArthur from command in Korea. Once again he was supporting the president.[12]

In December, 1970, the Appropriations Committee approved a $66.4 billion defense bill with the addendum "None of the funds appropriated by this act shall be used to finance the introduction of American ground combat troops into Laos, Thailand, or Cambodia." The next day Ellender requested a reduction of U.S. NATO forces in Europe.[13]

Ellender's constituents responded to the conviction of Lt. William Calley for his role in the My Lai massacre. "My office has been flooded with letters and telegrams supporting the lieutenant," he wrote. He theorized that President Nixon might intervene in Calley's behalf. Ellender said he was shocked to learn in June of extensive drug use by American troops in Vietnam. He criticized the New York *Times* and the Washington *Post* for publishing the Pentagon Papers, which exposed a number of administration untruths about U.S. involvement in southeast Asia. Yet Ellender refused to vote for Majority Leader Mike Mansfield's amendment to a Selective Service bill to pull U.S. troops from Vietnam in nine months. Fifty-seven senators voted for the measure.[14]

Like Johnson, Nixon courted Ellender and other southern leaders who chaired important congressional committees. Nixon needed funds to pursue the war in Vietnam; Ellender wanted to reduce the budget but generate

12. Ambrose, *Nixon*, II, 358, 387; New Orleans *Times-Picayune*, May 24, 1970, in "1970" Scrapbook, AEP; *New Republic*, October 24, 1970, pp. 18, 20; *Congressional Quarterly Weekly Report*, September 19, 1969, p. 1729; Fite, *Richard Russell*, 486.

13. United Press International wire copy, December 3, 4, 1970, both in "1970" Scrapbook, AEP.

14. "Weekly Report from Congress," April 10, 1971, Box 1509, June 26, 1971, Box 1504, both in AEP.

funds for projects in Louisiana. Both men would face reelection campaigns in 1972. They agreed on a need for law and order and for conservative justices on the Supreme Court. Both disliked demonstrations and antiwar protests and wanted to end the war with dignity.

Ellender liked Nixon's so-called southern strategy, a plan to slow the course of racial integration. He also approved Nixon's appointees to the Supreme Court. He was pleased when Warren Burger became chief justice, but termed Senate rejection of southerner Clement Haynsworth a "miscarriage of justice." When the Senate rejected another southerner, G. Harrold Carswell, Ellender was disappointed. Later he approved the nominations to the high court of both William Rehnquist and Lewis Powell.[15]

Protests by college students, Ellender thought, did not represent a groundswell of resistance against the war. Convinced the disturbances were caused by a small group of students who traveled from one campus to another, Ellender noted proudly that Louisiana campuses were quiet in May, 1970, when students across the country protested Nixon's invasion of Cambodia. Alarmed by the senseless arson and bombings in Washington, D.C., and elsewhere, Ellender refused to consider the Black Panthers and other black militants sincere protesters.[16]

Ellender's support for Nixon undoubtedly helped to get economic grants for Louisiana; others came simply because of his position on the Appropriations Committee. He obtained $5.4 million for housing construction at Fort Polk and a $10 million NASA grant for research in Slidell. He visited Nixon in June, 1969, to discuss foreign aid, cooked for the president in July, 1970, and rode with him to New Orleans on Air Force One in August while Congress was debating the farm bill. Aboard the presidential plane Nixon presented Ellender a plaque proclaiming him "Chef Supreme" for his culinary talents.[17]

After approving a military appropriations budget of $66.5 billion and pork barrel projects for Louisiana in 1971, Ellender had to stretch the truth a bit to claim he favored reducing federal spending. Starting in 1971, his

15. "Weekly Report from Congress," March 28, 1970, Box 1507, June 14, November 29, 1969, Box 1495, April 11, 1970, Box 1508, October 30, 1971, Box 1505, all in AEP.

16. "Weekly Report from Congress," March 15, 1969, Box 1495, May 9, 1970, Box 1508, May 1, 15, 1971, Box 1504, all in AEP.

17. New Orleans *States-Item*, August 14, 1970, in "1970" Scrapbook, AEP; "Weekly Report from Congress," January 18, June 7, 1969, Box 1495, June 27, July 18, August 22, 1970, Box 1508, all in AEP.

weekly reports mailed to Louisiana constituents included a box summarizing grants to the state.[18]

Ellender's leadership was more symbolic than real. Rather than challenge Nixon on Vietnam or domestic spending, he went along with administration policy. Anticipating his reelection campaign in 1972, he acquired monies for Louisiana projects and blamed troublemakers for antiwar protests. Now in a position to implement budget reductions he had long advocated, he backed away.

When his eighty-first birthday rolled around, Ellender planned to entertain Mrs. Nixon and Mrs. Agnew by cooking and serving an elaborate meal. Staffers Dan Borné and Carroll Trosclair helped him prepare pralines the night before the September 24 feast. When Ellender discovered that Louisiana Acadian fiddler Doug Kershaw was performing at the Cellar Door, a popular Washington night spot, he invited him to his party. Kershaw put on his usual energetic show for Ellender and his guests. Later that night Ellender took his entire office staff to the Cellar Door for more entertainment by Kershaw.[19]

Agricultural reformers renewed their efforts to impose a limit on farm payments in 1969 armed with new ammunition. Many counties where farmers received big payments had no food stamp program at all. Willing to expand the food stamp program, Ellender steadfastly resisted efforts to limit farm payments. Nixon favored providing free food stamps to the needy, but Ellender disagreed, partly because doing so would have been costly. If the stamps were free, Ellender said, the poor would use their money to buy street drugs, cars, and other nonessentials. Ellender's food stamp bill, S. 2547, lowered the cost of stamps but did not provide free stamps.[20]

For a limit on farm payments to work, the cotton snapback provision would have to be repealed, for it automatically excluded cotton from any limit. But southerners, who dominated agricultural committees, held food

18. "Weekly Report from Congress," October 10, 1970, Box 1508, April 17, 1971, Box 1507, and Box 1504, *passim*, all in AEP.

19. Dan Borné, interview, April 30, 1992.

20. Burt Shorr, *Wall Street Journal*, March 3, 1969; *Congressional Record*, 91st Cong., 1st Sess., Vol. 115, Pt. 12, June 10, 1969, pp. 15321–22, Pt. 8, April 30, 1969, pp. 10867–71, Pt. 12, June 16, 1969 pp. 15865–67; New York *Times*, March 11, 1969; "Food Stamp, Department of Agriculture" Folder, *passim*, Box 466, AEP; miscellaneous newspaper clippings, March–April, 1969, in "1969" Scrapbook, AEP.

stamp legislation hostage and blocked imposition of a limit on payments in 1969.[21]

In 1970 the agricultural establishment was unable to hold off the tide of reform, and Congress finally passed a law with a limit on benefit payments. Knowing Congress would impose a limit, farm leaders had concentrated on raising it to $55,000. "My gracious, if a farmer had six crops, he would get six times $55,000," Congressman Ray Madden of Indiana said in disbelief. But Congress permitted farmers to receive a maximum total of $165,000. Ellender grudgingly agreed the $55,000 was workable. President Nixon signed the farm bill on November 30, 1970.[22]

During the debate on the limit, Ellender became angry when midwesterners cosponsored a bill limiting benefit payments while they asked for high price supports on feed grains and no mandatory restrictions like those imposed on cotton and other commodities. "Almost a third of the amount of money that is paid out in subsidies is paid to six states in the Midwest which plant corn and other feed grains," Ellender said. In other words, the Midwest received its government bounty in the form of price supports rather than in direct payments from the USDA. Limiting big payments would not solve that problem, Ellender knew.[23]

Reformers realized early in 1971 how widespread circumvention of the payment limit was. Big growers planted enough cotton to get their $55,000 payment and rented or leased out additional acreage at six or seven cents per pound of cotton produced, the *Wall Street Journal* explained in January. This practice was likely to eliminate the anticipated $58 million to $171 million in savings to taxpayers.[24]

Meanwhile, Ellender spent many hours on other aspects of agricultural

21. *Congressional Record,* 91st Cong., 1st Sess., Vol. 115, Pt. 8, April 30, 1969, pp. 10867–71, Pt. 12, June 17, 1969, p. 16269; Burt Schorr, *Wall Street Journal,* October 13, 1969, p. 26; Ellender to L. M. Coco, July 10, 1969, in "General, Department of Agriculture" Folder, Box 464, AEP.

22. William Robbins, New York *Times,* April 20, 1970; *New Republic,* June 27, 1970, p. 11; *Congressional Record,* 91st Cong., 2d Sess., Vol. 116, Pt. 20, August 4, 1970, p. 27130, August 6, 1970, p. 27644; Warren Weaver, Jr., New York *Times,* September 15, 16, December 1, 1970; New Orleans *Times-Picayune,* October 7, 1970, in "1970" Scrapbook, AEP; "Weekly Report from Congress," October 10, 1970, Box 1508, AEP.

23. *Congressional Record,* 91st Cong., 2d Sess., Vol. 116, Pt. 17, July 8, 1970, pp. 23264, 23279–80; *Wall Street Journal,* July 9, 1970; "Weekly Report from Congress," July 11, 25, 1970, Box 1508, AEP.

24. *Wall Street Journal,* January 13, 18, July 20, 1971; Burt Shorr, *Wall Street Journal,* March 9, 1971.

policy. He heard again from dissident rice farmers in Louisiana and Arkansas, who suspected foul play when Korea received a special subsidy in 1971 under Public Law 480, the program to subsidize sales of surplus commodities to friendly nations overseas. "I feel that there is some collusion going on in connection with the sale," one wrote. Ellender asked Secretary of Agriculture Clifford Hardin for details about the Korean deal so he could explain matters to his constituents.[25]

Ellender thanked the Koreans for purchasing Louisiana rice. In identical letters to Korean president Chung Hee Park and Korean CIA director Hu Rak Lee, Ellender praised Tongsun Park, who negotiated the deal. "I am told he is a fine representative of Korea," Ellender wrote. "Louisiana is especially appreciative of his guidance and effort in servicing the problems of the transactions involving rice sales." Congressmen Edwin Edwards of Crowley and Otto Passman of Monroe would go to Korea later in the year, Ellender said.[26] When he became governor, Edwards had to explain mysterious cash gifts from Park to his wife, Elaine Edwards.

In 1969 a long-standing dispute between major utility companies and Louisiana electric cooperatives erupted into an open fight between Charles Roemer II, the chairman of the Board of Louisiana Electric Cooperatives (LEC), and Ellender. For years Ellender had supported the Rural Electrification Administration, a part of the Department of Agriculture. Roemer claimed Ellender now represented the utility giants. The controversy centered on the generating and transmitting (G&T) capabilities of the LECs.

Ellender had begun to question the need for lending money to cooperatives to compete against investor-owned utility companies. He feared co-ops were building oversize plants with low-interest REA loans. Then, the government had to sell surplus power to consumers in competition with private companies. The giant utilities themselves enjoyed low-interest REA loans, tax breaks, and a guaranteed profit from operations, REA director Clyde Ellis told Ellender. Ellender wanted proof co-ops could produce and distribute electricity at a lower cost than private sources.[27]

25. Walter Garic to Allen Ellender, March 16, 1971, H. G. Chalkley, Jr., to Ellender, March 10, 1971, and Ellender to Clifford Hardin, March 10, 1971, all in "Rice, Department Agriculture" Folder, Box 306, AEP.

26. Both letters dated November 23, 1971, in "Rice, Department Agriculture" Folder, Box 306, AEP.

27. Clyde T. Ellis to Allen Ellender, April 19, 1963, Ellender to Karl Geist, May 20, 1963, and Ellender to R. B. Fritz, September 9, 1963, all in "Department of Agriculture, Rural Electrification Administration, 1963" Folder, Box 345, AEP; Allen Ellender to deLesseps Morrison,

In January, 1969, Roemer criticized Ellender sharply, in *Rural Louisiana,* the LEC journal, for opposing G&T loans to the LECs. Ellender, responding in the March issue, justified his opposition, saying one-third of the energy would go to a nonfarm operation, a paper mill near Baton Rouge. Since 1964, when Congress appropriated $56 million in G&T loans, the LECs had refused Ellender's request to let him or Senate officials inspect their contracts. Only four of the twelve co-ops produced their own power; these had tie-ins with two cities and a private industry. Roemer, testifying before the Subcommittee on Agricultural Appropriations of the Senate Appropriations Committee, said LECs were forced into generating and transmitting because the big companies discriminated against them with high costs. The utility giants believed co-ops should not be in the power business "except to develop areas for company takeover when they become profitable," Roemer said.[28]

In 1970 Ellender once again was drawn into the perennial controversy between the REA and private energy companies. Roemer said an LEC manager had provided Ellender with secret information on G&T costs. Ellender suspected Roemer had leaked information about the controversy to syndicated columnist Jack Anderson.[29]

Ellender maintained close ties to his family, but the Senate took most of his time and energy. After Walterine, Claude, and Willard died, he adopted their families as part of his extended family. This was not because Allen Jr., his only child, had failed to provide him with grandchildren; Allen Jr. had thirteen children. The clan provided Ellender many youthful contacts. In time the children of the nieces and nephews—the grandnieces and grand-nephews—also became part of his extended family. When Ellender visited a newborn infant for the first time, he would briefly place its little feet in his mouth as he commented on how healthy and fine it was.

Ellender purchased nice gifts abroad for family members. He bought china for Claude's widow, Thelma, and oil paintings from Germany for others. Frequently he bought unusual semiprecious stones abroad and had them

---

May 20, 1964, deLesseps S. Morrison Papers, Louisiana and Lower Mississippi Valley Collections, Louisiana State University, Baton Rouge, La.

28. *Rural Louisiana,* XVIV (January, 1969), 2, (March, 1969), 6, both in "1969" Scrapbook, AEP; Allen Ellender to Charles Roemer II, January 31, 1969, in "Department of Agriculture—REA Co-Op" Folder, Box 544, AEP; mimeographed statement, April 17, 1969, in "REA, Department Agriculture" Folder, Box 466, AEP.

29. Allen Ellender to Al. J. Poiencot, January 20, 1970, in "Department of Agriculture—REA Co-Op" Folder, Box 544, AEP.

fashioned into gift rings. One old associate, who had seen critical articles about Ellender's junkets, did not consider him generous or magnanimous. He had read about Ellender keeping Army post exchanges open late at night so he could shop for unusual items, which he shipped home in diplomatic pouches, free from taxes and import duties.[30]

The nieces and nephews liked visiting with Uncle Allen, who greeted them enthusiastically "How are you? How are you? How are you?" in staccato fashion. He enjoyed his role as patriarch of the family and rarely overlooked their birthdays. Usually he gave a gift of twenty-five dollars; sometimes he found an unusual woodcarving or toy from some exotic foreign land. On observing a child opening a present, he pointed out unique features about the gift or commented, "Finest there is." When he encountered a child to whom he had recently sent a cash gift, he always asked whether the youngster had saved the money or used it wisely.

At a Christmas gathering Ellender once innocently turned Walterine's dinner plate down at her customary spot, which upset his late sister's husband, Charles Caillouette. Thinking Allen had made a callous and insulting gesture to his deceased wife, Charles never returned to the Ellender family gatherings. Later he accused Allen of trying to change Walterine's will when he suggested that Charles sell 278 acres he inherited from her to the children of Wallace Jr. and Willard.[31]

Ellender's fishing technique had not changed over the years. He still buried the hook deeply in the bait, and his cast was in the fifty-foot range rather than the hundred-foot category of the younger fishermen. He questioned why Irving Legendre, Jr., caught twelve fish to his two, but he did not change his technique even after frequent explanations about covering the barb of the hook. "I've been fishing since before you were born," he would say. When a fish rejected his sheathed hook, he always proclaimed in a surprised manner, "Doggone, I missed him."

At the Legendre camp, where the pace was slow, Ellender waved to passing boats, held court for admiring youngsters, and spoke French to the locals familiar with the Acadian patois. Although he was eighty-one, he still walked around the camp without a shirt. Sometimes he cooked a redfish courtboullion, a popular spicy south Louisiana dish with a tomato sauce. In the afternoon he usually took a one-hour nap, but he did not go to bed

30. Viola Lynch Ellender, interview, July 14, 1980; Thelma Ellender, interview, June 30, 1980; Irving Legendre, Jr., interview, July 10, 1980; M. L. Funderburk, interview, July 11, 1980.
31. Charles Caillouette, interview, November 23, 1979.

until at least ten at night. At four-thirty or five the next morning he was up and ready for another day's fishing after he had a cup of Ovaltine with honey for breakfast.[32]

Ellender kept a close watch on political developments back home. Louisiana would elect a governor in 1971, one year before he faced reelection. As usual he consulted political cronies about rumors of candidates, political alliances, and his own chances for winning. Newspapers announced that John McKeithen would run against him in 1972.[33] Edwin Edwards, the Cajun congressman from Crowley in the rice-growing section of southwest Louisiana, entered the governor's race against J. Bennett Johnston, a north Louisiana politician whose wife was from south Louisiana. Various other Longites and anti-Longites scrambled and jockeyed for position in a race Ellender observed with particular interest. Edwards defeated Johnston in a hard-fought contest. Then Johnston, who had name recognition after waging a vigorous campaign, decided to run against Ellender. Young and energetic, he could be a serious threat to the senior senator.

When Congress recessed for the Christmas holidays in 1971, Ellender had an opportunity to survey the political climate in Louisiana at close range. Energetic and alert as ever, he viewed J. Bennett Johnston as a real threat. No rival had out-hustled the veteran Cajun senator in the past, and Ellender was determined it would not happen in 1972.

32. Irving Legendre, Jr., interview, July 10, 1980; Mrs. Irving Legendre, interview, June 4, 1980.

33. Opelousas (La.) *Daily World,* February 10, 1970, Edgar Poe, New Orleans *Times-Picayune,* February 22, 1970, both in "1970" Scrapbook, AEP.

19

The Final Campaign
(1972)

$\mathcal{T}$he year 1972 promised to be anything but routine, for it featured a presidential election and an Ellender reelection campaign. Legislative agendas differed during election years; tax talk gave way to patriotic hyperbole. The war in Vietnam was going badly, agricultural reform was in the air, and the youth protest movement sweeping the country had produced a strange counterculture. Who could say what political strategy would work under such circumstances?

As president pro tem, Ellender had a chauffeur and a press secretary. He had hired press secretary Carroll Trosclair, a Cajun, who sent out news releases in which Ellender readily discussed the merits of ambitious Louisiana projects, implying that funds to implement them would be found.

Ellender's seventh campaign for the U.S. Senate promised to be his most difficult and expensive ever. After Edwin Edwards won the gubernatorial election. Johnston, who lost by only five thousand votes, decided to run against Ellender. Johnston had name recognition and momentum; he hoped conditions were right for an upset of the veteran senator, even if he was president pro tempore and chairman of the Senate Appropriations Committee.

Trying to make age a campaign issue, Johnston said Louisiana needed a young, energetic senator. Ellender replied, "I will be eighty-two in September, but I am in excellent health. I work hard every day. I exercise regularly. I watch my diet. I quit smoking and drinking many years ago." At men-only political gatherings he sometimes jokingly bragged that he was as good as any man there—"from the waist up."[1]

---

1. Campaign speeches, Box 1839, Allen J. Ellender Papers, Nicholls State University Library, Thibodaux, La., hereinafter cited as AEP; Dan Borné, interview, April 30, 1992.

Because his opponent was less than half his age, Ellender wanted to appear energetic and active. In February, he discussed a trip to the South Pole he had taken in December at the request of the National Science Foundation. "This was the most spectacular trip I have ever made," he said, proud of being the oldest person ever to visit the South Pole. Not surprisingly, he had brought his movie camera along and would soon have another film for public viewing.

Ellender spoke cautiously about the war in Vietnam. In January he seemed to approve Nixon's efforts to achieve peace through secret negotiations with the North Vietnamese. Convinced the president had acted in good faith, Ellender wondered how secret negotiations affected obligations of Congress and the people. In April he worried about the increased tempo of the bombing of North Vietnam but now said he favored withdrawing U.S. forces from the field.[2]

According to a poll Johnston released in March, many voters considered Ellender's age a disadvantage. Meanwhile, Ellender tried to show how active he was. Claiming Johnston had spent nearly $1 million to build a favorable image, Ellender said people would reelect the senior senator when they considered how much more he could do for them than a freshman senator. For the first time in an election campaign, Ellender faced a viable young candidate who had name recognition, a well-financed organization, and an opportunity to scrutinize Ellender's thirty-five years in the Senate. Johnston's appeal, however, was similar to Ellender's, and he was unlikely to criticize the senator's record. Ellender's office published "Profile of Allen J. Ellender," a fifteen-page booklet with photographs of him with President Nixon and important congressional leaders. It listed major legislation he had sponsored over the years and emphasized thirty projects funded for Louisiana.[3]

Ellender's platform included about twenty planks; it outlined plans he hoped to implement and American problems he hoped to rectify. He endorsed a proposed north-south highway traversing the state. He favored more aid to public education, especially vocational-technical programs. He wanted to expand the Red River waterway and a hurricane-protection system

2. Press Releases, January 10, 24, 26, February 4, 15, 17, 1972, Box 1496, AEP; "Weekly Report from Congress," February 4, 1972, and statement, April 17, 1972, both in "Speeches," AEP.

3. Statement, March 14, 1972, Press Release, March 20, 1972, both in "Press Releases" Folder, Box 1496, AEP; "Profile of Allen J. Ellender," April 5, 1972, and News Release, April 28, 1972, both in "Speeches," AEP.

for coastal Louisiana. He promised to create jobs, maintain Louisiana's military bases, and develop Louisiana's natural resources more fully. Ellender promised to fight inflation, crime, and narcotics, to cut foreign aid spending, to stop forced busing, to prevent waste and fraud in food stamp programs, and to withdraw from Vietnam in an orderly manner.[4]

"Race is not an issue in this campaign," Ellender announced. "I seek everyone's vote. I pledge to work for all our people." Promising not to vote against presidential nominees on the basis of race, Ellender said, "I intend to cast my vote on all nominations on the basis of merit—not on race."[5]

Although Ellender spent much of his political career criticizing wasteful government spending, he acquiesced to costly projects for Louisiana. What he saw as waste in other sections of the country he apparently could not pass up for Louisiana, especially during an election year. Reluctant to reduce farm spending while the rest of the country received funds for military, highway, health care, and other ventures, Ellender felt farmers should share in the national affluence. By the time he headed the Appropriations Committee, he had received a tremendous number of grants from the Johnson and the Nixon administrations in exchange for support of their Vietnam policies. He chose to receive these costly benefits to enhance his reelection chances rather than to implement genuine reductions he had called for over the years. When he was in a position to do something about spending, he squandered opportunities to cut expenditures.

Television had changed the nature of politicking, Ellender and his advisers realized, even in the bayou country of south Louisiana. The cost of campaigning had risen steadily over the years. Media experts, who created an image that could be marketed, did not come cheaply. They conducted polls and studies, devised overall strategies, and used television and radio to convey the message to the public. The campaign had to follow the advice of the experts. The "content of the entire media presentation must be coordinated and must carry out a central theme," Ellender told election supervisor Gilbert Dozier in June, 1972.[6]

Ellender engaged Innovative Data Systems (IDS) to plan overall cam-

4. Thibodaux (La.) *Comet,* July 27, 1972.
5. Allen Ellender speeches, Box 1839, Statement, June 21, 1972, Box 1840, and Press Release, February 17, 1972, Box 1496, all in AEP; miscellaneous newspaper clippings, 1972, in Elward Wright Papers, in the possession of Thomas Wright, Houma, La., hereinafter cited as EWP.
6. Allen Ellender to Gilbert Dozier, June 13, 1972, Box 1835, AEP.

paign strategy from headquarters at Scopena Plantation in Caddo Parish near Bossier City. Managing partner Charles Roemer III, known as Buddy, directed IDS. Buddy was the son of Charles II, the spokesman for the Louisiana Electric Cooperatives, with whom Ellender had clashed on a number of occasions. Roemer's approach to campaigning was untraditional, "but it works," he told Ellender assistant Guirard in April. Roemer promised to provide advice and counsel (based on polls), computerized historic and demographic data, mailing lists and recommendations for mailings, and a written analysis of campaign progress.[7]

The Ellender campaign also engaged the services of Bauerlein, which had done advertising work for Ellender during the 1966 race. Bauerlein coordinated schedules with television stations across Louisiana to broadcast Ellender's thirty- and sixty-second television campaign spots and one five-minute program. Television stations demand payment when they receive a schedule, the media manager for Bauerlein informed Frank Wurzlow, Jr. "We will need a check for $100,000 to cover the costs of these television schedules," she wrote. Bauerlein also prepared a 178-page analysis of the race based on a statewide poll. The race would be close, and Ellender's age was considered a disadvantage by many voters, the Bauerlein study indicated.[8]

Johnston said Louisiana was not getting its share of tidelands oil money and the state did not have a north-south expressway. Barge traffic on the Red River could not flow freely because the main channel of the stream needed dredging. On many issues, he simply promised to do a better job than Ellender had been doing. The Ellender campaign engaged still another firm, Guggenheim Productions of Washington, D.C., to prepare Ellender's television advertisements. By July, Wurzlow had paid Guggenheim sixty-five thousand dollars and owed the firm twenty thousand more.[9]

The senator himself could not resist campaigning in the old way. Visiting country stores (he always bought a tube of toothpaste or some small item) and courthouses, he talked to small groups, offering to help with their problems. If registrars, clerks of court, assessors, or sheriffs were not in when he came by, he slipped handwritten notes on yellow legal sheets under their doors.[10]

7. Charles Roemer III to James Guirard, Jr., April 10, 1972, EWP.

8. Norma Jones to Frank Wurzlow, Jr., July 19, 1972, and "The Climate of Opinion in Ellender-Johnston Race for United States Senator," n.d., both in EWP.

9. Unidentified newspaper clipping, July 28, 1972, in Press Files, Russell B. Long Papers, Louisiana and Lower Mississippi Valley Collections, Louisiana State University, Baton Rouge, La.; Frank Wurzlow, Jr., to Guggenheim Productions, July 25, 1972, EWP.

10. Dan Borné, interview, April 30, 1992.

The Ellender campaign fund had grown over the years. Money left over from one campaign was shifted to another account until a new campaign opened. The Ellender campaign account at the Bank of Terrebonne had a zero balance on January 3, 1967, at the end of the 1966 Senate race. On May 24, 1972, the Ellender Campaign Committee deposited $57,390.95 in the campaign account at the Bank of Terrebonne and used the same checkbook it had used in the 1966 campaign. By July 21, 1972, the Ellender campaign had collected $318,620.95 and had spent $172,620.79, mostly for television spots, posters, computer needs, and polling. Unpaid bills totaled $286,864.84. Wright recorded contributions in a notebook: $5,000 from a friend named Hart in March, and more than $13,000 in April from other friends of Allen Ellender. Old friends from the past contributed to the campaign chest. Houma banker M. L. Funderburk did not think Ellender needed campaign funds, but he contributed $1,000 anyway. The campaign had a deficit of about $140,000.[11]

Ellender answered Johnston's charges by showing what age and seniority could bring: chairmanships. "Anyone who intends to serve you in Congress should acknowledge the real power of seniority and chairmanships." The chairman of the Senate Appropriations Committee handled $200 billion per year, he reminded voters. "It took me 16 years to get on the Committee. It took 34 years to become chairman." Ellender explained, "I became chairman of Appropriations only 18 months ago. This is no time to give it up."[12]

Louisiana received an impressive number of grants in the summer of 1972. Press releases and announcements of grants filled a two-inch-thick folder for May. In June the folder was even thicker; in July the number declined a bit, but every corner of the state seemed to qualify for some $20,000 grant. Several cities received grants in excess of $500,000.[13]

During the campaign, Nixon excluded Ellender from a briefing of senators before visiting the Soviet Union in May, 1972. "I would prefer to work something out so that we didn't have to include Ellender," Nixon said. "But, of course, Ellender will cause us considerable problems and will bore the other senators even more than he will us in the course of the meeting," Nixon wrote.[14] Unwilling to share the limelight, Nixon refused to acknowl-

11. Checkbook, and spreadsheet listing contributors, July 21, 1972, both in EWP; M. L. Funderburk, interview, July 11, 1980.

12. Ellender speeches, Box 1839, AEP.

13. "Joint Announcements" Folder, *passim*, Box 1499, AEP.

14. Bruce Oudes, ed., *From the President: Richard Nixon's Secret Files* (New York, 1989), 440–41.

edge Ellender's success in opening dialogue and developing rapport with Soviet leaders, a factor that made Nixon's USSR trip possible.

If Ellender was aware of the Watergate break-in of June 17, 1972, he did not comment publicly when the *Times-Picayune* began reporting it on June 19. He was probably more interested in a June 20 news item outlining political endorsements. Governor Edwin Edwards' top adviser, Charles Roemer II, endorsed Ellender; the governor's legal counsel, Sheldon Beychock, endorsed Johnston; Edwards endorsed no one. During the campaign, Ellender aide Carlisle Morrison asked former Republican presidential candidate Barry Goldwater of Arizona to endorse Ellender and sign a telegram saying he was a good man who would safeguard taxpayer dollars. Morrison hoped to circulate the telegram among Louisiana Republicans as campaign literature. However, Goldwater declined to endorse Ellender or sign the telegram.[15]

All the while Ellender was maintaining an exhausting traveling and speaking schedule. July 8 to July 16 typified his frantic pace. On Saturday, the eighth, he left Houma at 7:30 A.M. for a flight to Columbia in north Louisiana. In the afternoon he dedicated a bridge over Interstate Highway 20 near Monroe and attended a banquet that night before flying back to Houma.

Sunday's schedule was simple: "Off—Get some rest and brush up on the little black book of speeches." Monday morning at eight o'clock Flo LeCompte drove him to New Orleans for newspaper interviews in the morning and a meeting with financial backers at noon. He visited sheriffs in the river parishes before driving to Baton Rouge for a Farm Bureau meeting attended by former secretary of agriculture Earl Butz. He spent the night in Baton Rouge.

On Tuesday, July 10, Ellender flew to Patterson and then drove to meet people in Morgan City before settling for the night in Lafayette. Wednesday was taken up with drives to Eunice and the Opelousas area before returning to Lafayette for the night. Thursday he spent the night in Lake Charles after visiting Sulphur and Cameron in the southwest corner of the state. On Friday he attended a ground breaking ceremony for a bridge in Jennings and returned to New Orleans in a Coast Guard plane. He met Lieutenant Governor Jimmy Fitzmorris, Jr., of New Orleans and other supporters and spent the night at the Roosevelt Hotel. On Saturday Ellender drove across Lake

15. New Orleans *Times-Picayune,* June 19, 20, 1972; Carlisle B. Morrison to Barry Goldwater, July 12, 1972, and Goldwater to Morrison, July 17, 1972, both in "Campaign, 1972" Folder, Box 1842, AEP.

Pontchartrain to visit Slidell, Abita Springs, and Covington before returning to Houma that same night. Sunday, July 16, was a casual day until 4:30 P.M. when he flew to Abbeville for a speech, after which he returned to Houma.[16]

In mid-July Ellender's closest friends—Flo LeCompte, Elward Wright, and Frank Wurzlow, Jr.—discussed the grueling pace of the campaign over coffee. Ellender's schedule was a hectic one, his advisers realized, especially for a man who was eighty-one. They worried because Ellender seemed determined to outwork the young upstart who was making age the main issue in the race. He could not appear to be tired or slowing down, no matter how exhausting the pace.[17]

Flo LeCompte was writing thank-you notes to those who had contributed to the cause on Sunday, July 23, when Ellender called the Houma headquarters to say he would fly to Grand Isle with Fitzmorris and campaign among the crowd gathered for the annual redfish rodeo. He wanted LeCompte to drive to the island to pick him up Sunday night. He hung up the telephone before she could learn just where on the island she was to find him.

Fitzmorris and Warren Harang, a Thibodaux sugarcane grower, spent Sunday campaigning with Ellender on Grand Isle, visiting from camp to camp, shaking hands and reminding voters of the good things Ellender had done for his constituents. Totally forgotten was the leisurely pace of the Irving Legendre camp where Ellender often relaxed and fished. Harang claimed Ellender exhausted him with his nonstop pace and boundless energy.[18] Before LeCompte left for Grand Isle, Ellender called to say he would fly to Houma in Fitzmorris' plane. Relieved at not having to search the crowded seven-mile-long island for the senator, LeCompte drove instead to the Houma airport on the old World War II naval base, a short distance from her house. Ellender disembarked saying he felt good enough to jump over a plane. Instead of going to his home, Ellender asked LeCompte to drive him to his campaign headquarters.

Later in the evening at his home, Ellender granted an interview to Houma *Courier* editor Ray Dill, even though he was tired. Dill stayed past ten. Ellender's shirt collar was open and his hair was uncombed, Dill noticed, and he bemoaned not having been able to get to a barber shop. Gesturing

16. Ellender Itinerary, Box 1835, AEP; Dan Borné, interview, April 30, 1992.

17. Florence LeCompte, interview, June 11, 1980; Claude Duval, interview, December 18, 1979.

18. Warren Harang, Jr., interview, June 10, 1980.

with his eyeglasses, which he took off and then replaced, Ellender bounced up from time to time to make long-distance inquiries when he could not otherwise provide the information Dill sought. He insisted on dialing and making his own connections.[19]

On Monday morning, July 24, LeCompte drove Ellender to New Orleans, where he boarded a plane for several days of campaigning in north Louisiana. With him was press secretary Carroll Trosclair, who planned to use Monroe as a base of operations for north Louisiana. Maintaining his usual thirteen-hour day campaigning, Ellender called LeCompte every day to report on his progress and inquire about developments in south Louisiana and in Washington. On Wednesday, July 26, Ellender ate gumbo in West Monroe and drove to Tallulah and Delhi. Later that night he attended a barbecue in Rayville. Although he had a stomachache, he consumed a bit of spicy food. Ellender suffered from diverticulosis and always removed the seeds from tomatoes as a precaution against an attack of diverticulitis.

Later that night he called Allen Jr. to say he had indigestion and it "won't let go." Aware of his father's periodic complaints of gas, which he attributed to overeating, spicy food, or diverticulitis, Allen Jr. suspected his father was suffering from angina, a progressive heart disease. Allen Jr. located a north Louisiana cardiologist who examined Ellender and urged him to enter the hospital immediately for a thorough evaluation. Promising to get a complete medical checkup in Washington, Ellender said he had to return to the Capitol for an important vote.

Early Thursday morning, when Trosclair called Ellender's motel room, the senator complained of terrific stomach pains, which he attributed to diverticulitis. He had not slept much the night before, but he still planned to fly to Washington to vote on an agricultural appropriations bill. Before leaving for Washington at about 11 A.M., he called LeCompte and asked her to send a courier to pick up campaign contributions from Otto Passman in Monroe. His stomach pain was severe, but he would fly to Washington to vote on the appropriations bill, he told LeCompte.

When Ellender's plane landed at Dulles Airport at about 3:15 P.M., July 27, his chauffeur drove him to the Capitol, where Dr. George W. Calver, the Capitol physician, examined him at 4:00 P.M. Ellender wanted to go to the Senate floor, but Calver, recognizing serious symptoms, insisted on immediate hospitalization. Seating Ellender in a wheelchair, he summoned the

---

19. [Alfred Delahaye] editorial, Houma (La.) *Courier,* July 30, 1972; Alfred Delahaye, interview, March 20, 1992.

ambulance kept at the Senate office building. Ironically, Ellender had frequently commented on the waste of having an ambulance standing by just in case a senator became ill. Now he was in the vehicle, speeding toward Bethesda Naval Hospital. Before leaving at 4:30, Ellender told Trosclair he need not accompany him to the hospital.

Ellender was having a major heart attack, doctors at Bethesda recognized immediately. They called Allen Jr. to tell him his father was gravely ill and might not survive the seizure. A short time later they called to say he had died of a coronary occlusion at 6:15. He had suffered for years from angina, an autopsy revealed, and it had reached an advanced stage. Even immediate hospitalization would not have helped much; Ellender's heart damage would have left him confined to a wheelchair had he lived.[20]

Allen Jr. decided his father would have a Catholic funeral, even though the senator, not a practicing Catholic, had listed his religion as Presbyterian in the *Congressional Directory*. Ellender had not been a practicing Presbyterian either, Allen Jr. knew. Since Ellender had been baptized Catholic, he would be buried in a Catholic ceremony, his devoutly Catholic son decided. Allen Jr. called First National Funeral Home manager M. J. Cortez, one of his dad's old fishing buddies, to inform him of the senator's death and ask his help with funeral arrangements.[21]

By Friday, July 28, funeral plans had been completed. On Saturday, Ellender's body would lie in state in the rotunda of the State Capitol in Baton Rouge from 10 A.M. until 6 P.M. On Sunday viewers could pay final respects in the Houma Municipal Auditorium, and from 9 A.M. until funeral time at 11 A.M. on Monday morning, friends and family members could see him for the last time at St. Francis de Sales Church in downtown Houma. In the rotunda of the Capitol Huey Long built with Ellender's help, visitors streamed past Ellender's mahogany coffin. Governor Edwards, a Cajun like Ellender, said he always spoke at least a few words in French to Ellender every time they met. A Baptist choir from Baton Rouge sang "Nearer My God to Thee." Lieutenant Governor Fitzmorris said, "He loved Louisiana. He loved this nation. He gave it the only thing he had. He gave himself."[22]

President and Mrs. Nixon, Vice-president and Mrs. Agnew, and prom-

20.   Allen Ellender, Jr., interview, June 6, 1980; Florence LeCompte, interview, June 11, 1980; Daisy Donnelly, interview, July 14, 1980; Bill Crider, "Ellender Worked Until the Last," in Bogalusa (La.) *Daily News,* July 28, 1972, Box 1, AEP.

21.   Houma (La.) *Daily Courier,* July 30, 1972.

22.   *Ibid.*

inent congressional leaders attended the televised funeral on Monday, July 31. Security precautions were elaborate. Dignitaries from Washington flew to Alvin Callender Field, across the Mississippi River from New Orleans. The president boarded a helicopter for the fifty-mile flight to the Houma airport. When the president's motorcade left the small Houma airstrip for the short drive into town, workers in nearby offices were directed to stay away from windows and keep shades down.[23]

Monday, July 31, was a solemn day in Houma, marked by celebrity and history—what some Louisiana reporters would call the greatest gathering of national officials in the state's history. An early morning thunderstorm dissolved into intermittent rain. Undeterred, people began to wait under umbrellas as early as 7 A.M. near St. Francis de Sales Church, three blocks from the senator's home and less than two from the parish courthouse.

Dark-suited Secret Service and security men were on the alert, some in the skeleton of the courthouse annex under construction across from the church. At about 10:30 thirty senators, several congressmen, and other Washington dignitaries stepped from two Greyhound buses. Vice-president and Mrs. Agnew entered the church at about 10:45. Ten minutes later, President and Mrs. Nixon alighted from their limousine to be greeted by Elward Wright. After briefly exchanging courtesies with nine or so priests, the Nixons took their aisle seats in the left front pew next to Dr. and Mrs. Allen Ellender, Jr. The Agnews and Governor and Mrs. Edwards sat directly across the aisle.

When New Orleans archbishop Philip Hannan recited the names of the nation's highest officials, as protocol required, many in the church and in the television audience realized that not only were the president and the vice-president on hand but also the second and third officials in the line of presidential succession, Speaker of the House Carl Albert and Senate president pro tempore James O. Eastland. Many of Ellender's Senate colleagues also attended.

After the archbishop eulogized the man who served under six presidents, the eighty-member choir directed by Ellis J. LaRose sang "The Battle Hymn of the Republic." The all-services honor guard floated the flag-covered casket out of the thousand-seat church and into the broiling sunshine. The Nixons left immediately to return to Washington and to such problems as the Watergate break-in, which had occurred about six weeks earlier, and the presidential reelection campaign.

23. Willis Brown, interview, April 10, 1990.

The Agnews, the congressmen, and other dignitaries rode along a seven-block route to the Belanger Street entrance of nondenominational Magnolia Cemetery. There was a profusion of flowers. The Fort Polk Army Band played. There was a rifle-squad salute and the sound of "Taps." The senator was placed near his brother Claude. His tombstone would read FARMER-LAWYER-STATESMAN.[24]

Wright received a poll several days after the funeral indicating Ellender would have won in a close race. Five months after Ellender's death, in December, 1972, in a final accounting of campaign finances, Wright listed a deficit of $45,000. Ellender had died intestate. His son was his only heir. Creditors demanded payment. In 1977 Allen Jr. paid Buddy Roemer of IDS $38,157 in an out-of-court settlement.[25]

Amiable, congenial, and unpretentious, Ellender had represented his constituents for thirty-five years. Newspaper and television coverage of his funeral alerted people, some for the first time, to his national and world importance. A Houma *Daily Courier* editorial best summarized local reaction to his death. "Although he was from the bayous, he knew the world. And he left his imprint upon it and upon America," the writer said. "We were proud of him and he of us. He was our Number One citizen and America's Number One senator. Few men of his stature ever pass our way. We of Terrebonne are proud and grateful—and sad."[26]

Harry and Bess Truman sent Allen Jr. a message of sympathy, for which he thanked them. He explained how his father had refused to be hospitalized until just before he died, even though he was seriously ill. Harry would no longer receive the customary Ellender gift of pralines on his birthday, Allen Jr. lamented. The Acadian senator had returned to the good earth—Terrebonne—along the banks of the bayou where he had been born eighty-one years before.[27]

24.   Mary Russell, Washington *Post,* August 1, 1972; New York *Times,* July 31, 1972; New Orleans *Times-Picayune,* August 1, 1972; Houma (La.) *Daily Courier,* July 30, 31, August 1, 1972; Stephen Ambrose, *Nixon* (3 vols.; New York, 1989), II, 582.

25.   Elward Wright, interview, November 8, 1979; Wright to various parties, December, 1972, and Frank Wurzlow, Jr., to Allen Ellender, Jr., April 7, 1977, both in EWP.

26.   [Alfred Delahaye] editorial, Houma (La.) *Daily Courier,* July 30, 1972; Alfred Delahaye, interview, March 20, 1992.

27.   Allen Ellender, Jr., to Harry and Bess Truman, August 31, 1972, in "General—Ell–Ellery" Folder, Post-Pres. Gen. Files, Box 87, in Harry Truman Papers, Truman Library, Independence, Mo.

Bibliographical Essay

Primary Sources

Collections

$\mathcal{T}$he voluminous Allen J. Ellender Papers at Nicholls State University, Thibodaux, Louisiana, contain the most significant primary materials used for this biography. The collection covers 1937 to 1972 extensively and the 1920s and 1930s intermittently. The senator seldom threw anything away. The two-thousand-box collection has nineteen divisions, including Departmental, Legislative, Data, and Miscellaneous. Ellender's personal files, travel records, diaries, films, scrapbooks, and photographs are also part of the collection.

Elward Wright's papers, which are in the possession of Thomas Wright, disclose much about the senator's finances, political philosophy, and 1972 reelection campaign.

The Orville Freeman Papers in the Minnesota Historical Society Collection, St. Paul, Minnesota, reveal much about Ellender's approach to agricultural legislation as seen through the eyes of Freeman, who was secretary of agriculture.

The Hubert H. Humphrey Papers, also in the Minnesota Historical Society Collection, contain correspondence with Ellender on farm policy in the 1960s.

I used photocopied documents relating to Ellender from the Lyndon Baines Johnson Library, Austin, Texas. In the Oral History Collection is an interview of Allen Ellender by T. Harrison Baker, July 30, 1969.

The J. William Fulbright Papers, in Special Collections at the University of Arkansas Library, Fayetteville, provide useful insights into foreign policy and agriculture. The Joseph T. Robinson Papers, also at the University of

Arkansas Library, provide information on Ellender's first contacts with New Deal congressional leaders.

The Harry Truman Papers at the Truman Library, Independence, Missouri, while used sparingly, afford interesting glimpses into Ellender's close personal contacts with Truman.

Several manuscript collections in the Special Collections, Howard-Tilton Memorial Library, Tulane University, New Orleans, Louisiana, deal with Ellender's political career. The papers of Hale Boggs, deLesseps S. Morrison, Sam Houston Jones, and F. Edward Hebert all contain correspondence with or about Ellender.

The Louisiana and Lower Mississippi Valley Collections at Louisiana State University, Baton Rouge, Louisiana, house the papers of Russell B. Long, John Fournet, Earl Long, Richard Leche, deLesseps S. Morrison, and T. Harry Williams; all these papers contain materials relating to Ellender. Interviews T. Harry Williams conducted for his biography of Huey Long are also in the collection, and many include information about Ellender's legislative career, especially interviews with Richard Leche, Allen Ellender, Harvey Peltier, John Fournet, George W. Wallace, and E. H. (Lige) Williams.

Federal Bureau of Information files (Nos. 62-81810, 9-2629, and 9-45583) and State Department files (Nos. 033.1100-EL/5-1855, 033.1100-El/9-1758, 003.110-EL/11-2158, F0001, and F0008) on Ellender, obtained through the Freedom of Information Act, were disappointing and skimpy. In some cases, so many names had been blacked out that the information was useless. However, revealing insights into the thinking of State Department and FBI agents on clandestine foreign operations emerge. These materials may be viewed in the archives of Nicholls State University.

Hugh Cates's "Allen Ellender, Oral History No. 149," April 20, 1971, in Richard B. Russell Collection, Richard B. Russell Memorial Library, University of Georgia, Athens, was informative.

The "Allen J. Ellender Oral History Interview" by Larry Hackman, August 29, 1967 (John F. Kennedy Library, Washington, D.C.; facsimile copy in Nicholls State University Library, Thibodaux, La.), provides insights into Ellender's dealings with the Kennedy administration on civil rights and agricultural policy.

The Southern Tenant Farmers Union Papers, Southern Collection, University of North Carolina, Chapel Hill, include a wealth of information on agricultural policy.

Two sets of Robert Ruffin Barrow, Jr., Papers, one at Nicholls State

University and the other at Tulane University, relate to Ellender's early legal career and his financial dealings with the controversial planter and canal tycoon.

The Joseph Francis Rummel Papers in the archives of the Archdiocese of New Orleans contain several exchanges with Ellender over the years.

Sacred Heart Catholic Church funeral records, in Montegut, Louisiana, have information about the Ellenders and other early Terrebonne Parish families.

The records of two United Brotherhood of Carpenters and Joiners locals, Local 2258 in Houma, Louisiana, and Local 1897 in Lafayette, Louisiana, include some information about organized labor's view of Ellender.

Public archives of Terrebonne and Lafourche parishes contain original documents on conveyance, marriages, mortgages, corporations, and other matters. They contain many transactions involving Ellender.

Printed Documents

The *Congressional Record* was the most commonly used printed document, along with various U.S. House and Senate reports. *Hearings Before the Subcommittee of the Committee on Appropriations,* 78th Cong., 1st Sess., and *House Reports,* 89th Cong., 1st Sess., No. 631, "Food and Agriculture Act of 1965," both deal with significant agricultural legislation.

Census records on microfilm provide background information on the first families to settle Terrebonne Parish. *Public Papers of the Presidents of the United States* (Washington, D.C., various dates) contain occasional statements by presidents about Ellender.

Ellender's role in Huey Long's impeachment is recorded in *Proceedings on Impeachment Hearings Before the Committee of the Whole of the House of Representatives, State of Louisiana* (transcript in State Archives, Baton Rouge, La.).

Interviews

I interviewed the people listed below, some of them more than once, for information about Ellender. Footnotes indicate exact dates.

George Arceneaux, Jr., Donald J. Ayo, Kermic P. Bajat, T. M. Barker, Randolph Bazet, Edmond Becnel, Jr., Dan Borné, Wallace Borne, Roland Boudreaux, E. J. Bourg, Willis Brown, Kirby Brunet, Charles Caillouette, Mrs. Charles Cain, Jack Carlos, Fay Chauvin, Oneil Colwort, Elton Darsey, A. J. Dato, Alfred Delahaye, Edmond Deramee, Godfrey Detiveaux, James Domengeaux, Mrs. Charles A. Donnelly, Jerome Drolet, Claude Duval, Allen Ellender, Jr., Ernest Ellender, Jr., Gerald Ellender, Henry Ellender, Jr., Thelma Ellender, Viola Lynch Ellender, Wallace Ellender, Jr., Madison L. Funderburk, Carolyn Glynn, Warren Harang, Jr., Nelo Hebert, Adam LaCosta, Frank Lapeyrolerie, Chester Lapeyrouse, Florence LeCompte, Nolan P. LeCompte, Jr., Byrne Ellender Legendre, Mrs. Irving Legendre, Irving Legendre, Jr., Charles Logan, H. L. Mitchell, Numa Montet, M. T. Nolen, Vincent O'Connell, Jean Ludwig Palmer, Thomas Payne, Henry Pelet, Royal Pellegrin, Ashby W. Pettigrew, Jr., Evans Pitre, Charles Plauche, Armond Porche, Riley Rhodes, O. J. Robichaux, Noble Rogers, Joseph Sagona, Jr., Dennis Sellers, Herman Sonier, Susan Ellender Stall, Dave Stoufflet, O. J. Thibodaux, Joseph Vath, Cyprian Voisin, Gerald Voisin, Elward Wright, Thomas Wright, Betty Wurzlow, Frank Wurzlow, Jr.

Newspapers

The Ellender collection's scrapbooks of newspaper clippings are arranged chronologically and sometimes topically. Occasionally I made runs in newspapers for specific events. The most frequently used newspapers were the New Orleans *Times-Picayune* (and its forerunners), the Baton Rouge *Morning Advocate,* the Houma (La.) *Courier* (later *Daily Courier*), the *Terrebonne Press* of Houma, the Thibodaux (La.) *Comet* (and its forerunners), the Napoleonville (La.) *Pioneer,* the Washington *Post,* the New York *Times,* and the *Wall Street Journal.*

Other

Other sources I found useful were Covington Hall's "Labor Struggles in the Deep South" (Typescript in Manuscripts Section, Howard-Tilton Memorial Library, Tulane University, New Orleans, La.); Rogers, *Directory of the Parish of Terrebonne, 1897, Containing a Historical Sketch of the Parish* (New Orleans, 1897); and P. A. Champomier, *Statement of the Sugar Crop Made in Louisiana in 1859–60* (New Orleans, 1860).

Secondary Sources
Books, Articles, Periodicals

Only the most significant secondary works are listed below. Footnotes provide exact citations.

On the Louisiana racial, social, political, and economic milieu into which Ellender was born, a number of works are revealing. For a description of Acadians (Cajuns), see especially Carl A. Brasseaux, *The Founding of New*

Acadia: The Beginnings of Acadian Life in Louisiana, 1765–1803 (Baton Rouge, 1987); Brasseaux, *Acadian to Cajun: Transformation of a People, 1803–1877* (Jackson, Miss., 1992); and Glenn R. Conrad, ed., *The Cajuns: Essays on Their History and Culture* (Lafayette, La., 1978). The following all deal with Ellender's career: Thomas Becnel, "The Ellenders: Pioneer Terrebonne Parish Family, 1840–1924," *Louisiana History,* XXVI (Spring, 1985), 117–27; Becnel, "Louisiana Senator Allen J. Ellender and IWW Leader Covington Hall: An Agrarian Dichotomy," *Louisiana History,* XXIII (Summer, 1982), 259–75; Becnel, "Allen J. Ellender, Consensus Politician," *Louisiana History,* XXXII (Summer, 1991), 229–38; Becnel, "Fulbright of Arkansas vs. Ellender of Louisiana: The Politics of Sugar and Rice, 1937–1972," *Arkansas Historical Quarterly,* LXIII (Winter, 1984), 289–303; Becnel, *The Barrow Family and the Barataria and Lafourche Canal: The Transportation Revolution in Louisiana, 1829–1925* (Baton Rouge, 1989); Becnel, *Labor, Church, and the Sugar Establishment: Louisiana, 1887–1976* (Baton Rouge, 1980).

William I. Hair explains Louisiana racial attitudes before and after the turn of the century in *Carnival of Fury: Robert Charles and the New Orleans Race Riot of 1900* (Baton Rouge, 1976) and *Bourbonism and Agrarian Protests: Louisiana Politics, 1877–1900* (Baton Rouge, 1969). C. Vann Woodward, in the *New Republic,* March 14, 1988, p. 40, gives a succinct explanation of how both North and South criticized Reconstruction. J. Carlyle Sitterson, *Sugar Country: The Cane Sugar Industry of the South* (Lexington, Ky., 1953), is the standard study of the early sugar industry.

On Huey Long and Longism, T. Harry Williams' *Huey Long: A Biography* (New York, 1969) is the work against which all subsequent studies of Long are measured. William I. Hair, *The Kingfish and His Realm: The Life and Times of Huey P. Long* (Baton Rouge, 1991), offers more detail and is more critical of Long's tactics and personality. Allan P. Sindler, *Huey Long's Louisiana: State Politics, 1920–1952* (Baltimore, 1956), describes the factionalism between the Longites and the anti-Longites. Michael L. Kurtz and Morgan D. Peoples, in *Earl K. Long: The Saga of Uncle Earl and Louisiana Politics* (Baton Rouge, 1990), explain the career of Ellender's longtime political ally. Glen Jeansonne, in *Leander Perez: Boss of the Delta* (Baton Rouge, 1977), outlines the career of Ellender's segregationist political crony; his *Gerald L. K. Smith: Minister of Hate* (New Haven, 1988) is a biography of Long's Share Our Wealth director. Mark T. Carleton, in "Four Anti-Longites: A Tentative Assessment," *Louisiana History,* XXX (Summer, 1989), 249–62, discusses modern Louisiana reform movements. Miriam G. Reeves, *The Governors of Louisiana* (Gretna, La., 1980), and Joseph Dawson III, ed., *The*

Louisiana Governors: From Iberville to Edwards (Baton Rouge, 1990), are handy references on Louisiana politics. Bennett Wall, ed., *Louisiana: A Narrative History* (Arlington Heights, Ill., 1984), summarizes many phases of Louisiana history.

A number of works explain Ellender's relationships with Presidents Franklin Roosevelt, Harry Truman, Dwight Eisenhower, John F. Kennedy, Lyndon B. Johnson, and Richard Nixon.

Aspects of the New Deal are covered by several works on Roosevelt's domestic and foreign programs. William E. Leuchtenburg, *Franklin D. Roosevelt and the New Deal, 1932–1940* (New York, 1963), is a useful short summary. The following deal directly or indirectly with Ellender: Harold L. Ickes, Volume 2 of *The Secret Diary of Harold L. Ickes* (2 vols.; New York, 1954); Pete Daniel, "Going Among Strangers: Southern Reactions to World War II," *Journal of American History,* LXXVII (December, 1990), 886–911; George G. Lewis and John Mewha, *History of Prisoner of War Utilization by the United States Army, 1776–1945* (Washington, D.C., 1955); Joseph Butler, "Prisoner of War Labor in the Sugar Cane Fields of Lafourche Parish, Louisiana: 1943–1944," *Louisiana History,* XIV (Summer, 1973), 283–96.

The following offer insights on the Truman era: Richard Davies, *Housing Reform During the Truman Administration* (Columbia, Mo., 1965); Barton Bernstein, "Economic Policies," in *The Truman Period as a Research Field,* ed. Richard Kirkendall (Columbia, Mo., 1967); Clark Clifford, *Counsel to the President: A Memoir* (New York, 1991); Robert H. Ferrell, *Harry S. Truman and the Modern American Presidency* (Boston, 1983); David McCullough, *Truman* (New York, 1992).

Dwight Eisenhower's biographer, Stephen Ambrose, is also Richard Nixon's biographer. Ambrose's *Eisenhower: Soldier and President* (New York, 1990) reveals Ike's style and temperament.

David Schoenbrun, "Casebook of a Southern Senator: Allen J. Ellender of Louisiana," *Esquire,* September, 1963, pp. 106–108, describes Ellender during the Kennedy era.

Lyndon Johnson's biographers all agree on his ability to work with people to achieve legislative goals. His meteoric rise to power is described best by Robert Dallek, in *Lone Star Rising: Lyndon Johnson and His Times, 1908–1960* (New York, 1991). Johnson's dealings with Richard Russell are outlined in Mark Stern, "Lyndon Johnson and Richard Russell: Institutions, Ambitions, and Civil Rights," *Presidential Studies Quarterly,* XXI (Fall, 1991), 687–704. LBJ's political growth is shown in Ronnie Dugger, *The Politician: The Life and Times of Lyndon Johnson: The Drive for Power, from the Frontier to*

Master of the Senate (New York, 1982) and in Robert A. Caro, *The Years of Lyndon Johnson: Means of Ascent* (New York, 1990). Kermit Gordon, "How Much Should Government Do?" *Saturday Review,* January 9, 1965, pp. 25–27, tells about government spending.

Richard Nixon's career is convincingly documented and interpreted by Stephen Ambrose in his comprehensive three-volume biography, *Nixon* (New York, 1989). Volume 2, *The Triumph of a President, 1962–1972,* includes some dealings with Ellender. Bruce Oudes, ed., *From the President: Richard Nixon's Secret Files* (New York, 1989), provides glimpses of a scheming Nixon.

FBI director J. Edgar Hoover is exposed at work by Kenneth O'Reilly in *"Racial Matters": The FBI's Secret File on Black America, 1960–1972* (New York, 1989) and "The FBI and the Politics of the Riots, 1964–1968," *Journal of American History,* LXXV (June, 1988), 91–114; and by Athan G. Theoharis and John Stuart Cox in *The Boss: J. Edgar Hoover and the Great American Inquisition* (Philadelphia, 1988).

General works on senators and the U.S. Senate abound. A basis for appraising Ellender's career is provided by Donald R. Matthews, *U.S. Senators and Their World* (Chapel Hill, 1960); C. Vann Woodward, *Tom Watson: Agrarian Rebel* (New York, 1938); Robert Garson, *The Democratic Party and the Politics of Sectionalism, 1941–1948* (Baton Rouge, 1974); James W. Hilty, *Voting Alignments in the United States Senate, 1933–1944* (1 vol. with appendix; University Microfilms International, 1979); Richard Lowitt, *George W. Norris: The Triumph of a Progressive, 1933–1944* (Urbana, Ill., 1978); Gilbert C. Fite, *Richard B. Russell, Jr., Senator from Georgia* (Chapel Hill, 1991); James T. Patterson, *Mr. Republican: A Biography of Robert A. Taft* (Boston, 1972); Joseph B. Gorman, *Kefauver: A Political Biography* (New York, 1971); Virginia Van der Veer Hamilton, *Lister Hill: Statesman from the South* (Chapel Hill, 1987); Walter Johnson and Francis Colligan, *The Fulbright Program: A History* (Chicago, 1965); Tristan Coffin, *Senator Fulbright: Portrait of a Public Philosopher* (New York, 1966); and Carl Grafton and Anne Permaloff, *Big Mules and Branchheads: James E. Folsom and Political Power in Alabama* (Athens, Ga., 1985).

The following deal with racial policies and politics: George C. Rable, "The South and the Politics of Antilynching Legislation, 1920–1940," *Journal of Southern History,* LI (May, 1985), 201–20; Michael I. Sovern, *Legal Restraints on Racial Discrimination in Employment* (New York, 1966); Louis C. Kesselman, *The Social Politics of FEPC: A Study in Reform Pressure Movements* (Chapel Hill, 1948); James C. Cobb, " 'Somebody Done Nailed Us on the Cross': Federal Farm and Welfare Policy and the Civil Rights Movement in the Mississippi Delta," *Journal of American History*, LXXVII (December, 1990), 912–36.

Many writers explain American farm policy: Gilbert Fite, *Cotton Fields No More: Southern Agriculture, 1865–1980* (Lexington, Ky., 1984); Jack Kirby, *Rural Worlds Lost: The American South, 1920–1960* (Baton Rouge, 1987); Pete Daniel, *Breaking the Land: The Transformation of Cotton, Tobacco, and Rice Culture Since 1880* (Chicago, 1985); James D. Holley, "Old and New Worlds in the New Deal Resettlement Program: Two Louisiana Projects," *Louisiana History*, XI (Spring, 1970); Allen J. Matusow, *Farm Policies and Politics in the Truman Years* (Cambridge, Mass., 1967); John A. Salmond, "Postscript to the New Deal: The Defeat of the Nomination of Aubrey W. Williams as Rural Electrification Administrator in 1945," *Journal of American History*, LXI (September, 1974), 417–36; Theodore Saloutos, "Agricultural Organizations and Farm Policy in the South After World War II," *Agricultural History*, LIII (January, 1979), 374–404; Saloutos, "New Deal Agricultural Policy: An Evaluation," *Journal of American History*, LXI (September, 1974), 394–416; Julius Duscha, *Taxpayers' Hayride: The Farm Problem from the New Deal to the Billie Sol Estes Case* (Boston, 1964); Reo Christenson, *The Brannan Plan: Farm Politics and Policy* (Ann Arbor, 1959); Murray Benedict, *Farm Policies in the United States, 1790–1950* (New York, 1966); Varden Fuller, "Political Pressure and Income Distribution in Agriculture," and Wayne D. Rasmussen and Gladys L. Baker, "Programs for Agriculture, 1933–1965," both in *Agricultural Policy in an Affluent Society*, ed. Vernon W. Ruttan *et al.* (New York, 1969); Edward L. Schapsmeier and Frederick H. Schapsmeier, "Farm Policy from FDR to Eisenhower: Southern Democrats and the Politics of Agriculture," *Agricultural History*, LIII (January, 1979), 352–71; Joyce Appleby, "Commercial Farming and the 'Agrarian Myth' in the Early Republic," *Journal of American History*, LXVIII (March, 1982), 833–49; Stephen Chapman, "Farming for Dollars," *New Republic*, July 19, 1980, pp. 12–14; George L. Baka, "Farm Subsidies: The Game Never Stops," *Nation*, August 16, 1971, pp. 114–15.

Duane Tananbaum, *The Bricker Amendment Controversy: A Test of Eisenhower's Political Leadership* (Ithaca, N.Y., 1988), and Stephen S. Rosenfeld, "The Travels of Allen Ellender," *New Republic*, September 27, 1969, pp. 25–30, discuss Ellender's thinking on foreign affairs. F. Ray Marshall, *Labor in the South* (Cambridge, Mass., 1967), is a standard work on the generally weak labor unions in the South. Julius Duscha, "Is the Food Stamp Plan Working?" *Reporter*, March 1, 1962, pp. 38–39, 41, traces early food stamp programs. Ronald Steel, "Harry of Sunnybrook Farm," a review of David McCullough's *Truman* in *New Republic,* August 10, 1992, pp. 34–39, contains useful insights for a biographer.

Theses and Dissertations

Charles T. Walsten, "Allen J. Ellender: Long Legislative Lieutenant, 1928–1936" (M.A. thesis, Louisiana State University, 1985), outlines Ellender's early legislative career. James Paul Leslie, "Earl K. Long: The Formative Years, 1895–1940" (Ph.D. diss., University of Missouri, 1974), explains Earl Long's evolution. Brady M. Banta, "The Regulation and Conservation of Petroleum Resources in Louisiana, 1901–1940" (Ph.D. diss., Louisiana State University, 1981), untangles the legal but unethical oil leasing practices of the Longs and their followers. Edward F. Renwick, "The Longs' Legislative Lieutenants" (Ph.D. diss., University of Arizona, 1967), discusses Long's associates.

Index